For G...

Victor Knowles

1 Cor. 15:57

★ ★ ★ ★ ★ ★ ★

VOLUME I
1945 - 1977

★★★★★★★ VICTOR

— SINCE 1945 —

HOW AN
AMERICAN
WAR BABY
BECAME AN
INTERNATIONAL
PEACEMAKER

VICTOR KNOWLES

COLLEGE PRESS PUBLISHING · JOPLIN, MISSOURI

VICTOR: Since 1945
How an American War Baby Became an International Peacemaker
Volume 1 (1945-1977)
Published by College Press

Copyright © 2011 by Victor Knowles

ISBN 978-0-89900-400-6
Printed in the United States of America

Cover and interior design:
Brett Lyerla - www.bhold-designs.com

For information:
College Press
2111 North Main, Suite C
Joplin, MO
1.800.289.3300
www.collegepress.com

Peace on Earth Ministries
Post Office Box 275
Joplin, MO 64802
1.417.627.0325
www.poeministries.org

DEDICATION

For Dale and "Dearie,"

my patient parents,

who raised me the best they knew how,

"in the nurture and admonition of the Lord,"

in the best years in America

a boy could have wanted to live:

the late 40s, fabulous 50s, and early 60s.

And for Evelyn,

my wonderful wife,

and the love of my life;

the perfect mother of our six children,

who kept the home fires burning

while I was gone preaching

more than I should have been.

★ ★ ★ ★ ★ ★ ★

For when the One Great Scorer comes
To write against your name,
He marks — not that you won or lost —
But how you played the game.

— Grantland Rice

CONTENTS

★   ★   ★   ★   ★   ★   ★

P R E F A C E

When I saw how my dear father struggled with writing his life story at the age of 90, I determined that I would start my own attempt a little earlier. I was happy to help my father achieve his goal, *One Life of Many*, which was published in 2005, four years before his death in 2009. A good friend and trusted colleague, William E. Paul, who has written the Introduction to this book, encouraged me to start writing my autobiography when I turned 60. And so, on January 1, 2005, I sat down and outlined what I would write; though I did not actually start the writing process until two years later. What you now hold in your hands is Volume 1 of my life story, *Victor: Since 1945*.

Why does anyone set out to write his or her own biography? I suppose there may be as many motives as there are authors. But as for me, I simply wanted to tell my story as I recall it happening. If it makes you laugh, think, or cry, then I will have considered it a success. Some parts of the book will appeal to some more than it will to others. My schoolmates and college chums may choose to stop reading after that part is covered. Those who know me from later years may skip over the first part altogether. I hope, of course, that you will read the whole book.

Victor is written through my eyes – as I saw life unfold. I will tell you from the outset that I what I have written has been written, "as best I recall." My own biases and prejudices will be fairly evident. I may have misjudged some people or events. While I hope that this

★   ★   ★   ★   ★   ★   ★

book will inspire people, it is not inspired writing like the Bible – not by any stretch of the imagination. But I hope it is honest. I trust it is sincere. I want it to be a blessing to you.

"Why two volumes?" some may ask. The simple answer is because I couldn't get it all into one. I could have left out a lot of stories and anecdotes, but I felt that would be shortchanging my life. I haven't told everything, but I have told much. Probably too much in some people's thinking! But it's my life, I only get one, and this is the way I have chosen to tell it. Volume 2 (1978-2012) is scheduled to be released in May 2012.

I like playing with words, so *Victor* had a lot to offer for a title. It's the name my mother gave me, but it has a lot of spiritual significance too, as I relate in Chapter 1. I've been around since 1945 so the add-on, *Since 1945*, was a natural too. Each person is his or her own business or industry. I tacked on, *How an American War Baby Became an International Peacemaker* at the urging of my friend Jerry Rushford, Director of the Pepperdine University Bible Lectures, who has a penchant for descriptive sentences.

I am among the last of the "war babies" born in "The Greatest Generation." This is my story. I hope you enjoy it.

> Victor Knowles
> Founder and President
> Peace On Earth Ministries
> Joplin, Missouri

★   ★   ★   ★   ★   ★   ★

FOREWORD

My wife and I affectionately refer to Victor Knowles as "Sir Victor." In turn, he has tagged us "Lord Burgess" and "Queen Esther."

Our paths first crossed in 1964, the year Victor graduated from high school in Illinois. It was the same year I graduated from Bible college in Portland, Oregon. Esther and I headed east to begin ministry in Indiana. "Vic" moved west to attend Midwestern School of Evangelism in Iowa. I participated in several events at Midwestern during his years at Bible college. That casual acquaintance has turned into 46 years of friendship that has become a relationship that is "closer than a brother."

Eventually Esther and I moved back to Oregon to minister with the church where her illustrious father, Archie Word, had been the preacher for 33 years. I was also teaching classes at Northwest College of the Bible when the faculty extended an invitation to Victor Knowles to become president of NCB in 1984. Victor and his family became a beloved and valuable part of our church at Crossroads.

That same year Victor and I were selected to meet with a group of leaders from the Restoration Movement that convened in Joplin, Missouri, for the first of 25 national unity meetings. Eight years later Victor wrote the outstanding biography of Archie Word: *Voice of Thunder, Heart of Tears* (College Press, 1992). I was somewhat aware of Vic's gifted writing style, but when I read his biography of my father-in-law, the appreciation I had for his ability to transport my mind into the heart and soul of another life was raised incredibly.

★   ★   ★   ★   ★   ★   ★

And now, once again, Victor Knowles has given us a powerfully heartwarming, humorous, real-life story that he has penned in his own inimitable style. Victor splendidly frames his story with a picture of world events around him while God was shaping his early life.

If you've ever wondered what is the real story behind a great leader, or would love to know how God weaves people and events into a life that leads to dramatic decisions, or are challenged and empowered by seeing how God can use a great tragedy and change it into a turning point, this book is for you.

If you are fascinated by the "Google Earth" panorama of life, but you also want to be able to "zoom in" on what we value most, this book is for you. If watching "small beginnings" transform into a worldwide influence inspires you, or if you value someone who is motivated by nobility, honor and virtue while being "truly human," this book is for you.

A lifetime of ministry with people has allowed me to discover that there is a language we humans speak that transcends the words we use. Victor is adept with words, but they become secondary to his ability to communicate the feelings and understanding of his journey with God.

In Volume 1 of *Victor: Since 1945* you will see how the Lord built a fabulous foundation for His greater achievements later in life. You'll have a new friend by the time you're finished reading this book. I am a better person because of the influence of Victor Knowles in my life.

Tom Burgess
Senior Minister
Crossroads Church
Portland, Oregon

★   ★   ★   ★   ★   ★   ★

INTRODUCTION

The story of Victor Knowles' life is related in vintage Knowles style, complete with anecdotes, wordplays and descriptive adjectives. The author's ability to recall the details of incidents, statistics, dialogue and emotions of his 65+ years of life is nothing short of uncanny!

Prepare yourself for a freewheeling, candid, and at times, a tad reckless ride. While the story could never be classed a "tell all" account, "Vic" is oftentimes quite "frank" in sharing the experiences of his eventful life. But being the autobiography of a preacher, one would expect it to contain a truthful profile, "warts and all."

Vic's prowess as a budding athlete emerges early in life as a talented baseball player. This interest expanded to include a remarkable knowledge and recollection of numerous major league players, their positions, teams, and statistics.

Many who now know Victor as a polished speaker, gifted writer and world traveler may be surprised to learn of his "talent" as a college prankster. But, as often happens, when God takes over a life in major league fashion, these tendencies often become channeled into productive endeavors.

Victor touches on the romantic interests in his early life also, but with a discretion that does not hide a certain amount of emotion.

As is customary in his writings, Vic displays an incredible memory of contemporary history. His reference to current music, movies, public figures and incidents helps place his life story in a perspective of the times. His extensive travels and varied ministry activi-

★   ★   ★   ★   ★   ★   ★

ties exposed him to an abundant array of interesting happenings in the lives of many individuals and churches, which he shares always in a positive light.

At the heart of this story is the commitment to Christ and Christian ministry. Victor shares an astonishingly busy schedule of preaching in churches, conducting revival meetings, speaking at camps, rallies and conferences, and writing and editing books and periodicals. And all the while he maintained a voluminous correspondence of encouragement to countless saints. Through it all, he manages to share glimpses of a loving family life. Here is a story to challenge and inspire youth and elderly alike, as they view a life totally committed to "spending and being spent" for the cause of Christ.

As they say, "You will laugh; you will cry." But, most certainly, you will receive a blessing from reading *Victor: Since 1945*, and hopefully you will be inspired to live out *your* life story to its very fullest, expending *your* energies for Jesus, being an influence for good in *your* world, and exalting Christ in all *you* do and say!

William E. Paul
Associate Editor
Bible Editions & Versions
Franktown, Colorado

★   ★   ★   ★   ★   ★   ★

CHAPTER ONE

CALL ME "VICTOR"

Franklin Pierce, the 14th president of the United States, was born November 23, 1801. William H. Bonney, better known as "Billy the Kid," was born November 23, 1881. I was born November 23, 1945. Are you seeing a pattern here? A friend once told me, "Victor, you're not as good as your friends say you are, but then you're not as bad as your enemies say you are either." An American president and a notorious outlaw remind me of that!

I was born on the 23rd day of the 11th month in 1945. It's an easy date to remember: 11-23-45. The only date that might be easier to remember would be 01-23-45. But I was not born on that date. If you were, congratulations!

When it came time for my arrival, my father bundled up my mother in their 1936 Chevrolet and drove her at a most reasonable speed to Memorial Hospital in Seymour, Indiana. My parents lived in North Vernon but there was no hospital there in 1945.

November is probably the least respected month of the year. As a poet once wrote:

Dull November brings the blast;
Then the leaves are whirling fast.

Dull November? Oh, great. But it has one redeeming quality: Thanksgiving Day. For that we can all be thankful.

★　★　★　★　★　★　★

I was born with a big head. My mother, who had studied to be an LPN, was worried when they brought me to her and she saw the humongous hematoma: a swelling composed of blood. Dr. Black, the man who delivered me, assured her that the swelling would go down in a few days, which it did much to her relief. My critics may suggest I still have a big head. Actually, my hat size is a very respectable 6 and 7/8ths. But who wears hats these days?

"CONQUEROR OF THE HILLS AND VALLEYS"

My father wanted to name me Arthur, after one of his uncles who was a famous auctioneer in north central Iowa. I'm sorry, but I just can't see myself as "Art" Knowles, can you? I thought not. (With apologies to anyone reading this who is named Art or Arthur, a perfectly fine name I am sure.) I'm glad my mother prevailed, insisting that I be named after my father. And so to this day I am Dale Victor Knowles II. Mom stuck the Roman numeral II on because she didn't want people calling me Junior. My mother was a very wise woman.

Although I seldom use my first name, I like the name my mother gave me. It even has some spiritual significance. "Dale" means "valley." "Victor" comes from the Latin and means "conqueror." "Knowles" is related to "knoll" and means "hill." I like to think that I am a conqueror of the hills and valleys that I have experienced in my life. I know full well, of course, that the power to conquer comes from above and not just from within.

When I was in England in 1989, I spent an afternoon in a quaint old library doing research on the Knowles name. It seems that a good number of our ancestors were ministers, poets, journalists, and biographers. There are two family coats of arms, one with a ram's head and

★   ★   ★   ★   ★   ★   ★

the other with an elephant. I told my father that our coat of arms was probably the one with the elephant since we are such staunch Republicans. Tusk, tusk!

My grandfather on the Knowles side was also named Victor – William Victor Knowles. He always went by "Vic" and so did I, clear through college. I never knew my grandfather. He was killed on December 10, 1943, while fighting a fire in his hometown of Hubbard, Iowa. You will find his name engraved on the Firefighter's Memorial Wall in Coralville, Iowa. He was the captain of the Hubbard Fire Department and I am very proud to wear his name, along with my father's. I also have a cousin named Victor – Thomas Victor Halatyn, who lives in the Washington, D. C. area. I understand that the name Victor was very common among the early Christians, and you can see why from New Testament passages like Romans 8:37 ("We are more than conquerors") and 1 John 5:4 ("This is the victory that overcomes the world, even our faith.").

MY QUAKER HERITAGE

John Knowles and his wife Mary (Benedict) emigrated from Manchester, England, to Ontario, Canada, sometime before 1850. He was my great-great-grandfather. John Philip Knowles, my great-grandfather, and his wife Amelia (Albery) moved to Hardin County, Iowa, about 10 years later. My grandfather Vic was born to them in 1881 and married my grandmother Mary Elizabeth (Hiserote) in 1906, the same year as the great San Francisco earthquake. In 1915, my father was born to Vic and "Lib," as she was called, the fourth of five children.

My father, Dale V. Knowles, grew up in Hubbard during the Great Depression years and was a top-notch athlete. I learned to play

★   ★   ★   ★   ★   ★   ★

baseball from him. A full-length photograph of him appeared on the front page of the sports section of the *Des Moines Tribune* when Hubbard was vying for the Class B Title in basketball in 1933. Following his baptism on Easter Sunday 1936, dad enrolled in Minnesota Bible College, graduating from Cincinnati Bible Seminary in 1940. While preaching in Fountain City, Indiana, dad met a beautiful young girl who swept him off his ministerial feet – Ethel Mae Wickersham-Brown.

My mother was born March 14, 1922, to John and Fannie (Russell) Wickersham. She was the 11th of 12 children. Her mother died when she was 12 years old. Soon thereafter Russell and Lettie Brown of Richmond, Indiana, adopted her. Following her graduation from Whitewater High School she entered a School of Nursing in Richmond. The Browns were the only grandparents I knew on my mother's side of the family. Nearly every summer we spent some time at Grandpa and Grandma Brown's home in Richmond.

The Wickershams came to America from Sussex, England. Thomas Wickersham, my maternal grandfather six times removed, sailed to America on the same vessel as did William Penn. He settled in Pennsylvania and was a prominent Quaker, as were all the Wickershams until my grandfather John broke the chain by living a very non-Quaker life. (On my father's side, all were also Quakers, or Friends, until a minister at the Christian Church in Zearing, Iowa, baptized my grandmother, Mary Elizabeth Hiserote,) One of my distant cousins, Dave Wickersham, played major league baseball from 1960-1969, pitching for the Kansas City A's and Detroit Tigers, putting together a respectable 68-47 career record.

★   ★   ★   ★   ★   ★   ★

LAST OF THE WAR BABIES

When my father and mother started courting, World War II was in full swing. They were married December 14, 1941, just one week after the Japanese attack on Pearl Harbor. Dad always called her "Dearie." Most people thought it was her given name. She gave up her career in nursing when they began their first ministry together on January 11, 1942, with the Southside Church of Christ, Danville, Illinois. On June 25, 1943, my sister Rebecca was born. She was the only one of us five children whom my Grandfather Knowles got to see before he was tragically killed later that year. He was just four days shy of his 62nd birthday. My parents moved to minister with the North Vernon Church of Christ about a year before I was born.

I believe that life begins at conception. If my mother carried me the normal nine months that means my life began somewhere during the third week of March 1945. What in the world was going on in the world at that time, while I was safe and snug in my mother's womb?

For starters, the Russian army liberated Auschwitz, that man-made hell, on January 27. The carnage they uncovered was enough to make case-hardened soldiers gag.

In March, two months before the liberation of Holland, a 14-year-old girl died in Bergen-Belsen. Young Anne Frank left a diary that closed with these words: "[I] keep on trying to find a way of becoming what I would so like to be, and what I could be, if . . . if only there weren't any other people living in the world." I think she meant *bad* people. (Since life begins at conception, my own life began about the same time Anne Frank's ended.)

★   ★   ★   ★   ★   ★   ★

Three powerful world figures joined World War II's 50 million dead in April. President Franklin Roosevelt died of a cerebral hemorrhage. Benito Mussolini died in a hail of vengeful gunfire. Adolf Hitler blew his brains out in a Berlin bunker. Also, the courageous German theologian, Dietrich Bonhoeffer, was hanged on orders from the Nazi secret police on April 9, a few minutes after conducting a Sunday church service for prisoners. Bonhoeffer had supported a movement to overthrow Hitler.

On July 1, Hank Greenberg, arguably the greatest Jewish baseball player ever, became the first major league player to return from duty in World War II – and hit a home run in his first game back!

In August, President Truman dropped the atomic bomb on two cities in Japan: Hiroshima (August 6) and Nagasaki (August 9). The devastation was beyond belief and brought a swift end to the war.

On September 2, General Douglas MacArthur received Japan's "unconditional surrender." Church bells tolled while citizens wept and cheered all over America.

In October the Chicago Cubs made it to the World Series. At this writing they have not made it back to the October Classic.

One month before I was born, October 23, Jackie Robinson broke baseball's color barrier when he was signed to a major league contract by the Brooklyn Dodgers.

Three days before I was born – another grim reminder of man's inhumanity to man. The Nuremberg War Crimes Trials began in Nuremberg, Germany – the very city where Nazi judges once ruled that Jews were subhumans.

With only 39 days left in 1945, I entered the world. But it is as though the umbilical cord linking me to 1945 was never severed.

★   ★   ★   ★   ★   ★   ★

In December, Cordell Hull, "the father of the United Nations," won the coveted Nobel Peace Prize.

My first Christmas was spent cradled in my mother's arms as a war-weary nation gratefully celebrated Christmas and the birth of the Prince of Peace. I would like to think that she sweetly sang to me:

Away in a manger, no crib for a bed,
The little Lord Jesus laid down His sweet head;
The stars in the sky looked down where He lay,
The little Lord Jesus, asleep on the hay.

Sometimes people who were born in 1945 are incorrectly lumped in with the Baby Boomer generation. Actually, we are a part of the World War II "war babies" generation, 16 million strong. With my birth coming so late in 1945, I was among the last of the wartime babies (people born between 1939–1945). Studies have been done to try to answer a question I have often pondered. "Did the wartime emotional stress of their mothers change their brain wiring in utero?" Perhaps that is why I have sometimes felt that the umbilical cord connecting me to 1945 has remained attached all these years. We World War II babies are sometimes known as "The Silent Generation," "Builders," or simply "Traditionalists." All three fit me to a T. (Though I am not being very "silent" here, am I?)

MY EARLY CHILDHOOD MEMORIES

I remember nothing of our brief stay in Polo, Illinois. Polo is about 15 miles north of Dixon, birthplace of President Ronald Reagan. We moved there in April 1946 and stayed there for about a year. We lived in a second-floor apartment over a downtown bank. I am told

★   ★   ★   ★   ★   ★   ★

that one day I tripped and fell, driving my front teeth up into my gums when I hit the windowsill. I bet they could hear me howl all over town. It's a good thing the window wasn't open or I would have been a goner, a spot on the sidewalk. Our uncle Troy Knowles lived in nearby Freeport, Illinois, and often came to see us. He had served in the Pacific during World War II. My father says it was one of his greatest joys to baptize his own brother in the Christian Church in Polo. My sister Rebecca loved to play hide-and-seek with Uncle "Snack," as he was called. One day she found a hiding place and yelled, "Come find me, Uncle Snack. I'm under the bed!"

From Polo we moved to Clay Center, Nebraska, in June 1947. We lived there until February 1949. My first memories are of beams of sunshine coming in through the stained glass windows of the church and of the swirling snow that swallowed up the figure of my father. I'm not sure which came first or even how old I was at the time. But I distinctly remember our family being caught in a snow-storm and my father getting out of the car to go for help. I was more than a little frightened as I saw him disappear into the driving snow. Dad believes that it was a bad storm in Colorado in November of 1947 or 1948. Anyhow, that is my most vivid early childhood memory. I would have been two or three at the time.

My sister Muriel was born February 23, 1948. My mother suffered what is now called postpartum depression after Muriel's birth. Mom was hospitalized in Lincoln for a time, and so we three children were taken in by loving Christians. A crippled woman, Nora Werner, cared for baby Muriel while Rebecca and I went to live on a farm with Henry and Beulah Shaw. Beulah made me a little sailor suit that I was very proud to wear. (That's me wearing it on the cover of this book!)

★   ★   ★   ★   ★   ★   ★

One day I did something naughty and was made to stand in a corner. A little later Beulah felt a tug on her skirt. It was I. I looked up at her and said, "I torry, Boo." (I couldn't pronounce my S's or her name.) She gathered me up in her arms and gave me a big hug. Maybe that was my first sin, confession, and experience of receiving forgiveness!

When mom came home from the hospital, both of my grand-mothers came (at separate times) to help with the children. One day when Grandma Brown was feeding me, I scarfed it down, stuck out my empty bowl and demanded, "'Mo!" I wanted more and I got it.

Dad also did some weeknight preaching for small rural churches in the area: Angus, Deweese, and Harvard. I remember going with him to some of those meetings. One of the first church songs that I recall being sung was "God Is Calling the Prodigal." Its haunting refrain remains with me to this day. *"Calling now for thee, O weary prodigal come."* I have loved the hymns of the church ever since.

In February 1949 we moved to Whiting, Iowa. About the only thing I can remember about the church is that the drapes behind the pulpit were purple. I could be wrong. I think the auditorium floor sloped to the front, as many did in those years.

My third and final sister, Bonnie, was born on August 12, 1950. I was a little put out because I wanted a brother. Being the only boy in the house with three sisters was a burden hard to bear, but I must say that I bore it manfully. Actually, I got along with my sisters pretty well. Bonnie, a "tomboy," was almost like having a brother. Dad called her "The Wabash Cannonball" because of the way she tore around the house. Dad had nicknames for all of us. Rebecca was "Keb" (Bec back-wards), Muriel was "Mayo," my brother David, yet to be born, was "Hoom," and I was "Lamb" or "Lamb-boy." I guess I crawled into

★   ★   ★   ★   ★   ★   ★

dad's study one day and he asked, "Are you my little puppy?" I answered, "No, I am your little lamb." I feel a little sheepish about it now.

I started school in the fall of 1950. I was not yet five years old. My teacher was Miss Mustard. On May Day I hung a May basket on her door, knocked, and ran like the dickens. I later told my parents, "Mith Muthard chathed me and caught me and kithed me." I had a tooth out at the time. This may be about the time that I bit myself on the arm and told my dad that Rebecca had bit me. What was I thinking? For when dad checked the bite marks, there was the evidence that I had bitten myself to spite her. So I got the spanking instead of her. It was kind of like Haman getting hung on the gallows he had built for Mordecai. Well, maybe not quite. I wasn't very smart in those days. One day Rebecca said to me, "Oh, Victor, you're so stupid." I padded into my father's study and asked him, "Dad, is 'stupid' good or bad?" I was beyond pathetic.

My father was an accomplished poet, composing about 3,000 poems in his lifetime, many of them about our family. One of them, "The Day Victor Started School," was 23 stanzas long. Here's the next-to-last stanza:

> Although the future is obscure
> I hope and trust and pray
> A wholesome, glad, triumphant life
> Is his beyond today.

As I write these words at the age of 62, I hope and pray that I have lived up to his hopes and prayers. I do know that I was born a Victor and a victor is a conqueror. I do feel that my life has been most-

★   ★   ★   ★   ★   ★   ★

ly "wholesome, glad, and triumphant" – though there have been times when I was none of the three. But through Christ, the greatest conqueror of all, I am a Victor and not a victim. As the hymn says, "He arose a Victor from the dark domain, and He lives forever with His saints to reign."

We had naptime in school. We were supposed to lie down on our little blankets and take a rest. It was probably for the teacher's benefit. I took one of my favorite toys with me to school that fateful day. It was a small cream-colored car, a convertible, with a green retractable roof. I was pushing it back and forth on the floor when it got away from me. I never saw it again. Some classmate probably snatched it up, stuck it in his pocket, and acted like he was asleep. I still think about that little car. And the dirty rat that took it home.

I had a habit of getting up and walking around during class. Must have been nervous energy. One day the teacher tied me to my chair with a tea towel. The ACLU wasn't around in those days, at least in Whiting. My parents would not have been inclined to sue the school anyway. So I dutifully did my time for my crime and learned not to go for a stroll when the teacher was calling roll.

My father saved most of my report cards from kindergarten to my senior year of high school. I got off to a fair start garnering B's in Reading, Literature, Music, and Writing. I got C's in Language, Social Studies, and Art. I was given a B for Conduct.

Dad brought the celebrated evangelist O. L. Mankamyer to Whiting to conduct a series of sermons on the Holy Spirit. After church one evening dad wanted to impress Brother Mankamyer with my budding Bible knowledge. He said, "Victor, tell Brother Mac the names of the three sons of Noah." I knew who they were but I froze up in the

★   ★   ★   ★   ★   ★   ★

presence of theological greatness. Brother Mac tried to help me out by stretching out the name of the first son, hoping I would pick up from there. He said, "Sham . . ." All I could think of was "shampoo," so, like a dork, I responded, "Poo . . ." From that day to the day he died Brother Mankamyer referred to me as Shampoo Knowles. It was a little embarrassing to receive letters from him addressed to "Mr. Shampoo Knowles" when I was in my first full-time ministry.

I believe it was in 1951 that my father was asked to speak at the "Christ for the World" Conference, hosted by First Christian Church in Inglewood, California. Dad took Rebecca and me along with him on the cross-country trip. I remember sitting in the balcony of that big church and hearing the great evangelist Archie Word preach, never dreaming that some day I would be the great man's biographer.

In August, 1951, just before I was to begin first grade, we moved again. I never thought much about all those moves until much later in life. I did not know that nearly everywhere thus far, with the exception of Danville, my father had experienced some opposition to his biblical preaching. Sometimes it was very strong. A woman who was not even a member of the Whiting church ran the Ladies Circle. Things went downhill from there. My mother, bless her heart, as gentle a Christian as ever lived, once stood up in a congregational meeting and sweetly asked a question that the troublemakers should have carried with them to their graves: "Why can't Christians just be Christian?" That is still a pretty good question for churches to ponder before asking a godly minister to leave.

HAPPY IN HAMBURG

My father had previously done some guest speaking at churches

★   ★   ★   ★   ★   ★   ★

in both Hamburg, Iowa, and Isadora, Missouri. Both congregations were interested in having dad come and be their new minister. Dad and mom liked both churches. Either one would have been fine with them. They put out a simple fleece: the church that was first to extend a formal invitation to them to come would be the indicator as to where God wanted them to go.

I have often wondered how different my life might have turned out if the good elder in Isadora had used the telephone instead of a 3-cent postage stamp. (I say that because the Hamburg Church of Christ was where I was ordained, married, and enjoyed two ministries.) So I believe to this day that it was providential that Faye Weatherhead (God bless him!), one of the elders in the Hamburg church, picked up the phone and made a long-distance call to my dad, telling him the good news that Hamburg wanted him to be their preacher. You didn't make long-distance phone calls in those days unless it was an absolute emergency. By the time the letter of invitation arrived from Isadora, my folks had already accepted the call from Hamburg. And so on September 2, 1951, began one of my father's happiest ministries and our family's most pleasant stays.

The church at 1305 Main Street became our entire life. I say that because we lived in a new addition to the back of the church. Mom made it into a nice home for us. My bedroom was curtained off from my sisters' shared bedroom. One Sunday evening I went to sleep in church and when I awoke the sanctuary was dark and empty. At least I didn't have far to go to find my own bed! Once I had a deep chest cold and mom applied a mustard plaster to my chest. (I preferred *Vick's* VapoRub of course.) The benefits of being sick and staying home in bed were that I usually got to

★   ★   ★   ★   ★   ★   ★

drink 7-Up or Bubble-Up. Mom used those drinks in a medicinal manner and that was all right by me.

Dad's study was stage right from the pulpit in the sanctuary. I loved the smell of mimeograph ink when he would crank off his paper *The Christian Campaigner.* Sometimes he would let us help him fold the paper. I loved how the sunlight came through the stained glass windows in his office and in the main sanctuary. I always felt like I was in "the house of the Lord" no matter where I was in the church edifice. One of my big thrills was getting to pull the bell rope in the vestibule on Sunday mornings. Sometimes it would lift me clear off the floor. I wanted everyone in town to hear the bell and come to church.

I went through my first three grades of school at Hamburg Elementary. The school was just a few blocks from the church. You had to climb some concrete steps from the sidewalk up to the school. I loved recess where we got to play ball in warm weather. One day I wasn't watching and someone swung a bat and got me right in the mouth. It's a wonder I had any teeth left. Where the playground ended there was a steep bank that contained loads of broken slate. Sometimes some of us boys went over the edge and stuffed our pockets full of the blue-gray slate. You could write on it with a piece of chalk, just like you could on a blackboard because it was made of the same stuff.

Today the elementary school is named after Marnie Simons. She was one strict, no-nonsense disciplinarian. She was my first grade teacher. I was just an average student under her tutelage, getting four C+'s, three C's, and one C- (in writing, to my shame!). One day in reading circle Gary Cradic and I were whispering. She came up behind, grabbed us by our hair and cracked our heads together. Another teacher was Miss Cane. One could say that if you misbehaved in either

★   ★   ★   ★   ★   ★   ★

class one would give you heck and the other would give you the cane! (We were not allowed to use the word "heck," "darn," "gee," "geemi-nee Christmas," "gosh," "gosh darn" or "Holy Smoke" in our house. We were taught that they were simply euphemisms for "hell," "damn," "Jesus," "Jesus Christ," "God" "God damn," and "Holy Ghost." "Judas Priest," I must confess, became my favorite "cuss" word. Maybe I felt it was the "safest.") During second grade, under Mrs. Collins, I earned three B's, five C+'s, and just one C (in spelling! Drat!).

My classrooms were typical of the times. A 48-star United States flag hung on the wall behind the teacher's wooden desk. Along with the letters of the alphabet, there were pictures of all of the United States presidents on the wall. Harry S Truman was president in 1951. In par-ticular I remember my third grade teacher, Miss Fern Wagner. She was also a member of the church where dad preached. Each school day began with Miss Wagner leading us in the Pledge of Allegiance, read-ing a verse from the Bible, and offering a brief prayer. Sometimes she would read to us from a children's book during the reading hour. My favorite was *Toby Tyler (Or "Ten Days with a Circus")*. It was about a boy who ran away from his foster home to join the circus. There he became attached to "Mr. Stubbs," a chimpanzee. I was so sad when Miss Wagner read to us about the chimpanzee's death at the hands of a hunter that I put my head down on my desk and sobbed. I cried myself to sleep for several nights. I have never taken the life of any animal with a gun, nor have I ever had a gun in the house (although I believe the Second Amendment allows for a citizen to bear arms).

I got my best grades under Miss Wagner. To this day I believe that when a teacher believes in you, you will believe in yourself. I was given four B's, two B-'s, one C+, and one C. I would not receive such

★   ★   ★   ★   ★   ★   ★

good grades (in my opinion) until we returned to Iowa after a disastrous academic showing in Idaho. Once I wrote to my father, who was
probably gone in a revival meeting who knows where. "Dear Daddy,
How are you? I am fine. I got a 90 in Arithmetic today. Today I pulled
my tooth, and it hurt. I did it by myself at school. Some men took Taffy
away Thursday morning. David's got the chicken pox and Rebecca's
got a fever. Did you know that the [Chicago] Bears beat the [Chicago]
Cardinals? I watched them play football over at Kyle Cook's [Koch's].
I went over to Johnny Huekel's and rode horses. Sincerely yours, R. C.
A. Victor." It's a wonder no one ever called me "R. C. A. Victor." Now
that the cat's out of the bag, probably everyone will! In my office today
I have a tin with the famous R. C. A. Victor dog "listening for his master's voice" over the old-fashioned phonograph player.

My favorite times of the school year were Thanksgiving,
Christmas, and Valentine's Day. I liked to paint with watercolors, and
I enjoyed the smell of construction paper and glue as I drew pilgrims
and turkeys and made snowflakes and valentines. On Valentine's Day
we made boxes to drop our valentines in. I had a special interest in
Emily Gound. In fact, Emily was the first girl I ever kissed. This must
have been around 1954, when I was going on nine. Emily did not
come to our church but lived just a block from the church. After
church she would come tripping down the alley where I would meet
her and we would tenderly kiss each other. An aside: years later, when
Evelyn and I were married and living in Hamburg, we attended a ball
game at Clayton Field one night. Emily Gound walked by and Evelyn,
never having seen her before or knowing our "romantic history,"
commented, "That woman has a beautiful mouth." I grinned and
said, "I know."

★   ★   ★   ★   ★   ★   ★

Television was still a fairly new invention in the early 50s, so we read lots of books. The public library was right next to the church building on Main Street. I was in the library most every day reading *Boy's Life* and checking out every book ever written by John R. Tunis who wrote sports fiction, specializing in books written about the Brooklyn Dodgers. I fell in love with Roy Tucker, Razzle Nugent, Fat Stuff, Highpockets, Spike Russell, Rats Doyle, and a host of his other memorable characters.

MY GLOVE AFFAIR WITH BASEBALL BEGINS

My lifelong love affair with baseball began in Hamburg. The town had a crackerjack town team. I loved to hear the crack of the bat when ash met horsehide. The smell of a leather glove is still one of the most wonderful smells in the world. I would pound the ball into the pocket again and again, wrapping the glove around the ball with rubber bands before I went to bed at night. I was too young to play organized baseball yet, but I often played catch with Dad in the back yard of the public library.

On October 1, 1951, almost exactly one month after we moved to Hamburg, one of the greatest games in baseball history was played at the Polo Grounds in New York between the Brooklyn Dodgers and the New York Giants. It was the third and deciding game of a three-game playoff to see who would go on to meet the Cleveland Indians in the World Series. The Giants' Bobby Thomson went to the plate in the bottom of the ninth with two men on and first base open. Ralph Branca chose to pitch to Thomson rather than Willie Mays who was on deck. Who can forget what happened next? Here's Russ Hodges, Giants broadcaster, to help you remember.

★   ★   ★   ★   ★   ★   ★

"There's a long drive . . . it's gonna be . . . I believe . . . the Giants win the pennant! . . . the Giants win the pennant! . . . the Giants win the pennant! . . . Bobby Thomson hit into the lower deck of the left field stands . . . the Giants win the pennant and they're going crazy . . . I don't believe it . . . I don't believe it . . . I will NOT believe it! . . ."

Thomson's home run became known as "The Shot Heard 'Round the World." If my dad had not himself been a baseball fan, I never would have heard that classic call on our old Crosley radio. With one crack of the bat I was hooked for life on the Great American Pastime. And who can forget the amazing over-the-shoulder catch made by Willie Mays in the subsequent World Series when he tracked down a long fly ball hit by the Indians' Vic Wertz?

There were lots of boys in the Hamburg church with whom I became fast friends: Gary Bryant, Gary Cradic, Kyle, Keevin, and Earl Koch, Steve and Phil Sheldon, Tim Wright, Johnny Huekel, Eddie Beam, the Zach brothers, and others. Johnny had some boxing gloves, and we used to go after each other like Joe Louis and Rocky Marciano. One Sunday afternoon he nearly knocked me out the open window of his second-story bedroom. Those of us who lived in town played ball all we could. The Koch brothers created a nifty rubber ball stadium in the back yard of their grandmother's house on Park Street. An old garage served as the backstop. The outfielder was the most important player; he had to be sure and snag the ball before it broke a window. The plastic fun ball and wiffle ball had not yet been created, so we used a small rubber ball, a littler smaller than a regulation baseball. It became one crimson blur when you really tagged it with the handle of

★   ★   ★   ★   ★   ★   ★

an old broomstick. Gary Cradic could throw a wicked curve ball that would drop right out of sight.

A long line of peony bushes separated the churchyard from the library grounds. It is a wonder that any of the peonies ever bloomed because after church was over on Sunday or Wednesday nights, we boys would pluck the round buds off and fire them at one another. If you ever got hit in the side of the head with a hard-thrown peony bud, you would never forget it. But it was great fun.

We boys all looked up to some of the older boys in the church: Marvin Oakes, Jan Clifton, Carroll Belle, Dale Emberton, and Rex Bryant (though I think Rex may have been in the army then). All the older girls raved about Marvin's good looks, handsome devil that he was. Jan was a big guy with a flattop haircut. One night after church he was blocking the door while shaking hands with dad. I reached up and tapped him on the hip and said, "Out of the way, small fry." Jan got a big kick out of that and never let me forget the incident. Dale started a Boys' Club just for us. On Saturday we would go to Ronald and Lorine Emberton's farm home, east of town. I remember in the fall how we would play touch football in the yard and then enjoy hot chocolate that Lorine made for us while Dale taught us a lesson from the Bible.

I liked football but not like I loved baseball. One Christmas I got a junior-sized Franklin football and I kicked the tar out that baby all Christmas vacation long in the big backyard of the library. The NFL had not fully developed in the early 50s so I did not follow any one team until a little later in my young life.

When winter came and we had a good covering of snow on the ground, every kid in Hamburg grabbed his or her wooden sled and headed for Dean's Hill. The city fathers would block off Argyle Street so

★   ★   ★   ★   ★   ★   ★

we could zoom down the hill at breakneck speed on our trusty sleds. There is nothing quite so exhilarating as the winter wind whipping you in your half-frozen face as you are zipping down Dean's Hill. I am happy to report that the city dads still block off Dean's Hill for the kids.

WHERE I FELL IN LOVE . . . WITH THE CHURCH

Dad had one of his greatest ministries in Hamburg. The church grew by leaps and bounds. Scores of people were baptized or transferred their membership. Dad brought in some great evangelists to conduct revival meetings. The ones I personally remember were Donald G. Hunt, Remi Duhon, and Ottis Platt. The sanctuary would be full to overflowing with men standing against the back wall. In the summer the windows would be opened and people would congregate outside to listen to the singing and the preaching. One of the elders, Ronald Emberton, loved to lead the church in singing "Power in the Blood." He could get as many as seven "powers" in the chorus.

Another elder, Raymond Wise, had such a unique way of phrasing his prayers that all of us boys could repeat it by rote. "Our dear kind and gracious heavenly Father, 'tis again that we assemble, thanking Thee for the many blessings Thou hast bestowed upon us." Ask any Hamburg boy worth his biblical salt to repeat it today, and he could do it at the drop of a hat. But who wears hats anymore?

Hamburg is where I fell in love with the church for which Christ died. That church had such a positive impact and influence on my life that I have carried a high view of the church ever since. Every New Year's Eve the church met upstairs to "pray in" the New Year at midnight. Every Sunday morning the choir led the congregation in singing the grand old hymns and anthems of the church. I loved to

★   ★   ★   ★   ★   ★   ★

hear Maude McSpadden and Frances Beam sing. Most of the time I sat with my mother in church, but sometimes she let me sit by Miss Barbara Foster. One Sunday Barbara was seated on stage in the choir. I reached into her purse and pulled out a package of Juicy Fruit gum. I held it up so she could see. She smiled and held up one finger. That meant I could have one stick of gum. I unwrapped it and popped it in my mouth. It tasted so good I went for another, and another, and another. Each time I thoughtfully held one up she frantically shook her head "no." I just kept folding them up and pushing them in until there was no more gum left in the package – and no more room in my mouth for any more gum. On our 40th wedding anniversary in 2007 she sent me a special gift – a pack of Juicy Fruit gum!

I loved Sunday School. Each Sunday morning, before the church service in the sanctuary below, we met in the new Sunday School addition on the second floor. We all sat in our little wooden chairs, prim and proper. We had visual aids in those days – flannel-graph lessons. We sang rousing choruses like "Boys and Girls for Jesus," "Climb, Climb Up Sunshine Mountain," and "I'll Be a Sunbeam for Jesus." A sunbeam for Jesus is all I've ever wanted to be.

A blind man tapped his way to church every Sunday morning. His name was Opie and he ran a little popcorn stand and candy store downtown. We called him "Opie the Popcorn Man." When church was over we all lined up in front of the church to get a free piece of candy from Opie. If you tried to get in line twice and snag a second piece of candy, the blind man could tell if you had already received your share.

One night after services the Aistrope girls climbed the stairs leading to the baptistery. Laurel got a little too close to the edge and tumbled in. Her sister Linda went running to her mother, crying,

★ ★ ★ ★ ★ ★ ★

"Mom, mom! Laurel fell into the 'baptism' – but it didn't do her any good!"

I remember three funerals my dad conducted in Hamburg. One was for Ida B. Wise, a woman of some renown in the national Women's Christian Temperance Union. I was once told that a correspondent for *Time* magazine covered the funeral. To this day there is a big rock in front of the church with a bronze plaque honoring the life of Ida B. Wise. We used to climb up on that rock and jump off after services. The second funeral I recall was that of Elmer Bryant, father of my good pal Gary Bryant. Brother Bryant was killed in an auto accident while driving three of his children, including Gary, to a country school. The church was as full as I ever remember it being. Dad told how Elmer had read his Bible and knelt in prayer as he always did the day of the fatal accident. The third "funeral" was that of "Dickie Bird," our pet canary, whose passing made me very sad. Mom tied a little red ribbon around his yellow neck and placed him in a matchbox lined with cotton. I burst into tears when we closed the lid on poor Dickie and we laid him to rest in the cold, hard ground of the churchyard. I can still take you to the spot should you be so inclined. Dad delivered a magnificent eulogy about how Dickie brought joy to everyone by using his God-given talent to sing, just as we should use our God-given talents to bless others. But I was beyond comfort.

Another bird story. One fine Sunday morning, a sparrow flew into the sanctuary. Faye Weatherhead was singing a solo. As he sang the sparrow continued to fly from one side of the vaulted ceiling to the other, desperate to find a way out. The eyes of every worshipper went back and forth, like spectators at a tennis match. When he was finished, Brother Weatherhead said, "Well, I think I chose the wrong song

★   ★   ★   ★   ★   ★   ★

this morning. I should have sung, 'His Eye is on the Sparrow.'" Everyone enjoyed a good laugh.

NO CREED BUT THE LONE RANGER'S CREED

It was at Faye and Julia's home that I saw my first scary TV program. I don't remember the name of the show. I just remember it had spooky organ music and kept focusing on a vase of flowers – lilies of the valley. I've never cared for those flowers since. I saw another scary TV show at the Sheldons. A deranged killer would dress as a woman, act like "her" car was broken down on a deserted stretch of highway, and then summarily dispatch (a nice word for "kill") the Good Samaritans who stopped to help. Maybe that's why I seldom stop to help strangers on the road! But these were child's play to the comic books I saw at one kid's house. I remember one where a mad sadist was cutting out the tongues of all his victims so they couldn't rat on him to the police. Pretty gory stuff for DC Comics, even in the 50s. The comic books I liked featured milder fare: Little Lulu, Porky Pig, Daffy Duck, Mickey Mouse, Donald Duck, et al. I guess their creators had a thing for alliteration. But what was with Porky Pig and most of the others going without trousers? Weird.

We did not have a television set in our home, but I would see TV shows from time to time in my friends' homes. The "Howdy Doody Show" was big then. I remember the dumb looking dog in an ad for Nestle's chocolate. "N-e-s-t-l-e-s, Nestles makes the very best . . . choclate!" I also liked the adventures of "Jungle Jim." But listening to broadcasts on the Crosley radio was where the real magic took place. "The Lone Ranger" was my favorite. To the strains of the William Tell

★   ★   ★   ★   ★   ★   ★

Overture, pounding hoofs, and blazing gunfire the announcer's voice thrilled my soul.

"A fiery horse with the speed of light, a cloud of dust and a hearty 'Hi-yo Silver!' The Lone Ranger. 'Hi-yo Silver, away!' With his faithful Indian companion Tonto, the daring and resourceful masked rider of the plains led the fight for law and order in the early West. Return with us now to those thrilling days of yesteryear. The Lone Ranger rides again!"

Brace Beemer was the radio voice of the Lone Ranger (Clayton Moore did the TV series). The bad guys were always whacking poor old Tonto on his topknot. The Lone Ranger always used silver bullets and never shot to kill. I loved it that the Lone Ranger's nephew, Dan Reid, had a horse named *Victor* (son of Silver)! Along with thousands of other boys, I took **The Lone Ranger Creed.**

*"**I believe** that to have a friend a man must be one.*

"That all men are created equal and that everyone has written within himself the power to make this a better world.

"That God put the firewood there but that every man must gather and light it himself.

"In being prepared physically, mentally, and morally to fight when necessary for that which is right.

"That a man should make the most of what equipment he has.

"That 'This government of the people, by the people and for the people" shall live always.

"That men should live by the rule of what is best for the greatest number.

"That sooner or later ... somewhere, somehow ... we must settle with the world and make payment for what we have taken.

★   ★   ★   ★   ★   ★   ★

"That all things change but truth, and that truth alone lives on forever.

"In my Creator, my country, my fellow man."

— **THE LONE RANGER**

I wasn't too big on Gene Autry (who rode Champion), but I did like cowboy shows featuring the adventures of Roy Rogers (who rode Trigger), Wild Bill Hickock (who rode Buckshot), Hopalong Cassidy (who rode Trooper), and Lash LaRue (who rode Black Diamond). I also liked the Cisco Kid, and the Range Rider and his sidekick Dick West. One Christmas I got a Western fort set, complete with plastic horses, corral fences, lookout posts, cowboys, Indians, teepees, and even a campfire. Cap guns gave off a specific smell of burnt powder. Gary Bryant and I used to play cowboys and Indians by the hour. We must have "killed" each other scores of times (in spite of the good example set by the Lone Ranger), only to be miraculously "resurrected" to fire away at each other again.

I remember, too, the radio signoff song sung by Roy Rogers and Dale Evans Rogers, "Happy Trails." My mother would often sing along with them as they sang:

Happy trails to you, until we meet again,

Happy trails to you, keep smilin' until then,

Who cares about the clouds when we're together?

Just sing a song and bring the sunny weather!

Happy trails to you, 'til we meet again.

THE DAY I PRAYED TO THE DEVIL!

Sometimes my mother would send me down to the market owned by Harvey and Mabel Thomas, who were also members of the church. Most of the time it was for milk and bread. I remember two

★   ★   ★   ★   ★   ★   ★

incidents that are kind of embarrassing to me. The first incident was when I got caught trying to leave the store without paying for something. Mr. Thomas had some novelty items and one of them was a child-sized ring with a beautiful fake blue stone set in the center. It seemed like every kid in class had one except me. I think it cost only a nickel, but I didn't have a nickel. I tried it on. A perfect fit! The temptation was too great. Mr. Thomas was up on a ladder, stocking the top shelf, his back to me. I turned to leave but was stopped in my tracks by the words: "PUT IT BACK!" I never knew little Harvey Thomas could have such a big voice. I put the ring back and slunk out the store, praying fervently that Mr. Thomas would not rat me out. He didn't. Stores should be so wise as to have cardboard cutouts of little Harvey Thomas with a battery-operated voice: "PUT IT BACK!" It might deter shoplifting.

The second incident, well, let the telling of it suffice. Mom sent me down to the Thomas' market, with the exact change, for some milk and bread. After paying for the groceries I was left with nothing except a strong longing for a piece of bubble gum. Alas and alack, what was I to do? There was no money left to buy a piece of gum. Mom knew how much money she had entrusted to my pudgy hands. I dared not try to pilfer anything ever again under the watchful eyes of Harvey Thomas. Therefore, I prayed to God for a miracle. Nothing happened. So I went over to the dark side. Yes, this is the day I, a son of a preacher man, prayed to the devil! In my childish stupidity I squeezed my eyes shut and prayed thusly, "O dear Devil, if you are real, give me a piece of bubble gum." I opened my eyes. And it came to pass, behold, at my feet ensconced in my Buster Brown shoes, lay a brand new piece of bubble gum still in the wrapper. Shocked and amazed, I picked it up, unfolded

★   ★   ★   ★   ★   ★   ★

the bright wrapper, and popped the gum in my mouth. Oh, the sweet taste of forbidden fruit! But when I got home, Mom spotted my carnal cud and said, "Where did you get that?" Behold, your sin shall find you out! I was stumped. What could I say? "Mom, I prayed to the devil and he gave it to me?" I don't think so! I stammered some lame excuse, all to no avail. Out came the paddle minus the bounce-back rubber ball. Over her knees I went. Whack, whack, whack! For the wages of sin is . . . a good paddling.

MY DAD, THE PEACEMAKER

In the spring of 1952 a terrible flood devastated the town of Hamburg. Dad drove us up to a viewpoint on a high bluff where we could look out and see nothing but water as far as the eye could see. South Hamburg was completely inundated and the turgid waters came right on down Main Street to the very steps leading up to our church. We had sandbagged the church in the event the waters might come that far. I thought it was pretty keen that the floodwaters were stopped at the Hamburg Church of Christ. It was like the angel that stayed the hand of Abraham when he was about to slay his son. It was as though God Himself spoke: "This far but no farther!"

Sometimes we accompanied dad on his trips to conduct revivals. He once held a meeting in Yellville, Arkansas, for O. L. Mankamyer. One afternoon a hornet stung me on my ankle. At one of the evening services a lady with a large goiter sat behind us. I kept turning around to stare, so intrigued was I by this fascinating specimen, especially when she sang. No one could sing like Brother Mankamyer. When he sang, "When They Ring Those Golden Bells for You and Me," you wanted to blast off for heaven on the spot.

★   ★   ★   ★   ★   ★   ★

One night dad took our family along to a church where he was to preach. I believe it might have been down near Rock Port, Missouri, the Nishnabotna church of which I will have more to say in the next chapter. A highway patrolman pulled us over. He walked up to the car and asked dad to get out. Our car had a taillight out, but I didn't know that. I thought dad was in big trouble. I stuck my head out the window and yelled, "Dad, is he going to put you in jail?" Dad and the cop got a big kick out of that. I think I may have listened to one too many episodes of "Boston Blackie."

My dad was a peacemaker. I have written about this in the story "Christmas Hero" which is in one of my books (*Christmas Tonight, Crosley Field*, 1993). It was Christmas Day, 1952, I believe, and I was out in the snow-covered backyard of the library, kicking my new football. I heard two cars squeal to a stop on the street side that was almost hidden by bare spirea bushes. I heard two men yelling at each other, swearing to beat the band. I sneaked up to the bushes and peered through. Now the men were slugging each other with might and main. I can still hear the sodden sounds of fist on flesh – can still see the spots of crimson blood splatter the snow. I hightailed on back to the church house and yelled for dad to come.

And I can still see the slight figure of my father, bareheaded in the winter wind, bravely approach those two men, who were still swearing like sailors and slugging each other like prizefighters. Dad said words to the effect: "Men, on this day, of all days, you should not be fighting. This is a day of 'peace on earth, good will to men.' Now why don't you quit your fighting and shake hands like good fellows." Then and there I saw a true miracle, a Christmas miracle. Before you could say "Jack Robinson," those men hung their heads in shame. One

*   *   *   *   *   *   *

stuck out his hand and the other grabbed it and murmured an apology. They got back in their cars and quietly drove away. Perhaps that was the occasion that sparked within me a desire to be a peacemaker. Imagine that – a war baby who became a peacemaker!

Another memorable Christmas in Hamburg that I have written about was "The Christmas That Stank to High Heaven" (*ibid.*), much too long to tell here. We drew names each Christmas and this particular year I got my mother's name. I went down to Wiig's Five and Dime and bought her a record by Spike Jones and his band, "I Saw Mommy Kissing Santa Claus." I was so proud of this purchase but when dad saw it he said that mom would probably like something else. I put my earmuffs and rubber boots back on and trudged through snow and slush back to the store in the gathering gloom in high dudgeon. "Stupid Christmas!" I muttered. I exchanged my lovely record for the first thing I saw – a bottle of perfume. But when mom opened her gift on Christmas morning, I knew I had made the right choice. She dabbed a little perfume behind each ear. She smelled so good. And when the Christmas text was read and explained that one of the three gifts brought was perfume (frankincense) I knew my choice was inspired.

"WHEN WE ASUNDER PART"

We all got a great gift on March 31, 1954, when my brother David was born. I was probably more excited than my sisters since I had *finally* gotten a brother, even though he was about nine years my junior. I pulled him around in my little red Radio Flyer wagon so he could see the sights of Hamburg whether the kid wanted to or not.

In May of that same year dad accepted a speaking assignment for a Bible conference at Boise Bible College, in Boise, Idaho. Not long

★　★　★　★　★　★　★

after he returned to Hamburg, a letter came from Boise inviting him to join Kenneth Beckman as associate minister at the church and join the faculty at BBC. If ever there was a decision my father would later regret making, it was this one. The Hamburg church was going great guns. We were one happy family there. I could have lived in Hamburg forever and ever and have been happy as a clam. To this day I remember with sadness our last day in Hamburg, a going-away picnic in the city park, pulling out of town in our car, looking back at the tear-stained faces of the church members and all my friends. For the first time in my young life I understood the words of a hymn I had heard sung at church again and again:

When we asunder part, it gives us inward pain;
But we shall still be joined in heart, and hope to meet again.

★   ★   ★   ★   ★   ★   ★

CHAPTER TWO

"GO WEST, YOUNG MAN!"

So I did. I took the admonition of the venerable Horace Greeley and accompanied my family on the long trek from Iowa to Idaho in our green 1950 Chevrolet. What else could I do? Hide in the basement of the Hamburg church? I don't think so! Do you remember Chevrolet's jingle? *"See the USA in your Chevrolet."* Our family did, at least part of it. We traveled through Nebraska, Colorado and Wyoming before reaching Idaho. In those days we stayed with friends along the way. I can only remember staying in a motel once in my younger years, in Kemmerer, Wyoming. I don't believe we frequented very many restaurants either. Most of the time we stopped at a grocery store and mom made sandwiches that we ate in the car or in a city park along the way.

I would like to say that I fell in love with the great American West on that trip, but I was probably carsick most of the way. I used to get terribly carsick, and dad would have to stop the car every so often just for me. The fresh air felt mighty good, and I'm sure the rest of the family was glad to get out of the car too.

LIFE AT WASHINGTON ELEMENTARY

We arrived in Boise, "The City of Trees," on August 18, 1954. Mom was somewhat disappointed because the new house that had

★　★　★　★　★　★　★

been promised by the powers that be was not there. Instead, we moved into an old house and made do with what we had. My three sisters and I were enrolled in Washington Elementary on North 15th Street, within easy walking distance of our house. About a month after we started school the phrase *"under God"* was added to the Pledge of Allegiance by an act of Congress. And so for the first time I pledged that we are "one nation *under God*, indivisible, with liberty and justice for all." Dwight D. Eisenhower was now our president having defeated Adlai Stevenson in a landslide. That was fine with me. Like millions of Americans, I liked Ike. (Eisenhower's irenic campaign motto was, "I like Ike.")

I had done fairly well in school up to this time, but I didn't do very well in Boise. I have joked that I liked fourth grade so well that I took it twice, but deep down I was more than ashamed that I was held back. That's what they did in those days. If you hadn't proved by your grades that you were ready for the next grade, you didn't get promoted. Arithmetic was my big undoing. I was fair with letters but not so good with numbers. Dad would sit down with me at the table after supper and try to help me with fractions and the like, but I just didn't "get it." I had a hard time even trying to tell time. Numbers were my downfall. Miss Reading was no Miss Wagner. One day she caught me passing a note to a girl and made me stand up and read it to the rest of the class. I racked up nothing but F's and D's in Arithmetic. Other than a B in reading (under Miss Reading!) the rest of my grades were C's.

My new best friend in school was Tony Stapello, an Italian kid who took me under his wing. I was the smallest kid in class but no one would pick on me as long as Tony was with me. The year I should have been in fifth grade Tony stuck by me. When some kid across the street

★   ★   ★   ★   ★   ★   ★   ★

yelled at me that I was stupid because I had flunked fourth grade, Tony took out after him. After that they let me alone. Except for the Scharf brothers, Ted and Gene. They lived down the street from us and they were poor and mean, a bad combination. Gene had green teeth but that was because he rarely brushed them. We got into a fight once, and I think I bested him. At least I gave him my best. Tony held Ted at bay until the fisticuffs had ended. An aside: Many years later I received a nice letter from Tony's mother, who had read one of my articles in the national weekly *The Lookout*. She told me Tony was a cop in Boise. Why was I not surprised?

Gene came to class one day with a poem he said he had written to complete an assignment. It was the famous poem, "A Dillar, a Dollar, a 10 o'Clock Scholar." He tried to convince Miss Heideman he had really written it. What a dolt. At least my poem was original. It was about the moon. Trouble was: each line ended with the same word – "moon." No wonder it rhymed so well!

I couldn't get music either. The music teacher provided us with "tonettes" (recorders), plastic wind instruments. I just couldn't learn to read music. When our class gave a concert, I stood there with the rest of the class and pretended I was playing. I felt like a first class idiot. My grades, however, improved the second time around in 4th grade: all B's and C's (even in Arithmetic and Music).

One time Tony and I got sent to the principal's office for throwing snowballs on the playground. Like we were the only ones throwing snowballs! I was impressed how Tony took his paddling like a man and so I braced myself and did the same. Then we went out and sat in a snow bank to cool down our warmed-up seats. In those days if you

* * * * * * *

got a paddling at school they sent a note home with you to your parents telling them about the incident. So, most likely, I got another paddling after I got home.

At our home mom and dad used "The Pink Board." That's all it was: a board that was painted pink. All I know is that it left us "in the pink" once it was used. I once wrote on it, "In case of fire, throw this in." Alas, there never was a fire, so The Pink Board remained. Actually, when we were disciplined at home, it was always done in love. Dad or mom would sit us down, tell us what we had done wrong, and then administer the spanking. It did no good to stick a book down the back of your pants. The sound of a board on a book is not the same as when a board meets the bottom! Sometimes dad would later come into the bedroom with a gumdrop or a cherry chocolate as a "peace offering." That took a little of the sting out of a spanking.

One of my new friends really got it one night. He had been pilfering pennies from the houses of his friends. His dad discovered his stash and made him visit each home on the block and return the loot. He had a big black belt with him, and after each "return deposit," he would whip the poor kid. I stood in wide-eyed wonder under the porch light and saw my friend cringe and cry each time the belt descended. I could hear him howling in the night as they went from house to house paying back and getting paid back. I was glad that our discipline was more loving and done in private.

One Halloween Muriel and I hid beneath a white sheet on the front porch. When trick-or-treaters came up and knocked on the door, we would jump up and yell "Boo!" at them. It scared one kid so bad he fell off the porch and broke his arm. We heard all kinds of horrible tales of what went on at Halloween in Boise. Like big kids catching black

★   ★   ★   ★   ★   ★   ★

cats, dousing them in gasoline and setting them on fire. I don't know if it actually happened or not, but it freaked me out just to think about it.

All was not bad at Washington Elementary. I couldn't wait for recess. We had a really neat ball field with a wooden backstop. On Saturdays we would return to the school just to play ball on that field. I was reading the life story of Babe Ruth then, and the way the Bambino described his school and ball field reminded me of ours in Boise. Despite my size I could hold my own with the best of them once I stepped up to the plate or put on my three-finger fielder's glove and took my place at third base.

Even though I couldn't read music, I could carry a tune. The whole school once put on a concert for the mothers, and I remember singing one song in particular: "Welcome, Sweet Springtime."

Welcome, sweet springtime,
We greet thee in song,
Murmurs of gladness,
Fall on the ear.
Voices long hushed,
Now hear full notes prolong,
Echoing far and near.

(This was before Barney Fife gave "second life" to this song on an episode of "The Andy Griffith Show." I've never quite forgiven Andy and Barney for trivializing the song that was special to me!) My mother sat in the front row with David on her lap and flashed her famous smile at me as I sang my heart out. Another song we sang was "Sixteen Tons" made popular by Tennessee Ernie Ford. I had no idea what it meant to owe your soul to the company store.

★ ★ ★ ★ ★ ★ ★

We studied about forestry in one of our classes, and I became very interested in the logging industry. "Smokey Bear" was big then and we drew posters of "How You Can Prevent Forest Fires!" A Christian man, Mr. Bob Beach, learned about my interest in logging and asked me if I would like to accompany him in his big truck on a log run. Would I? Would Custer have liked reinforcements? You bet!

So I got up early one Saturday morning and went with Mr. Beach deep into the forest to get a load of logs. We brought them down to the logging camp where the logs were unloaded in a big pond. Lumberjacks were everywhere, and you could hear the scream of the saw blades and smell the pungent sawdust. I wrote a report on my visit to the logging camp for school. For a time I flirted with the thought that I would like to be a forest ranger some day. On another occasion I was lying down on the grass in the backyard looking up at the sky and saw the jet stream of a plane passing overhead. I thought it would be cool to be an airline pilot too, but those were just fanciful childhood dreams. Some time after we left Boise, we were saddened to learn that kind Mr. Beach and his family were killed in a light airplane crash.

PLAYING MARBLES, SKATING, AND GETTING A "FREE SHOW"

In Boise I discovered a new love – the game of marbles. It seems that every boy on the block had a marble collection, so I started my own. I kept them in an old cigar box under my bed. When it was time to play marbles, I would spread my beauties out on my bed and carefully select the ones I wanted to risk (or not risk) in a game of "keepsies."

While the girls skipped rope at recess, the boys played marbles. We carried them in our pockets or in a small leather bag. A circle would be drawn in the dirt and you would try to knock the other fellows'

★   ★   ★   ★   ★   ★   ★

marbles out of the ring with your best shooter. I don't think we were allowed to play for keeps on the playground, but Saturdays was another story. We'd get up early in the morning, choose our marbles, and sally forth into the fray. You could go from one alley to the next in the years I lived in Boise (1954-1956) and find a game going in just about any alley. Sometimes we'd go back to the school ground at Washington Elementary and this time play for keeps. My favorite marbles were agates ("aggies") and oxbloods. Cat's eyes were cheap and easy to risk, especially when you played "pottsies." In that game you would dig a hole in the earth, put all the marbles you dared risk in the "pot," and then "pitch" (not shoot) for the jackpot. Mom had to patch the knees of my jeans because I would wear them out by kneeling down to shoot marbles.

Donald G. Hunt, the founder of Midwestern School of Evangelism (my eventual *alma mater*) once came to Boise Bible College to speak. He stayed in our home, and while he was there, he got down on his knees and played marbles with me. He "cleaned me out" but graciously allowed me to keep my coveted collection. He made a friend for life out of me just by playing marbles with a kid.

The sidewalks were full of skaters in our neighborhood. I don't know that I had skated before, but I took to this like a duck takes to water. You would fit your shoes into the metal skates, tighten down the clamps with a key, fasten the leather straps, and off you would go. The worst was when one of your skates came loose and banged you on the ankle. That could hurt like fury. Falling down and skinning your knee was child's play compared to a loose skate. Sometimes we'd have a friend pull us down the sidewalk while we would hang on to the back of his bike.

★   ★   ★   ★   ★   ★   ★

Some time after we moved to Boise, the Bryants came from Hamburg to visit us. My old pal Gary was fascinated with a pair of "spring shoes" I had picked up somewhere. They were red metal shoes that you stuck your feet in, only there were big coils on the bottoms of the shoes. You could bound down the street like some super hero. It was like having a pogo stick on each foot.

We had a horse chestnut tree on our block and we would take the larger chestnuts and make a slice in them with our jackknifes. Then we would take some kite string and fasten them in the slices and tie the strings to the four corners of a men's handkerchief. We'd fold the handkerchief up, put the chestnut in the middle, and throw it as high into the sky as we could. Poof! The "parachute" would open and float to the earth while we tried to shoot it down with a slingshot. Sometimes the parachutes would get caught up on a power line or in a tree and would swing there all summer as silent testimonies to our childlike imaginations and ingenuity.

Another friend from Washington Elementary I had was Mike, a little left-handed kid who pitched on our ball team. I wish I could remember his last name. Mike had a collection of plastic World War II soldiers, and we would often fight imaginary wars with his toy soldiers in his backyard. One girl on our block liked to "flash" us by suddenly showing up on the scene, pulling up her dress and giving us a "free show" whether we wanted it or not.

THE TERRIBLE CAR ACCIDENT

We had only been in Boise for about four months when something happened that nearly changed our lives forever. Dad was returning from his first preaching trip in Oregon. Perry Thomas, a fellow

★   ★   ★   ★   ★   ★   ★

teacher with dad at Boise Bible College, was driving dad's car. He hit a patch of black ice on Highway 20, about 30 miles west of Burns. Dad was thrown from the car, which rolled over once and came to rest on its top. Perry found dad lying unconscious and began to fervently pray that dad's life would be spared so that mom would not have to raise five children as a widow. Dad finally came to and was taken to a hospital in Burns. Kenneth Beckman came by our home to tell mom what had happened, but because he was always joking, she didn't take him seriously. When he finally got through to her, she broke down in tears. I remember going with her to the Boise airport a day or so later and saw my dad being carried from the plane on a stretcher to the car. It was cold and windy, and he couldn't walk because he had suffered broken ribs and a sprained ankle. He looked different because he hadn't shaved for several days. We were all glad to have him back home. Now I could breathe again because I thought for sure he was a goner. The Chevy was a total loss. Our new car was a 1953 DeSoto.

One Christmas my teacher asked the class, "Is there anyone here who doesn't have a Christmas tree?" Like the U. S. flag being raised on a flagpole, up went my hand. "Victor, you don't have a Christmas tree at your house?" Nope. But now we did. I dragged that evergreen all the way home and we had a Christmas tree that year. Mom decorated it with strings of popcorn and cranberries. Someone had sent us a box of Delicious apples and we used the crinkly paper the apples were wrapped in to make decorations for the tree.

THE BOISE BRAVES AND BASEBALL PERIOD

A celebrity lived at the end of our street. His name was Bobby King, and he played shortstop for the Boise Braves, a Class C minor

★　★　★　★　★　★　★

league baseball team in the Milwaukee Braves' farm system. Bob
Uecker was on that same team. Sometimes on Saturday nights, if the
Braves had played a day game, King would have the rest of the team
come to his home for a backyard barbecue. Tony, Mike and I would
peek through the bushes and watch the festivities. I saw Bob Uecker
drink beer before he ever pitched the stuff on national TV as a baseball
announcer. "Uke" may have been the only member of that team to
make it to the major leagues, where he hit a paltry .200 in 297 games
over a six-year span (1962-1967).

I'll never forget my first visit to the stadium where the Braves
played. It was a day game and the sun was shining brightly. I had to
pass a cold bottle of beer down the line to a paying customer in our
row and while I wasn't tempted to take a sip, it sure felt good to touch
something cold. If I remember correctly, I dropped it and the bottle
broke.

The Braves finished first in their division in 1955 and won the
Pioneer League championship in 1956. Other teams that were in the
league included the Magic Valley Cowboys, the Billings Mustangs,
Ogden, Great Falls, Idaho Falls, and Pocatello. I listened to many of
their games on the local radio station. One of the pitchers was a Negro
named Preacher Williams. I thought the announcer was saying,
"Williams goes into the *puppy* motion" when what he was really saying was, "Williams goes into the *pumping* motion."

I finally got to play organized baseball in Boise. I played third
base for a Little League team that was sponsored by United Airlines.
We had white T-shirts with blue letters on the front. We also got a blue
baseball hat. Most of us wore jeans and sneakers to complete the "uniform." Dad would come to my games and watch me play. One day he

★   ★   ★   ★   ★   ★   ★

was quite sick but came anyway. I came up with the bases loaded and cleared them with a long double to left. Dad stood up in the bleachers and shouted, "That's my boy!"

I believe it was in Boise that I started my baseball card collection. I bought them, a nickel a pack, at a little grocery store not far from our house. I could hardly wait to get home and open the packet of cards and see whom I had gotten. Topps cards was the leader in the field at that time although I had some Bowmans that I acquired in trades that went as far back as 1949.

How I loved those beautiful little pieces of pasteboard! I kept them in another cigar box under my bed. I would spread them out on the floor and categorize them according to position played or team played for. To this day I believe that the Topps cards for 1954, 1955, and 1956 were the most beautiful works of art in the world. The 1955 set was my all-time favorite set. Each card featured the team logo in the upper left corner, an action figure in the center, and a head shot on the right. The background was a colorful fadeout right to left. Over the action figure was a facsimile of the player's autograph. Even though the Indians were not my favorite team, I thought the Al Rosen card was the best of the lot in 1955. One day, in what can only be called a moment of temporary madness, I tore it in two. What was I thinking? I was horrified by what I had done. Who could love something so much that he would destroy it?

That same year, 1955, the Brooklyn Dodgers met the New York Yankees in the World Series. Because of Mickey Mantle I was a big Yankee fan, but I also had an affinity for the Dodgers largely due to the John R. Tunis books I had started reading in Hamburg about the beloved "Bums" of Flatbush. The Yankees, or "Bronx Bombers," pretty

★　★　★　★　★　★　★

well dominated baseball in the 1950s, winning six world championships. But the Dodgers rewrote the record book in 1955, beating the Yanks 4 games to 3, with Johnny Podres blanking the Yanks 2-0 in the final game. I got to see some of that World Series on TV and listened to the rest on radio. The Yankees bounced back in 1956 and got their revenge on the Dodgers. Who can forget game five? Don Larsen, a journeyman pitcher, threw the only perfect game in World Series history. Never in my wildest dreams could I have imagined that on May 17, 1998, I would be ensconced in Yankee Stadium to witness only the 15th perfect game, the Yankees' David Wells blanking the Minnesota Twins 4-0. Added irony: Wells attended the same high school in San Diego that Don Larsen had attended!

18TH AND EASTMAN

I can remember only one good friend that I had in the Boise church that met at 18th and Eastman. My best bud was Larry Lane, whose dad was one of the elders. Sometimes on Sunday afternoons the Lanes would take me home with them. After a big Sunday dinner we would play catch in the front yard, fool around in the barn, or spend some time in a tree house that Larry's older brothers had created. They had pinups on the wall, my first exposure to scantily clad women. One night I stayed over at the Lanes, and the mosquitoes were so bad that I couldn't even open my eyes in the morning. Perhaps it was divine retribution for peeking at those provocative pinups!

For some reason my only memory of church at Boise, the Church of Christ at 18th and Eastman that also housed Boise Bible College, was the night I got something stuck up my nose and had to be rescued by Larry's dad. Larry and I were sitting in the back of the

★　★　★　★　★　★　★

church peeling the foil off of gum wrappers while the preaching was going on. We made it into a good size ball, about the size one could stick up his nose if he was so inclined. I was so inclined. But I was "foiled" when the foil ball went up higher than it was supposed to. I panicked. Larry went for his dad who took me out on the front steps, under an overhead light, took out a pair of tweezers and performed a successful extraction. Whew! I could breathe deeply again.

I have a very bad memory of one night after church. Miriam Beckman, the daughter of the other preacher at 18th and Eastman, and some of the rest of the young people were playing in the yard next to the parsonage. I can't remember what was said or done but suddenly Keith, Miriam's older brother, charged out of the house and took a one-two punch at me. I literally saw stars from the force of the blows and went over backwards, hitting my head on the ground. I have no clue to this day what set him off. A sad aside: after we moved away from Boise, we learned that Miriam had drowned at a church camp. I felt bad for her parents, Kenneth and Martha. Martha was a very sweet woman.

Some of the students at Boise Bible College took a special interest in me. (At that time the college also met at 18th and Eastman.) Two young women who taught me in their Sunday School class were Neola Willey and Fern Marriott. To this day the two ladies are faithful supporters of our Peace on Earth Ministries. I also remember Dale and Linda Marshall, who have been missionaries in Southern Rhodesia/Zimbabwe for more than 40 years. Bob Granger was a cowboy from Wyoming and sometimes came over to our house. He wore tight Levis, cowboy boots, western shirts, and had an infectious smile. Since I liked cowboys, it was a big thrill to have a genuine cowboy right in our "bunkhouse."

★   ★   ★   ★   ★   ★   ★

We rented a TV for the 1956 Rose Bowl game. Dad was still a big Iowa Hawkeye fan, and we watched with pride as Iowa beat Oregon State 35-19. Because our house had no TV antenna, the players looked kind of "wavy" at times. We got to keep the TV over the weekend, and therefore I got to see one of the first episodes of Zorro. More waves. Mostly, however, we listened to the radio airwaves. I still liked the Lone Ranger, but "Inner Sanctum" gave me the willies. Dad subscribed to several magazines: *Saturday Evening Post*, *National Geographic*, and *Readers' Digest*. My favorite was the *Post*. I would read it while I was lying flat on my stomach on the living room rug. I especially liked the cartoons.

OUR ONE PERMANENT HOME

Grandma Knowles came to spend the fall and winter with us in 1954. How glad we all were to have her with us. But when she returned to Iowa in February, I was devastated. My dad tells the story of her departure and the effect it had on me in his biography *One Life of Many*.

Victor was so very sad to see her go that he became sick at school. His mother was called by his teacher to come and get him. Later we all went down to the depot in my car, waving goodbye to grandma as she headed for the train. Victor was just heart broken. He was still weeping so much that he ate no dinner. He then shuffled back to school with lowered head and quivering chin.

In the summertime we would drive back to Iowa to visit Grandma Knowles in Hubbard. I would still get carsick and make the trip unpleasant for everyone. I believe it was the second summer that my parents decided to leave me behind. I stayed at the Boise

★　　★　　★　　★　　★　　★　　★

Children's Home. I have no memories of my two-week stay there other than watching the horses in a corral from my perch on the top rail. Upon hearing of my perennial problem with carsickness, a neighbor lady suggested folding a brown paper sack into a square and placing it between my tummy and my T-shirt. Perhaps it was psychosomatic but it worked. I never got carsick again. Or maybe it was because I didn't want to get "left behind" again!

Grandma's house was special because it was the only home that never changed all through my childhood. It was permanent, it was secure, it was comforting, it was there and it would always be there and we five kids knew that. Grandma's house stood in the shadow of the town's twin water tanks, and we always tried to see who could spot them first when we got close to Hubbard.

Grandma Knowles believed in getting up at the crack of dawn. So, long before we had gotten out of bed, she had been out in the yard watering her flowers and going to the shed for kindling to fire up the old iron stove that she cooked on. We would have pancakes for breakfast. She called them "panny-cakes." When she made hamburgers, she would put a little bit of milk in them, and they were the best ever. Grandma also made the most scrumptious pies in the world, especially cherry pies.

There was no hot water heater in the house, so you had to warm a pan of water on the stove to wash up. Sometimes we would hang the area rugs over the clothesline and beat them with a carpet beater. We "painted" Grandma's front porch over and over, dipping our paintbrushes into old tin cans full of water. When we got thirsty or needed more water, we pumped it from an old iron pump near the garden.

★   ★   ★   ★   ★   ★   ★

There were all kinds of trees on Grandma's place, including fruit trees. Any time we were hungry, we could pick a plum, or an apple, or a cherry. Grandma grew every kind of vegetable imaginable, and her yard was a showcase of all kinds of bushes and flowers. My favorites were lilacs and the "Heavenly Blue" variety of morning glories. I liked to mow the yard – and it was a big one! – with her old push mower. The grass would fly as the blades of the mower whirred. The faster you went the more the push mower "sang" – until you hit a stick or a butternut that would stop you right in your tracks. A big ash tree was tempting to climb. My cousin "Zan" (Roseanne) fell out of it one day and broke her arm.

One day I did something naughty (imagine that!), and my mother sent me to the kitchen to pick out a small branch for my spanking. Grandma kept a box full of twigs and small branches for kindling next to the iron cook stove. When Grandma found out why I was there, she picked out the smallest branch in the box. I loved her for that although our little ruse did not work!

Grandma was a great patriot. She flew the American flag from a bamboo pole that she placed in an old iron pipe sticking up from the ground in the middle of the yard. On Memorial Day (she called it "Decoration Day") she was up before dawn and out on the lawn cutting fresh peonies which she then placed in a fruit jar filled with water. She then walked several miles to the cemetery on the edge of town and placed them on my grandfather's grave.

It was at Grandma's home in Hubbard that I became a St. Louis Cardinals fan. She had a ceramic cardinal on her windowsill that had these words painted on the base: "Stick by them Cards." So I did. Stan "The Man" Musial became my favorite Cardinal. He won seven batting

★   ★   ★   ★   ★   ★   ★

titles (back-to-back-to-back in 1950, 1951, and 1952) and was a three-time Most Valuable Player. Grandma's big yard was a great place to play ball. Because Mantle was a switch-hitter and Musial batted left-handed, I taught myself to bat from the left side of the plate. Grandma kept a bunch of old bats, gloves, and balls in the old shed, and even an old catcher's mitt, mask, chest protector, and shin guards, so we were well fitted to play.

Just like in Hamburg, the public library was right next door. My sisters and I would check out a stack of books and carry them to Grandma's house where we would camp out in our favorite place and read until it was too dark to continue. Some of the books I read were about great American heroes like John Paul Jones, Davey Crockett, Booker T. Washington, and George Washington Carver. Rebecca liked to read the last page first but I was a stickler for starting with page one. There was always a stack of old copies of the *Des Moines Sunday Register* on a footstool. I liked reading the funny papers and the "Big Peach" sports section. It was called the "Big Peach" because that section was printed on peach-colored paper. My favorite comic strips were "Blondie," "Dick Tracy," "Beetle Bailey," and Jimmy Hatlo's "They'll Do It Every Time." Grandma liked "Dennis the Menace."

In the evenings we would catch fireflies ("lightning bugs") and put them in a Mason glass jar. We had to go to bed early because Grandma did not want to waste electricity. Sometimes, if there was no ice cream left in the freezer portion of the small Crosley refrigerator, she would even unplug it to "save on electricity." When Daylight Saving Time was introduced Grandma kept her clocks set on "God's Time." That meant we would eat dinner one hour before noon, not at noon when the noon whistle went off. And dinner was not "lunch," it was dinner. Supper was the evening meal, not dinner. But Grandma

★   ★   ★   ★   ★   ★   ★

was always good for a "snack" and my favorite was peanut butter sandwiches, made with Skippy peanut butter and Wonder bread.

HEARING THE FIRST CALL OF GOD

We were always a bit sad to leave Grandma's house and make the long trip back to Boise. But life goes on. Dad continued his work with the Bible College and the church. He also held a good number of revival meetings throughout Idaho and Oregon. In one of them (Meridian, Idaho) there were 36 decisions for Christ. Early in 1956 Sherwood Smith invited dad to come to Cottage Grove, Oregon, and conduct a two-week meeting. It was during this meeting that I first felt the call of God on my life. The invitation was given one night, and I felt a strong desire to step out and give my life to Christ. But I held on to the pew in front of me with both hands until my knuckles turned white and did not walk down the aisle. I believe now that the Holy Spirit was beginning to do His work within me. I was just a little more than 10 years old at the time. It would be two more years before I would surrender my life to Christ. God knew I was Victor, but He wanted me to become a Victor, a Victor in Christ. Still, the Holy Spirit continued His work in me through our evening family devotions, my father's preaching, my mother's prayers, and the Sunday School classes that were taught by the young ladies of BBC.

Sometimes I marvel that I ever became a Christian, let alone a minister of the gospel (the Good News), because of some negative things that happened to my father during some of his ministries, Boise not excepted. In July my father was abruptly terminated from his position at the church and the college. Just like that. Three other teachers had earlier been given the pink slip. Mom was so discouraged. We had

★   ★   ★   ★   ★   ★   ★

already made another move while in Boise, this one to an even older house on North 18th Street. Now we had to pack our belongings once again. I don't know how she did it. When I got married in 1967, I made a promise to my wife that I would never allow her to endure what my dear mother had to go through as a minister's wife. Before we left Boise a good number of people from the church, including some of the church elders, and the college, including both students and teachers, presented dad with a "letter of commendation." We had $10 to our good family name. But a good Christian man from Rock Port, Missouri, Joe Wright, had sent us a check for $200 and that money, almost to the dollar, got us out of Boise and back to the Midwest.

FROM CITY LIFE TO LIFE ON A FARM

Our home for the next six months of my life was the Bernice Grable farm near Rock Port. Bernice was a widow who had a daughter, Janet Sue, who was about my age. Bernice's husband had been killed in a car wreck and she was doing her best to keep up the farm. She had heard about our plight in Boise and generously offered us her home as a temporary refuge. She gave dad and mom her own bedroom while she slept on a couch in the living room. My three sisters and Janet Sue shared two upstairs bedrooms. I didn't have a bedroom, but Bernice and mom created one for me on the upstairs landing, beneath a window. Sometimes at night I would stand on my bed and stare out into the darkness. I was used to living in town with streetlights. Out in the country, night is truly night. We lived right by a highway and the sounds of passing trucks and cars would gradually lull me to sleep.

Living on a farm was a new experience. We arrived in mid-October while the crops were being harvested. Bernice ran some cattle,

★ ★ ★ ★ ★ ★ ★

so there were always cows to be brought in from the pasture at milking time. We all learned to milk cows, not too unpleasant an experience. One of my jobs was to slop the hogs. I couldn't believe their lack of manners. Sometimes, in disgust, I poured the slop right on top of their hairy heads. Another task was gathering the eggs from the chicken coop. Coop rhymes with "poop" and that's what you had to walk through in the chicken yard to get the eggs. The brown eggs fascinated me. The cream separator that Bernice operated after we poured the fresh milk into it also amazed me. Having real cream on my Wheaties was supposed to be a real treat, but somehow I never developed a taste for cream.

The big old barn was a pleasant place. Up in the haymow you could lie back, chew on a stem of straw, and find some peace of mind. Down below the cows were munching away. I learned that they had four stomachs. No wonder they were always grazing! You could hear the gentle swish of their tails as they swatted away the flies. There was also a black bull that we named "Ferdinand." Dad nailed my old basketball hoop on the side of the barn so I could shoot baskets when the chores were done. Old pickup trucks and tractors were sitting around for me to explore. There were trails in the woods that I took to sometimes.

One of the cool things about moving back to the Midwest was that I was reunited with some of my old friends. Gary Bryant lived just a few miles from where we now resided, and it was great to take up where we left off when we moved from Hamburg. Rock Port and Hamburg are just a few miles apart, so we got to see lots of the Hamburg folks once again. Perhaps this was in answer to Bonnie's prayer not long after we arrived in Boise: "Dear God, watch over us until we visit Hamburg."

I had never ridden a school bus before, but that was now our method of getting to school in Rock Port. Janet Sue's cousin, Phyllis

★   ★   ★   ★   ★   ★   ★

Wolf, lived in the next house north, around a curve. She would holler at us "Bus coming!" when she saw it approaching. That way we were all ready for the bus when it pulled up in front of our house.

Another first was having to take my lunch to school. Always before we had walked home for lunch. Mom would pack my lunch box with a peanut butter or bologna sandwich, some potato chips, a cookie, an apple, and a thermos bottle of milk.

My fifth grade teacher was Mrs. Warren, and she took a special interest in me. I believe this was providential because of my unhappy school experience in Boise. I felt loved, safe and secure in her classroom. I viewed her as an angel sent from God. She was a beautiful woman and I may have even developed a "crush" on her. Even though we did not finish out the school year in Rock Port, it was a good time for me. I draw a blank when I try to remember any classmates from that short stint. I do not have my report cards from our last days in Boise or our short time in Rock Port. They probably got lost in the flurry of moving. But I am sure that my grades were an improvement over those in Boise.

Janet Sue was lot of fun to play with. One day we got "married" in a fake wedding ceremony on the lower landing of the stairs. I guess one of my sisters would have performed the "ceremony" since David was far too young to have done so. I conducted my first "funeral" in the backyard of the Grables. It was for a dead mouse we found one day. We posthumously named him "Squeaky" and then proceeded to bury him with great lamentation. I implored the Lord to receive the deceased rodent's soul into mousie heaven. A few tears were shed and then we all retired to the house for "fellowship." Somehow I always equated "fellowship" with potato chips – probably because of church

★ ★ ★ ★ ★ ★ ★

potluck dinners that included potato chips – so we may have had some potato chips that day.

One cold winter day I did something very foolish. I tried to lick some frost from the handle of an iron pump. The results were predictable, just like in the scene in the holiday movie that would be made some years later, "A Christmas Story." No fire truck was called to rescue me, however. My mother got a pan of warm water and carefully poured it over the frost-covered pump handle. Eventually my tongue was freed, although I left a little bit of skin on the pump handle when I pulled away. Another day we made an elaborate snow fort and stockpiled it with snowballs so we could fend off any invaders – should they be so foolish as to try to storm the Grable-Knowles Frozen Fortress.

WATCHING HISTORY UNFOLD IN BUDAPEST

Just down the road south from the Grables' house and around the bend was the home of Janet Sue's grandparents, Frank and Essie Erwin. Sometimes we would go there for a visit where I got to watch a little TV. It was on one of those occasions, or perhaps at the Grables, that I got my first lesson in world affairs. I watched in horror as Soviet tanks rolled through the streets of Budapest, Hungary. I saw young boys, not much older than myself, hurling homemade Molotov cocktails at the tanks, trying to blow the treads off to stop their advance. I saw hundreds of bodies lying in the streets, victims of ruthless Communism.

The date was October 23, 1956, one month before my 11th birthday. Then and there was born in my heart a desire to do something someday to help those living behind what Winston Churchill dubbed (on a visit to Fulton, Missouri) the "Iron Curtain." Thirty-four years later I set foot in Warsaw, Poland, one year to the very day after the Berlin Wall fell. TV can be educational and, on occasion, life-changing. It was for me.

★   ★   ★   ★   ★   ★   ★

THE CHURCH THAT MET IN A SCHOOL

When dad had ministered in Hamburg, a good number of people from Rock Port and Nishnabotna had driven to Hamburg to hear dad preach. He had also preached for them on Thursday nights. The congregation met in an old schoolhouse. The men of the church invited dad to be their preacher. You won't find Nishnabotna on the map. It was an unincorporated town near the Nishnabotna River, a few miles south of Rock Port. Eventually this hardy congregation would form the Rock Port Church of Christ and build a nice brick building.

I liked going to church at Nishnabotna. For one thing, I got to shoot baskets in the gym before and after the church services on Sundays and Thursday nights. The Rosenbohm brothers, Duane and Dennis, though older than me, let me shoot right along with them. Their folks, Virgil (everyone called him "Toots") and Esther, had a big farm home, and we often went there for Sunday dinner. One Sunday we got "snowed in" and got to stay there for an extra day. I also remember with fondness the Millers, Wrights, Adams, Wolfs, and other nice families.

Two humorous incidents took place at the Nishnabotna school/church. One summer night my dad was preaching. It was warm and the windows were open. Just as dad opened his mouth to say something, a wayward moth fluttered in . . . and took up residence in his stomach. We had a short sermon that night. One winter night I got too close to the pot-bellied stove that warmed the schoolroom. I had a red and green plaid wool coat on, wet with snow from a pre-church snowball fight. I backed up to the stove to get warm. Before long I – and everyone else – smelled something most unpleasant. The backside of my coat got a good scorching and everyone had a good-natured laugh.

Sometimes our family would accompany dad in his meetings. My favorite place to go was Nebraska because there I could play with the Brennfoerder kids, Gary and Dottie. Dad and mom were good

★ ★ ★ ★ ★ ★ ★

friends of Art and Evelyn Brennfoerder, who lived on a farm near Edgar. Evelyn enamored me: partly because she spoiled me rotten and partly because she was such a warm and loving person. Then and there I made a solemn, secret vow that some day I would marry someone named Evelyn. (And so I did in 1967.) Gary had quite a collection of toy tractors. Climbing up on a real one was even better. The Brennfoerders had something I had never seen before, except on *The Wizard of Oz*, and that was a storm cellar. It was there in case of a tornado but doubled as a fruit and vegetable cellar as well. Two older boys, Gary and Eddie Werner, from the church in Deweese, sometimes let me ride with them in their early 50s automobiles. That was a pretty big thrill for me. The dashboards always fascinated me. It was almost like being in the cockpit of an airplane. Cars were covered with chrome back then, inside and outside. I can still close my eyes and smell the interior of those 1950 hot rods. The car radio could pull in stations from Omaha and Lincoln.

NORTH TO IOWA (OR "THREE SCHOOLS IN ONE YEAR!")

Even though we were very happy in Rock Port and Nishnabotna, dad felt that he wasn't doing enough to support our family and that it wasn't fair to impose upon Bernice's gracious hospitality much longer. In the spring of 1957 he received a call from the Park Church of Christ in Goldfield, Iowa, to consider moving there. Not long thereafter we bid the folks at "Nishny" a bittersweet farewell and moved to Goldfield. It was in April, so I still had a month to go in the fifth grade. This meant that the Knowles kids would go to the same grade of school in three different states: Idaho, Missouri, and now Iowa. It's a wonder that any of us were promoted that school year (1956-1957), but by the grace of God we all were. Dad pointed the old DeSoto north to Iowa where I would spend the next five and-a-half years of my life. I believe they were the happiest of my growing up years.

★   ★   ★   ★   ★   ★   ★

CHAPTER THREE

STRIKING IT RICH
IN GOLDFIELD

We arrived in Goldfield, Iowa, in mid-April, 1957. The town of Goldfield, population about 800, was located in Wright County, about 60 miles north of Des Moines. Iowa had 99 counties and Wright County was the 99th one. You could tell what county a person lived in by the first two numbers on their license plate. Dad used to amaze us on trips by identifying the county merely by looking at the license plate on the car in front of us. He kept a little printed list of the counties on the visor. I would check it when we came up behind a car and he would reel off the name of the county. Sure enough, he was right.

I was mildly disappointed to discover that there was no gold in Goldfield. Its founder, Major O. M. Brassfield, originally named the town, the oldest in Wright County, Liberty. Legend has it that he named the town Brassfield but later the city fathers became a little embarrassed by the name Brassfield. They thought it sounded too cheap. So they renamed it Goldfield. A funny story, whether it's true or not. I felt that we had struck it rich by living in a town called Goldfield.

OUR NEARLY NEW HOME

We moved into an almost new parsonage, which was located right next to the church building. It was a modern brick ranch house

* * * * * * *

with a full basement and garage. We had sold most of our furniture when we left Boise. Dad took mom to Des Moines to buy new furniture for the house. Once it was all put in place, mom was really happy. Now she wouldn't have to share a house anymore.

Our new home had four bedrooms. Rebecca, now going by "Becky," had her own room. Muriel and Bonnie shared one, as did my little brother David and I. I stuck pictures of my baseball heroes on the wall, especially players from the Yankees and Cardinals. We had a set of bunk beds and I took the top so if David fell out, it wouldn't be too far before he hit the floor. Sometimes at night I would dangle my arm down, wave it back and forth, and make a ghostly whistle. It would scare him half to death and he would cry, "Dad, Mom! Vic's scaring me!" Of course I would always be "asleep" by the time they came in to check on the situation. Sometimes I would crawl on my stomach into Muriel and Bonnie's room once all the lights went out, and give them a good scare by rising up and yelling, "Boo!"

Every morning we would awaken to the sounds of WOAI on the Stromberg-Carlson floor model radio. WOAI was dad's favorite station. It broadcast from Iowa State University in Ames where my Uncle Lyle was a professor. Dad was a lifelong classical music buff. Sometimes he would put a rousing John Phillips Sousa march on the record player to help us wake up and get ready for the day. Nearly every evening at six dad would listen to Fulton Lewis, Jr., a conservative radio commentator heard on the Mutual Broadcasting System. His signature signoff was, "And that's the news as it looks from here."

In those days the family ate almost every meal together. Monday through Saturday we ate in the kitchen, but on Sunday, or when we had company, we used the dining room. Each meal would

★   ★   ★   ★   ★   ★   ★

begin, of course, with prayer. We had a chrome kitchen table with a red top and chrome kitchen chairs with red padded seats to match. I switched from Wheaties to Post Toasties when the latter started printing cutout baseball cards on the backs of their cereal boxes. When it came time for dad to mail out his monthly *Christian Campaigner*, we would fold and address them at the kitchen table. One night I was addressing one to a family friend, Belle Mossman. I was wont to read them aloud as I printed their name. I mispronounced Belle as "Belly" and dad got a good belly laugh out of that. On Sunday evenings after church he would often eat a big bowl of Corn Flakes – I mean a *big* bowl, a mixing bowl!

The public school was only about five blocks from our house, so we walked home at noon for lunch. It was great not to have to carry a lunchbox or ride a bus to school anymore. Sometimes when we came home from school in the afternoon, mom would have homemade doughnuts cooling on some wax paper on the kitchen counter. Is there anything more tempting to swipe or pleasing to the taste buds? But after the evening meal (called "supper" in our family) there were the dreaded dishes to do. Dad made a list of who had to wash and who had to dry, and it was on a rotating basis. At the bottom of the list were these words: "Do it cheerfully, promptly, and efficiently." On more than one occasion I must confess that I, without too much contrition, would check the list ahead of time and then slip out the bathroom window after supper to go play a game of work-up in the vacant lot across the street. I did it cheerfully, promptly, and efficiently!

In bad weather we could roller skate in the basement. I cut down a round cardboard canister of Quaker Oats and nailed it to a square piece of wood that served as a backboard. Then I nailed it to the wall

★   ★   ★   ★   ★   ★   ★

and presto – I had an indoor mini-basketball court. I used a piece of chalk to draw the free throw line and sideline boundaries. Muriel and Bonnie were my "cheerleaders" as I fired away at the makeshift basket, playing whole games and even "broadcasting" the game as I played.

Our living room was kind of a gathering point at night when the dishes were done. The radio or record player might be playing in the background while we worked on our homework at the dining room table or curled up in a chair and read a book or a copy of the weekly *Eagle Grove Eagle* or the daily *Mason City Globe-Gazette*. On special occasions dad would turn the lights down low and read to us a suspense-filled episode from *The Adventures of Sherlock Holmes*. He would develop a different voice for each character in the story, especially Holmes' nemesis, the evil Professor Moriarty. "The Hound of the Baskervilles" made the hair stand up on the back of my neck. Popcorn was our favorite after supper snack.

Just about every school night (except Wednesdays – church night, and Friday night – game night) we would end the day with family devotions. Most of the time we just used the Bible with each member of the family taking turns reading. Dad also bought each of us a copy of Donald G. Hunt's *The Unfolded Plan of God*, a handy overview of the Bible that I still use to this day. It took us awhile to get through that book but we did it. Then we would all kneel down and pray. My prayers were pretty pathetic at the time. Dad once called me "HFC" because my prayers went something like this: "Thank you for our home and food and clothing. Amen." Well, I was thankful for our new home, our food (especially those homemade doughnuts), and clothing.

I don't know how mom fed us on dad's salary of $50 a week, but she did. Mom was a dedicated coupon clipper and when we went

★   ★   ★   ★   ★   ★   ★

to Eagle Grove on Saturdays, five miles away, to get our groceries, she would always scout out the best bargains. While she was shopping for groceries, we kids would be at the library checking out stacks of books. About this time I read Walter Lord's blockbuster *A Night to Remember*, a chilling account of the sinking of the *Titanic*. I had no clue that some-day I would visit the shipyards in Belfast, Northern Ireland, where the *Titanic* was built.

We had a big garden in the backyard each summer and mom canned tomatoes, sweet corn, and green beans. Sometimes we would help her snap beans in the shade on a hot day. I wish now I had been more cheerful to do so. My dear mother was busy from dawn to dark for the sake of the family. On Sundays we often had meat loaf or pot roast potatoes with carrots. Sometimes we had chocolate cake and ice cream for dessert.

Mom had this "cruel rule" at our house: clean up your plate or there would be no dessert. Once we had diced beets. They were a pur-ple pain to get down. I would almost rather try to swallow a pair of dice than eat diced beets. But I wanted that cherry pie for dessert. So I took a piece of Wonder bread (you are about to find out why they call it "wonder"), cut off the crusts, put the despised beets in the center, and squeezed the bread into a ball. I popped it in my mouth, washed it down with milk, smiled at my mother and sweetly said, "Please pass the pie." I got the pie for, technically, I had "eaten" the beets.

Only once did I ever call my mother "the old lady." I don't know what got into me. I said, "Pass the meat, old lady." She passed the meat all right – the back of her hand to the side of my face. That was one side dish I did not like. But I deserved my just deserts.

★   ★   ★   ★   ★   ★   ★

Not long after we arrived in Goldfield we got our first family dog. She was a Mexican Chihuahua and we named her "Lady." She was fiercely jealous of her box that she slept in. All we had to say was, "Lady, I'm gonna' get your box," and she would jump in it and bare her teeth at us. If she were at one end of the house when the doorbell rang, she would tear down the hardwood hall and skitter into the wall every time before she could make the turn to see who had dared to enter her domain. We used to ring the doorbell just to see her hilarious act. Once I gave her a spoonful of peanut butter and had Bonnie ring the doorbell. She could hardly bark as she made her mad dash down the hall. Lady loved to curl up next to dad in the recliner when he was reading. Sometimes she violated this trust by violating the air. Dad would say, "Oh, Lady!" and would order her from the chair. Lady would lower her head in shame and slink to her box.

THE GREAT OUTDOORS

We had a nice front yard. It was long, like a football field. One of my jobs was to mow the lawn. I didn't mind. In fact, I had been begging and bugging dad to let me mow for some time. In time I got some jobs mowing other lawns in town. I think I charged a grand total of fifty cents an hour. I also turned the front yard into a fun ball stadium. This was before wiffle ball. Fun balls were made of plastic with dime-sized holes in them. You would take a piece of white adhesive tape (or black friction tape) and reinforce the seam to make the ball last longer. The left field wall was an old low fence that had grapes growing on it. The right field "fence" was the parsonage/ranch house itself. It was a "short porch" to right so I loved batting left-handed to put one over the roof. It was a "long launch" to left but I managed to put more than a few over the grapes as well.

★   ★   ★   ★   ★   ★   ★

The backyard was mom's domain. She planted a big garden each spring. It was off limits to us. David had a sandbox surrounded by tall sunflowers and castor beans that shaded him while he played in the sand. The side yard, between the parsonage and the church building, was where dad and I would often play catch. In the fall I would play football games by myself by throwing the ball up on the sloping roof of the church and then racing down the yard to "complete" the pass to myself by catching the football when it came off the roof. I had the Ohio State Buckeyes and the despised Notre Dame Irish going down to defeat at the hands of the Iowa Hawkeyes game after game. We never lost as long as I was the quarterback (Kenny Ploen) and the end (Jim Gibbons) all at the same time.

Another job I got but did not enjoy as much as mowing the lawn was shoveling sidewalks in the winter. It could really snow in north central Iowa and the mercury often plunged below zero. Sometimes the snow would drift pretty high. Once in awhile I would still be shoveling by the light of the street lamp. How good a cup of hot chocolate felt when I came in with my nose and toes tingling with cold!

I don't recall raking the leaves in the fall. Maybe that was because that's when the hobos and railroad bums were passing through town. I loved it when they showed up because my mother had another rule: "If any will not work, neither shall he eat." So she would assign "Hobo Joe from Mexico" (the name I assigned to all of them) to do some work first, like raking the leaves. That meant I didn't have to. Then she would prepare them a good lunch. Sometimes she allowed them to eat inside – if they were halfway tidy. But if they stank or were dirty they had to sit on the back porch steps and dine. I'll never forget one drifter who got to eat at the table. He wanted fried eggs, so mom

★   ★   ★   ★   ★   ★   ★

fixed him a couple. He had an "off eye," and I was fascinated by it. Somehow I came to associate fried eggs with off eyes and therefore did not eat any (eggs!) for some time. But after awhile I forgot about the guy with the bad eye and went back to fried eggs. I'm sure the hobos marked our house: "Beware! The woman here makes you work before you eat!" But it was good for them and even better for me. I sure miss those bums coming around.

I also had the task of taking the trash to the back alley and burning it. I liked to transform the trash into miniature cities created out of empty cereal boxes, wooden apple boxes, and the like. Then I would put a match to it and watch it burn like Nero watched Rome go up in flames. It was a pleasant task on a crisp fall night or cold winter evening.

OUR TOWN

Right behind our house and church was a small city park. This is how our church, Park Church of Christ, got its name. This was not Riverside Park of which I will tell you more later. Right next to the park was Memorial Hall. It had an old gym that was once used for basketball games. It was also used as fire station, jail, and city hall. At the time we arrived, it was used as a Youth Center where dances were held on Saturday nights.

During the summer there were band concerts. Some people sat in their cars on Main Street to listen. They would honk their horns as a courtesy to the band at the end of each number whether the band was any good or not. As night fell, the town kids would gather in the park and play "Red Rover" or "Kick the Can." My favorite was "Capture the Flag." I was fairly fleet of foot and could dart in, capture the flag,

★   ★   ★   ★   ★   ★   ★

and be back safe and sound before I was caught. I always went home with a sore midriff after trying to break the chain of linked arms in "Red Rover."

Main Street ran the length of the town, but I will only tell you of the "business district." Whyte's Garage sold and worked on cars. International Harvester had a store that sold farm equipment and hardware. Sometimes farmers would drive their tractors right down Main Street, flinging mud and manure into the air. I loved going to the store on Friday nights because they showed the Friday Night Fights on TV. My favorite boxer was Floyd Patterson. In 1956, the year before we moved to Goldfield, he knocked out Archie Moore to become the youngest boxer to win the heavyweight crown. I also liked Gene Fulmer and Carmen Basilio. The farmers would take over a row of wooden captains' chairs while the boys sat on old folding chairs or plunked down on a stack of tires. On Saturday afternoon we were back again for the Game of the Week with Dizzy Dean calling the action. The sponsors were Gillette Blue Blades and Hamm's Beer as I recall. As though it were yesterday I remember Don Buddin, a career .241 hitter, blasting a grand slam over the Green Monster at Fenway Park, to defeat my beloved Yankees.

I got my hair cut at a barbershop run by A. J. Cross. If you asked him how he was doing he always answered the same: "Got it in the guts." I guess he had a bad stomach. He also gave pretty bad haircuts. After awhile I let mom trim me up. The drug store was called Griffith's Sundries. They sold a variety of items including girlie magazines. One day I yielded to temptation and swiped one from the shelf. I endured several nights of guilt over my rash act of juvenile delinquency. Goldfield boasted two grocery stores back then. There was Jones'

★   ★   ★   ★   ★   ★   ★

Market that featured an ice cold meat locker and Baderschneider's General Store, which sold dry goods as well as groceries. I bought all my baseball cards at Baderschneider's and also started a football card collection when the NFL started printing them. My favorite candy bar was Pearson's Salted Nut Roll and I also liked the combo orange sherbet/vanilla ice cream bars. I think they were called Dreamsicles.

Sometimes on Saturday mornings the town kids would congregate behind Baderschneider's store for a daring BB gun battle. We must have been nuts. We would fort up behind big cardboard boxes and fire at each other with BB guns. "Whap, whap, whap." That was the sound of BBs imbedding themselves in the cardboard. Earl Baderschneider, who was in my class and lived with his parents above the store, only had one good eye. It's a mighty good thing none of us tagged him in his good eye with one of our shots!

Right across the street from Baderschneider's store was Schnell's Café. In the back of the café was "sin city" – a bar and a pool hall. Most of the "good" kids only frequented the front part of Schnell's. You were considered a "hood" if you passed through the batwings and entered the dark domain where local denizens smoked, chewed tobacco, guzzled beer, told off-color stories, and (gasp!) shot pool. Many a summer day I dropped into Schnell's Café with my ball playing buddies Dave Harvey and Scott Whyte for a cold bottle of pop. And I mean cold! The pop bottles were kept in an ice-cold cooler. Sometimes I would plunge my whole arm in and see how long I could keep it there. Most of my pals liked Pepsi (we were, after all, a part of the "Pepsi Generation"), but I always went for this off-brand pop that looked like gray dishwater. But it had a great citrus flavor and a strong kick when you took a big swig. Eventually we cooled off as we leaned

★   ★   ★   ★   ★   ★   ★

back in a booth and swigged pop under the welcome breezes of a slow-moving overhead fan. We liked to put salted peanuts in our pop to add to our treat. The pop cost only 10 cents.

Down the hill from Schnell's was the famous "Flow." The always flowing well produced water so cold it would make your teeth hurt. We would race our bikes down the hill, see which one of us could get to the flow first. A pipe stuck up out of the ground and the water was always flowing over the top. I've never tasted purer water anywhere in the world. It's still there if you want to have a drink today. At the other end of town, at the junction of Highway 3 and Highway 17, was the Dairy-Y. Sometimes I would walk out to the junction on a hot day just to get an ice cream cone or a root beer float.

MY FIRST KISS AND "SEX ED" IN THE 50S

I finished out fifth grade in the spring of 1957 under Mrs. Beckett. I am still amazed when I look at my report card and see how well I did in spite of all the moving that year. An A- (my first!) in Spelling, a B+ in Reading, a B- in Science, C+'s in Writing, English, and History, and C's in Geography and Arithmetic. I began a brand new school year in earnest in that fall. My sixth grade teacher was Mrs. Beulah Hinton, a rather large, buxom woman. Before I ever arrived on the scene, the boys had cruelly nicknamed her "Hitler." To come to her defense, however, she might not have been so demanding and commanding if they had not brought a dead skunk into the classroom one day.

Scott Whyte was the banker's son, and we struck up a friendship right away, mostly because we both loved sports so much. He had an even bigger and better front yard to play fun ball in. He also had an electric football game that we enjoyed playing in the fall. In years to

★   ★   ★   ★   ★   ★   ★

come we were on all the sports teams together. Bernie Bjorklund was another good friend, but he lived in the country so I didn't get to see him as much. Sometimes I rode the bus home with him and stayed overnight. We liked watching "Chip and Dale" cartoons. Since my first name was Dale, I called him Chip. He had a basketball rim in the hayloft of their barn where we would shoot baskets at night with the aid of a spotlight. I always connect him with a basketball. Perhaps this is because one day in gym I got mad at him and fired one at him. It left a welt on his forehead and, as fate would have it, it was school picture day. To this day there is poor Bernie with a knot on his head, courtesy of that new preacher's kid that moved to town!

We didn't have very many girls in our class: Holly Sorenson, Nancy Jewell, Phyllis Hefti, Bev Blumeyer (the superintendent's daughter), Nicole Smith, and Barbara Klaus. Barbara soon moved away leaving only five. I regret to say that we boys teased Barbara, pretending she had fleas and passing them around. One day our teasing got so bad that she threw up at her desk. Much later in life I learned that she had been killed in a grinding car-train collision. I wrote a story of contrition that was published in *Moody* and was then picked up by quite a few other Christian publications: "I'd Love to Say, 'I'm Sorry.'"

Nicole ("Nicky") and Bev were the only girls in our class who lived in town. Sometimes I would walk Nicky home and carry her books for her. One summer night she dared me to kiss her, so I did – right on her cheek. I remember two things about that kiss: how soft her cheek was and her merry trill of laughter as I pedaled my bike away from the scene of my evidently failed attempt at true romance. Phyllis seemed to be the class organizer. I remember several hayrides and wienie roasts that she had for us at her house in the country. She and Bev

★   ★   ★   ★   ★   ★   ★

were best friends as were Holly and Nancy. In junior high a new girl joined our class. Her name was Sally Dungan. She and her family had moved to Goldfield from Mechanicsville. She took our class by storm, at least the boys, because she was a nice-looking girl and was quite well endowed. Lots of guys wanted to carry her books home. Which leads me to my next story.

One day Mrs. Hinton came to class wearing a skirt and a pink sheer blouse. About mid-morning something happened that all of us remember to this day. Somehow one of her rather generous sized breasts slipped out of her brassiere leaving nothing to the imagination. The girls were too embarrassed to inform her of her "wardrobe mal-function," and the boys were not about to tell her. Before the day ended Mrs. Hinton caught me gazing in wonder, gave out a loud shriek, and fled the room. Someone had to be made the scapegoat, and the lot fell upon me to stay after class and clean the erasers and the blackboard. I guess it was to atone for the whole class's failure to notify her that she had given us a "free show" for most of the day! And they say we didn't have "sex education" classes in the 50s. We did that day.

The last day of school came and we all sang, "School's out, school's out, teacher let the monkeys out. No more pencils, no more books, no more teachers' dirty looks." I am sure Mrs. Hinton, God rest her soul, breathed a sigh of relief as we cleaned out our desks and departed the premises. My final semester grades in elementary school were just average: one B (Spelling) and the rest straight C's.

IN THE GOOD OLD SUMMERTIME!

That summer I got one of the biggest compliments of my young life. I played Little League baseball, like all the baseball-loving kids in

★   ★   ★   ★   ★   ★   ★

town, but one day I was asked to play on the high school team. They were short a man and needed an outfielder. I figured they would stick me out in right field where the dorks were sent, but instead they inserted me into the lineup in left field. That was pretty heady stuff for a kid who was not yet in junior high. For one beautiful day I was in the "big leagues."

Riverside Park was where the ballpark was located. The Boone River ran through the park (sometimes it went out of its banks and overran the park). Families used the park for picnics because of the many shade trees, but Riverside Park will always be a baseball memory for me. I played second base for awhile, got a new infielder's glove, and usually batted leadoff. When I went into junior high, I was moved to third base, the position I had played in Boise. I had a strong arm and could make the long throws to first from the "hot corner" position. In 1957 another one of my baseball heroes, Stan "The Man" Musial, won his seventh and final batting award, hitting .357 for my favorite National League team, the St. Louis Cardinals.

For our five-plus years in Goldfield, summer came to mean at least five things. I would go to Vacation Bible School at the Park church, attend Christian Service Camp at Dolliver State Park and/or Pine Lake State Park, play baseball, have a summer job, and go to each of my grandparents' homes for a visit.

Not long after we moved to Goldfield, two young women from Midwestern School of Evangelism, Anna Mae Ducommun and Letha Lu Solliday, came to conduct the Daily Vacation Bible School at the Park church. I memorized my first chapter of the Bible during this VBS – Psalm 1. In those days everyone used the King James Version. It was a good chapter to memorize and I have quoted from it many times

★   ★   ★   ★   ★   ★   ★

since. In my early days of preaching I developed a sermon from this text, "The Blessed Man."

THE SECOND CALL OF GOD

I will always have a warm place in my heart for Christian Service Camp because it is where I really learned what the Bible was all about and what God required of my young life. One of the first camps I went to was in the summer of 1957, a camp near Deweese, Nebraska. Dad was on the faculty and our whole family went. The next year my sister Becky and I attended Camp Diagonal, near Diagonal, Iowa. Some old friends from Hamburg were there that week – Gary Cradic and Gary Bryant. One night it seemed that God was calling me to preach His Word. I did not respond to the invitation publicly to answer this call for some reason, perhaps because I had not yet committed my life to Christ. I guess I was somewhat like young Samuel. He heard the call of God but did not yet know the Lord (1 Samuel 3:7). This was the second call of God I experienced (the first being in Cottage Grove, Oregon, in 1956). One of the faculty members at Diagonal was Bill Payne. He used to tease me saying that my sister Becky could hit the ball farther than I could. Becky played second base, as she did for the girl's softball team at GHS. Other faculty members I remember were David Kirk, Loren Daly, and H. N. Solliday.

Another camp I attended was held at Dolliver State Park, near Ft. Dodge, Iowa. This camp is memorable to me because of the "Morning Watch" service. One of the activities in our daily regimen was for each camper to get alone somewhere on the campground and just think about the Lord's return. After all, the Bible says we are to "watch and pray." So we were to watch for the Lord's return and think

*   *   *   *   *   *   *

about if we were ready or not. This was before the flag raising and breakfast. It was only a five-minute service but it was the longest five minutes of my life. I knew that the Bible taught that Jesus would return "in like manner," i.e., as He had ascended to heaven. I knew that His return would include clouds in the sky for the Bible said so (Acts 1:9). Even a little theology can have a profound effect on your life. On days that were cloudy I would be on better behavior than days when there was not a cloud in the sky! You must also remember that in October of 1957 Russia ignited the "space race" when they launched "Sputnik." One dark night dad pointed out the Soviet satellite to me in the heavens above. It was kind of spooky that Russia now had an "eye in the sky" looking down on us. Communism in the cosmos! Dad knew all the constellations. One night we got quite a show – the fabled *aurora borealis* (Northern Lights).

I GIVE MY LIFE TO CHRIST AT PINE LAKE BIBLE CAMP

But I guess Pine Lake Bible Camp, near Eldora, Iowa, will always be my favorite camp because that is where I gave my life to Christ in the summer of 1958. We had some great men of God who came to Pine Lake to teach and preach. Among them were Russell Boatman, Russell Casey, Hilliard Comeaux, and of course my dad. I still have the notes I took from Brother Boatman's class on "The New Testament Church." How could I know that Russell Boatman would assist me greatly when I wrote the biography of Archie Word? Or that his equally talented brother, Don Earl, would become a director of my ministry many years later? One year Donald Fream, a missionary from Jamaica, came to be the missionary speaker.

Pine Lake featured some great student-faculty softball games.

★   ★   ★   ★   ★   ★   ★

How we loved it when we could beat the faculty! We had chapel every morning. One day I sang my first "special number." I joined my good buddies Willie Williams and Joe Simcox from the Eldora church in a trio. We sang, "He Lives." I wonder how many millions of people have sung that same song? *"I serve a risen Savior, He's in the world today; I know that He is living, whatever men may say."* My mother was so proud of me, even if I couldn't hit all the notes.

No doubt we sang many good songs at camp, but one that is special to me to this day is the one James DeForest Murch wrote, "I'll Put Jesus First in My Life." This was a great song of consecration written by a great man of consecration. He served as editor of *Restoration Herald* and *The Lookout*, eventually becoming the managing editor of *Christianity Today*. His crowning work was *Christians Only*, the best book in my opinion ever written on the history of the Restoration Movement. To this day I have his picture in my office. The second stanza still touches my heart: *"The Lord Jesus died my salvation to win: He went in my stead to Calv'ry and bled; Redemption impels me to give up all sin: I'll put Jesus first in my life."* It means so much to me that I would like to have it sung at my funeral when that day comes.

And so it was that on Friday evening, June 20, 1958, at a "Galilean Service" at Pine Lake, I was won over by the love of Christ, and I surrendered my life to Him at His "third call" to me – just like Samuel! My dad "happened" to be the preacher that night. All of the campers were on one side of the lake and from the other side of the lake was a boat. A lighted cross, illuminated by a generator, was positioned upright in the boat. The light of the cross shimmered across the waves. Dad's sermon was "What Is Your Life?" When the invitation was given, I found myself stepping forward in the gathering darkness.

★   ★   ★   ★   ★   ★   ★

Milton Hendrickson, the minister at Waterloo, took my small hand in his big hand and I made the Good Confession. "I believe that Jesus is the Christ, the Son of the living God!" The following Sunday morning, June 22, my father baptized me in the name of the Father, Son, and Holy Spirit at the Park church in Goldfield. I was five months shy of my 13th birthday. My parents gave me a new King James Version of the Bible published by The World Publishing Company of Cleveland and New York. It had a center-reference column and the words of Jesus were printed in red. The Bible also contained famous art paintings of biblical characters and scenes by painters like Raphael. I could not begin to tell you how many Bibles I have owned since 1958, but I wish I still had that one. Whether I realized it or not at the time, I had been given two of the best gifts of my young life: the gift of salvation through Jesus Christ and the gift of the precious Word of God. I used that Bible until my father bought me a new one when I went to Bible College in 1964.

A motivational speaker once said, "I read the Bible and a daily newspaper every day. That way I know what both sides are up to!" All the newspapers in America in 1958 were covering the trial of Charles Starkweather, a 19-year-old serial killer who went on a bloody murder spree across Nebraska and Wyoming with his 15-year-old girl friend Caril Ann Fugate. Eleven lifeless bodies were left in their bloody wake. When the jury found him guilty and he was sentenced to death, my sister Muriel and I enacted what we thought should be his punishment. She turned on the electric stove and I stuck my head in the oven – for just a few seconds! I believe that Starkweather got the electric chair while Fugate was sent to prison. In 1976 she was paroled after serving 17 years as a model prisoner. Not long ago I met a Christian woman

⋆   ⋆   ⋆   ⋆   ⋆   ⋆   ⋆

who has ministered to Caril and she told me that Caril is truly reformed.

SUMMER JOBS

In the fall of 1958 I entered the "Big Time," Junior High. I started off on a good note with A's in Reading and English but wound up with B's in both subjects by the end of the school year. The rest were all C's and I could not believe it when I got a D in English! How could I do better in Math than English? You will have to ask Mrs. Robinson.

When I became a teenager, November 23, 1958, I got to do some things I had never done before. For one, I joined the Boy Scouts of America. I took the Scout Oath:

> *On my honor I will do my best*
> *To do my duty to God and my country and to obey the Scout Law;*
> *To help other people at all times;*
> *To keep myself physically strong, mentally awake, and morally*
>   *straight.*

Our Scoutmaster was a fellow named Joe, the local postmaster. I did my best to follow the Scout Law to be "trustworthy, loyal, helpful, friendly, courteous, kind, obedient, cheerful, thrifty, brave, clean, and reverent." I learned how to tie knots, tie off a tourniquet, tie my Boy Scout kerchief, and lots of other interesting things like how to build a campfire, set up a pup tent, and even dig a latrine! We also practiced the "manly art" of boxing. My reach wasn't very long, but I managed to get in a few good punches once in awhile. I had never been fishing until I became a Boy Scout. I caught a few blue gills at a "Camporee" and tried cooking them over a fire along with a potato

★   ★   ★   ★   ★   ★   ★

and corn-on-the-cob wrapped in aluminum foil. My botched "meal" made me hungry for mom's home cooking! On Memorial Day our scout troop would march from Memorial Hall to beautiful Glenwood Cemetery, along with the war veterans and the school band, for a memorial service. We stood at attention while "Taps" was played.

One summer M. J. Siemens, an elder at Park Church and our Sunday School teacher, took a bunch of boys to Minnesota, "Land of 10,000 Lakes," to do some serious fishing. We fished all day and had devotions around the campfire at night. I don't remember catching too many fish but I probably got a lot of mosquito bites in Minnesota.

I eventually worked my way up the labor ladder from mowing lawns and shoveling walks to walking bean fields with a crew of young people. Our field "boss" was Donna "Yogi" Carlson who lived across the street from us. She was called "Yogi" because she was the catcher on the girl's high school softball team. She could really "crack the whip" and sometimes cursed the crew like Captain Bligh if she thought we were not working like we should. Every morning we got up early and were driven out to some farmer's field where we walked down endless rows of dew-soaked soybeans, using our machetes to cut down milkweed, corn, and anything else that wasn't supposed to be there. I don't remember the pay scale, only that it was long, hard work. To this day I have an inch-and-a-half scar on my right wrist that I "earned" from this job. I slipped climbing over a barbed wire fence and sliced my wrist open. I took off my T-shirt and wrapped it around my bloody wrist. Someone drove me into town where Doc Basinger tended to my wound, tetanus shot and all. The thin, white scar will go with me to the grave. The bad thing was that my parents and sisters had just left for a vacation to Montana. I had opted to stay home and work during the

★   ★   ★   ★   ★   ★   ★

day and play ball at night. Now I couldn't do either one! Bummer! I spent a couple of weeks eating hamburgers and French Fries at M. J.'s "Shady Nook" café, listening to KIOA on the Stromberg-Carlson, and watching night games from a place I was not used to – the grandstand.

A VISIT TO SACRED GROUND – CROSLEY FIELD!

But in that splendid summer of 1958, I had a dream come true. It was August and we were in Indiana for our annual visit to Grandpa and Grandma Brown's house in Richmond when Dad asked me, "Son, how would you like to go to a major league baseball game?" Silly question! Would General Custer have liked reinforcements at the Little Big Horn? Show me the way to Cincinnati! We drove to the Queen City where we met up with one of dad's Oregon friends, Sherwood Smith, who was now teaching at Cincinnati Bible Seminary. I shall always cherish my visit to old Crosley Field, home of the Cincinnati Reds! Did you know it was named after Powell Crosley, Jr., American inventor, industrialist, and entrepreneur? (Think the Crosley automobile, the Crosley radio, and Crosley appliances.) It was a beautiful ballpark and I fell in love with it at first sight.

It may have been outside the ballpark that I saw my first Negro "live and in person." The old gentleman was wearing a stovepipe hat and was selling hot roasted peanuts from a pushcart that was mounted on big spoke wheels. I never smelled anything so good! I think they sold for 25 cents a bag. We walked up to the ticket windows and got our tickets. I still have my red ticket stub, faded now, pasteboard testimony that says I got in that night for a grand total of 75 cents! Dad bought a scorecard for 10 cents (I have it too), and then we entered baseball heaven. I shall never forget coming up the tunnel and getting

★   ★   ★   ★   ★   ★   ★

my first glimpse of a bona fide major league baseball field. It sparkled like a precious diamond under the lights. The outfield grass was emerald green and the amber infield looked like it had just been manicured. Dad said that my eyes nearly popped out of my head.

The Reds had several Negro players, men whom I had admired from afar: Frank Robinson, Vada Pinson, George Crowe, Bob Thurman, and Brooks Lawrence. The visiting Milwaukee Braves' roster included Hank Aaron, Wes Covington, Felix Mantilla, and Bill Bruton. Remember, the Boston Red Sox were the only team that did not include Negro players at this time. In 1959, twelve years after the Dodgers signed Jackie Robinson, Boston finally joined baseball and integrated. I thought it was funny that the man they signed was named Green – "Pumpsie" Green.

Don Newcombe, one of my heroes from the Brooklyn Dodgers, had recently been traded to the Reds. He took the mound against the visiting Milwaukee Braves. Leadoff man Bill Bruton clobbered the very first pitch I saw thrown in a major league game for a home run! We were sitting in the second deck on the third base side of the field, and I gazed in wonder as that white pellet arched its way in the night sky over the right field fence and fell into the hands of some fortunate fan. Joey Jay, a young flame throwing phenom, was pitching for the Braves. Would you believe I nearly saw a no-hitter that night? He gave up only one hit, a pinch-hit bloop single by Jerry Lynch in the sixth inning. Johnny Temple got kicked out of the game for kicking dirt on an umpire. Warren Spahn – Warren Spahn! – came in to pitch the ninth and seal the 3-0 victory for Milwaukee. The stylish southpaw was "poetry in motion." I saw four future Hall of Famers that night at Crosley Field: Spahn, Robinson, Aaron, and Eddie Mathews. It was

★   ★   ★   ★   ★   ★   ★

Gus Bell Night and the Reds gave Gus some kind of an award. My reward was just being there. I've never quite forgiven the Reds for demolishing those hallowed grounds in 1966 to go play ball in a sterile concrete bowl called Riverfront Stadium!

SEEING RICHARD M. NIXON

In November we went to Ft. Dodge for a big parade where we saw Richard M. Nixon, who was vice president under Dwight D. Eisenhower. I can't remember if Pat and their two daughters, Julie and Trisha, were with him or not that day. I thought they were a fine family and set a good example for all of America. Alaska became the 49th state in 1958 and Hawaii became the 50th in 1959. We knew our U. S. history in those days. In 2008, while campaigning for the presidency, Barack Obama told reporters he had been in 57 of the 58 states! Former geography teachers all over the United States nearly set off an earthquake by rolling over in their graves! The fawning media gave him a pass, saying he was "tired." That would not have cut it in Mrs. Robinson's class!

THE OTHER GAME

Up to this time I had not shown much interest in professional football, but in 1958 when the Baltimore Colts defeated the New York Giants 23-17 in sudden death overtime for the championship of the NFL, I "suddenly" got interested. The Colts had Alan "The Horse" Ameche (who scored the winning TD on a one-yard plunge), Gene "Big Daddy" Lipscomb, Gino Marchetti, Johnny Sample, and Raymond Berry. I really liked their drop-back quarterback, Johnny Unitas: crewcut, high top shoes, and all. The Giants, who eventually became my

★   ★   ★   ★   ★   ★   ★

favorite NFL team, boasted Frank Gifford, Charley Connerly, Roosevelt Brown, Andy Robustelli, Rosey Grier, and Pat Summerall. Expansion had not yet increased the size of the league. We knew most of the stars on all the teams. Besides the Giants and the Colts there were the Green Bay Packers and the Detroit Lions (who often played each other on Thanksgiving Day), the Cleveland Browns, Pittsburgh Steelers, Philadelphia Eagles, Washington Redskins, Los Angeles Rams, and San Francisco 49ers. Chicago boasted two teams: the Chicago Bears ("The Monsters of the Midway") and the Chicago Cardinals (who eventually moved to St. Louis and now play in Arizona). Only eight teams today remain in the cities where they were playing in 1958.

Sometimes Dad and I would listen to the LSU Tigers on WWL on Saturday nights. Dad had conducted a revival for Remi Duhon in Crowley, Louisiana, and had met a nice young man, Lynn LaBlanc, number 77, who played tackle for the Bayou Bengals. He was part of the famous "Chinese Bandits" defense. Dad also created an elaborate cardboard "spinner" football game that we played on the kitchen table. My team was always the Giants, and he would pick out one of the other teams. I also started collecting football cards but they never rivaled my baseball card collection. Goldfield did not have a football team, so the town kids usually got together on a Saturday morning, either at the school or some vacant lot, chose up sides, and played tackle football (with no pads). On offense I played halfback and on defense I played safety. I had an old blue and maize leather helmet (with no protective facemask) that I wore. Some of my buddies didn't even bother with a helmet. Mom must have had a hard time getting all the grass stains out of my jeans and sweatshirts.

★   ★   ★   ★   ★   ★   ★

LIFE AT THE PARK CHURCH

Now let me tell you about the Park Church of Christ where my father was the minister from 1957-1962. Goldfield had only four churches: the United Methodist Church, the United Presbyterian Church, the Christian Church (Disciples of Christ), and Park Church of Christ. Our church was started in 1949 when some members parted company with the Disciples Church over the United Missionary Society. The Christian Church eventually disbanded and some Lutherans bought their building and began Hauge Lutheran Church. Most of my friends in Goldfield went to one of these churches.

Each Sunday morning I would try to find the Sunday paper, the *Des Moines Register*, so I could read the comics and "The Big Peach" (the sports section), but Dad wisely hid it in a different place each week. I wore a white shirt and clip-on bow tie to church and, if it wasn't too warm, I would wear my suit coat as well. Woe be to any of us if we went to church without taking our KJV Bibles with us for Sunday School!

At the Hamburg church I had gotten to ring the church bell, calling people to worship. But in Goldfield I got to call people to church electronically. The church did not have a steeple or a bell tower (and, obviously no church bell), but it did have a modern public address system atop the church roof. Each Sunday morning I would go to the church, unlock the sound system cabinet, and turn on the record player. A green light came on and the air was filled with electronic incense, not unpleasant to me, while the machine was warming up. Then I would select a record that featured church chimes, place it on the turntable, carefully lift and lower the arm onto the record, and set

★   ★   ★   ★   ★   ★   ★

the volume. Outside, all over town, the "church bells" could be heard. I sometimes had fleeting thoughts of playing one of my favorite rock and roll songs like "Palisades Park" by Freddy Cannon to see what would happen. I'm sure it would have been the talk of the town. I would have been rocked and heads (at least *my* head) would have rolled!

SITTING IN THE "HEAVENLY PLACES"

The Park Church had a balcony, and I liked to sit up in the "heavenly places" and gaze down on all the congregants below. Usually an adult sat with us to make sure we paid attention and didn't sail any paper airplanes, made out of the Sunday bulletin, down into the unsuspecting congregation. One Sunday I noted that one of the older young people, Richard Stapp, was asleep on the back row down below. We called the back pew in the church "backslider's row." Ed Hebner, a big kid who played quarterback for the Boone Valley Bobcats, crossed his legs and accidentally dislodged a hymnal that was resting on the edge of the balcony railing. The blue hymnbook descended end over end and hit the floor twenty feet below like the crack of doom. The slumbering Richard came up out the pew like the dead will come up out of their graves on the Day of Judgment! It was not long after this incident I was made to sit in less heavenly places. I dutifully took my place with mom and the rest of the family in the main sanctuary. If you didn't behave, she would lovingly pinch us or give us a "thimble thump" with her index finger. Mom used thimbles for things other than sewing!

★　　★　　★　　★　　★　　★　　★

THE DREADED "PINK BOARD!"

One Sunday dad was gone holding a revival somewhere. We had a guest speaker that day, I believe it was Lyle Bartlett. In any event, all of us misbehaved in church. It wasn't a conspiracy or anything like that; it just happened. When we got back to the parsonage, mom "held court" and handed down the verdict: guilty of misbehavior in church in the first degree. Punishment: spanking with the Pink Board in the third degree. One by one my sisters entered the room of doom to take their medicine. Their cries began to remind me of the sobbing on the Sabbath made by the Jews at the Wailing Wall in old Jerusalem. When it came my turn, mom told me what she had told them. "If you can tell me one thing the preacher said in his sermon today, I won't spank you." Frantically my mind went into high gear. What had he said? I drew a blank. Up went the Pink Board.

"Wait, wait!" I cried. "Now I remember." The Pink Board slowly came down. "Well?" my mother asked.

"He told a story about a little dog that got run over by a car!" I breathed a premature sigh of relief. At last I would not get that spanking. But mom was not satisfied. "I want Scripture!" she said. Alas and alack, I could not think of one. Down came the Pink Board again and again. End of my tale. This is for all you preachers: put plenty of Scripture in your sermon lest some poor kid suffer the same fate as I.

GREAT SONGS OF THE CHURCH

Great Songs of the Church was the hymnbook used by the Park Church. It was published by Standard Publishing in Cincinnati but was edited by E. L. Jorgenson, a member of the Churches of Christ (a cap-

★   ★   ★   ★   ★   ★   ★

pella). It, therefore, was a significant and visible product of the unity effort between our Christian Churches/Churches of Christ fellowship and their fellowship of a cappella Churches of Christ. Although the two groups parted ways in 1906, efforts at unity had been made since the mid-30s by men like James DeForest Murch and Claud F. Witty, William Jessup and Earnest Beam, Don DeWelt and Carl Ketcherside, and several other key leaders from opposite sides of the keyboard. I tell you that to tell you the following story.

One fine Sunday morning a family visited the Park Church of Christ. It was a full house, as usual, so they took their place on the only pew that was rarely occupied – the front row. But the moment the pianist played the first note of the opening song, the father rose to his feet, picked up *Great Songs of the Church*, and slammed it down on the hardwood pew. *Crash!* Another "crack of doom" at the old Park Church! It seemed that every worshipper was lifted about an inch off their pews and the startled pianist nearly fell off the piano bench. The incensed father then marched his family out of the church building, informing the dazed deacon at the door that a *true* "Church of Christ" would *never* use "mechanical instruments" in "the worship." The slam of the front church of the door nearly sucked the oxygen out of the sanctuary. I had no idea what in the world was going on, but dad discerned that the family must have been from the South, perhaps Texas. And since the words "Church of Christ" were engraved on our church cornerstone, the man assumed that we were a Church of Christ just like the one he was used to back home. It is noteworthy that the song that took the brunt of the visitor's wrath was none other than M. C. Kurfee's "Unity Song." Think about the irony of the following words, printed on the inside back cover, being treated in such uncouth fash-

★　　★　　★　　★　　★　　★　　★

ion. *"How blest and how joyous will be the glad day, when heart beats to heart in the work of the Lord; when Christians united shall swell the grand lay, divisions all ended, triumphant His word!"*

There was a blind lady, Eva Christianson, who sometimes would favor us with a solo. I may be wrong but it seemed like every time she did it was: "Far and near the fields are teeming with the waves of ripened grain." Often we closed our Sunday evening service with "Day is dying in the west; heav'n is touching earth with rest; wait and worship while the night sets her evening lamps alight through all the sky." If the song leader dragged it out, the song could be quite mournful. I didn't care much for those two hymns, but there were others I really liked: "All Hail the Power of Jesus' Name," "All Things Are Ready," "Beulah Land" (although I wasn't quite sure what it meant), "Come, Thou Almighty King," "Faith of Our Fathers," "Home, Sweet Home," "Love Divine," "Marching to Zion," "The King's Business," "There Stands a Rock," "When All My Labors and Trials Are O'er" (even though it seemed that I did not have many at the time).

In addition to singing, our worship included "Responsive Readings," Communion, the offering, the sermon, prayers, and the dreaded "Birthday Offering." If you had a birthday that week you had to trudge to the front of the sanctuary, offering in hand, and stand there like a dork while the congregation chimed in as one: "Many happy returns on the day of thy birth, may sunshine and gladness be given. And may the dear Father prepare you on earth for a beautiful birthday in heaven." Then you dropped your offering in a little white plastic church, held by one of the church officers, and returned to your seat as fast as you could.

Sometimes we had missionaries come to Park Church, usually

★   ★   ★   ★   ★   ★   ★

on a Sunday night, and they would speak to a somewhat smaller crowd, show slides (most of them ended with a beautiful sunset), and make a heartfelt appeal to support their work. I'm not sure, but I believe Ralph Harter from India was one of those who came. Charles and Roberta Selby, preparing to go to the Philippines, came several times. A visiting missionary from a predominantly Roman Catholic country told hair-raising stories of religious persecution directed at all non-Catholics, including torture. I was appalled that people could persecute their fellow man and do so in the name of religion.

A NEW USE FOR A CHURCH HYMNAL

Doug Miller and I found a new use for *Great Songs of the Church* on Sunday nights. We both liked baseball. He was a huge fan of the Milwaukee Braves and of course I liked the Cardinals and the Yankees. On the back page of the Sunday bulletin we would write the names of our favorite players. Then we would create an entire season's records for those players. Let's say Doug picked Lew Burdette, a pitcher. Taking the hymnal between thumb and forefinger, between pages 1 and 30, he would riffle the pages and let them fall open at random. Since Burdette was a right-handed pitcher the corresponding number on the right hand page would stand for how many wins he racked up that year. If it was on page 23 ("Brightly Beams Our Father's Mercy") Burdette got 23 wins. The same for losses (page 18, "Be Not Dismayed Whate'er Betide," 18 losses for old Lew). Strikeouts could go as high as page 300 ("When the King Comes"). For batters the routine went pretty much the same. Home runs up to page 60 ("He Took Me Out of the Pit." But you wouldn't want to take anyone out of the game who hit 60!). RBIs up to 190 ("When Peace Like a River"). We knew our stats.

★   ★   ★   ★   ★   ★   ★

We knew that 190 was the record for RBIs (Hack Wilson, Chicago Cubs, 1930) and 60 was the record for home runs (Babe Ruth, New York Yankees, 1927). When Roger Maris hit 61 in 1961, we of course had to up the ante to 61 ("He Will Hold Me Fast"). Batting averages could go as high as .406 ("I Love Thy Kingdom, Lord") because that's what Teddy Ballgame hit in 1941. "At bats" could go clear to the end of the book, page 600 ("When He Cometh to Make Up His Jewels"). The amazing thing about all this is that I could still hear and retain enough of dad's Sunday evening sermon to be able to answer the inevitable quiz at the end of the day at the parsonage, while dad was having his corn flakes. "What was my text? Title? Main points?" But I also knew that Ken Boyer, on the back of the Sunday bulletin, had a good year: 45 home runs ("Fear Not, Little Flock"), 211 RBIs ("Sinner, You Have Sadly Wandered"), and a lusty batting average of .384 ("God Moves in a Mysterious Way"). I am sure that Fanny J. Crosby, Phillip P. Bliss, and Charles Wesley never dreamed their hymns would be used in such fashion. But then they probably never played baseball either.

THE GREAT CHURCH AND SOFTBALL SCHEDULE CONFLICT

My mother normally wore white gloves and a nice hat to church. Nearly all of the women did, and not just on Easter. Men usually wore suits and ties. We went to church in our "Sunday best." It was the way you did things in those days. It's been a long time since I've seen any woman wear either a hat or gloves to church. Now some churches urge you to "dress casual" and even call their services "casual worship." I don't wear a suit all the time anymore, but I hope my worship hasn't become "casual." After all, the Lord is still in His holy temple. Number 597. You could look it up.

★　　★　　★　　★　　★　　★　　★

My father kept his study, his *sanctum sanctorum*, at the church, stage left from the pulpit. Sometimes I would walk over from the parsonage and browse through his books while he was preparing for a sermon or cranking out *The Christian Campaigner*. The place had the smell of mimeograph ink, paper, and cherry chocolates that he kept on his desk. He had a blue cardboard sign on his wall that read, "I had no shoes and complained until I met a man who had no feet." That always stopped me in my tracks and made me think about the blessings that were mine.

Wednesday night was "Prayer Meeting Night." This presented a challenge sometimes because the church softball team, every once in awhile, also played on Wednesday night. Actually our team was called "Evergreen" because several of the men from the Park church played for the rural cooperative. Paul Siemens was the pitcher, his brother Frank played outfield, and I played third base. Since Paul was also the manager, sometimes he would go on out to the ballpark to get the field ready for play. But dad would not let me leave until the last "Amen" was said. By the time that happened – and sometimes "while the words were yet in his mouth" – I would be on my bike, pedaling furiously in the gathering gloom to the ballpark. On nights other than Prayer Meeting Night, Paul penciled me in the leadoff spot, but on Wednesday nights he put me at the bottom of the order because he knew I couldn't get there in time. Dad would eventually get there to see me play. Sometimes he would gently chide Paul and Frank for being AWOL, but he always rooted for us to win. And Evergreen usually won the league because we really did have a good team. Manning the "hot corner" was sometimes really hot when one of those husky farmers on the opposing team would rip one down the line. I loved

★   ★   ★   ★   ★   ★   ★

nothing more than going to my right on a screamer, digging it out of the dirt, and firing the ball over to first to get the runner by a step.

One night the United Presbyterians were short a man and so they called me out of the grandstands to play second base alongside my friend Dave Harvey at shortstop. We pulled off a nifty double play. I had never heard of the "ecumenical movement" before, but I guess you could say that this was that. My father took a dim view of it, but I told him that I had heard a call ("Who will play for us?") and I responded in Isaiah-like fashion ("Here am I; play me!").

HOLIDAYS AND RELATIVES

Every 4th of July, "Independence Day," the whole church was invited out to the farm of Bert and June Siemens for a grand picnic, games, and fireworks. We five Knowles kids really looked forward to this day because we seldom had pop at our house. But on the glorious 4th we could guzzle pop until we popped at the picnic. There were big galvanized tubs full of all kinds of bottles of pop immersed in ice cold water. Picnic tables groaned beneath the weight of fried chicken, hot dogs, potato salad, sliced tomatoes, baked beans, corn on the cob, and all kinds of delicious desserts: cakes, pies, doughnuts, and of course homemade ice cream. Dad would bring a short "God and country" devotion, and then we played games all afternoon, including a big softball game, which was right down my alley. Kids shot off firecrackers and nary a phalange was lost in the patriotic process.

On Halloween I went trick-or-treating with some of the town kids. We never did anything more serious than soap a few windows and screens. Well, once we tipped over an outhouse, but at least no one was in it at the time! Thanksgiving Day sometimes found our family

★   ★   ★   ★   ★   ★   ★

with another church family where, after a wonderful dinner, we watched the annual football game between Green Bay and Detroit. Christmas Eve was when we opened our Christmas gifts but never until Dad first read to us the Christmas story from Luke 2, a tradition I have maintained in my own family. We had several "Winter Wonderlands" in Goldfield on Christmas Day. My favorite Christmas song was Irving Berlin's "I'm Dreaming of a White Christmas." I loved the lines: "Where the treetops glisten and children listen to hear sleigh bells in the snow." On New Year's Day we often went to the home of Durwood and Pat Miller in Eagle Grove and watched some of the college football Bowl games. I was a big Iowa Hawkeye fan (and still am). From 1956-1960 the Hawks finished in the Top Ten four times, won three Big Ten titles, and earned two victories in the Rose Bowl.

It was always great when Grandma Knowles or Grandpa and Grandpa Brown came to stay with us for a few days. Grandma Knowles would spoil me with a homemade cherry pie. Grandpa Brown, who had a Case tractor dealership in Richmond, often brought me a shiny new toy tractor. I wish I still had at least one of them. Grandma Brown taught me to put peanut butter on a stalk of celery, a treat I enjoy to this day. Once dad and mom had to be gone for a week, so my aunt Lois and her husband, Harry Halatyn, came to stay with us. All of dad's brothers and sisters had nicknames when they were kids. Lois was "Pape," Dad was "Pearl," Boyd was "Toad," Troy was "Snack," and Lyle was "Camp." Aunt Pape always made things fun. Uncle Harry was a scholarly sophisticated sort and liked to smoke a pipe and read the *San Francisco Chronicle*. Dad was mad as hops when he got home and found out that Uncle Harry had smoked in our house and had actually kept beer in the fridge! But I must admit that I liked the smell

★   ★   ★   ★   ★   ★   ★

of pipe tobacco. It was a real treat for me to play with my cousin Tommy. Both of us had been given the same middle name, Victor, after our Grandpa William Victor Knowles. We played catch in the front yard and swapped baseball cards. Uncle Snack, who lived in Freeport, Illinois, often came to see us and always had some special treat for all five of us children. We were always sad when he said it was time to go back to his home in Illinois.

TRAVELS WITH DAD

Sometimes Dad took us calling with him. One day we were driving through the town of Pocohontas and Dad said, "Let's stop and see Matie Bailey for a little while." A chorus of groans went up from the back seat. Matie Bailey was a good Christian woman who lived alone in an old mansion that had deteriorated through the years. She was somewhat of an eccentric. The walls of her house were papered with old newspapers. If things got too boring, I could always read an old sports item. A fat cat was sitting in an old stuffed chair and would not surrender his throne. After visiting awhile, Matie told Dad she wanted to take us out for a treat. Where did we go? To a nice family restaurant? To a drive-in A & W where at least I could slouch in the back seat where no one could see me? Not on your life! With uncanny accuracy Matie directed Dad to the local teen hangout. Street rods surrounded the place like little pigs nuzzled up to their mother at feeding time. We found a booth but it was right next to the jukebox. Jerry Lee Lewis and Chuck Berry were blasting away for all their worth.

A gum-chewing waitress walked up to take our order. I swear she was smirking! Matie ordered ice cream all around. That was fine with me. But then she ordered a loaf of white bread too. Evidently she

★   ★   ★   ★   ★   ★   ★

enjoyed eating bread with her ice cream. Matie's voice was weak and she had to shout over the blare of the jukebox. All the local teens put down their cherry Cokes and French fries and stared at us in wonder. I slid down in the booth as low as I could go. Good old dad finally got the waitress to understand that Mrs. Bailey wanted a loaf of Wonder bread. So we had bread and ice cream that day. But Matie had a good heart and was often a benefactor to Bible colleges, including the college Becky went to following her graduation from GHS in 1962, Midwestern School of Evangelism.

Sometimes our family accompanied dad on one of his revival meetings. I met Terry Crist at Laurens, where Terry's dad, Paul, was preaching. Terry liked sports, too, and we became fast friends. We wound up going to the same college, roomed together one year, and were "best man" in each other's weddings.

One day Ron Carlson, a young married student at Midwestern School of Evangelism, visited our home. He took a "staged" picture of me drying dishes while reading a copy of his new youth magazine *Anchor*. I was the "cover boy" for the January 1962 issue. The caption read, "Everything stops when *Anchor* comes – even wiping the dishes." I would have preferred a picture showing me reading *Anchor* while perched on third base after hitting a triple!

Life rolled on. I can think of very few moments that I did not enjoy life in Goldfield. I have often thanked God that I was born when I was and that I grew up when I did and where I did. With the exception of our three years in Idaho, virtually all of my kindergarten to graduation years was spent in the Midwest – most of those years in Iowa. I was blessed with great parents, great churches, great teachers, and great friends. What more could a kid ask for? For those who look

★   ★   ★   ★   ★   ★   ★

down on that period of time and are dismissive of the "Ozzie and Harriet" families in that golden era, I say, "Get a life." We had one. And it was a good one. Life is what you make it. "Go thou and do likewise."

THE MUSIC OF MY LIFE

One day ("The Day the Music Died") I awoke to the news that Buddy Holly, Richie Valens, and "The Big Bopper" had been killed in a plane crash near Mason City, a town that we went to when Becky or Muriel marched in the marching band. Mason City was the inspiration for "River City" in the movie "The Music Man." The recording artists had sung the night before in Clear Lake. I have often said, "I grew up not far from where Buddy Holly went down." Clear Lake was a popular place to visit, especially in the summer. I went there a couple of times with my friends. I liked his song "Peggy Sue" partly because I liked a girl named Peggy, whom I met at a ball game, who lived in nearby Woolstock. In 1971, Don McLean came out with "American Pie," a tribute to the three fallen singers. I think it's the longest 45 RPM ever recorded. I don't think even Buddy could have figured out the lyrics. Why would you drive your Chevy to the levee? Why was the levee dry? Me, oh my! But don't think for a moment that the three men I admire most caught the last train for the coast!

My favorite male singer, however, was Roy Orbison from Wink, Texas. I still get chills down my spine when I hear that unique voice on songs like "Crying," "In Dreams," "Running Scared," "Blue Bayou," and "Only the Lonely." He was the first rock and roll singer to be backed up by orchestral strings and it was a stroke of genius. (Did you know he was a member of the Church of Christ? How ironic!) Don Gibson was a close second. Nobody does better than Gibson on "Sea of

★　　★　　★　　★　　★　　★　　★

Heartbreak, " "Lonesome Number One," "A Legend in My Time," and "Too Soon to Know." Other recording artists and/or songs I liked during this time frame included Sam Cooke ("Wonderful World"), Don Rondo ("White Silver Sands"), Larry Finnegan ("Dear One"), Lloyd Price ("Stagger Lee"), Johnny Horton ("North to Alaska"), Del Shannon ("Runaway"), and Bob Luman ("Let's Think about Living").

Connie Francis was my number one favorite female singer. She is the all-time most recorded singer in the world and can sing in an amazing number of languages. Her voice moves me to this day on songs like "Everybody's Somebody's Fool," "My Heart Has a Mind of It's Own," "Breakin' in a Brand New Broken Heart," and "Whose Heart are You Breaking Tonight?" I felt so bad for her the day I heard the news that she had been brutally raped by a stranger. I also liked Skeeter Davis ("Silver Threads and Golden Needles"), Gogi Grant ("The Wayward Wind"), Barbara George ("I Know"), Ketty Lester ("Love Letters"), and Brenda Lee ("I'm Sorry").

Instrumentalists that I enjoyed were The Ventures ("Walk, Don't Run"), Floyd Cramer ("Last Date"), Billy Vaughan ("Sail On Silvery Moon"), Dave "Baby" Cortez ("The Happy Organ"), Bert Kaempfert ("Wonderland by Night"), Kenny Ball and His Jazzmen ("Midnight in Moscow"), and B. Bumble and The Stingers ("Bumblebee Boogie"). The swaggering theme song from Peter Gunn was also one of my favorites. Groups that I liked included The Browns ("The Three Bells"), The McGuire Sisters ("Sugartime"), The Jarmels ("A Little Bit of Soap"), "The Platters" ("Twilight Time"), The Kingston Trio ("The Man Who Never Returned"), The Crystals ("He's a Rebel"), and The Tokens ("The Lion Sleeps Tonight").

Lest you be left with the impression that rock and roll music

★   ★   ★   ★   ★   ★   ★

was all I liked; I also developed an appreciation for some of dad's music! To this day I cherish an album of The Robert Shaw Chorale and songs I learned to like: "Aura Lee," "When You and I Were Young, Maggie," "Grandfather's Clock," "Bonnie Eloise," and "Seeing Nellie Home."

TV AND HISTORY

We still didn't have a TV in our home (in fact, we never did), but I still managed to see my favorite shows when I went to one of my friends' homes. Westerns that I liked included "Gunsmoke," "The Rifleman," and "Tales of Wells Fargo." Dad had many of the Zane Grey western novels that whetted my appetite for the Old West. Other TV programs that I enjoyed were "Dragnet," "Highway Patrol," "The Twilight Zone," and "Alfred Hitchcock Presents."

I have refrained from writing about each and every historical event that took place between 1957-1962 (the years we lived in Goldfield) because I think sometimes authors do that to make people think they had this great sense of geopolitical awareness, though but a fledgling youth. In reality, they were just drinking cherry Cokes and stuffing their face with French fries like the rest of us. But I do recall the presidential election of 1960 when Nixon and Kennedy were vying for votes. Some Protestants, including Norman Vincent Peale, were worried that JFK would take his orders from the Pope in Rome were he to be elected president. Out in Oregon the legendary Archie Word railed on the perceived Catholic threat to democracy in his paper *The Church Speaks*. I didn't see the famed TV debate between the two candidates. People who listened to the debate on radio thought Nixon won, but those who watched it on TV went for Kennedy. That might

★   ★   ★   ★   ★   ★   ★

say something about "style over substance." We were "rock-ribbed Republicans," so I know my parents voted for Nixon. My mother stayed up all night listening to the election returns on the radio. When I got up the next morning, to the news that Kennedy had eked out a win (by only 113,000 votes out of 68.3 million cast), I found mom asleep, her head on her folded arms, still sitting at the card table. She had kept tabs on a legal pad. I was later highly incensed to learn that the Democrats had stuffed the ballot boxes in Chicago's Cook County, in effect "stealing" the election. I have never liked the Democrats since, and I still admire Nixon for not taking the matter to court as Gore did in 2000. Nixon said that it would have torn apart the country, so he graciously conceded to Kennedy. Gore should have learned from his example. I believe that our country is still divided down the middle because of Gore's unbelievably selfish behavior. But I digress.

I also remember the tension that was caused by Russia shooting down one of our U2 spy planes, one piloted by Francis Gary Powers in 1960, but for some reason I do not recall much about the "Bay of Pigs" fiasco in 1961. Nor do I remember ever having to get down beneath my school desk in one of those simulated air raid warnings. Like a wooden desk is going to protect you from nuclear fallout anyway! But the Berlin Wall caught my attention. To this day one of my favorite novels is John LeCarre's *The Spy Who Came In from the Cold*. Sir Richard Burton starred in the gritty movie version of the international bestseller. (Speaking of movies, I never went to any until the summer of 1964 when I lived with my grandparents in Indiana, but that can wait until later. Going to movies or dances or playing cards were strictly off limits at our house.)

*   *   *   *   *   *   *

"MAZ," MARIS & MINNEAPOLIS

The World Series of 1960 was memorable because the students got to listen to some of the games over the school's public address system. Everyone rooting for the Pittsburgh Pirates sat on one side of the gym and those who were cheering for the New York Yankees joined me and most of my baseball-playing buddies on the other side. You can imagine our shock and dismay when the Bucco's Bill Mazeroski hit a walk-off home run off Ralph Terry to win the World Series. To add insult to injury, a cup of beer tipped over and rained down on the head of the dejected left fielder for the defeated Yankees.

Major league baseball history was made in 1961 when Roger Maris broke Babe Ruth's longstanding home run record with number 61 off Boston's Tracy Stallard on the last day of the season at the hallowed grounds of Yankee Stadium. But earlier in the '61 season Dad and a preacher friend (Ron Carlson), took me to Minneapolis-St. Paul in August where we saw the visiting Bronx Bombers beat the newly transplanted Washington Senators, at that time known as the Minnesota Twins. The day game was played at old Metropolitan Stadium. By this point in the season Maris had more than 50 home runs. It was actually "Roger Maris Day" at the ballpark because Maris was from nearby Fargo, North Dakota. Mom had made us some peanut butter and jelly sandwiches, but I was too excited to eat. I mean, here were my beloved Yankees just a few feet away from me. What a robust roster! "Around the horn" there was Clete Boyer, Tony Kubek, Bobby Richardson and "Moose" Skowron. Patrolling the outfield you had the "M & M" boys, Mantle and Maris, plus Yogi Berra, Bob Cerv and Hector Lopez. Behind the plate you had Elston Howard backed up

★　★　★　★　★　★　★

by John Blanchard. On the mound you had Whitey Ford, "Bullet" Bob Turley and Ralph Terry, with Ryne Duren in the bullpen. My hero Mantle clobbered his 48th of the year off Jack Kralick (he would wind up with 54). Howard and Lopez also went deep that day. And the Twins were not bad shakes either with hurlers like Camilo Pascual, Pedro Ramos and Jim Kaat, and sluggers like Harmon Killebrew, Bob Allison, Jim Lemon, Don Mincher and Elmer Valo. Lemon hit one clear out of the park, a gargantuan clout! Maris went 0 for 5, but I was one happy kid by the end of the game. Fathers, be wise enough to take your children to the Great American game. It will make a memory that will last them a lifetime!

NEW ADVENTURES IN SPORTS

Goldfield was a big basketball town. Everybody turned out to see the Goldfield boys (the Indians) and girls (the Indianettes) play. The high school girl's basketball team won the state championship in 1955. I had never played basketball before, but I tried out for the junior high team and made the squad. I played guard and made a few baskets now and then. What I enjoyed most was anticipating a pass, stealing the ball, and driving down the court for an easy lay-up. On March 17, 1960, I wrote my Grandma Knowles, updating her on my progress. "Our basketball team isn't having a very good season. We have a 1-6 record, and we have one game left. I have a total of 33 points so far. The next highest is 31 points. I play the guard position. The most I have scored in a game is 10 points." (In the same letter I wrote, "Did you know that Stan Musial will get $80,000 dollars this year?") I signed off: "Stan 'The Man' Victor Knowles."

★   ★   ★   ★   ★   ★   ★

When I played high school basketball we had a great coach in Ralph Voith. He really drove us hard, making us do wind sprints and bleacher runs until we thought our lungs would burst. In our warm-ups I got so I could actually jump up and touch the rim. After school was out, we had a spirited scrimmage each afternoon. I made the team and got into more and more games. I played point guard and had the job of bringing the ball up the court. I had to know all the plays and call them as Coach Voith signaled them to me. He wanted me to drive the lane ("bloody-nose lane") to draw a foul. I think the most points I ever scored in one game on the A squad was nine. I probably made more assists than points. One night I sank a shot from just over the half-court line. Swish! Don't think that didn't bring dad up out of his seat! My friend Dave Harvey, a grade or two ahead of me, was the big star on the team. His dad built him a wooden basketball court in his yard and we shot baskets there by the hours. My "finest hour" in basketball was in the Regionals at Belmond. Coach Voith pulled a starter in the decisive fourth quarter and sent me out onto the floor. It happened so fast that I hardly had time to be scared. This was the "big time" for me and I played my best even though we lost the game. At the end of the season Coach Voith took our team to Boy's State Championship at Vet's Auditorium in Des Moines. I bought a crazy bright yellow "scrunch" hat and had a ball.

I saw my first NBA basketball game, an exhibition game, at Ft. Dodge. The Philadelphia Warriors took on the St. Louis Hawks. Wilt "The Stilt" Chamberlain dunked the ball several times. During the warm-ups I yelled at the Warrior's Al Attles, trying to get his attention. He looked at me like I was nuts. Bob Pettit was the big star for the Hawks. He had more hair on his back than I had on my head. Which

★   ★   ★   ★   ★   ★   ★

wouldn't take much since I wore a flat top! Another time dad took us to see the Harlem Globetrotters. 'Meadowlark" Lemon put on quite a show. I almost felt sorry for the "stooge" team, the Washington Generals, who had to take it on the chin for the 'Trotters night after night. On another occasion we saw the bearded House of David team play the Globetrotters.

Another sport that was new to me was track and field. Our track coach was a nice soft-spoken guy named Dean Roosa, who also taught science and biology. He worked with me really hard to develop me as a sprinter. I did much better in track than I did in basketball. I ran the 50-yard dash, the 100-yard dash, and the 220-yard run (my favorite event). I went to State my sophomore year in the 100-yard dash. I had a wind-aided 10.4 in that event at one of our track meets in the North Star Conference. Coach Rosa also used me in the 880-relay and the mile medley. One night I was running the third leg, passed my opponent, handed off to the anchorman, and jumped up and down in delight when we won the race! I have a two-inch scar on my right leg where I once spiked myself when I was trying to shinny out of my warm-ups on a cold, raw day. I ran that leg with blood streaming down my leg, but I was a "gamer" and finished the race. I should mention that I could not afford a pair of track spikes. My friend Gary Smith, whom I somehow tagged with the unusual nickname "Roach Paste Caviar," loaned me his. One day, at the Pocohontas Relays, our miler ate a hot dog before the race and threw up all over the place. I bravely (but foolishly) volunteered to enter the mile run for good old GHS. I did all right the first time around the track, leading the pack. Then I ran out of gas! I was a sprinter, not a distance runner. But I "gutted it out" and hung in there to the bitter end. I was running next to a kid from

★   ★   ★   ★   ★   ★   ★

Rockwell-Swaledale. We got to know each other pretty well in that short time. He had a stitch in his left side. I told him I had one in my right side. The entire GHS track team ran up to the sidelines as we entered the last turn, side-by-side, to cheer me on. I think some of them were laughing! I said to my traveling companion, "I don't know about you buddy, but I'm sure not going to finish last in this race!" I put on a mighty kick and left him in the dust. That was my first (and last) time that I ran the mile run!

BASEBALL, THE THREE-SEASON SPORT

But it was baseball – always baseball – that drew me like a moth to the flame. Since Goldfield did not field a football team, we played baseball three seasons out of four: spring, summer, and fall. I believe I played one game at second base before I moved over to the hot corner. Once in awhile I was put in the outfield with my buddy Scott Whyte. One windy day, playing at Kanawa, we about wore ourselves out chasing wind-aided fly balls. I normally batted leadoff, and once I got on I did my best to steal second, and sometimes third. I managed to steal home in a game against Bancroft, who had a really good team. I can still see the catcher's look of surprise as I slid across the plate. Denis Menke had played for Bancroft. He made it to the major leagues where he played 13 years for the Braves, Astros, and Reds, getting into the 1972 World Series. I was a pull hitter and managed to hit several home runs. Our best pitcher was Al Rodriquez. Polio had left him with a thin left arm but there was nothing wrong with his right arm. Dave Harvey was the star of the team at shortstop. He gave me his old Rawlings glove and I wore it for several years. We had a big freshman kid, Steve "Rhino" Whyte, Scott's cousin, who batted left handed and

★   ★   ★   ★   ★   ★   ★

could hit the ball clear into the cornfield out in right field. One day we hosted Ft. Dodge, a big city school. They came to Goldfield in an air-conditioned diesel bus. They thought they were pretty hot stuff. Their pitcher was working on a no-hitter until I ruined it for him with a base hit to left field in the 7th inning. I may have even thumbed my nose at him from my perch on first base. My worst game was at Corwith-Wesley where I struck out several times, made an error at third, and got picked off first. I was feeling quite low and then a thought came to me out of the blue: "Heaven will be better." Even during a baseball game the Lord was working on me! My freshman year we were still wearing old, gray, baggy, wool uniforms but my sophomore year we got brand-new, fitted, white uniforms with blue piping. I was given number 1, the same number worn by Bobby Richardson of the Yankees. We had a new superintendent by this time, Mr. Huisman, and he had a son who wanted to play baseball in the worst way. Bill would constantly bug us to let him play with us, but he was too young at the time. Would you believe that Bill Huisman eventually was signed by the Chicago Cubs and played in the Texas League for many years? It was his misfortune to be playing second base when the Cubs had Glenn Beckert holding down that position, so he never got called up to the big time.

THE HOUSE THAT DAVE BUILT

In the summer our coach was Vince "Vinny" Saccento. He put me on the mound and tried to show me how to throw a curve ball. But I never could get the hang of it, so I didn't throw too many of them in a game. Summer also meant playing wiffle ball in Dave Harvey's fabulous wiffle ball stadium. For a time we played cork ball in Dave's

★   ★   ★   ★   ★   ★   ★

backyard. We would take a cork ball, about the size of a silver dollar, and wrap it in black friction tape. A ball hit against the garage in left was a single, on the roof a double, off the ridge of the roof a triple, and over it, of course, was a home run. But Dave felt the "stadium" was too constrained in size, so he built this awesome stadium at his grandpa's place on the far end of town. The Yankees had "The House That Ruth Built." We had "The House That Dave Built!" From the left field line to center field and to right center he constructed a fence made of chicken wire. An old chicken coop in right field completed the outfield fence. The foul lines were laid out with old clotheslines, straight as a string. Dave even mowed the infield grass short and laid out a nice pitching mound. An old oak tree served as the backstop. Since it was Dave's stadium, he was in charge of the show. And what a show it was! He took on Scott Whyte and me all by himself. He was always the New York Yankees and insisted that we be the Detroit Tigers. In 1961 the real Tigers won 101 games but finished in second place, eight games behind the real Yankees! We had to bat left-handed if the real Tiger we were representing like Norm Cash or Bill Bruton, batted lefty. Mercifully, we did not have to pitch lefty if our guy, like Hank Aguirre, was a southpaw. Pitching or batting, Dave was also the Voice of the Yankees, Mel Allen, calling the game even as we played it! He would ad lib as he "announced" the game. Just before he threw a pitch to the plate, he would say something so funny that we would laugh so hard we could hardly swing. No wonder the Tigers never beat the Yankees! The two of us could never top Dave.

Every summer I would spend at least a week or two at my Grandma's house in Hubbard. Even there I created a wiffle ball stadium. Home plate was in front of a lilac bush, and left field was the invit-

★   ★   ★   ★   ★   ★   ★

ing target of the fire department where the fire trucks were kept parked. If you hit one past the row of Grandma's peony bushes bordering the alley, you had a single. A double was off the wall of the firehouse, a triple off the roof, and a home run over the roof. Lonnie Lura, who lived a few blocks away, became my best friend in Hubbard. We would play ball by the hours or listen to a Cubs game on WGN before going out in the yard to play catch.

A SUMMER ON THE FARM

The summer of 1960, when I was 14 going on 15, I worked for a month or more on a farm near Indianola. While I really missed playing baseball, I did enjoy making a little bit of spending money. According to a post card I sent Grandma Knowles on August 10, I was making $20 a week "driving a tractor and picking up hay." I stayed with Jim and Phyllis Minnis. Jim worked for Evergreen Farms. Phyllis was the daughter of Henry and Beulah Shaw, whom I had stayed with for a little while when my mother was sick in Nebraska. She made really great sour milk cookies and I ate a ton of them. Most of my summer was spent putting up hay. Jim had a nifty little blue and gray Ford tractor that I got to drive. Sometimes I drove the tractor while Jim and a hired hand threw the bales on the wagon I was pulling. One day he told me to "cut up" the hill. I stood up on the tractor and starting "cutting up." Jim laughed so hard he could hardly throw a bale after that. He asked me one night how many bales I had thrown that summer. I said, "About 60 million, I guess." I began to see them in my sleep. Sometimes Jim sent me up in the haymow to catch the bales and stack them as they came off the conveyor belt. It was hot, scratchy work. Once in awhile you had to dodge some angry hornets. I also fed the chickens for Phyllis. Once I accidentally dropped a heavy jar of feed and it crushed

★   ★   ★   ★   ★   ★   ★

a little chick. I was sick at my stomach for causing the chick's death.

At night I would listen to the games of the Des Moines Demons over KRNT on my transistor radio. The Demons were an affiliate of the Philadelphia Phillies and played in the Class B Three-I League (teams from Iowa, Illinois, and Indiana). My little radio was shaped like a rocket ship and I pulled in the stations as I twisted the dial at the base of the red "rocket." I kept up on my batting skills after supper by going out to the pine grove and hitting small pinecones with an old broom handle. They would really "sing" when I zinged them just right. Of course I had to "call" the game, a la Harry Caray, as I played it out.

On Sundays, after church, I would go home with A. K. and Annabelle Miller for a nice Sunday dinner. I once asked A. K. what his name was. He told me it was Amos Kellogg. I replied, "No wonder they call you A. K." He thought that was pretty funny. A. K. always bought a *Des Moines Sunday Register*, and he loved to quiz me on the current standings and batting statistics of different teams and players. "Victor, who's in first place this week? How many home runs does Mickey Mantle have? What is Stan Musial's batting average this week?" He would check out my answers with the listings in "The Big Peach" sports section. He would get such a bang out of this game when my answers were nearly always right with what was printed in "The Big Peach." I will never forget what he once said to me. "Victor, I hope someday you will know the Word of God as well as you know all these baseball statistics." Folks like A. K. and Annabelle, Jim and Phyllis, and George and Melva Conz were such good influences on me that summer, and I shall always be grateful to them for taking an interest in such an immature teen-age boy as I was then.

★   ★   ★   ★   ★   ★   ★

BACK TO SCHOOL

I closed out Junior High by managing to run the scale from A to D on my report card: final grades of an A in Spelling, B's in Reading, Social Studies, and Health, C's in Science and Music, and D's in English and my old nemesis, Arithmetic. Now I was somewhat ready for the "Major Leagues," High School. I am so appreciative of the good teachers I had at Goldfield High School. My favorite was Barbara Sunner, my journalism teacher. She encouraged me to write for our school paper, *The War Whoop*, published weekly in *The Goldfield Chronicle*, a section of the *Eagle Grove Eagle*. Modesty prevented me from using my byline in sports stories that involved me, so I sometimes wrote with no byline or used a pseudonym. I was awarded a nice journalism pin for my work. Mrs. Sunner wanted me to pursue a career in journalism at Iowa State University, but providence took me elsewhere. Still, I owe her a big debt of gratitude for her patient work with me in developing some writing skills. Another teacher who was good for me was Callie Mandsager, our English teacher. I do regret that I, along with some other boys, sometimes made up "book reports" that we had to give orally. It isn't that I wasn't a reader; I was a voracious reader. My favorite book was a tossup between *Southpaw Flyhawk* by Addison Rand or *The Year the Yankees Lost the Pennant* by Douglas Wallop. I read both book so many times I could have quoted some sections verbatim. I can't remember if we got caught for making those "book reports" and disciplined or not. We should have been.

My sisters and I were the envy of the school the day "Putt" Mossman came to town and put on an amazing demonstration of his talent at a special outdoor assembly. He had been raised in Hubbard with

★   ★   ★   ★   ★   ★   ★

Dad and often stopped by to see us in Goldfield. Each time he did, he gave each of us a silver dollar. "Uncle Putt," as we affectionately called him, was a world-champion horseshoe pitcher and a world-famous motorcycle driver and Hollywood stuntman. He could throw "ringers" blindfolded. He could do outrageous things on his trusty motorcycle. I told everyone we knew him, but Ole Carlson doubted my word. I told Ole, "Ask him." Ole did and "Uncle Putt" said, "Of course I know Victor!" Don't think I didn't swell up at that confirmation. Sometimes it's not what you know, but *whom* you know! I had an extra swagger in my step that day. "Putt" Mossman eventually was enshrined in the Horseshoe Pitching Hall of Fame and the Motorcycle Hall of Fame (he went in the same year Steve McQueen was admitted).

One day Scott, Bernie, and I found ourselves in Superintendent E. J. Blumeyer's office, but not for anything bad we had done. We were commissioned by our class to go to him to ask permission to have a special class party. I don't remember which one of us did it, but right in the middle of our appeal one of us accidentally broke wind. It was really loud. We got to laughing so hard that we could not quit. Every time we thought we had gotten the situation under control one of us caught the other's tear-filled eye and we went into gales of laughter again. Mr. Blumeyer was not amused in the least. He stared at us like we were lunatics who had just escaped from an asylum. I actually had to lean against the wall lest I fall over. Finally Mr. Blumyer had had enough. He ordered us out of his office, and we sheepishly returned to our homeroom, "mission not accomplished." I'm not sure we told them why we had failed in our mission, but we were not very popular with our classmates for the next few days.

As sophomores we had to serve at the junior-senior banquet. The

★   ★   ★   ★   ★   ★   ★

theme had something to do with Rome, so we put on a skit we had made up especially for their entertainment. I was Julius Caesar and Bernie played the part of Brutus, who was supposed to "assassinate" me with a wooden dagger. However, all was not what it appeared to be. I yelled, "*Et tu, Brute?*" just like old Will Shakespeare wrote it, but then we changed the score. I ripped open my toga revealing the big red "S" of a Superman shirt I was wearing underneath. I was invincible to the thrusts of Bernie's dagger. My royal bodyguards then whipped out plastic machine guns (squirt guns) from beneath their togas and "mowed down" poor Brutus and his assassination squad like it was the St. Valentine's Day Massacre. We thought it was fitting since it was a banquet. I'm not sure our class sponsor agreed.

MY BRIEF MUSICAL CAREER

On Fridays we sometimes had talent shows in the music room. Scott and I did so well at "lip synching" some of the songs of The Kingston Trio that we were asked to perform "The Man Who Never Returned" for the ladies of the PTA one night. One day we were assigned to do takeoffs on popular TV commercials. Terry Trotter and I chose to act out a commercial for Colgate dental cream. Terry played the evil villain, "Mr. Tooth Decay," and I was "Happy Tooth," a shining example that comes only from brushing your teeth regularly with Colgate dental cream ("It cleans your breath, while it cleans your teeth!"). Mr. Tooth Decay foully leaped upon me from the top of the piano, but as I fell backwards, my knee caught Terry right in his crotch. He curled up in a fetal position, forgot his lines, and cried, "Oh, Vic! You got me where it really hurts!" The music room exploded in laughter. Poor Terry. I really did not mean to get him where it really hurts. Would

★   ★   ★   ★   ★   ★   ★

you believe that 50 years later I still use Colgate? I bet Terry doesn't!

I sang in Glee Club in Mr. Bailey's music class. I started out as a tenor. In college I wound up singing bass. One of the more nonsensical songs we sang included these lyrics: *"Zingy-wing, and Zangy-wang, and Zungy-wung and Zoom. Husky young mosquitoes, 'neath summer moon."* Why I can remember those zany lines after all these years is beyond me. One of my favorites was the Hanover Winter Song.

O, here by the fire we defy frost and storm
Aha! We are warm and we have our heart's desire
For here were good fellows, and the beechwood and the bellows,
And the cup is at the lip in the pledge of fellowship,
Of fellowship!

My sisters Becky (trombone) and Muriel (French horn) both played in band, and Mr. Opheim wanted me to play too. But I would rather play ball, so I declined the opportunity after a few music lessons on the tuba. Besides, I couldn't read music, and that was kind of important! I do regret not learning to play the piano when Becky offered to teach me at home. Again, the lure of a game of work-up after supper won out. These days I would love to be able to sit down at the piano and play something. I haven't played any organized ball since I hung up my spikes at 45 (church league softball).

My problems with math continued at GHS. Loretta Robinson was my algebra teacher, but despite her help, I got a big red F in algebra one semester. The next semester she took mercy on me and gave me a D minus-minus (you read it right) for effort, perhaps the lowest "passing grade" in the history of Algebra. John R. Jones helped me earn a respectable C in General Math by having me stay after school and work-

★   ★   ★   ★   ★   ★   ★

ing with me. I earned pretty fair grades in science and biology and probably got my best grades with anything that had to do with history, social studies, or writing. I also learned to drive by taking driver's education. I finally got my driver's permit and was looking forward to getting my driver's license so I wouldn't always have to double date.

ROBUST ROMANCE!

My first real "romance" happened at Pine Lake Bible Camp when I was about 15. Her name was Jeanie Kline, and I thought she was mighty fine, even divine. She was from the church in Waterloo, Iowa. I sat next to her one day in Russell Boatman's class on "The Church," and we passed a few introductory and inquisitive notes to each other. Just like the old song, I dreamed of Jeanie with the light brown hair! We sat together, a little closer now, in chapel and for the evening services. When I was playing softball or volleyball in the afternoon, I was always looking to she if she was looking at me. When we walked down to the lake in the moonlight for baptisms, we held hands. I thought I had died and was about to go to heaven. When the week of camp was over, we exchanged addresses. The letters flew back and forth for a year or so. One evening, her folks drove her from Waterloo to Goldfield just so we could see each other again. Eventually the letters slowed down and trickled to a stop. It wasn't because of the cost of postage stamps. They only cost 3 cents. I guess the flame of adolescent puppy love just flickered and died. I have no idea whatever happened to "Jeanine with the light brown hair."

Two girls had a "crush" on me, or so I was told by my "sources" (boys can gossip too). Kathy Hebner, a very nice girl from the Park Church liked me. The Hebners lived in the country and the kids actually attended another school, Goldfield's "arch enemy," the

★   ★   ★   ★   ★   ★   ★

dreaded Boone Valley Bobcats. I often went home with Kathy's brother, Larry, on Sundays, but for some reason I never responded to her shy glances. Kathy also went to Bible college, married, and suffered a tragedy on the mission field in Brazil when her husband was killed in an automobile accident. She returned to the U.S. and eventually married another minister. Nancy Jewell, another very nice girl, one of my classmates, also liked me. I think I may have hurt her a little by sitting with Peggy Schonfield, a girl from Woolstock, at a softball game one night. The girls in our class were a close-knit group and probably did not appreciate it when a boy in their own class turned his affections to a non-Goldfield girl.

My last summer in Goldfield I had a couple of dates with Doris Miller. Doris was one of the seven Miller girls from Des Moines. In fact, her oldest sister, Ruth, was married to Paul Siemens, who managed our church softball team. Doris came to stay with the Siemens for a few weeks and we hit it off. One night we were standing under the grape arbor, about to kiss, when Paul stuck his head out the upstairs bedroom window and yelled down at me: "Hey, Vic! It's getting kind of late. Don't you think maybe you'd better go on home?" Maybe we were "saved by the yell." Anyhow, Larry Hebner, who I was double dating with that night, took me home and I got in just before the midnight deadline.

"HOPE DEFERRED"

The Bible says, "Hope deferred maketh the heart sick: but when the desire cometh, it is a tree of life" (Proverbs 13:12). I soon found that to be true. My hopes were dashed and my heart was sick over the whole affair. Dad's friend Remi Duhon, whom he had held a meeting for in Louisiana, had moved to Mulberry Grove, Illinois, and was ready to move on. He recommended Dad to the Illinois congregation. They invited Dad to conduct a meeting. After the meeting they asked

★   ★   ★   ★   ★   ★   ★

him to move to Mulberry Grove. It was the first time in my life I really resented moving. I was 16 years old and really looking forward to my junior year in high school. I believed I would have been a starter on the basketball team. I loved my school. I had plenty of friends at both school and church. Life in Goldfield had been good, and I believed it would only get better. But it was not to be. My class had a nice going-away party for me, but I was beyond consolation. I am proud to say that even though I didn't get to graduate with them, they have always considered me a part of the Class of '64 and I am always invited to attend the class reunion.

In July 2005 something nice happened. The city of Goldfield celebrated its sesquicentennial. They pulled out the stops with a Civil War reenactment at Riverside Park, the unveiling of a statue honoring the town's founder (Major Brassfield), an Abraham Lincoln impersonator, a big parade on Saturday, and much more. I was invited to come as one of the "Authors of Goldfield." There I was right next to Mr. Roosa, my old science teacher who had written several books on ecology. About 10 of us autographed books at City Hall. I got to see Mrs. Sunner and a number of my old classmates. On Sunday all the churches dismissed services to meet in an outdoor service at City Park. I was asked to speak on the theme "One Lord, One Faith, One Baptism." I preached from a stage set up in the middle of the street, and several hundred folks brought lawn chairs or sat on the grass to listen. I shared several of my experiences preaching this same theme, and seeing its wonderful results, in different places around the world. The men of the Park Church of Christ were in charge of the Communion service. It was a great day. One of my classmates, Dean Richter, leaned over to Larry Rasmussen, and whispered, "Can you believe that he was one of us?" Thomas Wolfe was wrong. Sometimes you *can* go home again!

★　　★　　★　　★　　★　　★　　★

CHAPTER FOUR

TOWN WITHOUT PITY

Our family pulled into the town called Mulberry Grove in late August 1962. Our new home was a 4-bedroom parsonage right next to the church building. We unpacked our belongings and I fixed up my room with my usual sports paraphernalia and fine-tuned my radio to KMOX, the flagship station for the St. Louis Cardinals. Then I set out to explore the town. I was not too impressed. The main drag had only a few businesses: the Post Office, a feed store, an auto dealership, a car repair shop, a small grocery store, a barbershop, and little more. "Ripperdan's Funeral Parlor" conjured up images of Jack the Ripper preparing his victims for burial. One of the elders of the church, Eldon Sugg, had a corner Sinclair gas station where you could air up the tires on your bike and get a cold bottle of pop. I can't pass a Sinclair station today without thinking of Mr. Sugg, who was very kind to me. Saturdays the town came alive when all the farm folk came to town to do their shopping, buy groceries, or get a haircut. The first time I got a haircut in Mulberry Grove the song that was playing on the barber's radio was "I Can't Stop Loving You" by Ray Charles. I have no idea why I can remember that.

MY NEW SCHOOL

The new school where Muriel, Bonnie and I would attend was a combined junior high-senior high on the west edge of town. David, who was only a third-grader, would go to the elementary school just a

★   ★   ★   ★   ★   ★   ★

few blocks from our house. I checked out the school's baseball diamond, and while it was not as nice as the ones I had played on in Iowa, I deemed it sufficient. The pitching rubber was actually a section of an old tire. I didn't see a football field or a running track, so I figured it was a two-sport school. I was right. Just like that my track career was over and my football career would never start! Sigh. Right across from the school was "The Cowbell," a popular restaurant frequented mainly by high school students. Burgers, French fries, malts and shakes were the specialty of the house. The joint had a jukebox, several pinball machines, a long counter, and several booths. A tired looking but nice woman named "Gert" ran the place. Somebody was always feeding the jukebox a quarter. The songs that were the most popular of the patrons at The Cowbell in 1962 were "Sherry" by The Four Seasons, "Sheila" by Tommy Roe, and "Patches" by Dickie Lee. The latter was one of those sappy "suicide" songs. A girl, Patches, of "Old Shanty Town," had gone and jumped in the river, ending her life, so her boy friend decided he would too. Good grief! Other records that were played often by the jukebox junkies were "Let's Dance" by Dave "Baby" Cortez, "Ahab the Arab" by Ray Stevens, and "Town Without Pity" by Gene Pitney. "Oh, it isn't very pretty what a town without pity can do." As I was soon to find out.

The town's name was fairly obvious. There must have been a grove of mulberry trees somewhere at some time, but I never saw too many, if any. Later I learned that Mulberry Grove had also been called "Bucktown," "Houston," and "Shakerag." This was southern Illinois. I was no longer in northern Iowa. What few Negro families there were in Mulberry Grove lived on the other side of the tracks in Royal Lake, a government development just southwest of town. Most of the fami-

*   *   *   *   *   *   *

lies that lived in Royal Lake were from the East St. Louis area. I was told that sometimes they left town in the middle of the night. Sometimes they didn't want to leave but they did anyway. I did not like the sound of that.

My new school played in the Egyptian-Illini Conference. "Illini" was an abbreviation of the Illinois Indian tribe. All of southern Illinois is called "Little Egypt." In the 1830s a shortage of grain had forced those living in the northern part of the state to go to the southern part to find food for their families and seed for their farms, just like the Israelites had to go down to Egypt for grain in biblical times. Some towns were given Egyptian names like Cairo and Thebes, adding to the Egyptian mystique. The whole Egyptian thing was a mystery to me.

Soon after Labor Day the four of us Knowles kids enrolled in school. Becky had already graduated from high school in Iowa in 1961 and was now in her sophomore year at Midwestern. During the summer of 1962 the Supreme Court had ruled that prayer in public schools was unconstitutional, so this would be our first school to attend where prayer was not a part of the daily regimen. In 1963 the Supreme Court took it upon themselves to ban reading the Lord's Prayer and the Bible itself. This did not sit well with my parents, any of the churches, or the majority of the good citizens in Mulberry Grove who felt that the court had disregarded their rights and had given in to one disgruntled parent, an atheist, the infamous Madalyn Murray O'Hair.

Three weeks after I enrolled as a junior, James Meredith, a Negro student, enrolled at the University of Mississippi, creating a big uproar in that state. President Kennedy had to send in federal troops and U.S. Marshals to restore order. One day a new girl enrolled at MGHS. The teacher seated her next to me. I noticed that she did not

★   ★   ★   ★   ★   ★   ★

have any notebook paper or even a pencil, so I opened up my desk and gave her some paper and a pencil. To this day I remember her words: "Thank you, sir." *"Sir!"* This Negro girl called me "sir." I thought to myself, "Dear God, what is going on that she felt it necessary to call me, a 16-year-old boy, her equal, 'Sir'?" (Incidentally, thus far I am using the term "Negro" because that was the nomenclature of the 50s and early 60s.) The new girl was only with us for a few months, and then she was gone. I can't even remember her name. But I shall always remember her soft voice calling me "Sir."

Everyone was still talking about the mysterious death of Marilyn Monroe, who had apparently died of an overdose of pills in the summer of 1962. I felt sorry for poor old Joe DiMaggio, "The Yankee Clipper," who had been her husband at one time. I saw a picture of him in the newspapers and he looked so sad. I understand that for many years he would have a rose delivered every day at her mausoleum in Los Angeles. The "Boston Strangler" was still at large, and the media had a field day with that case too. He killed 13 women before the police finally caught him; some loser named Albert DeSalvo. The term "serial killer" was coming into vogue. "If it bleeds it leads" was the motto of the media.

"DOE" AND MY NEW FRIENDS

Although the population of Mulberry Grove was about the same as Goldfield (800), my new junior class had 44 members, compared to only 14 at GHS. I must say that my new class members made me feel welcome. Six of them were also members of our church, the Mulberry Grove Church of Christ. But my new best friend in our class was from the Baptist Church in Pleasant Mound, Larry Dothager.

★   ★   ★   ★   ★   ★   ★

Everyone called him "Doe," so I did too. We struck it off immediately. One day "Doe" asked me if I wanted a "sody."

I said, "A what?"

He said, "Do you want a sody?" I had no idea what a "sody" was. He finally explained to me that a "sody" was a soda pop.

"Oh," I said, "You mean a pop!" He looked at me like I was from another planet. But "pop" is what we had always called it in Iowa. Pop was pop as in, "Let's have a bottle of pop." But in southern Illinois it was soda pop, or just "sody."

So I said, "Yeah, I'll have a 'sody' with you."

I have often used "Doe" as an illustration of how to make friends. The Bible says that to have friends one must be friendly. "Doe" was that to me. He took the initiative and we became lifelong friends. Our new friendship gradually eased the sting of losing my old friends in Iowa.

My transcripts from Iowa showed that I had already taken several subjects that the juniors were taking, so I found myself taking several classes with the seniors. There, too, I was made to feel most welcome. Walt Leidner, a star on both the baseball and basketball teams, became my best friend in the senior class. He was a big fan of Elvis Presley and had just about every 45-RPM or LP album Elvis had recorded. Doug Ambuehl, the captain of the basketball team, was also very nice to me. My first date was with Elaine Beckert, a senior, who was also a member of our church. Dave Koertge, whose mom was the secretary of the school, was one funny guy. Naturally, he became my friend too!

Rusty Wilfong, a freshman, and son of one of the church elders, was my new best pal at church. Our church had a huge youth

★   ★   ★   ★   ★   ★   ★

group; I think that more kids went to our church than any other church in town. Rusty was short in stature but spunky as they come. My senior year he became my catcher when I pitched for the Mulberry Grove Aces. His nonstop chatter behind the batters would distract them. He would often signal me to intentionally throw a wild pitch over his head for my last warm-up pitch. When the first batter dug in, Rusty would tell him how I had hit some poor guy with a wild pitch and sent him to the hospital the previous game. Then I would "pull the string" and throw a change-up on the first pitch. Sometimes the batter was actually bailing out of the box when the pitch floated over the plate for a strike. Rusty would laugh his little red head off. His tale behind the plate was partly true. I did drill a batter at Patoka one day, and they had to take him to the hospital for examination.

STAREDOWN

Mrs. Florence Neathammer was one of my favorite teachers at MGHS. In my two years of school I had her for World Geography, American History, World History, Sociology, and U.S. Government. She knew her stuff and made history come alive. Some major events that would become a part of history were happening even as she was teaching and I was sitting in class. Among them were the Cuban Missile Crisis, JFK's *"Ich bin ein Berliner"* speech at the Berlin Wall, Buddhist monks setting themselves on fire in Saigon, MLK's "I Have a Dream" speech in Washington, and the bombing of Ebeneezer Baptist Church in Birmingham, where four little Negro girls were killed. Mrs. Neathammer was both a terrific and terrifying teacher. She did not want anyone distracting anyone else while she was teaching. If she caught you goofing off, she would immediately stop talking and stare

★   ★   ★   ★   ★   ★   ★

a hole through you that you could not fill even with the big green wastebasket that sat beside her desk. Many a student tried to "stare her down." None ever succeeded. I had heard of her famous stare-downs, so I never tried. Not that I did not enjoy it when someone else tried, of course!

Poor Dave Koertge was caught twice. One day he brought an oversized handkerchief to school. He coughed a few times to get our attention. Then he pulled out this big hankie and crisply snapped it open. This was all while Mrs. Neathammer was writing on the chalkboard with her back to us. That hankie looked as big as a parachute! He held it over his face and "honked" louder than a semi-truck passing by on the highway outside the window. Not once, but two or three times. On the third honk he was caught, stared down, and he meekly folded up the ridiculous rag and stuck it back in his pocket. On another occasion, Dave gave us "driver's education" right at his desk. The Cowbell was right across from the school, and often cars would pull out of the parking lot with a spray of gravel, shifting into second, and so on down the highway. Dave put a couple of books on the floor at his feet. One was the "clutch" and the other was the "gas pedal." A wooden ruler in his right hand became the "gear shift." When we saw, out of the corners of our eyes, a patron leave The Cowbell and get into his car, Dave went into action. He made the motion of starting the engine, putting the ruler into reverse, then shifting to low, all the while working the clutch and the gas pedal. His actions became more animated when the driver was someone like Gary Kious, a notorious "peeler." When Gary's car "backed off," far down the road, so would Dave. Alas and alack, he was caught once again. Sheepishly the books and ruler went back into his desk, and we all went back to work on our papers.

★　　★　　★　　★　　★　　★　　★

None of this should deter from what Mrs. Neathammer taught. She was an A-1 teacher even if I did not always get an "A" in one of her classes. Her class in geography opened up a whole new world to me, one that I would someday even travel far from home. Her classes in history, sociology, and government – especially history – would prove valuable to me. I don't know that she ever got to travel to those places she talked about, but I sometimes thought of her when I was in foreign cities like London, Havana, Warsaw, Moscow, Belfast, New Delhi, or Johannesburg. Years later I received a letter from her. She had a question about the Herod dynasty in the New Testament. She was retired from teaching, but still had an interest in history. I was thrilled to do some research and send it to her. One Sunday morning I was teaching the adult class where I was ministering in Oskaloosa, Iowa. The class was just ending when Mrs. Neathammer walked in. Between class and the worship service I visited with her. She told me that she had driven clear over from Illinois just to hear me preach. She said, "I always want to check up on one of my students who has made something good of his life." Think that didn't make me feel good? Before I preached that morning I introduced her to the congregation and told them why she was one of my favorite teachers. I had her stand up and take a bow. The church gave her a standing ovation! There were tears in her eyes when she left that day – and tears in mine as well. I am so thankful for her life and teaching and that I learned American history and world history before it suffered at the hands of politically correct revisionists and intellectually dishonest deconstructionists. I think Mrs. Neathammer, were she alive, would be very upset at the compilers of some modern textbooks that give more space to Lady Gaga than to George Washington. One thing I know: they would wither and die under her famous stare-down!

★   ★   ★   ★   ★   ★   ★

TEACHER'S PET

Another influential and outstanding teacher I had at MGHS was Mrs. Frances Fansler, my English instructor. Her first year of teaching high school English was my senior year. I think I became her "pet" student because her husband was also named Vic. ("Vic" is what I went by in high school and college days.) She had a pleasing personality and always seemed to enjoy seeing us blossom under her teaching. I had her for English IV, English Literature, and Vocabulary. I especially liked English Lit and Vocabulary. The works of Shakespeare were a challenge but I managed to do all right. To liven things up a bit, "Doe" and I would sometimes write funny captions under the drawings of some of Shakespeare's characters. I suppose you could call this "creative writing," but it was not. We would crack up at each other's hilarious entries. Whoever got our books the next year probably thought "Doe" and "Vic" were pretty weird guys. Short stories that remain with me are Jack London's chilling "To Build a Fire" and Frank Stockton's curious "The Lady, or the Tiger?"

I probably owe more to Mrs. Fansler than any other teacher I had when it comes to writing. I treasure my 12th year *Vocabulary Workshop* (Jerome Shostak, Oxford Book Co., N.Y.). Each week we would be quizzed on our vocabulary lessons. In 12 units I earned 10 A's. Both of us knew when I had not studied as hard as I should have. I doubt that many of the words I learned are being taught today. I don't know if Vocabulary is even a part of the modern curriculum. Perhaps it was this course that whetted my appetite for the *Reader's Digest* feature "It Pays to Increase Your Word Power." Here follows just a few of the words I was learning in Mrs. Fansler's class my senior year (1963-1964)

★   ★   ★   ★   ★   ★   ★

that I have since used in my writing. Abrogate, affront, bastion, bucolic, cacophonous, circumvent, decimate, dissemble, effrontery, embellish, feckless, germane, histrionic, idiosyncrasy, inexorable, invidious, jocular, laconic, largesse, mendacious, moribund, nadir, nuance, obtuse, pejorative, plenary, promulgate, quintessence, recrimination, sacerdotal, shibboleth, sumptuous, syllogism, tantamount, ubiquitous, untenable, virago, vituperative, wraith, and zephyr. In my writing seminars that I have conducted at several Christian colleges in America, I often quote from Jerome Shostak. "Words are power! They are the keys to a better understanding of ourselves and of the world around us. They are indispensable to vocational and social success."

The day President Kennedy was assassinated (a Friday) we were scheduled to have an English test. I was not prepared for the test like I should have been. Mrs. Fansler was afraid that some of us would be too emotionally upset to concentrate on the test so she gave us the option of waiting until Monday to take the test. She went around to each student and when she came to me I said, "No, Mrs. Fansler, I don't think I can take the test today." What I should have said was, "Mrs. Fansler, I did not study for this test. I can't take advantage of your generous offer. I will try to take the test." I am not proud of getting out of that test that day. "Remember not the sins of my youth." Through the years I have exchanged Christmas cards with Mrs. Fansler. She has always been supportive of my work and ministry in both word and deed. In 2008 I was invited to preach at the First Christian Church in Greenville. Mrs. Fansler came to hear me speak and afterwards pronounced my message "word perfect." It was like getting in an A in English all over again!

A third good teacher who invested her life in mine was Mrs.

★   ★   ★   ★   ★   ★   ★

Lorraine Hazlett, a first-year teacher my senior year. I took Advanced Typing and Bookkeeping under Mrs. Hazlett. I imagine that I have typed millions of words in all of the letters, sermons, articles, editorials, and books that I have written. Her typing classes really helped me start down this path that I am still on. She was very patient with me in Bookkeeping. I have always had a hard time with figures but she, like Mr. Jones in Goldfield, worked with me until I got a fairly good grade. Mrs. Hazlett was also an advisor to the *Messenger* staff (the school newspaper that I did some writing for). I have no idea of her whereabouts today. She probably has no idea of how much I appreciate the help she gave to me. I do hope she does not remember the winter day that I slipped off my penny loafers, put gloves on my feet, and walked up to her desk to have her help me with a bookkeeping problem. I thought Frankie Tomkins was going to fall out of his chair laughing!

FAST TIMES AT MULBERRY HIGH

Three of us in the Class of '64 were "PK's" (preacher's kids): Rita Grigg, Gary Royer, and myself. I must confess that they were much better Christian witnesses than was I. Everyone called Gary "Rev," but it was a term of endearment. Gary was voted class president as a junior and senior, so I know he had the respect of the class. Sometimes "Doe" and I would give him a ride home after a basketball game. One night it was raining and "Doe" and I were already in his old Ford pickup truck. We called it "The Black Bomb." Gary came running out of the gym in the rain, hunched under his raincoat, and headed toward us. "Doe" revved up the engine and took off a little. Gary yelled, "Wait, wait!" So we slowed down, only to speed up again when Gary got closer. We kept this up for quite some time. Gary kept yelling,

★　★　★　★　★　★　★

"Wait, wait!" until we finally let him in. He was wet as a fish. "Wait, wait!" became a byword between "Doe" and me from that night forward. "Rev" would even laugh and say, "Oh, you guys!"

On rare occasions I got to drive our car, a 1959 Rambler station wagon. We dubbed it "The Green Tomato Can." "Doe's" dad had a beautiful two-tone (aqua and cream) 1957 Chevy that "Doe" got to drive once in awhile. One Sunday afternoon "Doe" was going a little too fast on a gravel road and we slid right into a bridge abutment and crumpled one of the front fenders. "Doe" knew he was in big trouble. We didn't get to tool around in the '57 Chevy for some time! "Doe" knew every back road in Bond County and then some, but one night we actually got lost. We were double dating and that made it worse. Four sets of parents were quite upset that their children got in late. When we tried to explain that we *really* had gotten lost, no one believed us.

Four of the girls in our class were members of our church and were also cheerleaders for the basketball team: Janie Bea Johnson, Susan Hopkins, Lynda Jackson, and Sandy Siebert. Janie Bea's dad, Oliver "Twist" Johnson, was one of the elders of the church. We'd work on homework together or just go out for a joyride from time to time. We had some pretty deep conversations for teen-agers, and to this day I still rely upon her for advice (she serves on the Advisory Council of my ministry). Sometimes I'd go over to Susan's house to listen to records while her mom fed me milk and cookies. Lynda and Sandy both had steady boyfriends and wound up marrying them after graduation. Our whole youth group was a pretty tight-knit group. That's what made it so rough the next year when the church suffered a split, but I am getting ahead of myself.

★   ★   ★   ★   ★   ★   ★

Janie, Susan, Lynda, Sandy and I were all in the Junior Class Play, "Cupid in Pigtails." The industrial arts teacher doubled as director of the play. I'm sure he was a good industrial arts teacher, but he left something to be desired as a play director. Janie Bea and "Doe" had the lead roles and I played two parts – a lawyer and a killer in disguise, "The Mad Butcher." When playing that part I wore a black fright wig, a black leather jacket, and had a wicked assortment of deadly butcher knives. I promised the cast I was going to do some ad-libbing, and word got around to the rest of the school about my plan. During the matinee presentation I pulled it off, and the house came down. To this day Mulberry Grove is called "Sow-Pig Town" by some of us.

PLAYING FOR THE "ACES"

I made the baseball team easily. The coach was glad to see me come, but my days of playing third base were over. Another kid held down that position even though he wasn't much good (in my opinion). The same was true at shortstop, where I had also played before. A boy from our church, Tom Jackson, was the catcher. Walt Leidner handled the pitching chores and Doug Ambhuel played first base. Coach put me in the outfield, which I didn't mind. I did miss the "infield chatter" though. I asked for and got number 6, the number of my hero Stan Musial who was playing in his last year for the Cardinals. I had a beauty of a bat, a 32-ounce "Duke" Snider Louisville Slugger so "Doe" dubbed me "Duke." The 1963 *Mulberry Leaves* said, "Vic Knowles displayed base running ability which was as good as any to be found in the area; he also distinguished himself as a defensive outfielder." In one game I stole several bases and was itching to steal home, which I knew I could do, but the coach wouldn't let me try. I usually played centerfield, but

★　　★　　★　　★　　★　　★　　★

if a pull hitter came up, I would be switched over to either left or right to track down drives hit in that direction.

We beat Okawville 9-8 in the season opener, but then went on a four-game losing streak before besting Okawville 7-6 again, this time on their diamond. I pitched that game and got the win. D. O. Banks, a senior, was playing left field that day. A batter really tagged one of my fast balls and sent a long fly out to deep left. The outfield ended where a cornfield began. Banks, running at full speed, disappeared into the cornfield yelling, "I got it! I got it!" The batter circled the bases while D. O. was thrashing around, looking for the ball. Finally he emerged, grinning from ear to ear, dry cornhusks stuck under his hat, but ball in hand. "I got it!" he yelled one more time but the umpire was not to be fooled. "Home run!" he bellowed.

One afternoon we were traveling on the school bus to a game and D. O. had a box of raisins with him. Sitting up front, he stuffed his cheeks full of raisins and stuck the rest on his face. He turned around and looked at us. He looked like a chipmunk with smallpox. We all cracked up. On another bus trip D. O. entertained us by taking off one of his baseball stockings and pulling it over his head like a nightcap. The breeze blowing through the open bus window made it stand out almost straight. Coach was not amused. We had lost another game. But we thought it was funny as all get out. We ended the season at 3-7. I wasn't used to being on a losing team. I ended the year batting .292, scoring 7 runs, driving in 7 runs, stealing 7 bases, and tying for the lead in doubles (3). I actually wound up pitching more innings than Walt, going 1 and 3 and leading the pitching staff in strikeouts (14).

In spite of our lousy record, the Aces got to go to St. Louis to see the Cardinals play the San Francisco Giants. The Cardinals were still

★   ★   ★   ★   ★   ★   ★

playing in Sportsman's Park and it was one grand sight. Someone once called baseball stadiums "Green Cathedrals," and I don't think he was too far from the mark. For the first time I got to see Stan "The Man" Musial "live and in person." The Redbirds finished second to the Dodgers that year, racking up a nice 93-69 record. My man Musial, Curt Flood, and George Altman patrolled the outfield. Third to first it was Ken Boyer, Dick Groat, Julian Javier, and Bill White. Tim McCarver and Carl "Swats" Sawatski (from Shickshinny, Penn.) shared the catching duties. The pitching rotation packed a great one-two punch: two righties, Bob Gibson and Ernie Broglio, and two lefties, Ray Sadecki and Curt Simmons. I took my scorecard down to field level after batting practice and got an autograph, but it wasn't Musial's. You probably never heard of Harry "The Flame Thrower" Fanok. He was a rookie that year and had a 2-1 record striking out 25 batters in the 25 innings he pitched. But he walked almost as many. The next year Fanok pitched in only four games and that was the end of his major league career. I suppose "The Flame Thrower" went back to his hometown of Whippany, New Jersey. The Giants, we joked, gave you the Willies – Willie Mays and Willie McCovey! One of the guys bought some Philly Panatelas and passed them out when the coach wasn't looking. I thought they smelled pretty good but didn't care much for the taste.

I listened to a lot of the Cardinals' games on KMOX all summer long, sometimes keeping score in a blue-backed official Rawlings "Simplex Baseball Score Book No. 4" that I still have. One day Sawatski, a plodding catcher who had never stolen a base in his 11-year career, suddenly took off and stole second. I thought Harry Caray, the Cardinal's colorful play-by-play announcer, was going to fall out of the press box laughing. And before you knew it, the lumbering lummox

* * * * * * *

stole a second base! At the end of the year Sawatski retired and probably went back to Shickshinny. The next time I am in Pennslvania I will
have to pay a visit to Shickshinny. And Donora, birthplace of Stan
Musial.

HOOPS AND SMALL-TOWN POLITICS

Basketball season rolled around, I made the squad with no
trouble but quickly learned a hard lesson in small town politics. The
coach (the same one who coached baseball and whose name I have
arbitrarily decided not to mention) welcomed me to the team and
promptly sat me down on the bench. I knew I was a better player than
the senior who was playing guard. "Doe" (who "rode the pines" with
me and was a better player too) knew it, Walt and Doug knew it, and
most of the town knew it if they paid any attention at all to the games.
I believe the coach even knew it. But the senior's dad was on the school
board. I led the B team in scoring, usually scoring in double figures.
(Unlike GHS, MGHS had no girl's team, so the B squad would play
before the A game.) When the coach would finally put us in the A
game, "Doe" and I would sometimes rack up more points in one quarter than two of the seniors had scored the entire game. Nels Elam, a
grade school kid who idolized "Doe" and me, would plunk himself
down on the bleachers a few rows behind the coach. The little kid had
an unbelievably deep voice that echoed all over the gym. "C'mon
coach, put 'Doe' in! Put Vic in the game!" He was relentless. Sometimes
I think we got into the game only because the coach was tired of being
hounded by a grade school kid who sounded like John Wayne. The
Aces went 0-5 before we caught fire and finished a respectable 14-9. I was
delighted when Doug Ambuehl, the team captain, was named MVP. I earned

★   ★   ★   ★   ★   ★   ★

letters in both baseball and basketball my junior year, but the one I had mom affix to my letter jacket was the baseball letter.

After our basketball season was over, I got to see my first NBA basketball game. One of the teachers, Miss Kaye Boldt, who taught Home Economics and Family Living, invited "Doe" and me to join her and some of her girl students to accompany them to St. Louis. Why she asked us to go with them I don't know. Maybe they wanted some "body guards" because Keil Auditorium was a pretty rowdy place. In any event, we got to see the St. Louis Hawks host the Los Angeles Lakers. The Hawks had some pretty good players, guys like Bob Pettit, Cliff Hagan, and Richie Guerin. Clyde ("Boom-Boom") Lovellette had gone over to the rival ABA and was no longer with the Hawks. The Lakers had some really great players: Jerry West, Elgin Baylor, Frank Selvy, Leroy Ellis, Rudy La Russo, Don Nelson (a former Iowa Hawkeye), and Dick ("Fall Back, Baby!") Barnett. The latter got off some fantastic left-handed "fall back" jump shots from way out. It seemed like Baylor could almost suspend the law of gravity when he went up for a shot. As I recall, the Lakers won the game.

Some evenings, when I probably should have been working on my homework, I would listen to Buddy Blattner broadcast the Hawks games over KMOX. When someone made a good shot, he would yell, "Bingo! It's good!" In our basement at the parsonage I created a really neat miniature basketball court and would entertain myself by playing NBA games of my own, calling the game as I pitted one team against another. There weren't near as many teams then as there are today. You had the Hawks, Lakers, Boston Celtics, Detroit Pistons, New York Knickerbockers, Cincinnati Royals, Philadelphia Warriors, and Syracuse Nationals. The Warriors' Wilt Chamberlain scored 100 points

★　★　★　★　★　★　★

one night against the Knicks. That was in a *real* NBA game, not one of my wild shootouts in the parsonage basement!

HEARTBREAK

Another radio station in St. Louis, KXOK, played the latest hit songs. The wave of "surf songs" began in 1963 with the Beach Boy's "Surfin' USA" and Jan and Dean's "Surf City." I also liked "Donna, the Prima Donna" by Dion and The Belmonts, "Heat Wave" by Martha and the Vandellas, "He's So Fine" by The Chiffons, and "The End of the World" by Skeeter Davis. Some new groups were now hitting the charts, groups like Peter, Paul and Mary ("Blowin' in the Wind") and The Rooftop Singers ("Walk Right In"). Instrumental groups that I thought were cool were The Safaris ("Wipe Out") and the Chantays ("Pipeline"). At night you could also pick up KAAY ("The Mighty Ten-Ninety") in Little Rock, and once in a while you could pull in KOMA ("In Oklahoma!") way out in Oklahoma City.

I had noticed a very nice, quiet pretty girl in the sophomore class, Linda Roberts. We went out a time or two, and I really liked her. But Linda was a Catholic and her parents did not approve of her dating a Protestant. Of course, my folks felt the same about me dating a Catholic. A lot of the Catholic-Protestant tension went back to the Kennedy campaign. (When I got to Bible College, I learned it went back a lot farther than that!) Funny thing was, Linda had the highest set of moral standards of any girl I dated in high school. I believe it was Linda who called things off. For the first time in my young life it was my heart that was broken. But being young, it did not take long to heal.

★   ★   ★   ★   ★   ★   ★

"MURMUR" IN THE FIRST DEGREE

Not only was there schism between Catholics and Protestants, there was a division brewing in our own church. Dad had been assured that things were fine at Mulberry Grove and that the church had great potential. They did – as far as the young people were concerned – but with some of the "adults," well, that was another matter. Unbeknownst to dad the cauldron was about to boil over when he arrived on the scene. He soon sensed some of the problems and tried his best to address the situation in a Christian manner. In one sermon he nearly broke down when he urged the congregation to love one another as Christ loved them. He also warned them about the seriousness of the sin of division in the church. The faction that was stirring the pot, "The Loyal Sisters," would have none of it. They had "called the shots" for years and were not about to give up power. Some of the "elders" were that in name only, having been voted in without much thought being given to their biblical qualifications. My mother began to show signs of great stress and anxiety because of the situation in the church. "The Loyal Sisters" (some of whom were not even immersed or officially members of the church) had resorted to underhanded methods, like sending out a supposed "secret ballot" to every voting member of the church. But under each postage stamp on the return envelope that had been provided with the letter, they had written a number corresponding with the recipient's name. When the "secret" ballot was returned, they simply steamed off the stamp to see how each member had voted! They held secret meetings, apart from the male leadership of the church. Families were pitted against each other.

Things like this (and worse) took its toll on my mother's health.

★   ★   ★   ★   ★   ★   ★

One day, while Becky was home for college, my poor mother collapsed and was transported to the hospital in Alton. My mother spent 65 days in a mental institution (January 7 – March 13) where she was treated (as barbaric as it sounds today) with electric shock treatment. I believe all this was due in large part to the uncharitable, unchristian and downright ungodly behavior of "adult" church members like "The Loyal Sisters." No wonder, as I would later learn in Bible College, that Thomas Campbell called division "a horrid evil, fraught with many evils." For the first time I saw its bitter fruit in a town called Mulberry – a "town without pity" if there ever was one.

During all this time of turmoil and trouble Dad made 40 trips to Alton to be with mom. One day he took me with him. I took one look at her and another look around at all the other people there and thought to myself, "What in the world is my dear mother doing in this place with all these crazy people?!" Mom was so sweet and so concerned about how the other children and I were doing. Once again we had been "farmed out" for awhile. I stayed with Tom Jackson's parents, Roscoe and Imogene. They were very kind to me, and Tom and I had fun shooting baskets in his back yard and watching ball games on TV especially the exciting new American Football League (AFL). But life just wasn't the same without mom in the house. We all missed her, even Lady our dog! We were all happy when she came home from the hospital. And how did the faction in the church respond? They committed "murmur in the first degree." One week after she came home the murmurers called for a vote and split the church right down the middle. Some celebration! I am sure the angels rejoiced. (If you understand that there are evil angels too, well, "let the reader understand.") My classmate Janie Bea said my dad looked stooped with sorrow when the

★   ★   ★   ★   ★   ★   ★

division took place, and he left the church that dreadful night. About 100 souls left, but dad was not asked to be their preacher right away. We had to immediately vacate the parsonage and find another place to live. Dad found an old ramshackle farmhouse out in the country that became our new home. He and mom literally wore a path down in the yard where they would walk around the house praying, meditating, and talking. On top of everything else, our canary, "Dickie Bird," died. Dad wrote a story about him that became one of his best essays ever, "Sing When Your Trials Are Greatest." He sent a resume to several churches with no results. One church told him that at 48 he was too old for them. Eventually the new group, known as the New Testament Church of Christ, asked dad to preach for them. They bought some land and built a finished basement, hoping to build on to the new church later, which they eventually did, but not while we were there. So now we were an "underground church" so to speak.

OUR YOUTH GROUP

George and Sharon Carmen started working with our youth group. Some of our friends, perhaps because of parental pressure, remained with the factious group. I don't think we let it destroy or disturb our friendships, and we continued to get along at school and play. Everywhere but church. Somehow that doesn't sound right, does it?

In July Dad and Mr. Carmen took several of our youth group to a Christian service camp in Indiana. McCormick's Creek State Park, the oldest State Park in Indiana, was located near Bloomington. The faculty included some of Dad's preaching pals: Ed McSpadden, Gerald Stoltz, Ron Prilliman, Rex James, and others. Big Bob Doyle was the camp manager. These men all loved God and wanted us to do the

★   ★   ★   ★   ★   ★   ★

same. It wasn't Pike Lake but it was still a pretty good camp. Rusty and I enjoyed our time there, especially the student-faculty softball game. Rusty's cousin Ruth, who lived in St. Louis, came to Mulberry for a visit, and we started a long-distance romance, via letters. Stamps were now 5 cents and you had to use a zip code. Each letter smelled of perfume and each envelope that Ruth sent me had SWAK written on the seal of the envelope. I would almost go into orbit at the scent of this woman. Until I met Susan at college, Ruth was the best kisser I ever kissed!

Each month we received the attractive youth magazine *Anchor*, co-edited by Ron Carlson and Lafe Culver. A monthly feature, "We Asked YOUth," was probably my favorite. I got to know young people from around the country by seeing their pictures and reading their answers to the question of the month. Another feature I liked was "My Question Is . . ." where teens sent in questions they had to Donald G. Hunt who would then give his advice.

For several years our family had attended a preaching rally held in southern Iowa, the Centerville Rally. This year was no exception. The rally was held in the auditorium of the local high school. Donald G. Hunt was the main coordinator of the annual event. He would bring in "big name" preachers from the West Coast, men like Marion McKee, Archie Word, Don Jessup, and Warren Bell. Hunt and Burton W. Barber, co-founders and teachers at Midwestern School of Evangelism would join them. The rally was an opportunity for me to be reacquainted with some of my Iowa pals: Gary Bryant, Gary Cradic, and Terry Crist. I met Mike "Hoot" Gibson, a freshman at Midwestern, who would become a close friend in college. We were sitting towards the back of the sloping auditorium, and I passed the collection plate to

★   ★   ★   ★   ★   ★   ★

him. I let go too soon and the offering, most of it in coins, rolled down to the front. During the lunch hour we would all walk down to a local ice cream store where we would order burgers and malts. Sometimes we would go to the town square and eat at the Bluebird Café. I was fascinated by the big literature display of the *Voice of Evangelism* – rows and rows of books, booklets, charts, and tracts. I wondered, "How can they write all that stuff?" The college usually had a male quartet sing before each sermon. The Werner brothers, Gary and Eddie, made a lasting impression on me. They projected devotion and full dedication to God. After the evening service my friends and I would hang around and talk to some of the girls. Eileen Cox almost made me "promise" that I would come to Midwestern after graduation. It seemed like our family was always the last one to leave on Thursday night because Dad enjoyed visiting with others so much. We never left without being given several boxes of comb honey from Don Barber, a minister and bee farmer. Paul Gilliland always found our family a place to stay, usually with other Christians who lived in the city.

Leroy Waddelow was our high school Sunday School teacher at church. He had such a heart for us, and sometimes it seemed like he was on the verge of tears when he encouraged us to be good Christian young people. He was strong on our memorizing Scripture. This was because the man had memorized nearly the whole New Testament! His five children were required to memorize three verses a day. If they couldn't quote them to him before supper, there was no supper for them until they could do so. I don't remember much of what he taught us, only that he cared for us. He exemplified the saying "People don't care how much you know until they know how much you care." Brother Waddelow's oldest son, Harvey, became a missionary and

★   ★   ★   ★   ★   ★   ★

there is no wonder why in my mind. Harvey once told me that his dad had made so many notations in the margins and the spaces between verses that you could hardly even read the verses.

Glen and Pauline Miller had twin teenage daughters who were in our youth group. They lived near the school so sometimes I would go to their house when school was out. Mr. Miller drove a semi truck and asked me if I would like to accompany him on a run to St. Louis one night. I really enjoyed the midnight ride in the comfortable cab of his big rig. We sang as we listened to the radio. It reminded me of the short-lived dream that Bernie Bjorklund and I once had of co-owning a big rig and driving it around the good old U.S.A. I don't think truckers are as kind and courteous today as Mr. Miller was. Not everyone can say they went "on the road" and sang with "Glen Miller," but I can!

Rusty would absolutely crack me up at church. Sometimes when we were singing a hymn, Rusty would be whispering the words in an overdramatic, stagelike manner. Rusty's dad, Art, one of the elders, was a shoe cobbler by trade. He used a particular phrase in his prayers that perhaps only a fellow cobbler would understand. "Lord, we fasten ourselves over the loving tenterhooks of Thy mercy and grace." For a time I thought he was saying "tender hooks." I thought, "What in the world is a tender hook?" I guess a "tenter" is a sharp "hooked" nail on which one stretches out a piece of leather or cloth. Art and Leola always made me welcome in their home. I remember that he was always studying his Bible in the evenings after supper. Leola spoiled me rotten. We took our shoes to his shoe repair shop in Greenville when they needed to be resoled. The place smelled of leather and shoe polish and it was not unpleasant at all.

★   ★   ★   ★   ★   ★   ★

BOOKS, BEATLES, AND BIG TIME BOXING

We also went to Greenville to get our groceries because it was a bigger town (pop. 7,000), and mom could get better bargains there. While dad took mom shopping, we kids invaded the library and checked out books. I was still reading sports stuff, but I also remember reading *Silent Spring* by Rachel Carson, one of the first environmental books, and *Black Like Me* by John Howard Griffin, a white journalist who described his 6-week travels through the Deep South passing as a black man. The town had a nice town square with a Dairy Queen on one corner. Quite a few of the seniors who graduated from MGHS would go on to attend Greenville College, a 4-year Christian liberal arts college.

The "British invasion" took place early in 1964 when the Beatles came to America and appeared on the Ed Sullivan Show. At one time they held down the top five songs on the charts. The Dave Clark Five followed hard on their heels. I wasn't a big fan of the Liverpool sound because I still liked songs like Terry Stafford's "Suspicion," Dean Martin's "Everybody Loves Somebody Sometime," and the Rivieras' instrumental number "California Sun." One night, while dialing the tuner on my radio in my "new" upstairs bedroom, I "discovered" the Grand Ol' Opry on WSM in Nashville. I found a whole new world of music, singers like Webb Pierce, Ferlin Husky, George Jones, Marty Robbins, Ray Price, Jim Reeves, Faron Young, Leroy Van Dyke, Kitty Wells, Connie Smith, Jean Sheperd, and many others. On February 24 dad and I listened to a radio broadcast of the heavyweight championship fight in Miami Beach between defending champ Sonny Liston and a brash young boxer from Louisville, Kentucky, fast-talking, hard-

★   ★   ★   ★   ★   ★   ★

hitting Cassius Clay. When Liston could not answer the bell for the 7th round, Clay was declared the winner on a TKO. He danced around the ring, yelling, "I am the greatest." The next day Clay changed his name to "Muhammad Ali" and became a member of the Nation of Islam.

GOING STEADY

My senior year I started dating Linda Mayfield and before long we were "going steady." I gave her my junior class ring. We even bought matching shirts to wear on special occasions. Now that we lived in the country, David and the girls would ride the bus home, but I stayed in town after school for baseball practice. After practice I would either go over to Linda's house or Rusty's house until dad came in to get me. The Mayfields were a nice couple and treated me like I was part of the family. We would work on our homework, listen to records, or watch some TV. Mr. Mayfield ran a car dealership and sometimes let me drive one of the cars on the lot. The one I remember the most was a spiffy 1959 aqua and white Ford Galaxy convertible with dual glass packs. We turned a few heads riding around Mulberry Grove in that sweet ride.

At our first basketball practice the coach announced a new rule: no player could date at all during the basketball season. Nearly every senior the year before had dated, and most of them had steady girl friends. Now no one could. The ban included even the cheerleaders. We all vigorously protested the ban, but the coach would not let any of us play unless we promised we would not date. Well, I really liked Linda. I told coach I would not comply. In effect, he said, "Fine, you're off the team." I think he may have been looking for a chance to get rid of me because he didn't want to spend another season hearing Nels

★   ★   ★   ★   ★   ★   ★

Elam, aka John Wayne, bellow, "C'mon on coach! Put Vic in!" I have no doubt I deserved to be a starter. Several of the guys who took the pledge not to date went ahead and dated on the sly. That really didn't set well with me when I was sitting in the stands with my girl because I was honest and they were out there playing under pretense. The team lost their first 10 games in a row. I couldn't take it so I swallowed my pride and went to coach "hat in hand," promising to not date Linda until the season was over. He knew what I could do. As the physical education instructor he had recently seen me score 33 points in an intramural game. He "consulted" with his new assistant coach, a real suck-up, and together they said, "No dice." It was a bitter blow to me, and a stubborn and stupid death wish on their part. The Aces finished a dismal 5-19. Tom Jackson, however, set a scoring record when he rang up 49 points in one game.

Sometimes I was allowed to drive the car into Mulberry for the games. I took Muriel and Bonnie with me. After dropping Linda off at her house we had to pass a cemetery on the way home. One moonlit night I switched off the lights as we zoomed by the cemetery at 70-mph. My sisters' screams of terror and joy delighted me to no end.

Thirty days before my 18th birthday and in keeping with the Selective Service Act I went before the local draft board and registered for the military draft. I was granted a 2-D deferment, because I would be studying at a ministerial college. A 2-S deferment was granted to the male students in my class who planned to go to a secular college. I carried my draft card in my billfold for the next four years. I was never called up to go to Vietnam.

★   ★   ★   ★   ★   ★   ★

JFK

Friday, November 22, 1963. I was leaning against my hall lock-er talking to Linda Mayfield when Frankie Tomkins came running down the hall shouting, "Kennedy's been shot! Kennedy's been shot!" We didn't believe him, thinking this was one of Frankie's jokes. But then we heard the voice of our superintendent, Mr. Stanley Johnson, over the school intercom. "Would all students please go to your home rooms for an important announcement." Once we got there, Mr. Johnson connected his office radio to the intercom. About 1:35 p.m. (Central Standard Time) United Press International announced that the president had been pronounced dead by doctors at Parkland Hospital at approximately noon (CST). The next day, November 23, I turned 18 years of age. It was a somber birthday. In the days that followed we gradually became aware of some of the details of the assassination, including the name of the assassin: Lee Harvey Oswald. Whatever he knew about the dastardly deed he took with him to the grave when he was gunned down, live on national TV, by a seedy strip-club owner named Jack Ruby. We were just getting out of church when Oswald was shot.

On Monday afternoon Kennedy was buried at Arlington National Cemetery. I believe I saw some of the TV coverage of the funeral procession and burial on the evening news at Linda's house. I bought a memorial book, *The Torch Is Passed*, and an LP record, "John Fitzgerald Kennedy: A Memorial Album." I still have both of them. In the years to come I read a good number of books on the Kennedy assassination: *The Death of a President* by William Manchester, *The Day Kennedy Was Shot* by Jim Bishop, *Rush to Judgment* by Mark Lane, *Six*

*   *   *   *   *   *   *

Seconds in Dallas by Josiah Thompson, and of course, the controversial and flawed *Report of the Warren Commission.* The controversy will probably never end, in spite of one of the latest books *Case Closed* by Gerald Posner. I don't think the case will ever be closed in the court of public opinion. The amazing and relentless 16-mm Zapruder film footage of the president's head jerking violently *backward* at the moment of impact will always beg the question. So too the massive exit wound causing a portion of Kennedy's brains to go skittering off the back of the trunk with Jackie scrambling to retrieve the sliding horror. And how all that damage was done to both President Kennedy and Governor Connally's bodies by a single, pristine "magic bullet" is beyond me – and millions of other citizens. I have been to Dealey Plaza several times. It really is like stepping back in time for little has changed with the passing of the years. The motorcade route is still there; as are the Texas School Book Depository (now The Sixth Floor museum), the triple underpass, even the famous "grassy knoll" and picket fence. Only God knows the whole story of what happened there on Friday, November 23, 1963.

An interesting aside: the number one song on the charts that fateful day was "I'm Leaving It All Up to You" by Dale and Grace. Incredibly, the singing duo was in Dallas that day, standing alongside the motorcade route along with Dick Clark of American Bandstand. They waved as the Kennedys went by in the motorcade. Some years ago I started to write a novel, *Final Witness*, about a little boy who saw the second shooter that fateful day and spends his life tracking down the real killer. Like several other novel start-ups, it's still in a drawer of my file cabinet.

★   ★   ★   ★   ★   ★   ★

SAYONARA

The Senior Play found me playing the part of another lawyer in "Mountain Gal." This time I wore just a suit and tie ("The Mad Butcher" outfit having been "retired" in a trunk backstage). I played opposite Susan Hoskins, and the script called for us to kiss at the end of one scene. I didn't mind playing that part at all. In fact, sometimes at play practice, I would smile at Suzie and say, "I think we need to practice that scene again." She would stick her tongue out at me and say, "Oh, Vic! You're hopeless!" I played it close to the vest and did not surprise the play director with any preplanned ad-libs this time. Except for "the kiss" (the students yelling "woo-woo" from the audience) it was a pretty dull play.

Each year the seniors had "Tacky Day" when they could wear whatever they wanted to school. John "Mope" Edwards and Gary "Rev" Royer dressed up like the Beatles, the new singing sensations from England. A couple of guys actually came in "blackface" while several other guys came dressed as women. "Doe" and I played it "California cool" and wore white Levi's, bright colored Hawaiian shirts, tennies, and sunglasses.

I made the Honor Roll my senior year. I must not have had any math classes for me to pull that off. My parents were so proud of me. Mom said, "I always knew you could do it if you just applied yourself." I'm sure some of my teachers thought the same thing. Dad gave me $25 and I bought a new sport coat. We took our SATs and filled out questionnaires about our future plans. We were supposed to list three choices, so I put down Midwestern School of Evangelism (where my sister had gone and I was planning to go), Greenville College (because

★   ★   ★   ★   ★   ★   ★

a lot of my friends were going there), and Duke University (the latter as an inside joke on my seldom-used nickname, "Duke").

I took Linda to the Junior-Senior Banquet in Dad's new 1964 car. It was pretty slick looking for a Rambler – for a station wagon. At least it wasn't the ugly old "Green Tomato Can" and it had that fascinating "new car smell." The theme of the annual banquet was *Sayonara*. That was appropriate since our school days were coming to an end. Bruce Grigg, another preacher's kid, played the part of Confucius and gave "insight" into what the graduating seniors' future held in store. Bruce and I and our dates didn't stay around for the dance but went on a nice slow moonlight ride in the country instead.

THE FINAL SEASON

In the spring, when baseball season came around, "miracle of miracles" and "lo and behold," the dating ban was suddenly rescinded! Had the coach received some divine message? I knew full well that since my buddy Walt Leidner had graduated most of the pitching duties would fall to me during the spring baseball season. What a joke! On days I wasn't pitching, I played first base. I really enjoyed moving around on that side of the infield. I had now played every position on the diamond except catcher. I asked permission to catch at least one inning, but was denied the opportunity. The 1964 *Mulberry Leaves* carried a picture of me doing a follow-through after a delivery. "Vic Knowles provided most of the fire power from the mound for the Aces. Knowles not only was a frequent starter, but provided bullpen help in critical situations." Connie Mansholt, a sports lover, and a member of our senior class, wrote the copy. There was also a picture of Tom Jackson and me "poised to steal." "Tom Jackson and Vic Knowles, the

★   ★   ★   ★   ★   ★   ★

Ace's answer to Maury Wills and Willie Davis, led the teams in runs scored with 10 apiece. In stolen bases, Knowles racked up six, two more than Jackson with four." Another picture showed four of us holding out our bats to form a Y. "The Aces were not without their hitters. Leading the club in averages were Knowles, .379, Widger, .418, Goodman, .416, and Jackson, .376." I remember this picture because Connie wanted to take one of the top three sluggers. I told her that Tom was only three points behind me and that he should be in the picture too. So there we are, frozen in time, the Four Aces!

The '64 Aces were a young team. Tom, "Doe" and I were the only seniors on the squad. But we were "strong up the middle" when I took the mound. I had Rusty or Ron Shipley behind the plate, Tom at shortstop, Loren Widger at second, and "Doe" patrolling center field. "Poogie" Goodman, like Widger, a sophomore, held down my old position at third base and did a fine job. I usually batted third in the lineup. My fast ball was still my "meal ticket," and I had better control now. We didn't have a pitch count in those days, and the coach "used" my arm beyond what would be considered appropriate today, but I didn't mind all that much. Every pitch I threw was for the team, not him. For some reason there are no team records in our senior annual, so I can't even tell you what our final record was. I imagine with such a young team that it was not the best, but I will say that we all gave our best. Shipley certainly gave his best when he went off to Vietnam a few years later. He returned in a casket, just like two other underclassmen: Jim Scroggins and Mike Scott. Sometimes I rode on the bus with Jimmy. For a time it was believed that he was the last man killed in Vietnam. I have an etching of his name taken from the Vietnam Memorial, the "Moving Wall" version. I cried like a baby when I made

★   ★   ★   ★   ★   ★   ★

it. My wife had to help me to my feet. In 2008 I got to see the new memorial to the three fallen heroes that now stands in front of MGHS. Do stop and see it if you ever pass through. The engraving reads: ALL GAVE SOME, SOME GAVE ALL. These casualties of war helped me understand that the game of baseball is just that – only a game.

In spite of all our troubles in Mulberry, I believe my dad made every game, home or away. In his diary he wrote, "On May 1 I saw Victor play his last High School baseball game in which he hit the ball over the left fielder's head for a triple." From that first bases-loaded double in Boise when I played for United Airlines to my last extra-base hit for the Mulberry Grove Aces, Dad was there to see me play. Lots of guys' fathers never came to see even one of their son's games. I took off my number 6 jersey for the last time, hung it in my sports locker, tossed my spikes and glove into a duffel bag, grabbed my bat, took one last look around, and left. And no voice said, "Victor has left the building."

I still had one more bitter pill to swallow. I was planning to go to a major league tryout camp nearby. I would like to think it was the Cardinals but if I remember correctly it was the Pirates. It really didn't matter. I showed up at the appointed departure point bright and early that morning, only to discover that my ride had already left town without me for the tryout. I knew I wasn't late for the appointment. I couldn't believe what had just happened. I now know full well that I wasn't good enough to play big league ball (well, maybe Class D, if I was very lucky!), but I sure would have liked at least a chance to try. I'm sure I "kicked dirt" all the way home through the town without pity.

THE GRADUATE

In May Dad took David and me to St. Louis to meet my sister

★　　★　　★　　★　　★　　★　　★

Becky who was coming home for my graduation. We took in an afternoon baseball game at Sportsman's Park after we picked her up at the
bus depot. Once again the Cardinals were playing the Giants. David,
who by this time was playing Bantam League baseball, brought his
glove in hopes of catching a foul ball. I managed to snag another autograph before the game. We walked into the stadium and there was the
Giant's third baseman Jim Davenport, in full uniform, talking to another gentleman. When he was done visiting, I asked Mr. Davenport if he
would mind giving me his autograph. He said, "Sure, kid." Davenport
was one of those rare birds who played his entire 13-season career with
the same team. Such loyalty is unheard of today.

The '64 Giants had a star-studded team: Willie Mays, Willie
McCovey, Orlando Cepeda, Jim Ray Hart, and two of the three Alou
brothers, Jesus and Mateo. My guy Duke Snider, the Dodger superstar,
was finishing up his long career by pinch-hitting for the hated Giants.
Don Larsen, who had thrown a no-hitter for the Yankees back in 1956,
was now toiling on the mound for the Giants. Their top pitcher was
"The Dominican Dandy," Juan Marichal. The Cardinal's Musial, my
childhood hero who played 22 years for the same team, had retired at
the end of the 1963 season. Lou Brock had come over in a trade and
took the city by storm with his base stealing. That night I saw one of
the greatest catches I have ever seen, but it was not made by Brock or
Mays like you would think. Carl Warwick, a journeyman player, was
playing right field for the Redbirds. Someone hit a sinking liner to right
and Warwick raced in, slid like he was sliding into a base, caught the
ball at hip level, then came up in one fluid motion and threw a perfect
strike to nail the runner deader than a doornail. We also saw McCovey
hit a Ray Sadecki fastball clear onto the pavilion roof in right field, a

★   ★   ★   ★   ★   ★   ★

truly Ruthian blast. Sportsman's Park would be demolished two years later when the Cardinals moved into new quarters, Busch Stadium.

About all that remained was graduation and that day came before you knew it. Baccalaureate services took place on May 24. Muriel and Bonnie played in the band and Muriel accompanied the girl's chorus on the piano. I got quite a few graduation cards, and some of them contained $5 or $10 bills from the relatives or friends of the family who sent them. Graduation day, May 29, came all too fast. All my family sat in a section reserved for families of the graduating seniors. Dad was on stage to offer both the Invocation and Benediction. The Class of '64 marched down the aisle to "Pomp and Circumstance," received our diplomas, turned our tassels, and that was it. I said goodby to my favorite teachers, fellow grads, and underclassmen. Quite a few of my classmates have lived in Mulberry or Greenville ever since our graduation, but I was out of there pretty quick and for good. My plans called for me to spend the summer with my grandparents in Richmond, Indiana. Grandpa Brown had secured a good job for me that would help me pay for college. I did not even stay to go on the Senior Trip. It seems so strange to me now that my classmates rode a bus through the Deep South, all the way to Florida, going right through Mississippi in the middle of "Freedom Summer." The very same month (June) three young civil rights workers (a Negro and two Jews) were kidnapped and murdered by the KKK in Mississippi. The horrible incident was later made into a movie, *Mississippi Burning*.

500 MILES

The hardest part of leaving Mulberry, besides leaving my parents and family, was leaving Linda. She had been crying a lot the last

★   ★   ★   ★   ★   ★   ★

month or so, realizing this could be good-by forever. She still had several years of high school to go, and I was headed for four years of college. Her mother had kindly and wisely tried to prepare her for this
day that we all knew would come. I tell you, life is doubly hard when
you're young and in love. Songs like "I Only Want to Be with You" by
Dusty Springfield, and "500 Miles Away from Home" by Bobby Bare
sure didn't help the situation when we figured out that Richmond was
a 500-mile roundtrip from Mulberry Grove! Shakespeare wrote,
"Parting is such sweet sorrow." Old Will didn't know the half of it.
Rusty assured me he would look out for Linda, and he did, bless his
good heart. Mom packed my suitcase, I threw in my glove and baseball spikes, strapped my Duke Snider bat to the suitcase, and soon
I was heading for Indiana, where I had been born some 18 years
ago. Like that great philosopher Yogi Berra once said, "It's *déjà vu*
all over again."

★   ★   ★   ★   ★   ★   ★

CHAPTER FIVE

THE WHIRLWIND YEAR

Highway 40 runs across Illinois, through Indiana and on into Ohio. It took me right into Richmond, a city of about 40,000, located on the Indiana-Ohio border. Richmond would be my home for the summer of '64. I thought it was one big, beautiful city. Richmond is famous for its variety of roses and is called "The Rose City." It is the home of Earlham College and for many years the renowned Quaker theologian, Dr. Elton Truebood, lectured there. It is also the home of Rich Mullins, the late, great Christian contemporary music artist and humanitarian, who would have been about eight years old the day I rolled into Richmond. Other famous Richmondites include Orville and Wilbur Wright.

THE RICHMOND LIFE

My grandparents, Russell and Lettie Brown, lived at 310 Carol Drive. At one time they had lived at 1017 Peacock Drive. Now they were in their retirement years. Grandpa, who had large "loving cup" ears and a heart as big to match, had worked for the J. I. Case Company. Case made tractors and farm implements. Every Christmas Grandpa gave me a beautiful little orange Case tractor. Grandma was a retired schoolteacher. She loved to entertain in her home, but the summer I came, she was not well and spent most of the time in bed. Every morning and evening I could hear them reading the Bible and praying in their room next to mine.

★　★　★　★　★　★　★

I quickly set up my new room. All my baseball gear went into the closet, as did my hanging clothes. The rest I stuffed in the dresser drawers. I bought a radio, although I really wouldn't have needed to, and put it on my nightstand. Grandpa's house had a connected radio and intercom system that could be heard and used throughout the entire house. Linda sent me a nice studio 8 × 10 picture of herself and I placed it on top of the mahogany dresser. Several books that were in my room I read that summer. One was *The Last Days of Hitler* by Hugh Trevor-Roper. Grandpa had been in World War I. Another book I read that summer was *Man-Eaters of Kumaon* by Jim Corbett, a world-famous big-game hunter. Grandpa had a fantastic sun helmet, just like big-game hunters wore in Africa. He wore it when he was directing parking in the busy IGA store where he had secured me a job for the summer.

I liked my work at Cox's IGA store. Most of the time I sacked groceries but sometimes I stocked shelves. I made friends with some of the other sackers and stock boys. The store was elevated and had a long concrete ramp that you had to carefully negotiate when taking a cart of groceries down to the parking lot. You were in big trouble with the manager if a cart ever got away from you and went on a "ramp"-age! Some of the customers tipped their sackers and that was always appreciated because we were making a grand total of about a dollar an hour. One lady in particular was my favorite. She lived several blocks from the store, and I always tried to time it so I could sack her purchases. She not only gave a very nice tip, but she would offer me some cookies and a cold drink.

Grandpa did most of the cooking that summer. I liked that just fine because he bought lots of Pepsi, Ritz crackers, and Colby cheese.

★   ★   ★   ★   ★   ★   ★

We would sit in the living room together, TV trays in front of us, and watch two of his favorite shows: "Candid Camera" with Allen Funt and "The Red Skelton Show." My favorite that summer was "The Bob Cummings Show." In July we probably watched the evening news and saw LBJ sign into law the Civil Rights Act of 1964. No doubt we also caught some of the Republican National Convention that was televised from San Francisco. The Republican nominee, Barry Goldwater, said, "Extremism in the defense of liberty is no vice, and moderation in the pursuit of justice is no virtue." The media played up the first part of that quote and played down the second. If I got tired of TV, I would listen to the Cincinnati Reds over WCKY on my radio. Waite Hoyt called the play-by-play. He was a former Yankee pitcher, and would later (1969) be voted into the Hall of Fame. Hoyt would broadcast the game in the past tense. "Banks grounded the ball to second. Rose threw him out." I never heard anyone else call a game that way. I especially liked to listen to him when the Reds were in a rain delay. Hoyt would tell one story after another about when he played the grand old game with legends like Babe Ruth and Lou Gehrig. Frisch's Big Boy was one of the advertisers. I still stop at a Frisch's whenever I'm in Indiana for one of those great Big Boy sandwiches.

TWO DREAM STADIUMS

"All work and no play makes Jack a dull boy." I was not about to become a dull boy in spite of the good job I had. The boy next door, whose name escapes me, played American Legion baseball and urged me to try out for a city league team. And so that summer I played for the Richmond Lions in the nicest ballpark I ever played in – McBride Municipal Stadium. The stadium had a covered grandstand and seat-

★   ★   ★   ★   ★   ★   ★

ed about 2,500 spectators. It was built into a hillside and, like Crosley Field in Cincinnati, the outfield had a slight incline leading up to the outfield fences. I had never played in such a large park. I believe it was at least 400′ down each line, 450 to the power alleys, and 500 to dead center. I was told that Ted Klusewski, a big slugger for the Reds who hit 279 homers during his 15-year career, was the only player to hit a ball over the centerfield fence. So I felt pretty good one Saturday afternoon when I hit one that at least *rolled* all the way to the where the incline began in left-center.

My first game was a nightmare. I was very nervous at the "cat-calls" that came from the opposing dugout. My fastball was working, but I was wild as all get out. I think we were shut out, 9-0. But eventually I got my game together. I couldn't wait for work to end so I could head out to McBride Stadium on the corner of Peacock and NW 13th. I grew to love that grand old ballpark. Playing at McBride was as close to professional baseball as I would ever get. The Richmond Roses, a minor league club, had played at McBride. I think they were an affiliate with the New York Yankees. For many years I carried a newspaper clipping from the Richmond *Palladium-Item* in my wallet. It was a write-up of the last game I played for the Richmond Lions club. The clipping said I pitched a three-hitter, fanned 12 batters, and went 4-for-5 at the plate, rapping out a double and driving in five runs. I guess if you've got to go, that was the way to go!

Each Sunday I went to church with my grandpa at the Northside Church of Christ where grandpa served as an elder. I met a boy at church who was about my age, Gail Brown (no relation to my grandparents). We became good friends and he gave me rides on his motorcycle all over town and across the state line into Ohio. The min-

★   ★   ★   ★   ★   ★   ★

ister of the church, Hervey Sewell, was also very kind to me. One day he took me to Cincinnati to see the Reds play the Chicago Cubs. Before the game we went into a restaurant near Crosley Field to get a bite to eat. We were the only white people in the place. The overhead fans whispered softly in the air as we ate our BLTs and drank our pop. Most of the Negroes were talking quietly and drinking Schoenling beer from long-necked brown bottles. I don't remember who won the game but I was excited to see the great Ernie Banks, Ron Santo, and Billy Williams of Whistler, Alabama, playing for the Cubbies. Between the three of them they whacked 86 home runs that year. The Reds still had Frank Robinson and Vada Pinson, whom I had seen in 1958, but now they also had "Charlie Hustle" – Pete Rose. This would be my last visit to Crosley Field. It was torn down in 1966 so that "The Big Red Machine" could play in a sterile concrete bowl called Riverfront Stadium.

THE MOVIES OF MY LIFE

I had never gone to a movie in my life up to the time I moved to Richmond. The neighbor boy invited me to go with him to the movies. We saw *The Carpetbaggers* starring George Peppard and Carroll Baker. Everything was larger than life on the big screen.

A "parenthetical insertion" is due here. Through the years I have "caught up" on some movies I missed out on in my youth by seeing them on TV or DVD. Allow me to mention them here. Movies that were made before I was born that I eventually got to see and came to like would include *Good-by, Mr. Chips*, *The Shop around the Corner*, *Pride of the Yankees*, *The Ox-Bow Incident*, and *Double Indemnity*. Movies that would have been showing in my grade school years that I have come to like include *It's a Wonderful Life*, *Miracle on 34th Street*, *Quo Vadis*,

★   ★   ★   ★   ★   ★   ★

High Noon, and *Shane*. Movies I missed seeing in junior high include *Witness for the Prosecution*, *12 Angry Men*, *The Bridge on the River Kwai*, *Vertigo*, *The Big Country*, *The Inn of the Sixth Happiness*, *North by Northwest*, *The Diary of Anne Frank*, and the big screen epic *Ben Hur*. Twelve films that I never saw in high school but are among my favorites now are *Spartacus*, *Elmer Gantry*, *The Guns of Navarone*, *Judgment at Nuremburg*, *Bird Man of Alcatraz*, *Lawrence of Arabia*, *The Manchurian Candidate*, *The Longest Day*, *The Man Who Shot Liberty Valance*, *Seven Days in May*, *The Great Escape*, and *The Train*. Movie buffs will quickly recognize that my favorite actor was Burt Lancaster, who starred in five of my favorite films of the early 60s. Finishing out the 60s would have to include *The Spy Who Came in from the Cold*, *A Big Hand for the Little Lady*, *Where Eagles Dare* and my all-time favorite Western, *True Grit*. The only musicals that made my list are *Scrooge* and *Fiddler on the Roof*. Other movies from the 70s that I like are *Duel*, *The Odessa File*, *Papillon*, *QB VII*, *The Hiding Place*, *A Bridge Too Far*, *The Shootist*, and *Being There*. Films of the 80s and 90s are fewer because I think fewer good movies were being made. However, I still liked the following: *Somewhere in Time*, *Gandhi*, *Firefox*, *Shoah* [a 9 ½ hour holocaust documentary], *Hoosiers*, *Driving Miss Daisy*, *Awakenings*, *Avalon*, *The Remains of the Day*, *The Edge*, and *The Apostle*. The best actors I ever saw, besides Lancaster, were Jimmy Stewart, Gary Cooper, Henry Fonda, Charles Laughton, Alec Guinness, Gregory Peck, Cary Grant, Charlton Heston, Kirk Douglas, Maximilian Schell, John Wayne, Steve McQueen, Richard Burton, Albert Finney, Sir Anthony Hopkins, Sir Lawrence Olivier, Morgan Freeman, and Robert Duval. I have a shorter list for best actresses but they would include Greer Garson, Donna Reed, Maureen O'Sullivan, Kim Novak, Jean Simmons, Marlene

★   ★   ★   ★   ★   ★   ★

Dietrich, Ingrid Bergman, Jessica Lange, and Kim Darby – who should have won at least an Oscar nomination for *True Grit*. End of parenthetical insertion.

ONE SWEET RIDE

Back to life, real life in real time, in Richmond. Earning a weekly paycheck for the first time in my life gave me the opportunity to buy my own clothes. I bought some nice shirts, slacks, and a nifty windbreaker. I also purchased some LP record albums: The Ray Coniff Singers, The New Christy Minstrels, and one by Skeeter Davis, "The End of the Word." Uldene Cristenberry, our next-door neighbor, was also a member of the Northside church. She gave me a key to her house so I could listen to my records any time I wanted to on her stereo. Grandpa also let me drive his 1958 Chevy Impala as long as I put in the gas and kept it up. No worries there! I must have washed it in his driveway every other day! It was a very nice looking two-door, two-tone sedan (pink and white) with air vents on each of the front side panels. At last, no more wretched Rambler station wagons! I bought a furry white cover to dress up the rear-view mirror from which I hung my blue and gold graduation tassel. With the windows down, ensconced in luxuriant leather seats, and a V-8 engine purring under the hood, it was one sweet ride. I thought it would be cool to drive down the road smoking a cigarette so one day I bought a pack of (what else?) Kools. I choked on them and tossed them out the window after a few disastrous efforts at inhaling. I decided I could be just as cool without my Kools.

Having a car meant I could date. But what about Linda back in Mulberry Grove? I am truly embarrassed to say that I was not true to

★   ★   ★   ★   ★   ★   ★

her. Her letters kept coming to 310 Carol Drive but very few of mine went back in return. One day I received a small package in the mail. It was my junior class ring that I had given her to wear. I felt about two inches tall. She deserved better than me. Feeling quite guilty, I slipped the ring back on my finger and mailed her picture back to Mulberry Grove. My grandparents introduced me to a nice girl from the church. I think her name was Garnet Coffey. We went to her house after going out for supper one night and I met her parents. I dated another girl from the church whose name I cannot even remember. One night I took a checker from the IGA store, a little older than myself, to a movie. I think it was *Honeymoon Hotel* with Robert Goulet and Nancy Kwan.

My uncle, Bob Wickersham, lived in Centerville, a straight shot of about five miles from Richmond on Highway 40. Sometimes I would drive over to his house and visit with Bob and his wife Lucille. My "kissin' cousin," Judy and I would drive around town. One night we went to a drive-in movie. Uncle Bob was a car salesman and I enjoyed looking at all the cars on his car lot. Some Sundays I went with them to the Christian Church in Centerville.

THE SEYMOUR CONNECTION

That summer I also attended camp at Mahoning Valley Christian Service Camp near Rushville. I believe I went with Gail Brown on his motorcycle. I met another kid named Dave Weber and we became good friends too. The daily schedule of MVCSC was pretty much like other Bible camps I had gone to. Devotions, breakfast, classes, and chapel in the morning; lunch and sports activities in the afternoon; clean up, supper, and vespers in the evening. The students were divided up into teams and the team I was on put together a Bible

★   ★   ★   ★   ★   ★   ★

pantomime one morning. It was the story of David and Bathsheba but we toned it down. Some. I played the part of King David. I "arose from my bed" (a cot on the stage) and "from the roof saw a woman bathing." Actually there was no woman. Outside the open window a girl sprayed water in the air and "sang in the shower" to create the illusion of a pretty noisy bath. I looked down on nothing but a garden hose but stroked my non-existent kingly beard, arched my eyebrows, and inquired of my servant who this lovely woman was. Well, you know the rest of the story. I sent a kid who played the part of Uriah off to war to be killed so I could have Bathsheba for my own. Another kid played the part of Nathan the Prophet who came on stage in his bathrobe and read me the riot act for my selfish sin. The baby Bathsheba and I had (a child's doll bundled up in a blanket) died, and I fasted and repented of my sin. Some of the judges (the faculty) thought it quite creative and others thought we were pushing the envelope.

I met Ann Seymour at Mahoning Valley. She was from the Grand Avenue Church of Christ in Connersville and was there that week with her twin sister Jan. I gave Jan a ride on Gail's motorcycle one afternoon, but it was really Ann who I had my eye on. I mustered up enough courage to ask her to sit next to me at vespers and she accepted the invitation. The rest of the week we spent a lot of time walking around the campground or sitting on a picnic table and just talking. At the end of the week I got her address, and from then on just about all my spare time was devoted to driving about 20 miles from Richmond to Connersville to see Ann.

Jan and Ann had a sister named Zoe. None of them had a middle name. I thought that was really odd. I thought that maybe "fate" had brought Ann and me together since I was born in Seymour and her

★　★　★　★　★　★　★

last name was the same. We dated the rest of the summer. Sometimes Gail and I would go to Connersville on his motorcycle and other times I would drive Grandpa's '58 Chevy. One night at the county fair I proceeded to win a good number of stuffed animals for Ann by shooting lopsided basketballs through a tilted rim or knocking over weighted milk bottles with an equally lopsided softball. When we returned the next night, the vendors would not accept my money. The kids we were with thought that was most unfair so they rigged up a disguise for me to wear. But I was so nervous that I would be "found out" by the vendors that I couldn't manage to win a single prize. So I ditched the disguise, and we went on the Ferris Wheel for a ride.

CINCINNATI BIBLE SEMINARY

Some of the kids I had met at church camp were planning to attend Cincinnati Bible Seminary in the fall or were already students there. They encouraged me to visit the campus, so one day I accompanied some of them to CBS. My father had graduated from the seminary in 1940, and I was shown a picture of his graduating class on a wall. Someone talked to me about playing for the Golden Eagles. CBS had both men's baseball and basketball. That sure appealed to me! I was taken to the men's dorm, and I went so far as to pick out a room that I thought would do for me. I indicated that I would like to enroll but that I would have to talk to my parents first. Years later I was told that a professor of the college once said that I was "the one that got away." I was just a small fish in a big pond, but it made me feel pretty good to hear that. I wrote dad and told him I wanted to attend CBS. I was somewhat surprised when he said no. So I called him on the phone. Again he said no. I was terribly disappointed. I did not get to attend Cincinnati Bible Seminary,

★   ★   ★   ★   ★   ★   ★

but I would have been proud to. It was my dad's alma mater, they had a great faculty, and I think I would have fit in just fine had I gone to CBS. I have since returned to the seminary on several occasions: speaking at a Restoration Forum, conducting a Christian Writer's Seminar, and most recently, preaching at their fall 2009 Bible conference "Impact!"

The summer wound down, and it was getting time to leave Richmond. My grandmother had the whole church over to her home one night for a party. I helped her serve all of the guests and did some sketch art of some of them. One afternoon I brought Ann to meet my grandparents. I was proud of her and I was proud of them, and I wanted them to meet each other. On occasions like this my grandmother would get out of bed, dress up in her "Sunday best," and entertain visitors like she had done so often in the past when she was well. I think it did her good. Ann skipped her junior class trip just to be with me on our last date. She stood under a shade tree in their front yard and waved good-by to me as I drove away, and I have never seen her since. For a few months we exchanged letters, and then the summer romance was over. However, we have remained good friends through the years, and every year her Christmas card is the first that we receive.

So, why did I return to Illinois and from there go on to Iowa where I eventually enrolled at Midwestern when in my heart of hearts I wanted to go to Cincinnati? For one thing, dad's situation at Mulberry Grove was still tenuous. Mom's hospital bills were high, and he just didn't have much money to help me go to Cincinnati where the tuition was considerably higher. He did concede that if I would go to Midwestern for one year, I could transfer to CBS the second year. Another factor was an unexpected visit one afternoon from some newlyweds who were attending Midwestern, Ken and Deana Mickey. Ken

★   ★   ★   ★   ★   ★   ★

was to be a senior and Deana a sophomore. They were in the area, heard that I was in Richmond, and stopped by to see me. Ken spoke glowingly of his three years at MSE and encouraged me to come to Midwestern. It finally came down to a biblical maxim I had learned long ago: "Honor your father and your mother, that your days may be long upon the land . . ." (The Fifth Commandment, Exodus 20:12). My parents thought it best that I go to Midwestern, so off to Midwestern I went.

THE WHIRLWIND BEGINS

Each school year at Midwestern School of Evangelism was kicked off by a big preaching rally in nearby Centerville, Iowa. As we had done in the past, our family attended the event August 25-27. In 1964, however, the rally had moved from the high school auditorium in Centerville to a brand new 700-seat wooden tabernacle that had been erected on the grounds of Sharon Bluff Bible Camp just outside Centerville. It was named Sharon Bluff because it bordered Sharon Bluff State Park. It was the 20th anniversary year of the rally and folks came, literally, "from coast to coast and border to border." I was reacquainted with Mike "Hoot" Gibson, a returning sophomore, whom I had met at the rally the previous year, and also met some incoming freshmen. They included Eileen Cox from Iowa, Sam Brown from Kansas, Sharon Agenter from Arizona, Kerry Conaway and Lois Williamson from Nebraska, Jenifer Bradley from Oklahoma, Roger Deys and Rich Geringswald from Florida, Heriberta Olmo from New York City, and my future brother-in-law Gary McGlumphry from the Iowa City area. Our freshman class (39) made up more than half of the entire student body that year (75).

The keynote speakers that year were Donald G. Hunt, Archie

★   ★   ★   ★   ★   ★   ★

Word, and Don Jessup. I had heard Hunt and Word speak many times before, but this was my first time to hear Jessup, minister of the Workman Street Church of Christ in Los Angeles, Calif. I was enamored by his use of the English language, especially his wordplay. He would say things like, "The apostle Paul had a thorn in the flesh but he did not go around tooting his own thorn." Sometimes he would have a student come up on the platform and have him write a word on a big blackboard to help him illustrate a point. I was glad he did not call on me. Sometimes his face would get beet red when he was making a point. He had a great smile that would just disarm you. He had two college-age sons, Graydon and Wesley, who were superb athletes and were as tall and handsome as their illustrious father. Jessup, who had been converted to Christ by Archie Word, was a great athlete himself, turning down an athletic scholarship to play football at Southern Cal and going to San Jose Bible College instead. I went away thinking, "This guy is all right." I was honored beyond words some years later when the great Don Jessup invited me to come and hold a revival for him.

When the rally was over, my folks drove me to Ottumwa, home of Midwestern, to get moved into the men's dormitory; a big three-story white house located at 319 West 5th Street. My room was a large one on the second floor, which I would share with Darrell Bridgewater, a senior, and two other freshmen: Leon Hansen and Bob Goetz. Darrell was a returning senior from Indiana. As such, he was in charge of leading the morning devotions. Leon was from Council Bluffs and Bob was from Pittsburgh, Pennsylvania. The poor fellow had suffered shell shock in the military and acted a bit strange at times, but he had a good heart.

Once I was settled in, dad and mom drove me to the beautiful

★　　★　　★　　★　　★　　★　　★

old mansion at 908 North Court Street that had served as the school's administration building since 1952. When you walked in the doors, it was really something. Everything was done in walnut trim, including the staircase railing that led up to the second floor. Every classroom had a marble fireplace. The chapel had theater seats arranged in a semi-circle. The library was on the second floor. So were the production offices of the *Voice of Evangelism* as well as the faculty's offices. After getting the grand tour, it was time for my family to leave. I walked them out to the car but declined a ride back to the dorm. Mom cried as she hugged me, and I found myself fighting back tears. They drove away and I went back into the chapel to collect myself. Now I was really "on my own." Up to this point in time I had always lived with my parents or grandparents. Now those ties were severed forever.

OFF TO A BAD START

Orientation Week was August 31-September 4 with classes getting underway September 8. However, I missed part of Registration Day because I was at City Hall paying a fine for careless driving. Leon had loaned me his car to drive to the A & W to get a sack of burgers. It was dark, I was not familiar with the city, and I got lost on the way back. I was frustrated and went around a corner with tires squealing. Wouldn't you know it, a policeman spotted me, pulled me over, and wrote me a ticket. So while my classmates were getting registered for classes, I was paying a visit to municipal court – not the best way to start your collegiate career, especially at a Christian college!

Probably sensing that I needed a little extra oversight, Mr. Hunt chose me to be in his 7:30 A.M. prayer group. After a few weeks of calling him "Mr. Hunt" he told me one day, with a smile, "You can call me

★   ★   ★   ★   ★   ★   ★

'Brother Hunt.'" And so I did. Just listening to his prayers was an experience. He was a devout, consecrated Christian man. Of course I had no
idea then that some day I would deliver the eulogy at his funeral and
write a book about his life (or co-author a book about the college itself).

On the second floor were two Prayer Closets with drop-down
shelves. Faculty and students alike were encouraged to use the prayer
closets from time to time. This was based on Matthew 6:6, "When thou
prayest, enter into thy closet, and when thou has shut thy door, pray to
thy Father which is in secret . . ." (I'm using the King James Version
here because that is what everyone used in the 60s at Midwestern.) I probably used the prayer closet more on the day I had a tough test coming
up! Prayer Meeting night was on Thursday at the Pennsylvania
Avenue Church of Christ where most of the students attended. Richard
M. Ellis, one of the faculty members at Midwestern, was the minister
of the congregation.

"THE DUKE OF OTTUMWA"

My freshman class schedule included Bible Geography and Life
of Christ under Ellis, and Old Testament History, Homiletics, and
Essentials of Correct Speaking with Lafe Culver. In the afternoons I had
Voice with Margaret Hunt. The class I remember the most was Life of
Christ. Ellis was a tough teacher but a good one. Our textbook was a
big red 743-page book, *The Life of Christ,* written by Adam Fahling. His
explanation of how God sent Jesus "in the fullness of time" captured
my imagination. I got B's in Homiletics and Speaking and C's in O. T.
History and Life of Christ. However, at the end of the second semester
I received an Incomplete in Life of Christ for failing to write out from
memory the famous yet fearsome "Bird's-eye View of the Life of

★   ★   ★   ★   ★   ★   ★

Christ," an eight-page, single-spaced outline containing 176 events (including 72 geographical locations). Our textbook in Bible Geography was *Baker's Bible Atlas.* I scored in the mid-to-high 90s on my maps in Geography but must have failed to get some final work in because I also received an Incomplete. Rats and double rats! All that work for nothing.

Lafe Culver made the Old Testament come alive with his humor and descriptive stories. One day we were going through a list of the "dukes" in Genesis 36:40ff (KJV), and I happened to whisper to Gary McGlumphry that my nickname when I played baseball at Mulberry Grove was "Duke."

"Really?" Gary whispered back.

"Yes," I replied in a hushed voice.

"Then I pronounce you 'The Duke of Ottumwa,'" Gary said.

My sister Muriel even wrote "The Duke of Ottumwa" on the envelopes when she wrote to me from California!

In Culver's Homiletics class I learned that a sermon is an oral address, based on a biblical text, treated elaborately yet aimed at the average mind, and delivered with a view toward persuasion. We also learned the seven parts of a sermon outline and the difference between a topical, textual, or expository sermon. Dad gave me two books from his library on homiletics: *How to Prepare a Sermon* and *How to Prepare an Expository Sermon* by Harold E. Knott. Of course Culver also stressed the preacher's personal and spiritual life as well. Speech class stressed the importance of enunciation, pronunciation, and the like. I learned that I should always speak so that the person at the back of the auditorium or sanctuary could hear me and never, but never, drop my voice so low that people had to strain to hear what I was saying. I was told

★   ★   ★   ★   ★   ★   ★

that I had a natural "radio voice" and, indeed, in years to come, my voice would go out over the radio airwaves in many places, including New York City.

"VICTOR SANG BASS"

After a few lessons in Voice, Mrs. Hunt selected me to sing bass in the Freshman Quartet. The other members were Sam Brown, Roger Deys, and a boy from Vermont, Raymond Johnson. When we sang in chapel, we wore black slacks, white shirts, and black neckties. One afternoon I was visiting with David Solliday who sang in the Senior Quartet. David's dad, H. N., and my dad were fast friends, and I had been at the Solliday's house several times. David had quite a collection of LPs featuring men's gospel quartets like The Blackwood Brothers, The Statesmen Quartet and The Oak Ridge Boys. I was fascinated by their unique styles of singing and soon started a record collection of my own. My favorite group was The Blackwood Brothers (James and Cecil Blackwood, Bill Shaw, J.D Sumner, with Wally Varner at the piano). I loved hearing their 5-minute and 53-second rendition of "The Old Country Church." If you had told me then that some day in the future James Blackwood, "the father of gospel music," would sing a special number just before I would preach at a Bible conference in Branson, Missouri, I would not have believed you.

GOING TO CHAPEL

Each day, following Prayer Time, we had Chapel. It was not optional as it was in some Bible colleges. Each student was required to take notes on the sermon. At the end of the semester we turned the notebooks in for credit. I still have many of those spiral notebooks and

★   ★   ★   ★   ★   ★   ★

I am glad we were required to take notes. Wouldn't you know that the first sermon I heard in chapel, after my speeding incident, was Brother Hunt's "To Hurry or Not to Hurry – That Is the Question." I am not kidding. The second, by Culver, was "Why God Wants You to Change." Was God trying to tell me something? The third was "The Damascus Road and You" by Ellis. I was surely on some kind of road! In addition to sermons presented by the faculty and senior ministerial students, we often had guest speakers. My own father had been a frequent guest speaker in the past. Guest speakers I remember hearing during the first semester of my freshman year were Malburt Prater, Ed McSpadden, Lt. Col. (retired) L. H. Tyree, Don Pinon, and William Pile. (One of the men in that list of dukes in Genesis 36 was "Duke Pinon," and I got a big kick out of that.)

MY NEW DICKSON BIBLE

Dad had ordered a new Bible for me to use in Bible College. It arrived from the John A. Dickson Publishing Company in Chicago sometime during the first semester. Dad had ordered it from Gene Lockling, A. K. Miller's son-in-law, who preached in Yale, Iowa, and was a Dickson sales representative. In 15 years of selling Dickson Bibles he sold more than 3,000 of them! *The New Analytical Bible* was thumb-indexed and was bound in "Genuine Morocco." It must have cost dad a pretty penny. It was, of course, the King James Version, but it also featured, within brackets, the more correct renderings of the 1901 American Standard Version. I had never seen a Bible like this. For my analytical mind it was a perfect match. It contained 800 pages of different helps and features including a Harmony of the Gospels and all the teachings of Jesus arranged by topic. On the front page I wrote some

★   ★   ★   ★   ★   ★   ★

words that I had heard somewhere: "This book will keep me from sin, or sin will keep me from this book." In years to come I would add other sayings I had picked up:

• "As you become less spiritual, the Bible will become less interesting."

• "Praying will make one cease from sinning, and sinning will make one cease from praying."

• "The most important time of day is when I read and when I pray" (Donald G. Hunt).

• "He is no fool who gives what he cannot keep to gain what he cannot lose" (Jim Elliott).

• "Unless there is within us that which is above us, we shall soon yield to that which is about us."

• "By not making a decision for Christ you have made a decision."

• "The cross is God's plus sign on the skyline."

• "The philosophy of today's classroom will be the policy of tomorrow's government" (Abraham Lincoln).

• "We do not preach a Christ who was alive and is dead; we preach the Christ who was dead and is alive" (Dyson Hague).

• "No minister of Christ has any right to smooth off the corners of the cross" (Dyson Hague).

I used that Bible to preach from until the early 1980s. It has more underlining, markings, and writings in the margins than any other Bibles I have in my library. To this day I can mentally picture where just about any verse is on the pages of that well-worn Dickson Bible, right down to the color of ink I used to mark it with.

★ ★ ★ ★ ★ ★ ★

LET THE GAMES BEGIN!

One fine fall afternoon we had a big game on a softball field about a block from the campus. The whole student body, including the faculty, turned out for it. This was high-octane fast-pitch softball. Donald Hunt was pitching, I was catching and visiting speaker Don ("Duke") Pinon was playing second base. Someone attempted to steal second, and I fired a rocket down to second. Poor Brother Pinon couldn't get his glove up in time and took the rocket – right in his eye socket! The maimed minister had to wear sunglasses the rest of the week to cover up the terrible black eye I unintentionally gave him. I was just glad he didn't suffer any broken bones or lose his eyesight. Perhaps he should have been the one wearing the catcher's mask that day!

We also played football on that same field. Terry Paul, a senior, had been an All-State quarterback at Orlando, Florida. Michael Harris, another senior, had been an All-City tackle at Madison, Illinois. Other upperclassmen who could really play the game included Mike Gibson, Henry Neff, Ted Stolz and Ken Mickey. Freshmen who joined in, besides myself, were Sam Brown, Kerry Conaway, Roger Deys, Ray Johnson, and others. Harris was playing fullback that day, and he charged through the line, bowling over one player after another. I was playing safety and tried to make an open field tackle on the big bruiser, and the next thing I knew I was "coming to" on the sidelines. The year before I came to school, Paul, Harris, Gibson, Art Deys and others took on the State Champion Ottumwa Bulldogs high school football team and beat them without the benefit of shoulder pads or helmets. Whoever said only "pantywaists" went to Bible College had obviously never been to Midwestern!

★   ★   ★   ★   ★   ★   ★

POLITICIANS AND PREACHERS

That fall we also had a "work week" on campus. Classes were dismissed and we all, students and faculty alike, worked on fixing up the administration building. This kept the buildings and grounds up and our tuition down. There was a great spirit of unity as we worked. Terry Paul and I climbed up on tall aluminum ladders and did some plastering and painting. One day I got the bright idea of going up on top of the three-story building, clear to the top of the cupola, and attaching a Barry Goldwater flag on the spire. Lots of the upperclassmen had Goldwater stickers on their bumpers – AuH_2O in '64. (Au was the chemical symbol for gold and H_2O was the symbol for water.) Even though I was not yet old enough to vote, I thought I would do my part. A few days later someone (probably a closet Democrat!) pointed out the flag to Brother Hunt. With a twinkle in his eye he told me that perhaps it would be best if the flag were removed. So once again I "scaled the utmost heights" and took down the flag, just like Lyndon "Landslide" Johnson took down Goldwater the second Tuesday in November. Later in the year I bought a book that had just been published in 1964, *The Challenges We Face* by Richard M. Nixon, devoured it, reinforcing my staunch admiration of the Quaker politician.

There were lots of extracurricular activities going on at Midwestern. One Saturday a month an area church hosted a Youth Rally. One Sunday afternoon a month another area congregation would host a Singspiration. I went to many of these with my fellow students. The local church, the Pennsylvania Avenue Church of Christ, also had Tuesday night preaching services as well as the regular Sunday and Thursday services. Twice a year, in the spring and fall, they would have a high-powered evangelist like Carol J. Lankford, Marion McKee, or Archie

★   ★   ★   ★   ★   ★   ★

Word come in for a two-week revival meeting. The auditorium would usually be jam-packed. Churches in the area were also having revival meetings, so sometimes it was hard to get your homework done with all these events going on.

THE FAIRER SEX

I liked a girl in our class, Jenifer Bradley, but she didn't think I was spiritual enough to date her (and she was right). Jenifer worked as a receptionist at the school in the afternoons. One day I called from the boy's dorm, posing as a lineman from the Bell Telephone Company. I told her we were cleaning out all the phone lines on North Court Street that day and asked her to place the receiver on her desk and cover it with a handkerchief so the dust wouldn't blow all over the place. Some of us hopped in a car and raced to the administration building. We doubled over with laughter when we walked in and there was Jenifer at her desk, the phone receiver off the hook and covered with her handkerchief. I guess after a stunt like that you could see why she thought I wasn't mature enough to take her out! We did, however, walk around town some evenings with Gary McGlumphry and Susan Wood (who would eventually marry) and had some nice visits.

Once I borrowed Kerry Conaway's bright red convertible, a Ford Falcon, and took Heriberta (pronounced Eddie-Velta) Olmo to a church-sponsored hayride and wienie roast. She was a little Puerto Rican girl from New York City who barely came up to my shoulder. One night we were standing together on a bridge overlooking the duck pond at Memorial Park on the North Side. I noticed two "women" sitting on a park bench not far away. They seemed quite amused by something. Later I discovered that Mike Gibson and Mike Frances had

★   ★   ★   ★   ★   ★   ★

dressed up like bag ladies and were following us around town on our date. Heriberta stomped her foot and told Gibson, "Oh, Michael, you make me so mad!" A married couple, Doug and Sue Gilliland, invited Sharon Agenter and me to their apartment for a supper date one evening. For a while I dated Karen Corder, a sophomore from Moline, Illinois, and even went home with her one weekend to meet her parents and younger brother.

GOING TOO FAST

On October 18 I was going too fast on a gravel road near Abingdon and I flipped Kerry's convertible. I was not wearing a seat belt and was thrown into the back of the car and knocked unconscious. When I came to, I smelled gasoline. The engine was still running. I had enough sense to turn off the ignition. Fortunately, I was able to crawl out through the driver's side window. Providentially, I had left the top up even though it was a beautiful sunny day. A motorist came by and called for an ambulance. I was taken to the Ottumwa Hospital where I was kept for a few days for observation and recovery from bumps and bruises. Mike Gibson worked as an orderly at the hospital and took good care of me. Dad called from Illinois. Many students came to visit, as did Brother Hunt. He walked in my room, took off his hat, and sat down beside my hospital bed. After taking a sympathetic look at me, he said, "I think you have suffered enough. There will be no fine." (I was off campus without permission.) I breathed a sigh of relief. Good old Brother Hunt! (He was all of 42 then, but he seemed "old" to me). Mike found me an old-fashioned, cane-bottomed wheel chair with big wheels. After the nurse saw me popping "wheelies" in the hall, she told the doctor I was ready to be released.

★   ★   ★   ★   ★   ★   ★

"I LIKE MIKE"

Mike and I became fast friends. Perhaps it was because he loved baseball too. He was a great southpaw pitcher who could really bring it. We would play "burnout" on the sidewalk in front of the dorm and he would win every time. Sometimes I went home with him on weekends. He lived on a farm near Bloomfield and it was good to get out of the city and into the country. He took me rabbit hunting one day. Some nights we would go "bushwhacking." That meant borrowing Gary Cradic's car and roaming the countryside in search of parked cars in some secluded "Lover's Lane." Once a car was spotted, we would turn off the headlights and drift up slowly behind the unsuspecting victims. Then we would turn on the headlights and lay on the horn! Usually the startled lovers were too shocked to do anything, but one night a guy threw his car into reverse and chased us all over the countryside before we finally lost him in the dust. One night we ran out of gas going up the incline of Highway 63 past the girls' dorm; Mike put the car in neutral, and we rolled back down the highway at a pretty alarming rate of speed, cars swerving to miss us. Mike was laughing like a madman, and soon I nervously joined in although I was scared out of my skin.

Mike's fiancée, Judy Buzick, had graduated the year before and was serving the Lord in faraway San Juan, Puerto Rico. Mike missed her mightily and maybe that is why he was so restless and in search of something to do. I was only too happy to be his willing accomplice. As Mike and Mike Frances had tailed me on a date, we decided to tail Midwestern students on their dates. Mike would drive and I would put a scarf on and tuck some padding under my shirt in the appropri-

★   ★   ★   ★   ★   ★   ★

ate places to look like I was Mike's "date." Or vice versa. One time we hoofed it, sans the costumes, kind of like plainclothes detectives. Graham's Dairy Freeze was a popular place for everyone in Ottumwa. It was located on West 2nd Street, right across from the Post Office. Bob Goetz and his girl Jean Eakins walked to Graham's one fine Friday night, and we stalked them every step of the way. We climbed up on the roof of Graham's and started tossing pieces of gravel down on Bob's head. He couldn't figure out what was happening. Then he spotted us, although he did not recognize who we were. About that time a police car cruised up to the curb. Maybe the cop wanted an ice cream cone like everyone else. Bob rushed over to the car and yelled, "Officer! Officer! There's two men on the roof throwing rocks at me!"

Mike and I leaped off the roof, crossed the alley with lightning speed, and started running up a heavily wooded hill to get out of there as fast as we could. The policeman was running after us yelling, "Stop, stop!" For the first time in my life, I intentionally disobeyed the law. I kept going and so did Mike. It was pitch dark and all I could hear, besides the pounding of my heart, was Mike fighting his way up the hill like Teddy Roosevelt and his Rough Riders going up San Juan Hill. We finally made it to the top of the hill, spotted an old pickup truck, jumped in the back and laid down to catch our breath. When we felt that the coast was clear, we walked calmly back to the boy's dorm. In the distance we could hear the wail of a police siren, but we kept our cool. We made it back safe and sound, and Bob never suspected a thing when he came in later. We innocently asked him, "Bob, how was your date?" He said, "Fine, but there were these two crazy guys who . . ." We just smiled as he recounted the story we had just lived.

★   ★   ★   ★   ★   ★   ★

READY TO RUMBLE

Mike would always head to my room when he got off work at the hospital at 11 P.M. He would open the door a crack, poke his head in, and whisper, "Vic, are you still awake?" Of course I was always awake and ready to rumble. Compact cars were the rage then, and it seemed like everyone in college drove either a VW Bug or a Corvair. Darrell Bridgewater drove a VW Bug, and one morning he found it on the front porch of the dorm. The look on his face was priceless. Of course for that event Mike and I had to enlist a few helpers. Late one cold winter night we crept into Darrell's room, got four old neckties, and proceeded to carefully tie Darrell's wrists and ankles to the four corners of his top bunk. Then we opened the second floor window, carefully crept out on the icy roof and scooped up a wastebasket full of snow and snapped off several large icicles hanging from the eaves. Darrell's pleasant dreams were suddenly interrupted by two hooded fiends "torturing" him with handfuls of snow and "wanding" him with icicles. "Oh, boys!" he cried, "Have mercy, have mercy!" Of mischief we had plenty; of mercy we had none. But Darrell was a good-natured fellow, and so we were grateful that he did not squeal on us.

My fellow classmate from Florida, Rich Geringswald, also received a visit that same winter. Someone had built a large snowman on the front yard. Mike and I managed to remove its ample mid-section and lug it up to the second floor. All under the cover of darkness. We muscled it into Geringswald's room, lifted it up and carefully placed it at the end of his bed. About one in the morning Mike Harris, sleeping on the bottom bunk beneath the slumbering freshman felt the drip, drip, drip of cold water on his forehead. Frosty the Snowman, at

★ ★ ★ ★ ★ ★ ★

least his midsection, had melted and Rich somehow had not been disturbed by this cold, dismembered, uninvited guest!

Henry Smith, an upperclassman from Sacramento, also fell victim to our seemingly nonstop nocturnal nonsense. Henry was snoring away on his bunk, his mouth wide open. Mike had some baby powder, and we carefully poured a small amount on Henry's tongue. It looked like a little mountain of snow. A feather under Henry's nose did the trick. "Achoo!" A puff of white smoke and the deed was done. All Henry could say, once he was fully awake, was "Oh, you crazy guys!"

TWO GLORIOUS BATTLES

One winter day we had a heavy snowfall. The snow was perfect for packing snowballs. The Great Snowball Fight started after lunch at the girl's dorm when Mike Harris caught me full in the face when I stepped outside, bloodying my nose. The fight was on! It seemed like it was Gibson and me against the whole school. Now why would anyone hold a grudge against us? But they had forgotten that Mike and I had both been pitchers on our high school baseball teams. We fought our way down the hill, across Highway 63, snowballs whizzing left and right. Then we started uphill to the boy's dorm, nailing this one and that one with hard-thrown, well-aimed snowballs. Mike Frances, safe on the second floor (he thought) went to the window and threw up the sash. Pow! A blazing snowball drove him clear back across the room. The air outside was just white with snowballs. It was one grand and glorious day.

In the spring it was The Great Water Gun Fight. This started when Mike brought home from the hospital some large empty lotion bottles that he used when he gave back rubs to patients. When filled

★ ★ ★ ★ ★ ★ ★

with water and squeezed, they delivered a powerful jet stream of water. Other guys armed themselves with pitiful little squirt guns you could buy for a quarter at Woolworth's. They were no match for our weapons of war. Then someone started lobbing water balloons. You never knew at night who was going to open your door and let you have it with a water balloon. But even this was not enough. (Who started all this anyway?) Now it was large wastebaskets filled with water. Poor Henry was the first to get doused when he was taking a nice, warm bath. I got it from Gary McGlumphry in the same manner. Ted Stolz took a dousing on the top of his head from the roof as he was leaving the dorm to go to work. I caught Kerry Conaway coming up the back steps and washed him off his feet back down the back stairs in a truly amazing wave of water thrown from a huge garbage can. One day I was trying to escape someone's impending attack, slipped on the wet linoleum, and put my knee right through a wall. The next morning I got up early and went to "confession," telling Brother Hunt what I had done and that I would fix or pay for the repair of the damage done. Later a stool pigeon knocked on Brother Hunt's office door to rat me out. I loved it when Brother Hunt told him, "Now, Victor has already admitted to what was done and has offered to make things right." That was one case where the early bird truly got the worm! Finally the faculty found it necessary to make a special announcement in chapel: no more water fights. We surrendered our water weapons and went back to our desks to study. But every time the door opened behind you, you still flinched.

THREE MEMORABLE CHAPELS

One morning in chapel Roger Deys was singing the special number. He chose "The Great Judgment Morning." It is a dramatic

★   ★   ★   ★   ★   ★   ★

song with some dramatic lines. But he botched one of his lines. He was supposed to sing, "forever in hell they will sink." But instead he sang, "forever in hell they will *stink*." It wouldn't have been nearly so funny if he had not quickly corrected himself: "forever in hell they will stink – *sink*!" The follow-up "sink" sent us into gales of laughter. Mike laughed so hard he nearly fell out of his theater seat. Throughout the rest of the song and the sermon to follow Mike and I could not keep a straight face. He was sitting next to the window and he would turn his head that way, but I could still see his reflection in the window. Have you ever tried to hold in laughter when you are dying to laugh? Then you will know what we experienced that day. It was wonderful and it was horrible.

Something that appeared to be really horrible took place in chapel one day. Right at the end of the service Deana Mickey screamed, "He shot him!" Five Ottumwa High School seniors had staged a fake shooting on the corner of North Court Street and Pennsylvania Avenue. Through the tall floor-to-ceiling chapel windows Deana saw one boy jump from one car and another boy from another. The first boy took out a gun and shot the other, who then fell to the ground as though gravely wounded. Two other boys then jumped from the car to help their "wounded" friend into the car while the shooter fled the scene. Mike and I saw the whole thing play out too. It looked pretty real to us. Someone called the police. Mike raced out of chapel, got into Cradic's car and tore off in hot pursuit of the shooter. Soon our campus was swarming with police, sheriff's officers, and an emergency ambulance. The boys were arrested and turned over to juvenile authorities. The "smoking weapon" turned out to be a cap gun. The pranksters insisted the act was "unrehearsed and unpremeditated." The story

★   ★   ★   ★   ★   ★   ★

made the papers, including the *Des Moines Register*. The headline read "Shooting Staged; Capture Isn't." The report credited the students of Midwestern for turning in the alarm. Mike was the real hero, however, because he, having no idea the gun wasn't real, blocked the "shooter's" escape with his car until the police appeared to apprehend him.

Since I was taking voice lessons from Margaret Hunt, I, like Roger, was chosen to sing a solo in chapel. The day that was supposed to take place I developed a severe case of stage fright. I remained in my dorm room and did not attend chapel that day. About the time chapel was to start, I heard footsteps in the hall. I peeked out the door and saw Brother Culver. I thought, "Oh, no. They really take singing in chapel seriously. He has come to get me and make me sing!" But all he was there for was to conduct the daily inspection of the dorm rooms. Relieved, I suddenly recovered from my stage fright and made it to school in time for classes. But to this day I have never had the nerve to sing a solo, and I guess I never will until I get to heaven.

MORE MISCHIEF AND A DILEMMA

One afternoon I took a novelty item I had bought at Woolworth's, a piece of rubber vomit, and placed it in the water fountain at the foot of the stairway. Wouldn't you know my first victim was none other than faculty member and co-founder of the college, Burton W. Barber. Nearly all of us walked in fear of him. He went to the fountain, bent over, hesitated when he saw the rubber vomit, and then went ahead and took a drink. He straightened up, looked around, and saw me. Boy, was I in for it now. But all he did was say, with the very faintest hint of a smile, "Better get that thing removed." I was most glad to do so.

★   ★   ★   ★   ★   ★   ★

Gary Cradic and I decided one night to climb the tall radio tower that was located at the top of North 5th Street. I only made it halfway up, but Cradic went clear to the top, where the beacon's red light was constantly glowing. In the distance we heard the sound of a police siren. We figured someone must have spotted us and turned us in. We came down the tower much faster than we had gone up!

In October I was faced with a dilemma. Both teams I had rooted for all my life – the Cardinals in the National League and the Yankees in the American League – won the pennant in each league! Now which of the two teams was I going to root for? I almost made this a matter of prayer (I said *almost*!). This was like Solomon deciding what to do with the baby. You can't have your Kate and Edith too. What was I to do? I decided to just go with the flow and may the best team win. The Cardinals' Ken Boyer had led the league with 119 RBIs. The Yankees' Mickey Mantle had slugged 35 home runs. The Redbirds' Bob Gibson went 19-12 (Ray Sadecki topping him with 20 wins) but the Bombers' Whitey Ford went 17-6 with a winning percentage of .739. (Incidentally, my cousin Dave Wickersham, pitching for the Detroit Tigers, went 19-12 that same year, the best year he ever had.) I was sorry that Stan Musial had retired the year before and would not be in the Fall Classic. And a Fall Classic it was, going the full 7 games, the Cards edging the Yanks 4 games to 3. Boyer's grand slam won game 4. Gibson pitched game 7, striking out 9 for a series record of 31. Mantle hit 3 home runs. Richardson set a series record with 13 hits.

Around Halloween some of the guys convinced some of the gals to visit an old house, an ex-nunnery, on the posh North Side that was reputed to be haunted. Tall bushes surrounded the house on all four sides. If you laid down on the ground you could see the house

★   ★   ★   ★   ★   ★   ★

fairly well. Someone thought they saw a figure with a candle moving around on the second floor. The wind sighed in the trees and someone stepped on a dead branch. One of the high-strung girls couldn't stand the tension any longer and let loose with a bloodcurdling scream that was loud enough to wake the dead, so we had to get out of there.

ODD JOBS AND OTHER JOBS

Each week I would receive a letter from dad, and usually there was a little check with the letter to help on my tuition. (I have kept nearly every card or letter that my father ever wrote to me.) Gary and I raked leaves in the fall and shoveled walks in the winter. One rich but eccentric lady actually wanted us to rake the leaves that had fallen in her yard from her neighbor's tree back over into her neighbor's yard! She also wanted me to rake "faster." She would come out of the house and just before getting into her Jaguar she would yell, "Faster, faster!" I finally couldn't take it any more and threw my rake up into the air and walked off the job. Gary and I also learned to build limestone walls for Raymond Lyon, a landscaper who also preached at What Cheer. Some of those beautiful rock walls are still standing in Ottumwa, proving that not everything I did in those years was foolish. Doug Gilliland, a senior, worked for Coca-Cola, and sometimes I helped him on his deliveries to restaurants. I learned that restaurant kitchens are not always the cleanest places in the world. Many times the *Ottumwa Courier* would hire some of us to do a special job. We would stand at a long counter in the press room and stuff circulars in the daily paper. Finally, I caught on with a Hy-Vee grocery store on the North Side and later switched over to work for Easter's Super-Valu on the South Side. I left Hy-Vee because the assistant manager insisted that we should

*   *   *   *   *   *   *

have a perpetual smile on our faces. It's not easy to smile all day long. In both stores I sacked groceries, unloaded trucks, stocked shelves, and did some checkout work. Little did I know that right next door to Easter's Super-Valu lived the girl whom I would marry in 1967.

LIFE IN "LITTLE CHICAGO"

The Des Moines River separated the city of Ottumwa, at that time boasting a population of about 35,000. Ottumwa (an Indian word meaning "rippling water") is today known as "The City of Bridges." At one time it was called "Little Chicago" because when the heat was on in Chicago, Al Capone and his cronies would take the train to Ottumwa and lay low until things cooled off in the Windy City. The boys' dormitory was just a few blocks north of Lowenberg's Bakery. About four in the morning the delicious aroma of fresh bread baking would often awaken us. It was hard to go back to sleep. Most of us couldn't afford fresh pastries so we would stuff our faces with day old stuff.

I took my meals in the school's cafeteria, located on the main floor of the girls' dormitory, on 421 North 5th Street. Nathalie Smith was the main chef. You had to cross Highway 63, a 4-lane highway, in order to get to the girls' dorm. That was sometimes an adventure. Every student loved going to The Canteen in the Alley in downtown Ottumwa for a Canteen (maid-rite) and a Mountain Dew. The seating was in a horseshoe shape. The owner decorated the walls with pictures of presidents, but only Democrats earned their spot on the wall. Sometimes we would banter politics with the little old ladies who slapped together our sandwiches (crumbled hamburger, a dash of salt, a paddle splat of mustard or ketchup). It was (and still is) a popular place where sometimes you'd have to stand in line to get a seat. I believe

★   ★   ★   ★   ★   ★   ★

it was also in Ottumwa that I had my first McDonald's hamburger. I would work at McDonald's my sophomore year. Richard and Nancy Ellis invited some students to their house one night, and I devoured 13 tacos. Every winter during my four years of college the students would be invited to Lafe and Anita Culver's place in the country to ice skate and then enjoy a cup of hot apple cider. As a hungry 125-pound freshman I quickly learned never to turn down an invitation where free food might be served.

WILD RIDES

One night I ate way too much. After I had devoured a big helping of tuna and noodles at the cafeteria, I got hungry. So Gary McGlumphry and I drove to McDonald's to get something else to eat. From there we drove to the A & W to get even more to eat. We must have been flush with money that week. Driving down North Court Street, however, I suddenly felt a bit flushed and had the urge to roll down the window to get some fresh air. It was too late. Gary thought I was just faking until I turned around and he saw noodles coming out my nose! That just about freaked him out! We stopped at the school to hose down the exterior of the passenger side of the car, but there was no garden hose available. So we took off one of the hubcaps, filled it with water from an outside spigot, and used it to wash off the evidence of my culinary excess.

Gary and I were doing our laundry at the Laundromat on East Second Street one afternoon. Three girls from the school were doing the same. We offered to give them a lift back to the girls' dorm in a car Gary had borrowed from Ray Stevens. It was a Corvair, and the front hood was missing. We placed the plastic baskets filled with freshly

★   ★   ★   ★   ★   ★   ★

folded laundry in the trunk (which of course in a Corvair was in the front). Jenifer Bradley and Susan Wood jumped into the back seat, so poor Dorothy Gorham had to ride in the trunk with the laundry baskets. Well, I could have, but I wasn't about to give up my "shotgun" seat in the wild ride that was ahead. Instead of taking the girls directly to the dorm, Gary drove right through the downtown district in spite of Dorothy's shrieks of dismay: "Oh, you boys are terrible!"

The guys (and some of the more adventuresome gals) liked to go "hookybobbing" in the winter when the streets were packed firm with snow. I feel sorry for those who have never experienced the wild thrill of "hookybobbing." You would get behind a car, "hook on" to the rear bumper, crouch down and then take the ride of your life. Sometimes the driver knew there was a "hookybobber" hanging on, and sometimes they didn't know. When a car went around a corner too fast, we would often lose our grip and go tumbling head over heels "laughing all the way." We also got some large cardboard boxes from the grocery store, flattened them out, and used them to sled down the steep banks on either side of Highway 63. One evening our sliding path got so slick that I broke through the big ridge of snow created by the snowplows and slid out into the northbound lane of the highway. A big car swerved to miss me. I remember looking up just as it shot by and noticing that it was a Buick Park Avenue. It's funny how when your whole life is flashing by, your brain is still registering earthly things like that. "Hey, that is one nice car!" It's a wonder that I survived my freshman year, it really is.

Some of the girls worked the night shift at the Jefferson Square Manor, a nursing home. Most of them did not have cars, so they would ring the boys' dorm to see if someone was willing to take them. Gary

★　★　★　★　★　★　★

and I were always willing. One evening we answered the call for Jean Eakins who worked at the Ottumwa Hospital. I crouched down in the back seat with a ladies' nylon stocking pulled down over my face. I must have looked like a deranged Chinese bandit. About halfway to the hospital, I sat up and stuck my fright face in her face. Without batting an eye Jeanie just said, "Oh, Vic, sit down!" I must have been so notorious that I was getting monotonous!

VICTOR IMMATURE

Evidently my hi-jinks had caught the attention of the faculty. I don't think they had ever encountered a student like me. Several years later I learned that they had actually had a special meeting where they discussed whether or not to dismiss me from school. That would have broken my dad's heart, and maybe that is why they decided not to do it. One day Brother Hunt invited me to lunch at his home in the country. After lunch Margaret left the room and it was just Brother Hunt and me, man to boy as it were. He told me, firmly but in a kind manner, that I should be more disciplined and serious, that the faculty expected more of me, that God expected more of me, all of which was true. I wasn't exactly Victor Mature (an actor in the 50s). I was more like Victor Immature. Brother Hunt even brought up Vietnam and the draft. I guess he meant that if I left school, my 2-D status would be revoked and I would have to go to Vietnam. That thought didn't bother me at all because I would have gladly gone to Vietnam where my high school buddies were fighting for our country and where three of them paid the supreme sacrifice. I was not in college merely to evade the draft. My father's great uncle had fought in the Civil War, my Grandpa Brown had fought in World War I, my two uncles Boyd and

★   ★   ★   ★   ★   ★   ★

Troy had fought in World War II, and my father had served in the National Guard. In the end, however, I promised him that I would try to be a better student. In the years that have followed my graduation, I have always tried to be an "ambassador of good will" for Midwestern.

A postscript: a few years ago Lafe Culver, who had recommended my dismissal, apologized to me. He said, "Oh, Victor, if we had dismissed you, none of this great work you are doing would have ever been done." I assured him that had they done so, it probably would have been the right thing to do and not to feel bad for having once considered my dismissal. I freely affirm that I was full of mischief, but I frankly deny that I ever did anything that was malicious.

"I WANT TO PREACH"

Sometime in September or October of 1964 I had the first of three "Turning Points" in my life after "matriculating at Midwestern." Dewey Lalk was preaching at a Tuesday night service at the Pennsylvania Avenue church. The topic he spoke on that evening was "The End of the World." When a man who is nearing his own end (he was literally dying of cancer) preaches on the end of all things, one listens. His message was so convincing and convicting that I found myself walking down the aisle at the invitation. I heard footsteps coming behind me. When I got to the front of the auditorium, I made way for Gary Cradic, my old pal from Hamburg. Richard Ellis led us into a small room at the front of the building and asked us what was on our heart. Unbeknownst to each other we had both come to dedicate our lives to the preaching of the gospel. I spoke four words that would alter the course of my life in years to come: "I want to preach." I didn't know

★   ★   ★   ★   ★   ★   ★

how to preach, but I knew that somehow I must preach. In my heart I felt what Paul must have felt when he said, ". . . for necessity is laid upon me; yea, woe is unto me, if I preach not the gospel!" (1 Corinthians 9:16). It would be another two years or so before Gary and I would begin preaching on a regular basis, but the die was cast that never-to-be-forgotten night.

I am sure my decision shocked some of my fellow students. "What's a goof-off like him doing making a decision like that?" But Paul also wrote, "For the gifts and the calling of God are irrevocable" (Romans 11:29). Matthew Henry said, "For whom God calls He qualifies." That was good enough for me. I had at last responded to that mysterious call to preach that had come to me at Camp Diagonal in 1957. Would you believe whom I was sitting next to that long ago night at Camp Diagonal? Brace yourselves for this one. The one and same . . . Gary Cradic! Truly, "God moves in a mysterious way, His wonders to perform" (William Cowper). And will those wonders never cease? God's spokesman that night, Dewey Lalk, was at that time establishing a new church in nearby Oskaloosa – a church where I would, from 1977-1984, have my longest and most fruitful ministry!

MINISTRY IN CALIFORNIA AND MARTYDOM IN THE CONGO

In November my father finally secured a new place to minister – the Broad Street Church of Christ in far-off San Luis Obispo, California. My parents, Muriel, Bonnie and David stopped by in Ottumwa on their way to California on my 19th birthday, November 23. I was working at Easter's Super Valu and my mother came in and bought me a chocolate cake. It was great to see them once again and, of course, I was sad to see them leave. I will say that the Broad Street church, of all the

★   ★   ★   ★   ★   ★   ★

churches I had gone to as a "preacher's kid," was the only church to regularly contribute financially to my college education. Sometimes churches in the Midwest suspected that West Coast churches were "liberal." Well, "Broad Street" was well named: they were "liberal" all right – liberal in their giving to a kid whom they had never even met and was not officially a "Timothy" of the church, let alone a member. In the years to come I would hold at least three revival meetings for the good folks in San Luis Obispo.

The day after my 19th birthday something took place in the Republic of Congo (the former Belgian Congo) that I was not aware of at the time. Phyllis Rine, a 25-year-old student from Cincinnati Bible Seminary, where I had registered but never attended, was murdered in Stanleyville. Insurgent Congolese rebels had seized the city and taken about 2,000 Americans and Europeans hostage. Some of them, like Phyllis were missionaries. After 111 days of being held hostage, an attempt was made by U. S. planes and Belgian paratroopers to rescue them. But it was too late for poor Phyllis Rine. The rebels mowed her down with machine-gun fire along with 250 other souls. If only I had bought a copy of *Time* on December 4, 1964, with the face of Dr. Paul Carlson, another martyr of November 24, on the cover. If only I had read the story, it just might have sobered me and caused me to be more serious as a student. Today Phyllis Rine is remembered as the first female martyr from the Restoration Movement. I recently sent a gift to Cincinnati Christian University to help renovate a girl's dormitory named in her memory.

MY FIRST SERMON

I preached my first sermon at the B Avenue Church of Christ in Council Bluffs on Sunday evening, November 29, 1964. I was barely 19

★   ★   ★   ★   ★   ★   ★

years old. My sister Becky was studying to be a nurse at the Jennie
Edmundson School of Nursing in Council Bluffs and was a member of
the church. Leon Hansen, my roommate, had invited me to go home
with him for Thanksgiving. When the minister of the church, William
Payne, heard that we were coming he asked Leon and me to conduct
the evening service. Leon was scheduled to lead the singing and sing
a solo and I would preach the sermon. I borrowed a typewriter and
typed out my sermon. I decided I would take my text from Joshua
7:11ff, "Israel hath sinned . . . therefore the children of Israel could not
stand before their enemies . . ." I settled on my title: "Sin in the Camp."
Why did I choose that particular text and theme? Nearly half a century later I really could not tell you. Perhaps it was because in Old
Testament History we may have been discussing the story of Achan,
the man who was "aching" to get his hands on some silver shekels, a
chunk of gold, and a "goodly Babylonish garment."

That night Brother Payne introduced us as "The Hansen-
Knowles Evangelistic Team." I think he was joking. Leon led some congregational songs, sang a solo, and then it was my turn. I was nervous
as a cat on a hot tin roof. I had Becky time me, and I think I managed
to go a little more than 20 minutes before calling for Leon to lead the
invitation hymn. Robert York, a man in the congregation who often
recorded big-name evangelists like Archie Word and Marion McKee at
preaching rallies, was on the front row, headset on, professionally
recording my sermon for posterity on his very expensive reel-to-reel
recording machine. I still have it somewhere (the recording, not the
machine!). I also have the two yellowed pages of typewritten notes.
"First" seldom means "best." It was my first attempt at preaching and
that was about it – an attempt. But after the benediction many people

★　　★　　★　　★　　★　　★　　★

came up and shook my hand and patted me on the back and told me I had done a good job. May God bless all the small churches everywhere that have endured such meager fare and yet have offered kind words to 19-year-old "preachers." Surely they shall not lose their reward.

CHRISTMAS IN CALIFORNIA

During the Christmas break I got to go to California with fellow students Don and Margaret Stephens who drove from Ottumwa to Sutter. I took a bus from Sutter to San Luis Obispo arriving at 3:15 in the morning. I was able to spend a week or so with my family in their new home at 1961 Oceanaire Drive. I got my first view of the Pacific Ocean on January 1, 1965. Since dad had paid for my new Dickson Bible, I had him sign it on the presentation page on that same day.

One day I asked mom where my collection of baseball cards and marbles were. She "confessed" to me that when they packed up to leave Illinois for California she had given them the old heave-ho. I yelled, *"You what?"* She smiled that famous smile that could just melt your heart and replied, "Well, Victor, the Bible says, 'When I was a child, I spake as a child, I understood as a child, I thought as a child: but when I became a man, I put away childish things.' You are a man now, so I just 'put away' your 'childish things' for you!" I couldn't argue with her logic, especially since she was quoting from 1 Corinthians 13, but I still couldn't believe she had thrown away my beloved baseball cards and pitched my magnificent marbles. I guess that was the day I discovered that I had "lost my marbles!" I felt like hopping a bus and heading for Mulberry Grove to sift through the town dump to find poor old Joey Almafitano, Bobby Del Greco, "Minnie" Minoso, Billy Consolo, "Rip" Repulski, Ray Jabolonski. Ray Narleski, Wilmer "Vinegar Bend" Mizell, Willie

★   ★   ★   ★   ★   ★   ★

"Puddinhead" Jones, "Sad Sam" Jones, Harry "Suitcase" Simpson, Harry "The Golden Greek" Agannis (who died of leukemia at 25) and hundreds of other pasteboard pals who had helped me through puberty. The thought of them molding in a dump almost made me ill. The trading cards have long since disintegrated but I hope whoever has my marbles today is enjoying them!

BACK TO ILLINOIS

One day I read in the school's weekly paper, *Evangelism from the Heart of America*, that there would be a Youth Rally in Mulberry Grove. And so in mid-February I went back to my old haunts with several students from MSE. Don Jessup's son Graydon was one of the speakers, and the other was Tom Burgess. After the rally I decided to stay on a few extra days. I stayed at Rusty Wilfong's house and also went to a party where I saw a number of kids who had been underclassmen when I was a senior. At the party I saw Linda Mayfield, my old steady, but she was kind of quiet and cool toward me. And why shouldn't she have been? I left the party with Janis Ennen, who would graduate that spring, and she drove me to Rusty's house where we "necked" a little. I needed to get back to college, so Rusty's dad loaned me 20 bucks to take a bus the 220 miles back to Ottumwa. This time Thomas Wolfe was right. "You can't go home again."

THE "UNDERGROUND CHURCH"

I got the same grades the second semester that I had received the first semester – two Cs and two Bs. Guest speakers in chapel included Tom Burgess, Eddie DeVries, Dale A. Williamson, and Fred P. Miller. Much later I would work with all four men in kingdom activi-

★   ★   ★   ★   ★   ★   ★

ties. One day we had a special guest speaker, "Brother Andrew." I believe it was Terry Paul who first sparked my interest in the "underground church" movement behind the Iron Curtain, for it was he who was responsible for bringing "Brother Andrew" to town. He had achieved worldwide fame as "God's Smuggler," transporting thousands of Bibles into Eastern European countries that were controlled by communism. I bought his book by the same title. We heard much about communism in those days. Burton W. Barber, an ardent anti-communist, had a literature display in the back of the chapel where you could buy all kinds of books like *I Was a Slave in Russia* by John S. Noble, *The Naked Communist* by Cleon Skousen, *None Dare Call It Treason* by John A. Stormer, and *Masters of Deceit: A Study of Communism in America and How to Defeat It* by none other than J. Edgar Hoover, director of the FBI. If memory serves me correctly, Terry also arranged for Paul Vorenoff, a Russian, to speak on the dangers of communism.

MY FIRST CAR

I was getting tired of walking or having to depend upon someone else for a ride. Not too many guys probably wanted to loan me their car, speed demon that I was! I had my eye on a beautiful green MG convertible, an English-made car, but I knew I couldn't afford it. Brother Ellis agreed to co-sign for me at the bank. We went down to Vaughan's Chevrolet and picked out a nice 1962 two-door Chevy Corvair Sport Coupe, sometimes called "the poor man's Porsche." It was cream colored and had a three-speed gearshift on the floor. The Corvair was different from standard cars in that the 6-cylinder engine was air-cooled, made of aluminum, and was mounted horizontally in the rear of the car. I had to put some sandbags in the front end because

★   ★   ★   ★   ★   ★   ★

when I started out in low and shifted into second I could almost lift the front of the car off the ground. Not long after I got the car, I challenged Gary McGlumphry to a drag race on the edge of town. He was behind the wheel of a 1965 Ford Falcon. We revved up our motors and took off, rear tires squealing, leaving the air befouled with burning rubber. Well, one of us did. I had the gearshift in third instead of first! I "took off," lurching and lunging like a wounded turtle. Gary remembers looking in his rear view mirror and watching me loom larger until I shot by him like a bat out of Hades. I washed and waxed my new ride and put Baby Moon hubcaps on the wheels. Sam Brown bested me, however, when he bought a shiny gold Corvair Spyder with a turbocharger, a really hot looking car.

Beneath the dash of my Corvair were powerful air vents. When I was giving a girl a ride to school or to work I would ask them to reach under the dash and open the air vent. Whoosh! A jet stream of outside air would blow their skirt up over their knees! They would shriek and say, "Oh, Vic!" Of course I never peeked. I'm sure Sam never pulled the same trick on his female passengers. Sam's devotion and dedication to the Lord really impressed me. His dorm room was covered with Scripture verses he had printed on index cards in order to help him to commit them to memory.

SEEING SUSAN

The first week in March, I walked into Mrs. Hunt's music room where Susan Hand was practicing the piano. I had become attracted to this blue-eyed blonde, a senior, from Sidney, Ohio. I brashly leaned on the piano and struck up a conversation with her. She was 21 but would turn 22 on March 7. I was 19, going on 20. In addition to her physical

★   ★   ★   ★   ★   ★   ★

beauty, Susan was a very nice girl, quiet, sometimes shy, at other times bubbling over with laughter. I asked her if she would like to go out with me sometime, and she said yes. I wanted so much for this relationship to be a good one. That may be one reason why shortly after we started seeing each other that I decided to be immersed a second time.

Sometimes a number of the young people who came to Midwestern would be "rebaptized." Most of them would say that they were too young to understand the meaning of baptism when they had been immersed or that they didn't really know what they were doing. In my case I began to question whether or not I had understood the meaning of repentance. I knew that the Bible said, "Repent, and be baptized every one of you in the name of Jesus Christ for the remission of sins, and you shall receive the gift of the Holy Spirit" (Acts 2:38). Had I truly repented back in 1958? (I wasn't sure. Had I even committed enough "sin" to repent of when I was 12?) I visited with Brother Ellis about some of these matters and then decided that I would be baptized again. But before I did so, I went into Brother Culver's office, got down on my knees and confessed every sin I could remember ever committing. I told God I was truly sorry for my sins and asked Him to help me live a more consecrated life. I did so want to present myself as a "vessel of honor" to Susan as well.

With the passing of time, however, I have come to believe that my first baptism was indeed valid. Baptism, among other things, is for the forgiveness of sin, and forgiveness takes place in the mind of God. After one is baptized, there will still be the need for repentance and confession of sin. The apostle John wrote (to Christians), "If we confess our sins, he is faithful and just to forgive us our sins, and to cleanse us from all unrighteousness" (1 John 1:9). That is what I needed to do the week

★   ★   ★   ★   ★   ★   ★

of March 7, and that is what I did in Brother Culver's office. Repentance is not a fixed act in God's wonderful plan of salvation. As long as we are in the flesh, we will need to repent and confess our sins to God.

Now that I had given myself to God, I was ready to give myself to Susan. We started sitting together in chapel. That was a good start. Sometimes in the evening we would walk back to the administration building and sit on the veranda and just talk. We dated as often as the rules on dating would allow at Midwestern. One cold night we went ice-skating, and I gallantly knelt down and laced up her white skates. On another occasion the famous Blackwood Brothers were in town and we went to their concert. Like nearly every couple at Midwestern, we went to The Canteen and had dessert at Graham's Dairy Freeze.

Susan's best friend was Bonnie Stolz from Florida. One afternoon I was sitting on the landing of the boys' dorm talking to Bonnie on the phone about Susan. I had this habit of nudging my class ring up above the knuckle of my ring finger and circling it around with my thumb when I talked on the phone. To my horror (I can still see this in slow motion) the ring sailed off my finger, bounced down three steps and disappeared forever through a crack between the molding and the wall. I was thunderstruck. Now I could not give my class ring to Susan as I had planned.

Every freshman student was issued Barber's booklet *Friendship, Courtship, Engagement, Marriage*. These were the "4 Spiritual Laws" at Midwestern long before Bill Bright ever came up with his own set! I moved through the first two like Sherman marched through Georgia. I should have taken more time but I was accustomed to doing every thing fast – playing burnout, racing cars, and seeing Susan.

★   ★   ★   ★   ★   ★   ★

Ken and Deana Mickey invited me to their apartment for supper one evening. Ken wanted to talk to me about taking his job at Johnson's Funeral Chapel once he graduated in May. Seeing how happy Ken and Deana were made me long for what they had. One weekend I took Susan with me to Hamburg. I wanted her to see the people in the church that meant so much to me. I also wanted them to see what a find I had in Susan.

A BIG YOUTH RALLY

In April I attended the famous Lexington Youth Rally in Lexington, Nebraska. Lois Williamson's dad, Dale A. Williamson, was the preacher there and had a great love for young people. He had built up the rally that was attended by several hundred young people from all over the Midwest each spring. I wanted to go because Sam, Roger, and Gary had all been asked to give testimonies. Sam had become a Christian at the rally the year previous and he was to speak on "My First Year as a Christian." Gary Werner, who had made such a good impression on me earlier in my life, was also one of the speakers. Brother Hunt was the keynote speaker. I enjoyed the theme of the rally ("Traveling Life's Journey") and was challenged by the zeal and ardor that everyone seemed to project. The rally took place just a few days after our freshman class had received quite a jolt. On March 28, Peggy Wyatt, Sam Brown's cousin, died of a brain aneurysm at a hospital in Kansas City. She had become mysteriously ill not long after she enrolled and had to return to her home in Ashland, Kansas. Many years later, at Sam's own funeral, I visited Peggy's grave and wept for the years she never had.

Little did I know that in a few years I would succeed Brother Williamson at Lexington and would direct the Lexington Youth Rally

★   ★   ★   ★   ★   ★   ★

for three years. On the way back to Iowa one of Kerry Conaway's lungs collapsed and we had to take him to a hospital.

MY CHAPEL SERMON

I knew that soon I would have to preach in chapel as the freshmen did each spring. Fifteen of us preached that year. I began my sermon preparation and came up with what I thought was an ingenious outline. My theme would be "In-Sins" and I would develop three main points, all starting with the prefix "in" – inconsistency, ingratitude, and indifference. One afternoon I took my sermon to the school and knocked on Brother Hunt's office door. Above the door was an open transom. On the frosted glass the words *Voice of Evangelism* had been professionally painted. I cautiously asked him if he would vet my sermon, and he graciously took time to do so. Then he cleared his throat and said, "Victor, we usually start a sermon with a text." Good night! I had been so caught up with my wordplay I had forgotten what I had learned in Homiletics. "A sermon is an oral address, *based on a biblical text . . .*" I'm sure my countenance fell. But Brother Hunt raised my spirits when he said, "Let's go to the Word of God and see what we can find." In no time at all we had a text that would serve as a springboard into the sermon. "For *in* many things we *offend* all (James 3:2 KJV). "In-Sins." Perfect! Thank you, Brother Hunt! He must have been just as delighted because he not only published my title in the May 12 *Evangelism from the Heart of America*, but he also mentioned all three points.

A SAD CHAPEL

I never got to sit under the teaching of the great Burton W. Barber my freshman year. He was planning to move to Puerto Rico in

★　★　★　★　★　★　★

the summer and kept busy on the second floor doing the layout and printing of the *Voice of Evangelism*, a weekly paper that he had started with Donald Hunt in 1947. There was also some tension between some of the upperclassmen and Richard M. Ellis. They felt that his teaching was not challenging enough. (If anyone should have complained, it should have been the freshman Life of Christ class. It was way too challenging for most of us!). A few of the upperclassmen went to the faculty with their complaints. This, however, did not sit well with the majority of the students. Soon a petition was circulated. It stated that "a gross injustice" had been done to Brother Ellis by having his teaching ability defamed and that the undersigned gave their "sincerest vote of confidence" to him. Forty-one students signed the petition including Ken and Deana, Susan, myself, and just about every member of the freshman Life of Christ class. All of this turmoil was very unsettling to me and to many of the students. I had known Hunt and Barber for years. Ellis was my preacher at Pennsylvania Avenue and had co-signed for me so I could buy a car. I had been in all of their homes that year. I liked all of them. I couldn't understand why they couldn't get along together. If it is "good and pleasant" for brethren to dwell together in unity, then how "bad and unpleasant" it is when they don't.

The week of May 18-21 Brother Ellis preached what proved to be his final series of chapel messages. At the end of chapel of May 21, as dismissal was about to be given, John Bell, a married student, said, "We're not finished here yet." He went to the stage and read the petition. No one went to class that day. The extended chapel went on until noon with much discussion, pro and con. I sat there with Susan wondering what the Lord thought about all this. What a way to end the school year with graduation just four days away! In spite of the show

* * * * * * *

of support from the majority of the student body, both freshmen and upperclassmen, Brother Ellis was summarily relieved of his teaching duties. Years later I would begin addressing the issue of division in my paper *Vanguard*. It caught the attention of Don DeWelt in Joplin, Missouri and . . . . Well, that story will have to wait until Volume 2!

A WEDDING AND AN "AMBUSH"

My first year of college was almost over. The smell of apple blossoms was in the air. Soon Susan would receive her diploma and would return to her home in Ohio for the summer. There is no doubt in my mind (now) that I was on an emotional roller coaster ride. The weekend before graduation I accompanied some students to Granite City, Illinois, for the wedding of Robert Landreth and Joyce Parsley. Susan did not go because she was busy preparing for her graduation. Seeing Robert and Joyce standing together hand-in-hand at the altar only made me long for Susan all the more.

On Sunday morning, something totally unexpected happened. Fifteen minutes before the services started, the preacher, Delmer Rhodebeck, tapped me on the shoulder and said, "You're preaching this morning." I turned around to protest but he was gone. Frantically I tried to remember as much as I could from the sermon that I had preached the previous November in Council Bluffs. Somehow I managed to "preach" the morning message – a message I was totally unprepared to deliver. I am sure it was intended to be a good learning experience for me. I don't think it was. From the very beginning I wanted to be prepared when I went into the pulpit. I have always enjoyed the preparation of a sermon every bit as much as the delivery.

★   ★   ★   ★   ★   ★   ★

"WILL YOU MARRY ME?"

Graduation Day finally arrived, Monday May 25, 1965. The services were held at the Pennsylvania Avenue church. Thirteen seniors received their diplomas (the largest graduating class in the history of Midwestern until our class topped them by one in 1968). I bought Susan a nice corsage and sat in the large audience of families, friends, and fellow students, my eyes on her, my blue-eyed blonde in her pretty turquoise dress. She sang in a trio with her best friend Bonnie Stoltz and Sherrill Johnson. Ken Mickey, who had played a part in my attending Midwestern and would be joining Deana's parents in the traveling Prater-Evangelistic Team, gave me a big bear hug and wished me well.

Susan and I drove out to Memorial Park and spent hours walking hand-in-hand. She would be leaving for Ohio in the morning. This was all ending so fast. For once in my life I didn't like fast. We had been seeing each other for three months and now she was leaving. Her summer plans included teaching VBS in Ohio and Indiana and working as a staff member of a Christian camp in far-away Florida. On impulse, but straight from the heart, I asked Susan, "Will you marry me?" I had just started my job, had no engagement ring to offer her, or anything else except my love. After what seemed to me like an eternity, Susan smiled at me and said, "Yes." Happy as a lark, I drove her back to the girls' dorm in the wee hours of the morning, apologizing profusely for keeping her out so late when she had such a long trip to make in the morning. I promised to come and see her as soon as I could, and I did keep that promise.

The next night I phoned my folks in California. Dad was gone preaching in Los Angeles, and so I told mom that I had asked Susan,

★　★　★　★　★　★　★

whom she had never met, to marry me. My mother said, *"You what?"* I was kind of hurt. I think I said, "Don't you want me to be happy?" She replied, "Of course, but son this is so sudden and so unexpected. And you are so young." (I was 19 years and five months old. Mom was just 19 when she married dad!) She told me to give it some time, which, of course, was always good advice for anyone contemplating marrying someone for life. I phoned dad a few nights later and told him the same thing. I do not recall his reaction or advice, but it was probably the same as my mother's.

I did not want Susan to forget me so I went to a photography studio and had a picture taken. I signed it "With all my love," meaning every word, and mailed it to Susan in Ohio. The June 23rd issue of *Evangelism from the Heart of America* carried the pictures and plans of the 13 graduates. On the front page was Susan's lovely picture and summer plans, including this line: *"Is engaged to ministerial student Victor Knowles."*

We never made it to the altar.

★   ★   ★   ★   ★   ★   ★

CHAPTER SIX

AFTER THE STORM

Johnson's Funeral Chapel was located on Church Street on Ottumwa's South Side. Johnson's rivaled two big funeral homes on the North Side, Jay's and Reece's. Don Johnson was now running the business, succeeding his father Carl. He and nearly all the men who worked there were heavy smokers. Right across the street was a Rexall's Drug Store where we would go to take a mid-morning break. Just down the street was Henry's Hamburgers where I would often go for lunch. Like all students at Midwestern I had to find housing elsewhere since the dorms were closed for the summer. After staying with Gary Cradic in his apartment for awhile, George and Marge Scott, some very nice people who attended the Pennsylvania Avenue church, offered me a basement room in their home at 1813 Asbury Avenue on the South Side. I was glad to rent it from them, although I did not see much of them with all my comings and goings. Their son George Jr. was in high school and had a red motorbike. Sometimes I let him drive my Corvair while I drove his motorbike.

LIFE AND DEATH IN 1965

Johnson's kept a fleet of gleaming white vehicles that had to be kept spotless inside and out. Before and after each funeral it fell to me to wash, dry, and vacuum each vehicle. The fleet included the hearse, family car, and a van. As soon as each funeral ended, it was my job to put all the flowers in the van and get them to the cemetery before the funeral

★   ★   ★   ★   ★   ★   ★

procession arrived. This meant that I had to know the way to each cemetery and take short cuts to get there. I was never picked up for speeding
while driving for Johnson's but I easily could have been. If I hadn't gotten all the flowers placed at the graveside and vacated the cemetery by
the time Don drove in with the procession, I knew I was in for it.

The funeral home also had an ambulance service, so I had to
keep that vehicle up as well. We were on call 24 hours a day. One night
we had to go pick up a man who had been killed in a terrible car wreck.
He had evidently gone to sleep at the wheel and had hit a concrete
bridge abutment head on at a high rate of speed. It seemed like forever
before we were able to extract his body from the accordion that was once
a car. Ordinary death calls were much easier on my psyche. However, I had
not realized that when some people die they evacuate themselves. No
wonder the veterans at Johnson's lifted the head and back while I got the
bottom and legs! (So much for all those romantic death scenes of someone dying in their lover's arms in the movies.) I also learned what the
expression "dead weight" means. Corpses do not help you at all when
you are trying to lift them like live persons can when you are lifting them
up off the bed.

When we arrived back at Johnson's with a body, the ambulance
would be backed up to the funeral home and we would wheel the body
on the stretcher to the elevator. The embalming room was on the second
floor. The corpse would then be carefully placed on the embalming table.
I did not stay for that process! The man who did the embalming would
often play Country Western music as he did his work. Sometimes I could
hear the rhythmic "thump" of the embalming machine from down
below. Sometimes it was almost in beat with the song that was playing
on the radio. That was weird. Another weird thing was the shoe room.

★   ★   ★   ★   ★   ★   ★

Family members of the deceased would bring shoes along with the deceased's favorite outfit. Since the lower end of the casket was always closed, the shoes never went on their feet. I was told I could pick out any shoes that were my size. It was like a regular shoe store. I think I picked out one pair but never wore them. The thought of wearing someone else's soles made my soul a little uneasy.

Anytime we had a body in the building, it was standard policy that someone spend the night at the funeral home. I slept on a cot in one of the offices in the rear of the building. Sometimes we would have as many as three or four bodies in the "slumber chambers." After visiting hours were over, I emptied the wastebaskets and vacuumed the carpets. Before I went to bed, I would lock all the doors, close the lid of each occupied casket, and turn off each rose-colored floor lamp beside the casket. After one or two evenings of visitations you almost felt like you knew the departed.

"Pleasant dreams, Mr. Smith."

"Sleep well, Mrs. Green."

"Good night, Mrs. Calabash, or whoever you are!"

THREE FRIGHT NIGHTS

I remember three unusual nights at Johnson's Funeral Chapel. The first was of my own doing. I conspired with a friend to play a trick on some of the girls from college who were still in town that summer. I put my friend in an empty casket and rolled him into a slumber room. Then I called one of the girls and asked her if she and some of her friends might like to come over for a "tour" of the chapel. When we walked into that particular slumber room, my friend let out with a moan and sat upright in his casket with arms extended. The girls screamed like mad

★　　★　　★　　★　　★　　★　　★

and then chased the two of us all over the place, beating us with their purses. I thought I would die laughing right there in the funeral home!

The second unusual experience was the night I forgot to lock the front door on the Church Street side of the home. Visitation hours were over, and I was already in bed. Suddenly I heard footsteps coming down the hall. I got out of bed and peeked around the corner. I saw a shadowy figure in the hall who, like myself, was probably frozen with fear. He must have realized his mistake. Visiting hours were over. About the time he turned to go, I cleared my throat. That did it for him. He wheeled and raced out of the chapel while I raced down the hall after him to lock the door! I don't know which one of us was scared the most.

The casket display room, like the embalming room, was also on the second floor. A long, wide flight of stairs led up to the display area. One night we had a terrible thunderstorm and Don called me and told me to go upstairs and make sure the roof was not leaking on any of the caskets. I was about halfway up the stairs when a crash of thunder nearly scared me out of my skin. I raced up the stairs, did a quick inventory, and headed down the stairs. About then a bolt of lightning lit up the place like the noonday sun. I happened to glance over to my right and saw a corpse on the embalming table. I had forgotten all about him. The sight of a bald, dead man lit up by a streak of lightning kind of does something to you. It was like a scene out of Frankenstein. I reached the bottom of the stairs in record time and was back in my bed with the covers over my head in no time flat.

The bookkeeper at Johnson's was a little old lady who got on the nerves of some the staff. At least once a week she would go upstairs to inventory the caskets. She would clasp her stenographer's notebook to her breast and announce, "Well, I'm off to the regions above." As soon

★   ★   ★   ★   ★   ★   ★

as she was out of earshot one of the disgruntled staff would say, "I wish she'd be off to the regions below!" I presumed he meant that he wished she would go to that place that none of us want to go to.

TWO SAD FUNERALS

The strangest and perhaps saddest moment at Johnson's was the funeral of some indigent whom nobody knew or claimed as a relative. The day of his funeral, no one came. Not a solitary soul. Don crushed out his cigarette and said, "O.K. boys, it looks like it's us. Let's go." So we all got up, adjusted our ties, marched single file into the chapel and took our places on the front pew. A minister delivered a funeral sermon for a man he did not know. The staff of Johnson's served as the man's pallbearers. We carried him to the hearse just like we would have for any other soul. At the grave it was just the minister and us. I had the thought, "Dear Lord, I don't ever want to go like this."

On another occasion, we had to call a doctor to give a grieving woman a sedative. I knew her – in fact she had worked as a checker at the Hy-Vee grocery store when I was a sacker. Her teen-age son had drowned in a swimming accident. She was so overcome with grief at the graveside service that she had to be restrained lest she leap into the grave on top of the casket. She cried over and over, "I'll never see him again! "I'll never see him again!" I have since thought of what Paul said, "But I do not want you to be ignorant, brethren, concerning those who have fallen asleep, *lest you sorrow as others who have no hope.*" When it comes to the end of life, faith in Christ makes all the difference.

SEEING SUSAN AGAIN

Susan and I continued to correspond with each other every

★ ★ ★ ★ ★ ★ ★

week. But letters weren't good enough. One weekend in June I was able to drive to Sidney, Ohio, to see her. I asked Gary McGlumphry to go with me on the quick trip. We left on a Friday in my Corvair and drove straight through to Sidney, a trip of some 400 miles. We stopped only to put gas in the car and at the same time grab a bite to eat. We did not even stop to change drivers. When I was tired of driving, I would flip backwards over the driver's seat into the back seat while Gary would slide over and take the wheel. This was before the seat belt law was enforced. We got some mighty strange looks from motorists we were passing when we pulled that stunt.

The city of Sidney was named after Sir Philip Sidney, a well-known poet and member of the British Parliament. Voted an "All-America City" in 1964, Sidney is the hometown of Paul Lauterbur, Nobel Prize winner in Medicine and developer of the MRI. Oddly enough, the little town of Sidney, Iowa, just a few miles from Hamburg, was named after the much larger Ohio city. But I really didn't care about any of that. I just wanted to see Susan again. Susan introduced me to her mother, Willa Hand. I thought it sounded like "wilted hand" and we had a good laugh at that. Susan's parents were divorced; her father having left home when she was just nine. Mrs. Hand made pies at a well-know restaurant, "The Spot." In fact, she made over a half-million pies there! In his 2004 re-election campaign, President George W. Bush stopped at "The Spot" for a piece of Mrs. Hand's pie.

Susan and I sat down after supper (and probably had a piece of Mrs. Hand's famous pie) and talked about our wedding. I wanted to get married in November, shortly after Thanksgiving, but Susan wisely thought we should wait until the spring of 1966. After she fulfilled her obligations for the summer with VBS and camp, she planned to get a job

★   ★   ★   ★   ★   ★   ★   ★

and start saving for our wedding. We talked about our future together late into the night.

I went to church with Susan on Sunday morning where Gerald Stoltz preached. Gary and I had spent the night at the parsonage. We had to leave right after church since both Gary and I had to be back at work on Monday morning. I was pretty torn up and could hardly eat the meal that Susan prepared for me. I tearfully kissed Susan good-by never dreaming that we would never wed. The return trip to Iowa was made in the same manner as the trip out to Ohio. I wrote to dad and told him that we had agreed to delay the wedding until the following spring. I believe that Susan wrote to him as well. On July 5 dad wrote back, "I believe you are very wise in delaying the wedding date . . . haste in marriage is not good."

A RESTLESS WIND

Late in June I came down with a bad case of strep throat which resulted in my being hospitalized for about a week. I had a lot of time to think, maybe too much time. I was sad that Susan and I would not be married in the fall after all. I missed her and all my friends from my freshman year. I was sick: physically sick, emotionally lovesick, and even homesick. On June 30 my sister Becky, a student nurse in Council Bluffs, wrote inquiring about my health. Evidently I had written her about my extreme sadness and loneliness because she wrote, "So you're finding out Ottumwa is a pretty lonesome place during the summer. You'll have to come and see me some weekend."

I guess I was too much like the person Gogi Grant sang about in her song "The Wayward Wind." I was a "restless wind that yearns to wander." One day early in July I suddenly quit my job at Johnson's and

★   ★   ★   ★   ★   ★   ★

moved to Hamburg, Iowa. Don Johnson, who paid me well, had even talked of sending me off to embalming school to learn the fine art of being a mortician. I would like to say that I had decided I would "let the dead bury the dead," as Jesus said, to "go and preach the kingdom of God." But that would be too noble and just not true. I was simply irresponsible. In spite of my bravado, the job of dealing with the dead was getting on my nerves. Like a wayward wind, I was out of there.

Everyone at Hamburg was a bit surprised to see me come but seemed glad to see me back again. I moved into the back of the church with my long-time friend, Gary Bryant. I was glad to see the Koch brothers too. So much would happen that summer that Gary dubbed it the "endless summer." It was kind of like "coming home" to me because our family had lived in these same rooms from 1951-1953.

THE ENDLESS SUMMER

I didn't have too much trouble getting jobs that summer because there were plenty of opportunities to put up hay and walk bean fields. I bucked bales for several farmers including Raymond Wise, Dale Emberton, and a man named John Brown. Raymond pampered his work crew, often taking breaks for iced tea and sandwiches. I found a new friend in Gary Sebeck, a local Hamburg boy, who also was on the crew working for Farmer Brown. Sometimes we would get to laughing so hard in the haymow trying to catch up with all the bales that were shooting off the conveyer belt, that we could hardly stand up. Gary was dating a local girl and eventually married her. His father-in-law, however, did not like Gary at all and even threatened his life. One day Gary turned up missing, and he has not been found to this day. Talk around Hamburg is that Gary's father-in-law did what he had threatened to do

★   ★   ★   ★   ★   ★   ★

– murder him and scatter his body around Fremont County. Just a few years ago a skull and some bones were found in the Loess hills surrounding Hamburg. Everyone thought it might be Gary, but forensics proved to be inconclusive. Some day "truth will out" when the murderer of my good friend will stand before the Judge of all.

Gary Bryant and I put up hay for Dale Emberton, Ronald's son. Dale had taught our boys' youth club when we were kids. He drove us a little harder than Raymond had. An older man, Harvey Buxton, also worked for Dale. He had a problem with booze, but could still throw hay bales clear over a loaded hay wagon even when he was "loaded." He cursed something awful, so we nicknamed him "Foul Mouth" Buxton. One evening, after a long, hot day of bucking bales, Gary and I and the Koch brothers were sitting in the grandstand at Clayton Field watching a baseball game. Old "Foul Mouth" had been driving up and down Main Street, drinking and singing a boozy song. The batter hit a foul ball that went backwards over the backstop. It took one bounce on the sidewalk, went directly through Buxton's open driver's side window, and hit old "Foul Mouth" right in the teeth. We about fell off the grandstand laughing. It seemed fitting that "Foul Mouth" Buxton be smacked with a foul ball right in his foul mouth! The next morning he was back heaving bales clear over the wagon even with his usual hangover and his now puffy lips!

I also walked the endless bean fields with the Koch brothers: Kyle, Keevin and Earl. This time I managed not to maim myself as I had done at Goldfield a few years earlier. One night we decided to go to Municipal Stadium in Kansas City and see the Kansas City A's play. As soon as we had cleaned up after work, the four of us piled into my Corvair and took off for Kansas City, 120 miles south of Hamburg.

★   ★   ★   ★   ★   ★   ★

Keevin was driving and we were all having a grand time until one of the front tires on the Corvair blew at 70 mph. How Keevin ever kept that car under control must have been a miracle. The Corvair, with its light front end, swerved from one side of the road to the other until Keevin finally got it stopped by the side of the busy highway. We jumped out, shaking like leaves, and opened the trunk to put on the spare tire. Except there was none! We took the wheel off and I hitched a ride with a trucker into the outskirts of K. C. to get a new tire put on the rim. All we could find was a thief who knew a stranger when he saw one and was glad to "take him in." It took all our money to buy a nearly bald tire and have him put it on the rim. By the time we got it on, the game was half over, so we drove home at a greatly reduced rate of speed, lest this wretched excuse for a tire also blow. We got to bed in the wee hours, only to arise at 5 A.M. to walk the endless bean fields once again.

I BREAK OUR ENGAGEMENT

But what, you may ask, about sweet Susan in Sidney? None of our letters remain to tell the story or even to nail down a definite date with their stamped postmarks. Long ago they were discarded or burned to ashes in the fire. True, we were still writing back and forth about our future lives together. On June 27 Susan was in Florida and was a brides-maid at the wedding of her best friend Bonnie Stoltz who was united in marriage to her sweetheart Stuart Fitzgerald. I am sure she had dreams of our marriage then just as I did when I had attended the wedding of Robert and Joyce in Illinois in late May. She remained in Florida for a youth camp June 28-July 3 and then returned to Ohio to secure a job and start saving for our marriage and life together.

A letter postmarked July 14 arrived from my father. He had just

* * * * * * *

heard (but not from me) that I had quit my job in Ottumwa and moved to Hamburg. He wrote, "Remember that yours is a nature to be hasty, impulsive, and changeable." He also wrote, "Don't confuse your first breath of the loveliness of marriage with the flower itself." But it was too late. I had already written Susan, breaking our engagement. Long years later she told me that my letter was so "final" in its wording that she did not even write back. Today, as I write these words, I am still so ashamed of the cold and callous way I ended our relationship. What is worse, I cannot even recall the rationale I gave her. Whatever words I wrote no longer exist to bear witness against me or explain what I was thinking (if I was thinking at all) at the time. I could blame it on my youth or any number of convenient excuses, but I won't. The words of a Frank Sinatra song come to mind.

"Call me irresponsible." (Leaving my job in Ottumwa was irresponsible.)

"Call me unreliable." (Leaving Brother Ellis to make my car payments proved me unreliable.)

There should have been another line in that song – "Call me reprehensible." What I did to Susan was simply reprehensible.

I did not tell my parents about our breakup. Dad found out several weeks later, "via the grapevine," and on July 29 he wrote me a blistering letter for what I had done. I deserved every word of his literary tongue-lashing. He demanded a "frank and quick reply" to why I had broken my engagement to Susan. I wish now that he had saved my letter so I could tell you what my thinking was. When Susan did not write back, I assumed, wrongly, that she must not have been hurt too bad. So like the fool that I was, I just went on with my life. The words of an old Elvis come to mind: "Don't be cruel to a love that's true." Susan was true

★　★　★　★　★　★　★

to me but I was cruel to her. We would never walk up to the preacher and say, "I do." This is one of the darkest chapters in my life, but I will not cover it up or try to whitewash my actions.

Two years after our broken engagement Susan earned a degree in nursing at the Dayton School of Practical Nursing. In 1969 she married Chester Mullins, a member of my old quartet at Midwestern, had three children, and then went through a painful divorce in 1981. The day after her divorce was finalized (though I did not know this at the time) I ran into her at the Centerville Rally. She looked so lonely and sad. I told her, way, way too late, how sorry I was for my awful behavior. Susan, who remarried in 1984 and is happily married today, and still lives in Sidney, was as gracious as she could be. She murmured something like "You were so young at the time and we didn't know each other very long." Being young, however, does not give one the right to dash someone's hopes or break someone's heart. Neil Sedaka once sang, "Breaking Up Is Hard to Do." Unfortunately, I found it all too easy to do. I now had the unenviable reputation of being a "heartbreaker," and it is a wonder that anyone even dated me from that point on, let alone ever considered marrying me. I "swore off" girls when I returned to Midwestern in August.

An aside: I knew nothing then of the famous "four tempera-ments" but since have learned that I am mostly melancholy and partly choleric. A melancholy's weaknesses include being moody, self-cen-tered, and being off in another world. A choleric can be unsympathetic, rude, and impetuous. That may explain (but not excuse) my behavior to a "T" in the summer of 1965.

Sometimes we sang a hymn in the church at Hamburg that I should have paid more attention to. I don't know how I could have sung "An Evening Prayer" after what I had done to Susan.

*   *   *   *   *   *   *

If I have wounded any soul today,

If I have caused one foot to go astray,

If I have walked in my own willful way,

Dear Lord, forgive!

"If?" I hardly think so. I had indeed wounded a soul. I had most certainly walked in my own willful way. I can hardly sing that song today. Nor can I tell you how many times I have prayed the prayer of David whenever I think of Susan: *"Remember not the sins of my youth."*

MY FIRST CONVERT

The minister at the Hamburg Church of Christ was Eddie DeVries. He saw some potential in me in spite of my obvious immaturity and glaring flaws. If he talked to me about Susan, I do not recall what he said. In time he became a mentor to me (although that word was not in vogue in those days). His wife Betty was also very nice to me, taking me "under her wing" along with their five children. Preachers were about at the bottom of the pay scale back then, and I was surprised to see how little food they had to eat. None of them had a problem with being overweight, that was for sure. When the food was passed around the table, I took smaller portions than I normally would. The older boys all had jobs and were hard workers.

A little chorus that we sometimes sang at the close of a Sunday evening service went something like this:

Lord, lay some soul upon my heart

And love that soul through me,

And may I ever do my part

To win that soul for Thee.

★　★　★　★　★　★　★

But I had yet to win that soul for the Lord. That all changed when I accompanied Eddie and Betty and the whole DeVries family to Etterville, Missouri, for a week at Sho-Me-Mo Bible Camp, July 18-23. Eddie was the night speaker, and there were eight baptisms that week. I had been to many camps before, but this was my first time as a non-camper. Eddie wanted me there with him like Paul wanted Timothy to accompany him on some of his trips. It was at this camp that I led my first person to Christ, a girl named Becky Crouch, from Olean, Missouri, who was probably about 12 years old. The evening service was over and most of the faculty and campers were down at a nearby stream for some baptisms. I asked Becky if there was anything that kept her from giving her life to Christ. After talking for awhile she decided there was nothing to hinder her. Then and there she surrendered to the call of God. When the others returned from the baptisms, I told Eddie what had happened. Eddie, author of *Techniques for Snatching Them from the Flames*, and the best personal worker I had ever seen, was pleased as punch. He wanted me to baptize Becky, but I had not yet had a lesson in how to immerse someone, especially at night and in running water at that. So we all returned to the "cleansing stream" where Eddie baptized Becky. When camp came to an end, I encouraged her to continue in the faith. I followed up with a few discipling letters to let her know that I was praying for her in her new life in Christ. As I recall, she did not come from a Christian home. I hope to meet her again in heaven.

A MEMORABLE MEETING

Another highlight of that summer of 1965 was when the celebrated evangelist Marion McKee from The Church on Imperial Highway in Inglewood, California, came to Hamburg for a two-week

★   ★   ★   ★   ★   ★   ★

revival meeting. Brother McKee was a former night club entertainer who had been converted to Christ in 1936. Since 1941 he had won tens of thousands of people to Christ. Each night the church building was filled to overflowing. McKee would make his grand entrance about halfway through the song service, walking down the aisle carrying his Bible and black briefcase, smiling and nodding at the people. The congregational singing would finally pick up again when he took his seat on stage. McKee's preaching style was like none I had ever heard up to then. He had a flair for the dramatic and knew the power of the pregnant pause. He began one famous sermon by just looking out at the audience for the longest time. At last he spoke – one word – "BABYLON!" The three-syllable word seemed to echo forever around the auditorium. After more silence, he began preaching. The big oak semi-round pulpit at Hamburg was built for a man like McKee. He looked like Elijah the Prophet mounted in his chariot on his way to heaven. Sometimes he would use a lower shelf inside the pulpit to stand up on with one leg and raise himself in the air to accentuate a particular point. He preached sermons like "Payday, Someday" and "A Little Is a Lot about the Lot of Mrs. Lot" and "Sliding into Hell from the Church Pew." One of his sermons was preached entirely from the piano bench. McKee, an accomplished musician and singer, told the story of his life while playing the piano, singing songs from his youth, from his days in show business, his conversion, and his ministry of preaching the Word. He kept a green tank of oxygen on the stage and sometimes would pause in his preaching to take some deep breaths of oxygen. No one could keep the congregation's attention or extend the invitation like McKee.

McKee also stayed in the back of the church building in a room right next to where Gary and I were staying. We could hear every word

★   ★   ★   ★   ★   ★   ★

of his prayers both morning and night (we also could hear every word of his conversations on the phone with his wife back in Los Angeles). It was our job to take his suits to the dry cleaners every morning. The church was not yet air-conditioned, and it was mighty hot and humid in Hamburg in the summer of '65. The great man would not only sweat through his long-sleeve, cufflinked dress shirts, but through his suits as well. He tucked multicolored silk handkerchiefs in his breast pocket and would often whip them out with a flourish to mop his brow in the middle of his sermon. He had a big stylish mane of hair and we were stunned to discover that he used hair spray when he sent us down to Stoner's Drug Store to get some along with a copy of the daily *Omaha World Herald*. When the oxygen tanks ran low, we went to the hospital to get more.

"UNSAFE AT ANY SPEED"

During McKee's meeting I was injured in a car wreck (my second in 10 months) and was taken by ambulance to the local hospital. I was driving down the hill that went past the DeVries's home, going way too fast, and hit a car broadside in the intersection. Carl McSpadden, one of the members of the church, was sitting on his front porch and about fell out of his rocking chair when he saw the accident unfold. The front end of my car, having no engine, crumpled like an accordion. This was the same year (1965) that Ralph Nader, the consumer advocate guru, came out with his book *Unsafe at Any Speed*. He indicted the Corvair in particular. Actually, I was the one who was "unsafe at any speed!"

The doctors at the hospital thought that my spleen might have been ruptured but that test proved to be negative. I was kept in the hospital overnight for observation. Brother McKee came to visit me along

★   ★   ★   ★   ★   ★   ★

with Brother DeVries. The great man took my hand and prayed something like: "O Lord, hear my prayer today. Preserve this boy's life! Raise him up from this bed of sickness, and may he someday be a proclaimer of Your Holy Word!" When someone like Marion McKee prays for you, you get well! I did and was back the next night to hear more from this master expounder of God's Word. On a much sadder note, I learned that on August 10 my Grandma Brown had suffered a severe stroke that left her nearly completely paralyzed. I was devastated.

THE "ENDLESS SUMMER" ENDS

Lorine Emberton, Dale's mother, and one of my mother's dearest friends, took me on as a serious "spiritual son" project and encouraged me to give my best in the service of Christ. She had written several Christian choruses that were published in *Anchor*. One of them was a song called "Dare to Be a Christian." It encouraged all young people to be "Pure in heart and mind . . . / Strong in faith and purpose; humble, meek and kind . . . / Strong and brave and true . . . / Dare to be a Christian, God has need of you." For twenty years or more this godly woman was like a mother to me. Her letters of encouragement that often contained a nice check continued right up to her death. I cried like a baby the day she died, August 27, 1982.

When late August rolled around, I got my Corvair out of the body shop, filled her up with gas at Earl Geyer's DX service station, and headed east to Ottumwa. I had a nice suntan, I had let my hair grow out (no doubt influenced by Marion McKee), and I had a little money that I had earned that summer. (I had to pay Brother Ellis back for the two monthly $50 car payments he had covered for me in July and August.) But I had earned something else too – the unenviable reputation of being a repre-

★　★　★　★　★　★　★

hensible heartbreaker. I was ready for my sophomore year at Midwestern. Whether Midwestern was ready for me remained to be seen.

"ME AND BROTHER MCKEE"

I was glad that seven members of the youth group from Hamburg were enrolled for the 1965-66 school year: Sylvia Braman, Gary Bryant, Gary Cradic, Kyle Koch, Kathleen Peterson, Benny Rippey, and myself. Actually Bryant, Kathleen, and I were listed as being from California, but we all claimed Hamburg as our church home. Gary was a transfer student from Fullerton Community College, Kathleen had moved to Iowa with her grandparents from Los Angeles, and I was listed as being enrolled from San Luis Obispo since dad was now preaching there. We were a close-knit bunch. Hamburg's preacher, my mentor and friend Eddie DeVries, had been added to the faculty and took the train from Hamburg to Ottumwa to teach two days my sophomore year. He stayed in the boys' dorm and was willing to stay up all hours to answer our questions or just talk to us man-to-young man.

As always, the school year began with the Centerville Rally. I sang in a male quartet for the first time, but what stands out in my mind to this day is some of the best preaching I have ever heard in my life. The positive theme "Victory in Jesus" was developed by three homiletical heavyweights: Don Jessup, Marion McKee, and Archie Word. Both Jessup and McKee were from the Los Angeles area where just two weeks prior to the rally race riots in the Watts section had left 30 people dead, hundreds more injured, and millions of dollars in property damage. Each evangelist preached three powerful sermons. Talk about a theological trifecta! They were all great, but I shall never forget McKee's second

$\star$ $\star$ $\star$ $\star$ $\star$ $\star$ $\star$

sermon, "Victory over Philosophical Attachment." He was quoting from Bertrand Russell's book *Why I Am Not a Christian*, responding with Scripture to refute Russell's arguments point by point. At one point he paused, looked up from Russell's book, and asked the audience, "Am I boring you?" A thunderous "No!' went up from the assembled multitude, and so he went on meticulously dissecting the renowned British agnostic's rationale. Later I bought a copy of Russell's book and became convinced that every young Christian should familiarize himself or herself with it before going off to college, especially if going to a secular university. To be forewarned is to be forearmed. The rally supercharged me for another year of school.

It would be a few more years before Janis Joplin would go to the top of the charts with "Me and Bobby McGee," but as far as I was concerned, 1965 was turning out to be the summer of "Me and Brother McKee," and that was just fine with me. Immediately following the Centerville Rally he came to Ottumwa where he conducted a three-week revival meeting for Dick Ellis and the Pennsylvania Avenue church. One night I was part of a male quartet that was to sing before his message. I was on stage sitting right next to him. It was a spirited song service and McKee was slapping his leg in time with the music. When he got tired of slapping his leg, he reached over and started beating out the time on my leg! I was wearing one of those dark green iridescent suits that were in style back then. The auditorium was packed and it was pretty warm and humid. Just before he got up to preach, Brother McKee leaned over to me and said, "Victor, you look like a million tonight."

Somewhat flattered, I responded, "Why thank you, Brother McKee."

He smiled and said, "Yes, all green and wrinkled!"

★   ★   ★   ★   ★   ★   ★

There were 33 decisions for Christ in that meeting. I never saw anyone who could conduct an invitation service like Brother McKee. An elderly man, a Mr. Ives, had come to each service of the meeting, but had not surrendered his life to Christ. Sam Brown and I and many of the students had been earnestly praying for Mr. Ives' salvation. On Sunday morning, after delivering a powerful message, Brother McKee went into the invitation something like this.

Do you see that hand? It is reaching out for you. Do you see that hand? It is the nail-scarred hand of Jesus! He died for you! How can you reject him? Reach out – reach out and put your hand in the nail-scarred hand of Jesus. Come to Jesus today. Say, 'I'm coming home, Lord! I'm coming home to you!

I was watching old Mr. Ives out of the corner of my eyes. His lower lip started trembling, his eyes welled up with tears, and then he threw up his hand in the air, as though taking the hand of Jesus, and stepped out into the aisle. "I'm coming!" he cried as he made his way to the front. "I'm coming!" Years later McKee wrote an article in the *Voice of Evangelism* on how to extend an evangelistic invitation. I clipped it out and kept it in the pulpit during my first full-time ministry (where McKee had also had a ministry) but I never could match McKee in bringing men and women to surrender their lives to Christ. Few men could. Fewer today even try.

Some of the best advice I ever heard came from one of his sermons when he leaned over the pulpit, eyes twinkling, and said, "Be winsome! If you are winsome you will win some to Christ!" Years later I wrote an article that was published in *The Lookout*, "The Best Advice I Ever Received." An important part of personal evangelism is in being *person-*

★   ★   ★   ★   ★   ★   ★

al to the ones we are trying to win for Christ. During one of my ministries I created a character whom I named "Sir Winsome Churchfill" and said that if we were all like Sir Winsome it would not be long until our church would be filled with new converts. We were, and the church was filled, just like McKee said it would be.

MIMICKING McKEE

Throughout the first semester of my sophomore year we had contests in the boys' dorm to see who could imitate McKee's preaching mannerisms the best. With no modesty at all may I say that I won every such contest. I would make my grand entrance into the room carrying a big Bible and briefcase, nodding and smiling to the "congregation." I would lean over the lectern (an old music stand or an ironing board) with my right arm extended and my left leg kicking the air behind me. With a great flourish I would pull out a silk handkerchief and dab my brow. I would grip both sides of the "pulpit" with my hands, a la McKee, and use my best McKee voice to use his best line: *"Keep pressing on to that land of full blessing and salvation!"* My crowning achievement was when I flopped down in a chair, "exhausted" from my "preaching," and reached for my "oxygen" – an Electrolux vacuum cleaner, turn the switch on, and hold the hose to my face. If anyone could somehow match this performance, I would then proceed to do the entire creation *in reverse*! The right arm would go *backwards* and the left leg would shake violently *forwards*. None of this was ever done to make fun of the man. "Imitation is the highest form of flattery."

McKee often quoted poems in his sermons. One was "When Jesus Came to Birmingham" by G. Studdart-Kennedy and another was "When I Met the Master." After McKee had returned to Inglewood, I wrote

★   ★   ★   ★   ★   ★   ★

him a letter, thanking him for his preaching, and asking him if he could send me those poems. I was happy as a clam the day a letter arrived in my mailbox from Brother McKee. Included with his letter were the two poems I had requested. I was the envy of the dorm. I still have that letter, dated November 15, 1965, in which he wrote as follows:

"Dear Victor,

Thank you so much for your letter at the close of the meeting.

I am thankful God was able to use the preaching to encourage you to be faithful to the Lord. It is my sincere prayer, Victor, that you will let God use you in a very definite way to the upbuilding of His Kingdom. Remember, it is not what we say that counts the most; it is what we do.

We need never be ashamed of having a tender heart at any time, or being emotional about the work of Christ.

I appreciated your singing in the meeting, and I trust that all your talents will always be surrendered to Christ.

If I can ever be of help to you in any way, Victor, please let me know.

Yours in the love of Christ,

Marion E. McKee

One evening Gary Bryant and I recreated the story of Abraham sacrificing his son Isaac. I played the part of Abraham and Gary was the "ram in the thicket." When I raised my hand to slay the sacrificial lamb

★   ★   ★   ★   ★   ★   ★

(Gary, lying on a table in the middle of the room as the lamb), the "lamb" let out such a pitiful bleat that my hand froze in mid-air. I said, "I can't do it! Back on the altar, Isaac!" The "audience" rolled on the floor with laughter. I recently heard that someone actually recorded the whole thing. That performance, however, was strictly for the boys' dorm on a slow night. I would never have tried that in chapel or anywhere else! I do believe that those who stand behind the "sacred desk" have a solemn responsibility. That does not mean that the use of humor is ruled out, but humor should never rule the sermon.

MY SOPHOMORE YEAR BEGINS

All returning full-time students were required to sign a statement promising "not to criticize the school nor its faculty members and their decisions." Failure to do so would result in "dismissal from the school." This, no doubt, was in response to the student petition signed by 41 of us in support of Richard M. Ellis. I did not like the idea of signing and briefly considered transferring to Central Christian College of the Bible in Moberly, Missouri. (Why CCCB and not CBS? I cannot remember what my thinking was.) In the end I signed the document but still felt it was an infringement on free speech. It was not long until the demand was put to the test.

To add insult to injury, an incoming freshman, my old pal Terry Crist, was assigned to be room captain. That honor normally went to the sophomore. Terry was kind of embarrassed about it and never once exercised his "powers." I was delighted to have him as my roommate. He was already on fire and ready to preach, and it was not long until he landed a little house church in Ridgeway, Missouri, for his preaching point. Terry was a real go-getter. He got a nice job as a salesman in the

★   ★   ★   ★   ★   ★   ★

men's department at J. C. Penney. He also went head-over heels for Karen Runner, a preacher's daughter from Minnesota. To get ready for his first date, he rushed home from Penneys to clean up. Some of us decided to "help" him get ready. We filled his shampoo jar with cold cream, his deodorant bottle with black cherry pop, and backed up a quarter inch of Brylcreem into his tube of toothpaste, so it took the poor fellow a while to clean up. We told him we had saved him a Cream Puff from supper, and he was so grateful. So gullible, too! He took a big bite and then spat it out for we had replaced the whipped cream with shaving cream. Still, his first date with Karen was a success. All was forgiven when he came into our room just before the dating deadline ended, giddily gushing about Karen like a true freshman.

My sophomore classes included Cults taught by Lafe Culver. Our textbook was *The Chaos of Cults* by Jan Karel van Baalen, who was Christian Reformed. We learned how and why groups like the Jehovah's Witnesses, Mormons, Seventh-Day Adventists, and Christian Scientists differed from orthodox Christianity. A highlight of the class was making a trip to Nauvoo, Illinois, where Joseph Smith and his followers had started to build a Mormon Temple. I earned a B in this class.

I struggled mightily with Greek I under Donald G. Hunt for some time before having to admit, "It's Greek to me" and dropped the class.

I got another B in Acts class. The new Acts instructor was Dewey Lalk. Brother Lalk was suffering from cancer, and sometimes it was painful just to watch him try to teach. When we got to Acts 2:22, 23, where Peter accused the men of Israel of crucifying Jesus of Nazareth, Dewey said, "Now that's personal preaching!" I wrote down the words "personal preaching" in the margin next to those verses. We used J. W. McGarvey's commentary on Acts as a textbook.

★   ★   ★   ★   ★   ★   ★

I also had Brother Lalk for General Epistles (James through Jude). I do not recall what textbook, if any, we used. I got a C in this class. That surely wouldn't qualify anyone to write a commentary on 1 and 2 Peter, but that is exactly what I did for College Press in 1986. Poor Brother Lalk was now in advanced stages of cancer and sometimes he was doubled over in pain at the desk. We were watching a dying man pouring out his soul as an offering to God. I am sure when he came to the next-to-last verse in Jude, that it meant far more to him than to us. "Now unto him that is able to keep you from falling and to present you faultless before the presence of his glory with exceeding joy."

I had another new instructor, Jerry Weller, for two classes that year. I got my only D in my four years at Midwestern in his Poets class (later renamed Wisdom Literature). The class was an overview of Job, Psalms, Proverbs, Ecclesiastes, and Song of Solomon. I am embarrassed to admit that I do not have one conscious memory of being in this class. It's like I wasn't there (maybe the D I got stood for "daydreaming"). I also had Brother Weller for 1 and 2 Corinthians. My Bible probably has more underlining and markings in those books than any other, which proves that I was working hard in this class, yet I received an Incomplete. Apparently I did not get some assignments handed in on time.

Eddie DeVries was my third new instructor my sophomore year. I took his second semester class on The Divine Church and received a C (showing that Brother DeVries didn't play favorites!). I believe he used a set of notes developed by James R. McMorrow. Brother McMorrow, a co-founder of Midwestern, had converted Eddie and was his instructor when Eddie attended college. I already loved the church for which Jesus

★   ★   ★   ★   ★   ★   ★

died, but this class gave me even more appreciation for the body of Christ. Timothy Dwight, while president of Yale University, wrote a great song about the church.

I love Thy kingdom, Lord, the house of Thine abode;

The church our blest Redeemer saved with His own precious blood.

I love Thy church, O God! Her walls before Thee stand,

Dear as the apple of Thine eye, and graven on Thy hand.

BUILDING A LIBRARY

In addition to the textbooks and class notes I was beginning to accumulate, I started to purchase books for my personal reading and study. I joined a religious book club and bought *The Encyclopedia of Religious Quotations* by Frank S. Mead. I have nearly worn the cover off that book. I did wear the cover off *Cruden's Complete Concordance* and *Roget's Thesaurus*. Other than the Bible itself, I have used those two books more than any other books in my 40-plus years of ministry. Other books I obtained in 1966 included: *Halley's Bible Handbook, The Interlinear Translation of the Greek New Testament*, the complete works of *Josephus, World Aflame* (Billy Graham), and *The Christian Persuader* (Leighton Ford, Graham's brother-in-law, and the best book I ever read on personal evangelism). In the next two years I added several more books including *Clarke's Commentary, Barnes' Notes on the New Testament, The People's New Testament with Notes* (B. W. Johnson), and *Sacred History and Geography* (Don DeWelt).

Midwestern also had a nice bookstore, and I purchased several tracts, charts, booklets, and books by Donald G. Hunt and Burton W. Barber. I bought Hunt's *52 Simple, Stimulating Studies, Backsliding*, and two more in his "Simple, Stimulating Studies" series: *Christian*

★   ★   ★   ★   ★   ★   ★

Stewardship and *The Life of Saul of Tarsus*. I also obtained *The Wallace-Barber Debate* (on the instrumental music question) and Barber's *What Determines Acceptable Aids in Matters of Religion?* (another book on instrumental music). Barber was a notable debater and had even debated the celebrated W. Carl Ketcherside at Midwestern several years before I enrolled.

LEAN TIMES

I really missed Mike Gibson who had left Midwestern to go to Puerto Rico where he could be closer to his fiancée. Maybe that is why I applied for an orderly position at St. Joseph's, a Catholic hospital. I didn't get that job, but I did work at three different jobs during my sophomore year. The first was working at a McDonald's restaurant on West Second Street. If memory serves me correctly, hamburgers sold for 15 cents, French fries went for 10 cents, soft drinks were 15 cents, and shakes were 25 cents. One of my jobs was to go down in the basement and bring up heavy burlap bags full of potatoes, which then had to be peeled and washed before being put in the potato slicer. George Petersen, a freshman from Tilden, Nebraska, also worked at McDonald's. We got our meals at a reduced price. One evening George was going off duty as I was coming on. He ordered a hamburger to go. About that time a moth fluttered into the hot bubbling grease where the fries were cooking. The unfortunate moth was instantly cooked. I fished out the crisply done moth, put it on George's hamburger, squirted some ketchup and mustard on it, covered it with a pickle, wrapped it up and handed it to George with a smile. We watched him stroll down the street munching merrily on his "special order." He never knew a thing and we never told him. I am sure that a nicely deep-fried moth contains much

★   ★   ★   ★   ★   ★   ★

good protein. McDonald's became a public company in 1965, selling shares for $22.50 each. I would be a rich man today if I had invested in those shares, but at that time I could barely afford the meals we got there at half price.

Sometimes Gary Bryant and I had to literally pool our pennies and divvy up our dimes just to buy a hamburger and a drink. He would put his 1956 Chevy in neutral when we were going down a hill to save on gas. We once survived a weekend in the dorm on a jar of Skippy peanut butter and a box of Ritz crackers. We didn't even have any change to buy pop in the pop machine. We managed to pry the caps off the captive bottles, insert a straw, and drink the pop in that fashion. We figured if King David, who was also hungry, could enter the sanctuary and eat the consecrated bread – which was not lawful – we could do something similar! We paid back every dime for the "pilfered pop" when we got our next paychecks.

During the Thanksgiving break I found myself "home alone" in the dorm, my family in far away California, probably feasting on turkey while I, like the Prodigal Son, was about to "perish with hunger." A married student, Ralph Smoot, lived with his wife "Cookie" in a downstairs apartment. His wife was off visiting her parents in Chicago or somewhere. Ralph must have heard my pacing on the floor above because he came upstairs and asked me if I wanted to join him for lunch. Did I ever! We dined that Thanksgiving Day on bologna sandwiches garnished with mustard and lettuce and washed down with a big glass of cold milk. Never did bologna taste so good. I felt like the rich man in Luke 16 who "fared sumptuously." To this day I am wont to say, "Sumptuous repast" after a particularly satisfying meal. The Bible says, "In everything give thanks." I gave thanks with every bite, believe you me! When

*　　*　　*　　*　　*　　*　　*

our Thanksgiving "feast" was over, I thanked Ralph for his hospitality and went back upstairs to hit the books and count the hours until Gary would return and we could go down to St. Mary's outdoor basketball court and shoot a few hoops.

A GIRL REMEMBERED

Many of the students at Midwestern enjoyed going to Des Moines on Saturday nights to hear nationally known gospel quartets sing at the KRNT Theater. The events were billed as "Singathons" and were promoted heavily by a big-time radio personality named Smokey Smith. When a handbill popped up on the bulletin board in the main lobby of Midwestern announcing a big Singathon on October 23, I was intrigued. Kerry Conaway and I decided we would go, but we wanted to take some girls with us. He had his eye on Kathleen Peterson, but it took him forever to get up the courage to call her on the phone. He ran through a couple of "dry runs" on the phone, but he was so nervous he kept pronouncing her name "Kafreen." "Kath-LEEN," I would yell at him. "She's not a cup of coffee (caffeine) Kerry, she's a girl named 'Kath-LEEN!'" The poor guy finally managed to make the call and danced a merry jig when she accepted. Now it was my turn. Who would I ask?

I had not dated anyone at school since I had broken my engagement to Susan Hand in July. But I remembered a girl whom I had met at a volleyball game earlier in the year on a lovely spring day, a Sunday afternoon to be exact. I was at the dorm doing some reading or studying when one of the students came running up the stairs and told me that there was a big volleyball game going on at Wildwood Park on the South Side. A young people's group from an a cappella Church of Christ had invited us to come and join them in the game. So several of us piled into

★　★　★　★　★　★　★

our cars and drove to Wildwood Park. Mike Gibson was with me. When we got out of my car and saw that the game was co-ed, I said to him, "Oh, great. I thought this was going to be a *real* game. Come on, let's go back to the dorm." But Mike prevailed upon me to stay, and so we joined the church youth group for the game. Good thing for me that he prevailed as you are about to see.

When I played ball, I always played all out; there was no give-and-take. Right across the net from me was a pretty girl, a brunette, whom I thought was very attractive. No matter! When I spiked the ball, she would duck her pretty head and just laugh. She was wearing a black scarf, a white blouse, and a black skirt. Once I spiked the ball off her head with such force that her scarf fell to the ground. I picked it up and hung it on the net for her to retrieve. One of the girl's sisters later said that I was a "clown," and she was right.

Several months later I was driving on the South Side when I spotted the dark-haired girl and one of her sisters walking near the Fareway Grocery Store. I whipped my car into the parking lot, rolled down my window, and visited with them for awhile. I learned that her name was Evelyn Saylor and that she lived next door to Easter's Super-Valu, where I had once worked. Something clicked in my mind. I remembered that she often came into the store to buy a few items. After visiting for awhile, I asked them if they would like a ride home. Gloria, Evelyn's sister, said no. (Later, Evelyn confessed to me that she really would have liked a ride home, but not because she was interested in me. She was tired, carrying a big package, and would have liked a ride!). I bade them farewell and drove off, almost hitting a light pole in the process! I can't swear to it, but I thought I heard a faint trill of laughter behind me.

★　　★　　★　　★　　★　　★　　★

OUR FIRST DATE

So, after two or three chance encounters earlier in the year, why did Evelyn Saylor, of all girls, come to mind? I never had thought of her in any romantic way when Susan and I were going together. I have to say that because someone had started a rumor that Evelyn was the reason I had broken up with Susan. I also figured I was *persona non grata* with any of the girls from Midwestern. Providence is the only explanation I have to offer. It wasn't fate, or luck, or anything other than the providence of God. Unlike Kerry, I had no problem making the call on the first try.

"Hello, my name is Vic Knowles. May I speak to Evelyn please?"

Evelyn's mother had answered the phone. She called Evelyn to the phone and handed the receiver to her.

"Hello, Evelyn. This is Vic Knowles." Pause.

"I met you at a volleyball game earlier this year. I'm the guy who knocked your scarf off. And nearly drove into a light pole at Fareway." Recognition.

"I was wondering if you would like to go with me and another couple from Midwestern to the Singathon in Des Moines this Saturday night." Another pause.

"Well, I'm already planning to go with someone else," she finally said.

I hadn't figured on this! But then she explained. "I'm going with my dad and some of my sisters."

I plunged into what seemed to me to be chilly waters. "Well, wouldn't you like to go with me instead of your dad?" After all, nothing ventured, nothing gained.

Believe it or not, it worked! She accepted my invitation and I told her when we would come by to pick her up.

★　★　★　★　★　★　★

I hung up the phone and said to Kerry, "Now, *that's* how you do it!" But inwardly I was relieved the call was over. What if she had said, "No, I would rather go with my dad"? That might have ended everything right there.

Evelyn later told me that her mother said I had a nice voice.

And so it came to pass that on a pleasant Sabbath evening, October 23, 1965, we had our first date, or to be technically correct, our first double date. We picked up Evelyn right on time. She was wearing a dark brown skirt, a yellow blouse with tiny brown polka dots and a bow at the collar. I wore a sport coat and tie. I probably splashed on a little extra Aqua Velva Ice Blue. As the ad said, "There's something about an Aqua Velva man!" Confession: I'm still using Aqua Velva Classic Ice Blue. Do you think I'd ever use anything else after that first date?

The KRNT Theater was the largest theater in the Midwest. It was located at 10th and Pleasant Street in Des Moines and seated more than 4,000 people. The domed ceiling was studded with thousands of tiny lights. It had been designed by an astronomer to duplicate a summer night's sky. Four groups were performing that night. The Frost Brothers were the opening act, followed by the Elmer Childress Family, and then The Plainsmen Quartet. The headliners were David Ingalls and The Vanguards. I couldn't believe the sound coming off that big stage. These guys were good! I especially like the last two groups.

At intermission I met Evelyn's father, Bob, by chance. We were washing our hands in the men's room. He was one big man, about six foot-two inches tall and weighing in at over 300 pounds. I can't remember if he said "How do you like the singing?" or "How do you like my daughter?" Either way, I liked them both just fine.

On the drive back to Ottumwa, Kerry pulled in at a Dairy Queen.

★   ★   ★   ★   ★   ★   ★

We went in to get some refreshments for the girls. When I got back into the car, I reached over and pinched Evelyn's nose. She told me later that she thought that was pretty fresh of me and I guess it was. At first I thought she had green eyes but later discovered that they were actually hazel. They sure did compliment her almost olive skin and beautiful long brown hair.

"SUZIE" AND THE SAYLORS

Evelyn Sue Saylor was born in Ottumwa on March 10, 1946. Her father worked at John Deere and her mother was a homemaker. Evelyn was the sixth of eight children. In time I met her brothers, Paul, Bobby, and Kevin, and her sisters, Priscilla, Lauraly, Gloria, and Eva. The family lived in a big two-story house on 202 N. James Street. Within walking distance was the church they attended, the 100-member Church of Christ on the corner of Finley Avenue and Adella Street. The church had no paid minister, and Evelyn's father did some of the teaching and preaching. The Saylors, like the Knowles family, were a close-knit bunch and enjoyed singing together. I always felt welcome in their home during the nearly two years that Evelyn and I were dating.

Evelyn's father and I hit it off real well. He was a Renaissance man and that appealed to me. He was well read and could discuss any topic you wanted to talk about with confidence and knowledge. Despite his size he could do something I could not do – bend over and touch the floor. He was quite athletic and loved to bowl, pitch horseshoes, and play volleyball. He also loved words and could beat anyone at the game of Anagrams or Scrabble. One of the things I liked to do with Bob was take the test in *Reader's Digest*, "It Pays to Increase Your Word Power." One month I would read them to Bob and he would guess, and the next

★   ★   ★   ★   ★   ★   ★

month he would read them to me and I would guess. He always beat me by one or two words. I also got to hear him speak a few times at the church on Finley and Adella. He was a gifted orator and could make the Word of God come alive when he spoke. The other speakers, although earnest, were kind of boring.

Evelyn's mother, Ethel, took a while to warm up to me. She was so concerned that her daughter was now going with a boy who was "not one of us" ("us" being the Church of Christ). "Now, Suzie," she would say, "You must be careful." "Suzie" was what she called Evelyn since her middle name was Sue. Even though she thought I had a nice voice, she was not so sure about my salvation (because I went to a church that used instrumental music). But Ethel was a good woman at heart and was never anything but kind and gracious to me when I was in her home. She loved the Lord and sometimes wrote poetry or songs to express her love for Him. Late at night, after everyone had gone to bed and the dishes were done and the house was tidied, Ethel would read her Bible at the dining room table. Sometimes she would fall asleep at the table as she read the Word of God beyond the midnight hour.

We found it interesting that our mothers had the same first name (Ethel) and that Evelyn's mother's maiden name was Black whereas my mother's (adopted) maiden name was Brown. My father was 26 and my mother was 19 when they were married, and Evelyn's father was 19 and her mother was 26 when they were married. Both men were preachers (Bob, non-salaried) and both women were homemakers.

I liked all of the Saylors. Paul, the oldest, was a good conversationalist and had a zest for life. Bobby was an athlete, and I took to him right away. That winter we went sledding at Wildwood Park. We found an old refrigerator door and went down a steep hill standing up in our

★   ★   ★   ★   ★   ★   ★

super unit. Sledders scattered left and right when they saw us coming down on this monster ride! Kevin was still in high school then and worked at Easter's Super-Valu where I had once worked (and would return to work in May). One day the store was robbed while Kevin was carrying out groceries for a customer. Kevin met the thief when he was coming out the door. Not knowing what had happened inside, Kevin said, "Thank you, come again." The robber said, "I don't think so." All of Evelyn's sisters, except Gloria, were married so it took me longer to get to know them. I liked Gloria the best. She was more my age and was with Evelyn a lot. For some reason I started calling her "Glorified Rice." That was a special dessert dish my mother used to make.

On our second date I took Evelyn to Molly's Restaurant, the nicest and most popular place in town. I got a nice window seat where we could see the swans on the lagoon. From then on it seemed that our lives started flowing together just like a river. For our 40th wedding anniversary I wrote Evelyn a poem which I titled "One Rolling River." The first two verses of the poem read:

> *There comes a point where two lives meet*
> *And never are the same,*
> *And so it was with you and me*
> *The day we one became.*
>
> *Around a bend we met that day*
> *Two lives became a team,*
> *I a raging rapids*
> *And you a gentle stream.*

A river, however, does not always flow smoothly. Our personalities and our temperaments were not the same. I was a melancholy/chol-

★ ★ ★ ★ ★ ★ ★

eric, and Evelyn was a sanguine/phlegmatic. (Neither of us, of course, knew much about the four temperaments at this point in our life.) Evelyn was, by nature, cheerful, optimistic, friendly, sympathetic, kind, and reconciled to life. When we talked about a future family, Evelyn, coming from a large family, wanted children, lots of them. I, however, was thinking in terms of one or two at the most. I wanted to give her lots of nice things, but "things" were not what she was interested in. She was (and remains) a "people person." She loved people, made friends easily, and always wanted to do something for others. And even though we came from the same religious heritage, we also had some differences there that needed to be addressed. And something else.

THE CONFESSION

After we had been going together for awhile, I felt that I must confess to Evelyn how I had treated Susan. Although I appeared pretty "happy-go-lucky" to most people, my conscience was still accusing me. One night, while driving down Madison Street, I told Evelyn that I had to tell her something. I would start to talk and then stop. I just couldn't get the words out. Evelyn began to wonder if it was something really horrible, like I had committed murder or was on drugs or some such thing. (Not that breaking an engagement is not a horrible thing to do.) Finally I told her what I had done. I wanted her to know what she was getting into. I was certainly not the nicest guy in the world. She needed to know that before things went any further. After I had finally finished with my confession, Evelyn gave me a hug and thanked me for my raw honesty. I think she was just relieved to know she was not in the same car with a serial killer like the "Boston Strangler!"

*   *   *   *   *   *   *

FIRST KISS

We continued to see each other through the fall. Sometimes we went to parties or the park, and other times we went on drives and had long talks. I was trying very hard to overcome my impulsive nature. I would not even tell Evelyn that I loved her. I would tell that her that I "lived" her – a word I coined from "liked" and "loved." I told her that my feelings for her were more than "like" but less than "love." She stayed with me anyway. I refused to even kiss her. She began to wonder if she had bad breath or something. She did not. I just did not want to push things as I had done before and ruin everything. Slowly but surely I was learning.

I liked going over to her house after work most of all because it wasn't officially considered a "date" by the rules. Some of the guys in the dorm "gnashed their teeth" over this "injustice," but was it my fault they were dating girls who didn't live in Ottumwa? I think not. Evelyn would fix me a hamburger while I read the *Ottumwa Courier*. Sometimes we would listen to records. The Plainsmen, whom we had heard at the KRNT Theater, was one of our favorite groups. We still like to put an LP record on and listen to songs like "Touch the Hand of the Lord," "Wasted Years," "There's a Light Guiding Me," and "When I Stand with God." We also liked "Back Beat Symphony (Rock and Roll in the Sound of Symphony)" by 101 Strings and Montovani's dreamy "Greensleeves."

Our first kiss, however, was not on a romantic song like "Greensleeves" but a song that just happened to be playing on the console radio in the living room at that magic moment. The song was "Apache," a big instrumental hit for The Ventures in 1962. Every time we hear it we smile and kiss – unless I am driving down the road. Then we just smile.

★   ★   ★   ★   ★   ★   ★

THE WHIRLWIND YEAR COMES TO AN END

In December I was invited by George Conz to preach in Albia, Iowa. Sam Brown, on his way to preach in Knoxville, dropped me off in Albia. (Many years later I learned that George Bennard, author of "The Old Rugged Cross," had once lived and preached in Albia.) I had developed a brand new sermon which I titled "Judas, the Devil." This was based on the words of Jesus in John 6:70, "Have not I chosen you twelve, and one of you is a devil?" Before the service started I went outside and earnestly prayed that God would help me preach a good sermon. And I believe he did. George and Melva had me over to their house afterwards, and we had a great time of fellowship while waiting for Sam to pick me up. I'm forever thankful for men like Brother Conz who gave me a chance to preach when others would not give me the time of day.

Several days after Christmas I received a wonderful letter from Beulah Shaw in Phoenix, Arizona, that she had written on Christmas Eve. Beulah had taken me in as a little boy when my mother was in the hospital for several months when we lived in Clay Center, Nebraska. She praised me for my progress at school and apologized for forgetting my birthday in November: "Spankings are for 'little boys' and I feel you have outgrown such." She also wrote, "Be kind to the girls and I dare say they will return like treatment." She closed with words that tugged at my heart: "Be good, Victor. Seems like I'll always remember you as part mine." That letter got me through the blue Christmas holidays, as I could not afford to be "home for Christmas" in California as I had the year before.

On New Year's Eve Evelyn and I attended a party sponsored by one of the members of the Finley and Adella church. We sang, played

★   ★   ★   ★   ★   ★   ★

games, and had hot chocolate at an old-fashioned taffy pull. It was a pleasant way to bring 1965 to a close. But what did God have in store for me in the New Year that was to come? Good things, bad things, things that made me happy, and things that made me sad. Through it all I recalled the words of Paul. "And we know that all things work together for good to them that love God, to them who are the called according to his purpose" (Romans 8:28). All these things would help me become "more than a conqueror." A kid named Victor was about to become more than a Victor in a way that only God could do.

TWO PREACHERS AND A RUNAWAY ROLLAWAY

The first Sunday in 1966, January 2, I went to the Pennsylvania Avenue church "as was my custom." That particular Lord's day we had a special guest speaker, and he made a big impression on me. He was F. J. Winder, the father of Nancy Ellis, and minister of the Alberta Street Church of Christ in Portland, Oregon. I sat in rapt fascination as he preached on "The Love of God" – with nothing but an open Bible in his hand and open tears in his eyes. To this day I do not recall hearing a better sermon on God's love for lost mankind and for the church of God which He purchased with His own blood. Later, I obtained his famous book of sermons, *That They May Be Won* (first issued in 1936) and used it for many years. I was always honored when he – an elder statesman – wrote to me, a young preacher. I learned from Brother Winder that preaching does not have to be aggressive in order to be effective: that preaching from the heart is what reaches the hearts of the hearers. I know he reached mine that day.

The annual January Gathering, a big preaching rally held at the Pennsylvania Avenue church that always kicked off the second semester,

*   *   *   *   *   *   *

rolled around at the end of the month. The special guest speaker that year was William E. Paul from the Union Park Church of Christ in Orlando, Florida. Like Eddie DeVries in Hamburg, Brother Paul was responsible for sending many young men and women from his church to his alma mater in Ottumwa. I was a good friend of his son Terry and was glad to hear his father speak. All of the messages were from Paul's second letter to Timothy. Was I the only one who saw irony in a preacher named Paul, who also had a son named Timothy back in Florida, and had sent many home-grown "Timothies" to Midwestern, preaching from the apostle Paul's letter to Timothy? Brother Paul had a keen, analytical grasp of Scripture and a dry sense of humor. I appreciated both. Soon I started receiving his monthly paper *News & Truths*. The man knew how to write, and that was a third reason why I liked him. Thirty years later the two of us would coauthor a 373-page hardback book that was published by College Press, *Taking a Stand: The Story of the Ottumwa Brethren.*

During the Gathering we had out-of-town guests stay at both dorms. We needed an extra bed at the boys' dorm for a guest, so Keevin Koch and I were commissioned to go to the girls' dorm and bring back a rollaway bed. We got the bed and started carefully walking it down the hill. Between the two dorms stretched Highway 63. Suddenly the rollaway bed developed a mind of its own and became a runaway bed. Bad bed! We finally caught up with it, hopped on, and took a wild ride down the hill and across the busy four-lane highway, cars honking and brakes screeching. We sailed across the "finish line" unscathed. Keevin's recollection is that I grinned at him and said, "That was fun! Let's do it again!"

★   ★   ★   ★   ★   ★   ★

A TOOTHLESS GURU AND A NEW JOB

One day in January Gary Cradic had all his teeth pulled. While he was waiting for his new set of dentures, he was most miserable. He could not eat solid food. Sometimes I would bring him a bowl of soup or a malted milk. Even in his "infirmity," however, he managed to entertain the boys in the dorm. He would sit cross-legged on a bed with a blanket draped over his shoulders, looking like some guru from the Far East. He had a great spiel on "Life" that went something like this. "Without teeth, there can be no chewing of food. Without the chewing of food, there can be no digestion. Without digestion there can be no nourishment. Without nourishment there can be no life. There is no life without teeth!" We would howl with laughter and beg him to do it again.

Sometime in January I returned to Easter's Super Valu on the South Side. You don't have to have a degree from Yale to figure out why I made this move. Evelyn lived right next door to the grocery store. Mom sent me some white shirts so I would look spiffy on the job. Most of the fellows in the dorm hired one of the girls in school to iron their shirts. One day someone noticed what a nice job I did ironing my shirt (my secret was plenty of Niagara Spray Starch). I charged them 25 cents a shirt. I even ironed a blouse for Evelyn one day. Her brother Kevin was a sacker at the store and her aunt Vi worked in the office. She recommended me to management to be a cashier so I got an "insider" promotion. The only bad thing was I couldn't carry Evelyn's purchases home for her. Not that she needed any help in carting home a half-gallon of milk or a loaf of bread!

In one of her rare but greatly appreciated letters that I received from mom she wrote, "Go easy on the matrimony. Give yourself time to

★   ★   ★   ★   ★   ★   ★

grow up. These teen marriages don't turn out so good you know. You are not a teenager now, but not far removed!" I did not remind her that she was 19 when she married my father! I wanted those shirts to keep coming.

THE NEGRO WHO CAME IN FROM THE COLD

One cold winter night there was "no room in the inn" for a guest. One of the fellows from the dorm brought in a Negro man whom he had seen hitchhiking on Highway 63. He had compassion on him and brought him to the dorm, as any of us would have done. Somebody ran down to the Canteen and got the man a couple of sandwiches. Somebody else filled the bathtub with hot water so he could take a nice bath and warm up. Somebody else started to make up a bed so he could have a comfortable place to sleep that night. Somehow word of what we were doing got back to the powers that be. Someone either came (or called) and issued a stern directive that we could not allow the man to stay in the dorm. This set off a firestorm of protest by nearly all of us, but all to no avail. We had to send the man back out into the cold. Terry Crist gave him his own Bible. Someone gave him a heavy winter coat. Someone gave him a blanket. We stuffed his pockets full of candy bars and gospel tracts and took up an impromptu offering. We gathered around him and prayed for him before he left. We apologized to him that he could not stay with us that night. He said something like, "Now, boys, that's all right. These things happen." And then he vanished into the cold dark night.

The final straw was when someone decided that the bathtub in which the Negro had taken a bath must be scrubbed with Lysol. We just about lost it. We raged up and down the halls yelling about the injustice

★   ★   ★   ★   ★   ★   ★

of it all. We went to bed fuming, thinking of the man who was sent back into the cold. The next morning in chapel we nearly had an insurrection. We sat there with sullen faces, arms crossed, barely listening to the sermon. This went on for several days until one of the faculty members got up and told us to cut it out. "What was done was done." We did, but not with any joy or enthusiasm. We could not understand what was going on. We knew that Negroes had a tough time down south but this was Iowa. This was a Christian institution. Although we did not have any Negro students the four years I was in school, others had been at Midwestern as far back as 1949. Patricia Estes, sister of the world famous baritone and opera singer Simon Estes, had gone to Midwestern. I had purchased an LP record of Marshall Keeble's sermons in the school's bookstore (Keeble, a Negro, was a famous Church of Christ preacher). We were not accusing the faculty of being racist; we just wanted an explanation. Since we never got one, at least to our satisfaction, here is what I finally surmised.

There was lots of racial tension in the 60s, including race riots in Watts, Detroit, Chicago, and other cities. The year before, in Selma, Alabama, Dr. Martin Luther King Jr. and more than 700 marchers were arrested for protesting discrimination in the voting process. Sheriff's officers used cattle prods and billy clubs on the marchers. Malcom X, a rival to Elijah Muhammad, was gunned down in Harlem by someone from the Nation of Islam. Then came the historic 50-mile march from Selma to Montgomery. King and Ralph Abernathy led 25,000 civil rights demonstrators on that famous "Freedom Walk." But some people saw King as a stooge for the communists. I heard one area preacher refer to him as "Martin Lucifer Coon." As I look back on the incident today, it may not have been political or racial at all. It could have been as simple as they

★　★　★　★　★　★　★

were looking out for our best interests. They didn't know the stranger from Adam (and neither did we). In fact, in June of 1966 a man named Richard Speck crept into a women's dorm in a nursing school in Chicago and murdered eight young nurses. I suppose something like that could have happened in our dorm in "Little Chicago" (Ottumwa). Still, what happened that night never sat well with those of us who protested what happened. None of us were dismissed from college for our little "Civil Rights" demonstration.

THE BEATLES VS. JESUS

Other things aroused our sense of righteous indignation in 1966. One was when John Lennon of the Beatles told the press, "We are more popular than Jesus Christ." The trouble was, Lennon was probably speaking the truth. They *were* more popular than Jesus was with many young Americans. Some used the incendiary quote to rail on the Beatles in sermons. That was in March. In April an occultist named Anton S. LaVey shaved his head, grew a goatee, and founded the Church of Satan in San Francisco. He conducted satanic baptisms, funerals, and even a "Satanic Mass." Later he came out with *The Satanic Bible*. This was just too much. We felt like this was a frontal assault on Christianity, and so he, like Lennon, became grist for the preaching mill.

I had purchased a nice reel-to-reel tape recorder and was anxious to try it out. I drove to Hamburg one weekend in April to attend a preaching rally and record the sermons of Don Pinon and Lafe Culver. When the rally was over Brother Culver complimented me on my grow-ing interest and involvement in spiritual things. Mark Twain once said, "I can live for two months on a good compliment." That compliment buoyed my spirits more than he could ever know. I think I knew how

★   ★   ★   ★   ★   ★   ★

Timothy must have felt when the great apostle Paul wrote to him, ". . . that your progress may be evident to all" (1 Timothy 4:15 NKJV). Even my roommate Terry, whom I had been so terrible to on the night of his first date, invited me to preach at Ridgeway, Missouri. We got up early that Sunday morning in April and made the trip. I preached in the morning and he preached in the evening, and we kept each other awake on the 90-mile return trip to Ottumwa by singing several songs made famous by The Blackwood Brothers.

CONTRASTING COUNSEL

By the end of April, Evelyn and I had decided that we wanted to be married some time in the future. I wrote my parents and told them of our desire to be one. Dad wrote back, "Between you two there is a bond of troth already forged." He cautioned against going public with an "official" engagement notice. No doubt he had in mind my broken engagement with Susan Hand. We took his advice to heart and settled on an "agreement" to marry.

In May the Prater-Mickey Evangelistic Team rolled into town for a two-week revival at the Pennsylvania Avenue church. Ken Mickey was the song evangelist and his father-in-law, Malburt Prater, was the preaching evangelist. One night he was really into his message on the works of the flesh. He grabbed the pulpit with both hands, leaned over, and thundered, "I'd rather be an adulterer than a 'homo.'" Gary Bryant and I were sitting next to each other, and one of us whispered to the other, "Who wouldn't?" Not that either one of us had any intentions of being an adulterer!

There was a packed house every night. Evelyn's father came to some of the services. Most of the students, including Evelyn and me,

★ ★ ★ ★ ★ ★ ★

attended as many nights as we could. Some people were concerned because she was from a Church of Christ that opposed instrumental music. They reasoned, falsely, that such a congregation could not be the "one, true church." Of course, there were many on her side of the aisle who were concerned that I was from a Church of Christ that used instrumental music. They reasoned, just as falsely, that such a congregation could not be the "one, true church." One afternoon Brother Prater asked us to meet with him for a counseling session. Very seriously he advised us to break up our relationship because, in his view, such a union would just not work. It was not like I was dating an unbeliever, a Roman Catholic, or even a Southern Baptist! I knew that Evelyn was a good girl, with a good heart, who came from a good family, and worshiped at a good congregation that was part of our shared religious heritage, and had the highest principles imaginable. I was somewhat offended but managed to keep my feelings under control. As I look back on it, I am sure that Brother Prater was as sincere as he could be in his feelings and felt compelled to counsel us as he did.

The counsel we received from Eddie DeVries, however, was entirely the opposite. He patiently helped us work through some of our religious differences. He even came to Evelyn's home and had several studies with visiting preachers who happened to be in town for a gospel meeting at her church. These meetings were conducted in a fine spirit even though one preacher got up abruptly and left the house. Where others saw no hope, Eddie was extremely hopeful. In fact, on numerous occasions, almost like a prophet, he told us that he felt that God had caused our paths to cross in order to accomplish something significant for the kingdom some day. He would often remind us of the story of Esther and would quote Esther 4:14, ". . . who knoweth whether thou art

*   *   *   *   *   *   *

come to the kingdom for such a time as this?" He believed in us and believed that something good and even great was going to happen. I couldn't help but think of Brother Eddie when Evelyn and I were presented with the "2004 Spiritual Development Award" for "continual efforts to uphold the unity of believers as prayed for by Jesus" at the Pepperdine University Bible Lectures. Howard Publishing Company (eventually taken over by Simon and Schuster) sponsored the award. Little wonder, then, that I asked Eddie to be one of my groomsmen when Evelyn and I were married a year or so later.

"PUSHING DRUGS"

My sophomore year ended and I secured a new and better paying job at Hoffman Drug. The Hoffman building was the tallest building in town, located in the heart of the city, and was a hub of activity. An elevator took folks up to their apartments or offices. Sometimes I spelled the elevator operator so he could get a bite to eat. The main floor was the big drug store, pharmacy, and lunch counter where patrons could order sandwiches and coffee. The food was prepared in the basement kitchen and was brought up by a dumbwaiter. I liked working for Dick Hoffman who was a real gentleman and a scholar. Part of my duties was helping create window displays. But my favorite part was delivering prescriptions around town.

Many people around town preferred to phone in their prescriptions. When the order was ready, Mr. Hoffman would ring the bell and I would hop in Hoffman's white Willys Jeep, drive to the address attached to the red and white paper sack, collect the money and hand over the drugs or medicine. I have joked that I "pushed drugs" in the 60s to work my way through college. In time I got to know every street and

★   ★   ★   ★   ★   ★   ★

back street in Ottumwa. I loved roaring around the town in that zippy little Jeep. It had a canvas top that could be removed in nice weather giving me free and natural "air conditioning." Any time I was in the area where Evelyn was babysitting, I would whip the Jeep up to the curb, hop out, and pop in to say a quick hello.

A BITTERSWEET SUMMER

Sometimes I would attend a Sunday evening service with Evelyn at her church. The place was usually packed because they had a large youth group at that time. The congregation was the oldest of any in the Restoration Movement in the city (established in 1880). Evelyn's maternal grandfather, Burley Black, had been one of the principal leaders in the church. When Scripture was read at the beginning of the service, the one who read the Scripture would say, "Thus, if correctly read, is . . ." and would then name the text read. Everyone was friendly to me. (Still, after all these years, I have never been called on to even offer a prayer. That bothers Evelyn more than it does me.) One night we attended a "gospel meeting" (what "our" churches would call a "revival meeting") at a rural church and heard one of their best-known speakers, Fred Kirbo, preach. It may have been at Savannah, Iowa. I enjoyed his preaching but was somewhat bemused when the song leader announced, before leading the congregation in a hymn, "Now, on this verse we will change it from 'Where the glad *harps* ring' to 'Where the glad *voices* gladly sing.'" The hymn, "A New Song," was actually based on Revelation 14:1-3. Not to harp on the incident but I thought that came pretty close to "taking away from the words of the book" (Revelation 22:19) or at least editing the word of God.

Dewey Lalk's valiant two-year battle with cancer came to an end

★   ★   ★   ★   ★   ★   ★

on June 16. Brother Lalk had been a living legend in the fellowship of churches in Iowa. He was one of the first students to enroll at Midwestern (1947). All the young people who had sat under his teaching and preaching in Christian Service camps especially loved him. No doubt that is why his funeral was conducted at Sharon Bluff Bible Camp, a camp that he had spent hundreds of hours in building. Evelyn and I attended his funeral service along with scores of other students and hundreds of mourners. Donald G. Hunt officiated. Brother Lalk, who had been converted to Christ in 1946, had just 20 years to preach the gospel. He was only 44 when he died. That fact was not lost on me.

On a happier note, Evelyn and I attended the wedding of my old pal Gary Cradic and his bride-to-be Sherril Johnson on July 30. I bought a new suit for the occasion. Eddie DeVries, Gary's preacher at Hamburg, officiated at the wedding. It was the longest wedding sermon that I have heard to this day! At the reception I presented Gary with Billy Graham's new book *World Aflame*. Evelyn thought that a book was kind of an odd gift for a wedding present, but I assured her this wasn't just any book. I had a copy of my own, and I figured what was good for me was good for him. I guess Evelyn was thinking of Sherril!

My sister Muriel had graduated from High School in California in May and by mid-July – accompanied by Juli Winder, daughter of F. J. Winder – came to Ottumwa for a few days before winging her way to join a mission team in San Juan, Puerto Rico. She was the first of our family to meet Evelyn. I was pretty proud of her for taking such a big step in her life. She was a missionary at 18 while I, "The Duke of Ottumwa," had not yet caught fire at a ministerial school. Muriel met several people in Puerto Rico whom I knew including my pal Mike Gibson who by this time had married Judy Buzick.

★   ★   ★   ★   ★   ★   ★

Archie Word was holding a revival meeting in August in Hamburg, so one weekend Evelyn and I drove over to hear him preach. Before the services Eddie DeVries introduced Brother Word to Evelyn, explaining that she was from a Church of Christ whose practice was to use one cup in the communion service. Evelyn was not too impressed when Brother Word harrumphed and said, "I guess they must have used a bathtub for communion in Jerusalem!" He walked off leaving both of us speechless. I thought, "This was not exactly the way to 'win friends and influence people.'" In years to come, however, she called him, affectionately, "Old Jerusalem Bathtub."

It was at Hamburg, however, that Evelyn had an epiphany. Instrumental music in worship had never bothered her that much because she saw it as a nonissue. But since her church always used one cup in the communion, and communion was the holiest part of worship, she was reticent to worship where tiny individual communion cups were used. Brother DeVries assured her that she would be served the communion in one cup following the morning service. The three of us went into a side room (which would become my office in 1968) where Brother DeVries prayed over the elements. When he presented the communion tray to her, with a solitary individual cup in the center, she was startled. At first, she felt betrayed because the cup was the same thing that everyone else was using. But then immediately the thought came to her, "It is one cup and everyone else had taken one cup too." The cup, whether large or small, was the precious fruit of the vine that symbolized the precious blood of Christ. From then on she was at peace with the way we partook of communion.

★   ★   ★   ★   ★   ★   ★

A FAMILY REUNION

I had not seen my parents and family in California for more than a year-and-a-half, so I was glad to see them when they came to Iowa in August. Bonnie was now 16 and David was 12. The California kid had already managed to break his collarbone twice while skateboarding. I joined them for a nice visit with Grandma Knowles in Hubbard. Uncle "Snack" came over from Illinois. One afternoon we took down a huge limb off the big ash tree that had been damaged in a storm. When the limb came down it took down Grandma's clothesline – laundry and all! Someone snapped a picture just as the event happened and we all had a good laugh when we saw the snapshot. Dave and I made up for lost time and played several fast and furious games of wiffle ball in my old "stadium." On Sunday we went to church in Goldfield at the Park church where dad had preached and I had spent 5 ½ happy years. Dad preached in the morning service, and I preached in the evening service. My logbook says that I preached a sermon called "Faith Like the Devil" from James 2:19. So for the first of several times, dad and I preached together the same day from the same pulpit.

I was eager to introduce my family to Evelyn when they brought me back to Ottumwa. They met her for the first time August 6 at her home on 202 North James Street. Mom had made black and white gingham checked shirts for dad, David, and me and used the same material to make dresses that she and Bonnie wore. Evelyn was impressed with our family love and solidarity, and was pleased to meet them. My parents were very impressed with Evelyn's natural beauty and inner grace. Mom told me later that I had found a rare treasure and that I had better not let her go. I was not about to. A day or so later we all attended the

★   ★   ★   ★   ★   ★   ★

Centerville Rally together and heard Word, Hunt, and Rodney Reyman, a successful Bible salesman from Reno, Nevada, develop a nicely balanced theme "The Case *For* and the Case *Against*."

MY JUNIOR YEAR BEGINS

Bidding my family a fond farewell, I registered for my junior year at Midwestern. I was delighted that Evelyn also enrolled with me. Some of the girls told her, "Boy, Vic sure has changed since he started dating you. You should have known him before!" My maturation process had begun, but I was still a long way from becoming "Victor Mature." They were right on both counts. Her favorite class was Old Testament History with Lafe Culver. I think I know why. I had noticed that at her church they only kept New Testaments in the racks on the back of the pews. Very little, if any, teaching or preaching was done from the Old Testament. Brother Culver's class opened up a whole new world to her, and she reveled in his entertaining survey of those 39 books of the Bible. She also enjoyed Life of Christ with Donald Hunt and a brand new class, Bible Fundamentals with Culver. Confession: as an upperclassman I was slated to take Hebrews, but instead I opted for Bible Fundamentals because that way I could be with Evelyn in class. My three other yearlong classes were Restoration History and Church History, both with Hunt, and Christian Evidences with Culver. I was determined that this school year was going to be my best ever and I did not disappoint my instructors nor myself.

THE ELISHA ROOM

One Sunday afternoon, as Gary Bryant and I were lying on our bunks reading, we both nearly had collective heart attacks when a low-

★   ★   ★   ★   ★   ★   ★

flying jet roared over the dorm. We both thought the Second Coming was underway! The noise on the second floor (that I used to help create) now started bugging me (as I had bugged many before). I asked permission to have a room for myself on the third floor so I could have uninterrupted time for study. None were available but Brother Hunt pointed out a nice gabled corner with a window where I could place a desk and chair against one wall and a twin bed against the other. It wasn't much, but I was happy with it. I got a small bookshelf for my growing library, hung a rod between the gables for my hanging clothes, and put a small nightstand with a lamp at the head of the bed. I was pleased as punch with my "Elisha Room." In 2 Kings 4 a "notable woman" of Shunem made a "small upper room on the wall" and put in it "a bed . . . a table and a chair and a lampstand" for the prophet Elisha. I got more studying done in my "Elisha Room" that year than I had done in my first two years of college. Brother Hunt once said, "I can give no greater advice to young men entering the ministry than to obtain a few good books and study them thoroughly with a daily schedule of study time." Now I was taking his advice to heart. I also wrote to Archie Word out in Portland, Oregon, and asked to be placed on his mailing list for his paper *The Church Speaks*. Our textbook for Restoration History was Robert Richardson's two-volume (1,225 pages!) work, *Memoirs of Alexander Campbell*. For Church History it was *Christianity through the Centuries* by Earle E. Cairns. For Christian Evidences it was *Evidences of Christianity* by J. W. McGarvey. I still have those three books, and I still smile when I see how many times I wrote the name "Evelyn" in different scripts in each one of them. I was a "goner" for sure.

★   ★   ★   ★   ★   ★   ★

THE "CHAPEL CHALLENGE SERIES"

The 1966-67 school year marked the 20th anniversary of the founding of Midwestern School of Evangelism. Brother Hunt crafted a special "Chapel Challenge Series" that ran the entire school year. Each chapel sermon was designed to deal with the kind of workers God wanted us to be. So each sermon title was prefaced with the words "Workers of . . ." That year we heard challenging messages from the faculty on being workers of consecration, industry, knowledge, humility, self-examination, desire, assurance, contentment, vision, courage, trust, growth, grace, leadership, dedication, self-sacrifice, spiritual depth, prayer, patience, responsibility, optimism, gratitude, dauntlessness, brotherly love, peace, intercession, joy, compassion, impartiality, reverence, virtue, faith, cleanliness, honesty, orderliness, steadfastness, example, harmony, godly fear, daring, abstinence, hope, zeal, etc. Who couldn't "grow in the grace and knowledge" of Christ hearing messages like those four mornings a week? To this day I am thankful that chapel was four days a week, that it was mandatory, and that we were required to take notes. (I have since preached on some Christian campuses where even some of the faculty did not attend.) I looked forward to each chapel service and am still forever grateful that Brother Hunt envisioned that vital series of sermons.

A NEW CHURCH BEGINS

In September a new church was being planted in nearby Fairfield, home of Fairfield College. For several Sundays I joined Darrell Bridgewater, Sharon Agenter, Leland Vandeveer, and Karen Runner in this evangelistic effort. One Sunday Darrell asked me to lead the morning worship

★　★　★　★　★　★　★

service, something I had never done before. I remember selecting "The Old Rugged Cross" for the communion hymn. Afternoons were spent in canvassing the city and making "cold calls." Brother Ellis had already trained some of us at Pennsylvania Avenue to do this, but I was never comfortable with going "two-by-two" and knocking on the doors of total strangers. Actually, they were not strangers; they were in their own homes. The people knocking on their doors were the strangers. In later years I learned the value of calling by appointment and experienced far better results by using that method. As Ben Merold has said, "Methods are many, principles are few; methods may change, principles never do."

And so, while the Gemini 11 spacecraft hovered 850 miles above the earth on its 44th orbit, all seemed well in my world. My world must have seemed very small to the astronauts. It probably looked small even to others who were earthlings. But I was starting to get it together. I had a different attitude, I was going slow and easy with Evelyn, and I was starting to get involved in the work of the church, even though I was not yet preaching as I had promised God I would do back in October 1964.

Then, three weeks into September, something dreadful happened that became the third and final "turning point" in my years at Midwestern.

★   ★   ★   ★   ★   ★   ★

First baby picture, 1946. Add a cigar
and I'd look like Churchill!

A proud father!

May 1947, Polo, Illinois.

I never joined the Navy,
but I did marry a Saylor!

First family picture.
Rebecca is behind me.

My first car! May 1947.

★   ★   ★   ★   ★   ★   ★

*Fall 1947,
Clay Center, Nebraska.*

*With Muriel & Rebecca, 1949,
Whiting, Iowa.*

*My first grade teacher,
Mrs. Simons, 1951,
Hamburg, Iowa.*

*Bonnie (on dad's lap),
1951, Hamburg.*

Third grade, 1953, Hamburg.

★ ★ ★ ★ ★ ★ ★

*Grandma Knowles' house,
Hubbard, Iowa.*

Grandma in rocker.

Hamburg Church of Christ.

*With my forelock, I look like
Hitler, Jr.! Boise, Idaho, 1955.*

*My favorite picture:
Fourth grade, Boise, Idaho.*

Putting our best feet forward, 1958.

★ ★ ★ ★ ★ ★ ★

My brother David in front:
Goldfield, Iowa.

At Camp Diagonal, 1960.
Gary Cradic wants me back
in the game!

Park Church of Christ
(and parsonage),
Goldfield, Iowa.

Cover boy of Anchor
(photo taken in 1961).

At Pine Lake Camp, 1962.
(With Willie Williams & Roger Rash).

★　★　★　★　★　★　★

Freshman, GHS.

Sophomore, GHS.

In my new
baseball uniform,
GHS.

I'm #21. GHS finished 19-5.

Junior, MGHS.

★   ★   ★   ★   ★   ★   ★

Goofing off at Midwestern, 1964.

Senior, MGHS.

*Freshman quartet
(with Ray Johnson,
Roger Deys, Sam Brown),
1964-65.*

*Our traveling quartet (Leland
Vanderveer at piano, Chester Mullins,
Henry Neff, Terry Crist), 1967-1968.*

My alma mater.

★ ★ ★ ★ ★ ★ ★

At age 19.

Evelyn Saylor at "sweet 16."

Evelyn at 18.

*We started dating in 1965 —
this is in 1966.*

*Evelyn held out her arm and
took this photo, Summer 1966.*

★　　★　　★　　★　　★　　★　　★

275

*Picture Day at Midwestern,
May 1967.*

*Having fun with
my brother David.*

*Wedding Day —
August 7, 1967.*

*We were married in
the Hamburg Church.*

*What were we thinking?
(I was preaching at Promise City now.)*

★   ★   ★   ★   ★   ★   ★

Preaching at Hamburg.

Working together, Summer 1968.

First full-time ministry, Lexington, Nebraska (1969-1972).

First family picture with Mindy, 1969.

With Dave and my parents, 1969.

★   ★   ★   ★   ★   ★   ★

*Bridget joined our family
in 1971.*

*Second ministry,
Eugene, Oregon (1972-1975).*

*Lincoln and Amanda joined
our family in Oregon.*

May 1975 (at my brother's wedding).

*Emily (on Mindy's lap) joined our
family in West Concord, Minnesota
(1975-1977).*

Portia made it six in 1977.

★　　★　　★　　★　　★　　★　　★

VICTOR: SINCE 1945

★ ★ ★ ★ ★ ★ ★

CHAPTER SEVEN

TURNING POINT

September 1966 began with a bang. Pakistani troops entered Kashmir on September 2. Four days later India responded by invading Lahore. On September 9 the Dodger's Sandy Koufax threw a perfect game against the Chicago Cubs. (I wasn't paying near the attention to baseball that I once had.) On the same day Hurricane Betsy roared into New Orleans with 145-mph winds, causing 76 deaths and 1.42 billion in damages, earning itself the nickname "Billion Dollar Betsy." On September 14 the fourth and final session of the Second Vatican Council opened in Rome. A coup failed in Iraq on September 16. None of these events altered my life in Iowa in the least. On Sunday afternoon, September 18, our new church in Fairfield hosted a monthly singspiration and we were pleased that 115 people came. Then came September 21, 1966.

The sun came up that morning with every good promise of a beautiful day. By the time it went down many lives were altered, my own included, and two beautiful young co-eds from Midwestern were in the city morgue. It was the saddest day of my life up to that time.

THE WRECK

I had known Carolyn Daly since we were young. Her father, Loren Daly, was a good friend of my father. In fact, Loren, like myself, was a "Timothy" of the Hamburg Church of Christ. Since we were both "PKs," Carolyn and I had a natural affinity, as preacher's kids are wont

★　★　★　★　★　★　★

to stick up for each other. Carolyn had an identical twin sister, Marilyn, who had also gone to Midwestern. Carolyn had married Leon Hansen, my roommate from my freshman year, and was carrying their first child.

Susan Wood, a brown-eyed girl from Lexington, Nebraska, had enrolled with me as a freshman. She was a fun-loving girl who caught the eye of my friend Gary McGlumphry. Her best friend was Jenifer Bradley, and sometimes the four of us had walked around town just talking and laughing during our freshman year. Gary and Susan's first wedding anniversary was just four days away. Their adorable little girl, Kristi, was just nine months old. No one could have guessed what would happen, and none of us were prepared for what did happen.

Late that afternoon the two young women, one a new mother and one a mother-to-be, decided to go to Chillicothe, east of Ottumwa, to pick some apples. Because Carolyn was nearing full-term, and could not easily bend over to pick up the apples, Susan went along to help. Susan had planned to take little Kristi with them, but at the last minute decided to leave her with Virginia Johnson, a next-door neighbor. It was the first time she had ever used a baby sitter.

About 7:30 P.M., just a mile from the McGlumphry's home, a drunk driver slammed into their car on the crest of small hill. Carolyn was thrown out of the car and was killed instantly along with her unborn child. Susan was wedged in the car, unconscious. Because there were so many "gawkers" that appeared on the scene, the emergency vehicles could hardly make their way to the scene of the accident. Some of the bystanders were actually picking up apples that had spilled from the car and were eating them as they watched. It took 40 minutes for the emergency workers to extract Susan and rush her to

★   ★   ★   ★   ★   ★   ★

the Ottumwa Hospital where she was pronounced dead. Poor Gary had to identify Carolyn. When told that Susan was dead too, he asked, "What about the baby?" The air went out of the room. "What baby?" they asked. Gary, not knowing that Susan had dropped Kristi off at Virginia's, thought their little girl had been in the car. Something told him to call Virginia, and he immediately made the call and was relieved to know that their baby was safe. The drunk driver was let off with a fine, never served a day in jail, and several years later killed two more women in another car crash while driving drunk. MADD (Mothers Against Drunk Driving) was still 14 years down the road.

Someone brought the shocking news to the dorms and every student was instantly overcome with sorrow. Terry Crist was just getting off work, and I told him the news as soon as he got out of his car. I can still see the look of shock on his face as he stood under the street light, a sack of Canteens in his hand that were never eaten that night. School was canceled for the rest of the week, although a special memorial chapel service was held. We took up an offering to help Leon and Gary with the expenses we knew they were going to incur in the next few days and weeks. The headline in next issue of the weekly school paper, *Evangelism from the Heart of America*, read . . .

TWO BEAUTIFUL LIVES END IN TRAGEDY

"The worst tragedy of its kind in the history of the school occurred Wednesday night, September 21, when an automobile accident snuffed out the lives of two of the students' wives," the article began. The entire issue was given over to the lives of Carolyn and Susan, ending with these words. "Both young ladies have left behind a large group of sorrowing friends in their home communities, at the

★   ★   ★   ★   ★   ★   ★

school, and wherever they were known. They were fine Christian young ladies, much too young to be taken, and happily settled in marriage."

Evelyn and I attended the double funeral service that was held three days later at the Pennsylvania Avenue church. Since Leon and Gary were such good friends, I drove to Council Bluffs for Carolyn's service and burial, and from there on out to Lexington for Susan's service and burial. By the time I returned to Ottumwa I was pretty well wrung out from the emotion of both of those funerals and burials. I called my father in California to talk about everything. He later wrote in his diary: "Vic was so badly shaken by those deaths."

THE AFTERMATH

Just as September 11, 2001, would later be a "wake up" call for America, September 21, 1966, became my personal "wake up" call. The two young ladies' sudden deaths reminded me of the brevity and uncertainty of life. Three years later, to the very day, I wrote, "Their deaths hit me hard; nothing ever shook me more than did the events of that night." I wasn't so concerned about meeting God unprepared, but I was troubled that I, as of yet, had not fulfilled my desire to preach the Word of God as I had publicly stated nearly two years before. At the double funeral in Ottumwa, Johnny Henshaw, a Midwestern graduate who was preaching at Modale, Iowa, and was moving to Lincoln, Nebraska, told me that he had been unable to find anyone to take his place. Instantly I asked him if he would give me a chance. He agreed, but eventually the job went to one of my classmates, Richard Geringswald. At first I was disappointed, but when invitations started coming in later to preach here and there, I was glad that I had the free-

★   ★   ★   ★   ★   ★   ★

dom to move about among the churches and preach. I have always had a kingdom heart that is larger than the local church.

I plunged into my studies with a fervor I had never possessed before. My grades for the first semester were unlike any I had received in my first two years at Midwestern. I received an A in Restoration History, another A in Church History, another A in Christian Evidence, and a B in Bible Fundamentals. I was so upset that I had received a B in this new class, designed for lower classmen, that I redoubled my efforts and got an A the second semester in that class. I also began work on a special sermon, inspired by the deaths of my classmates that would become my "signature sermon" for several years to come: "Just One Glimpse."

NOT AGAIN!

But while all this was happening, I did something strange and foolish. For whatever reason, toward the end of September, I stopped seeing Evelyn. Was I just too caught in my studies or was something else at work? Was I lapsing back into the darkness of my melancholy/choleric negatives that had ended one relationship and was now threatening another? I suspect it may have been a combination of both. Evelyn was cut to the quick, just as Susan had been. The girls in the dorm rallied to her defense and tried to console her. Some of them really let me have it for breaking up with her.

"Vic Knowles, you ought to be ashamed of yourself!"

"Vic Knowles, are you going to do this *again*?" (An unveiled reference to my broken engagement with Susan.)

"Vic Knowles, don't you realize that Evelyn is the best thing that ever happened to you!'

★   ★   ★   ★   ★   ★   ★

"Vic Knowles, are you crazy or what? You must be nuts!"

On October 18 my father wrote, "I noticed you said nothing about Evelyn in your last letter (October 4)." My sister Becky was more forthright. On October 26 it was her turn to send me a "blistering" letter. "I was *sick* to hear that you and Evelyn have parted company. Do hope you know what you're doing. I suppose you realize you'll never find as nice a girl as she is. And from a female's viewpoint it would serve you right if someone you're crazy over just drops you flat on your face one of these days."

All of my family had fallen in love with Evelyn. Even my little brother David had a crush on her. "Vic, she's the best!" he wrote. And now here I was falling out of love with her. I must have been out of my mind.

Of course I didn't date anyone else during the month or so that I stopped seeing Evelyn. I am sure that if I had been stupid enough to venture over to the girls' dorm and ask any girl on campus for a date that she would have yelled, "I wouldn't date you if you were the last man in the world!" And every window in the girls' dorm would have been thrown open and I would have heard a chorus of, "That goes for me too!"

One Saturday in October I drove to Orleans for a youth rally. It was a beautiful day, a nice picnic was spread for everyone who came, and the singing and the preaching were great. But it just wasn't the same without Evelyn sitting next to me. I probably talked to myself all the way back to Ottumwa.

"Vic Knowles, you ought to be ashamed of yourself!"

"Vic Knowles, are you going to do this *again*?"

"Vic Knowles, don't you realize that Evelyn is the best thing that ever happened to you?"

★   ★   ★   ★   ★   ★   ★

"Vic Knowles, are you crazy or what? You must be nuts!"

Where had I heard all this before? Was there an echo chamber in my Corvair?

THE VERSE THAT BROUGHT ME TO FULL SURRENDER

On October 23, one year to the day after Evelyn and I had gone to the KRNT Theater in Des Moines on our first date, the celebrated evangelist Carol J. Lankford began a two-week revival meeting at the Pennsylvania Avenue church. He also spoke three times in chapel while he was in our fair city. I never saw anyone stand so tall and erect in the pulpit. He had a mane of beautiful silver hair to boot. Brother Lankford was not only a great communicator, with a deep bass voice, but was also an accomplished soloist and had recorded several LP albums. His wife Donna accompanied him at the piano. At one service he sang "The Great Judgment Morning" (and never sang "stink" instead of "sink" as Roger Deys had done our freshman year). I believe he also sang "I Walked Today Where Jesus Walked." I had been reading a passage in Luke that started to convict me. In the old King James Version it reads, "O Jerusalem, Jerusalem, which killest the prophets, and stonest them that are sent unto thee: how often would I have gathered thy children together, as a hen doth gather her brood under her wings, and ye would not!" I began to see myself as a wayward child whom Christ wanted for His very own.

There were 25 decisions for Christ in that meeting – and I was one of them. I walked down that aisle and told Brother Ellis: "This is the last time I'm walking down this aisle. I am here and now rededicating my life to Christ!" And so I did. I made things right with God and I eventually made things right with Evelyn. I later underlined Luke

★   ★   ★   ★   ★   ★   ★

13:34 in red and wrote in my Bible: "The verse that brought me to full surrender to Christ." Years later I would reflect upon the following comments on that pivotal passage written by the renowned Scottish commentator William Barclay. "Nothing hurts so much as to go to someone and offer love and have that offer spurned. It is life's bitterest tragedy to give one's heart to someone only to have it broken. [*Don't think I didn't wince when I read that sentence!*] That is what happened to Jesus in Jerusalem; and he still comes to men, and still men reject him. But the fact remains that to reject God's love is in the end to be in peril of his wrath."

TOGETHER AGAIN

I started showing some attention to Evelyn again. She insists that I actually "flirted" with her. Whatever. I do know that one day while she was standing at the foot of the main staircase I intentionally (not accidentally) brushed up against her. Evelyn later told me that she thought she had just about gotten to the point where she could have gone on living without me when I started paying attention to her again. She wasn't sure that she should respond to my overtures.

But by mid-November we were together again.

> *Together again, my tears have stopped falling;*
> *The long lonely nights are now at an end.*
> *The key to my heart you hold in your hand,*
> *And nothing else matters now we're together again.*

(The above song, "Together Again," first sung by Buck Owens, was released in 1964, the year I first noticed Evelyn at a grocery store, and went to #1 on the country charts. In 1966, the year we got back

★   ★   ★   ★   ★   ★   ★

"together again," Ray Charles took it to #1 on the adult contemporary charts. Life can be stranger than fiction.)

As I look back on the whole matter, I now believe that someone must have been praying for us. I know my family was. I know others were too. That was the key to our reunion. Tennyson said, "More things are wrought (accomplished) by prayer than this world dreams of." When I get to heaven, where "we shall know as we are known," I will seek them out and fervently thank them for their intercessory prayers. Never underestimate the power of intercessory prayer.

I BEGIN TO PREACH

"From that time Jesus began to preach . . ." (Matthew 4:17). Jesus of Nazareth had a beginning point in His preaching ministry and so did I. My preaching career began in earnest in October 1966. Good old Terry Crist invited me once again to his preaching point in Ridgeway, Missouri, where I preached a brand new sermon, "A Verse to Remember," from Luke 23:34, "Father, forgive them, for they know not what they do." I had heard my own father preach from this text several times, and now I was following in his footsteps. Terry had me back later in the month to preach again.

In November Brother Hunt asked me if I would be willing to fill in for him one Sunday morning while he was preaching elsewhere. I could barely stammer out that, yes, I was willing. To be invited to preach was one thing, but to be invited by Donald G. Hunt was quite another. I knew that he was putting great trust in me. His new church plant in Des Moines was only about nine months old and was meeting in the Polk County Farm Bureau building on East Euclid Avenue in the northern part of the capitol city. It was to this congregation that I delivered for

★   ★   ★   ★   ★   ★   ★

the first time the message that God had laid upon my heart after the deaths of Carolyn and Susan, "Just One Glimpse." The title was inspired from the third stanza in the hymn "When We All Get to Heaven."

> *Let us then be true and faithful,*
>
> *Trusting, serving every day.*
>
> *Just one glimpse of Him in glory*
>
> *Will the toils of life repay.*

What would happen, I asked, if God would give us just one glimpse of Calvary, just one glimpse of the Judgment and Hell, and just one glimpse of Heaven? When the invitation was given a young man came down the aisle and rededicated his life to Christ. Leonard Harris, who had grown up in Brother Hunt's church in Orleans, had graduated from high school and was working in Des Moines. I stood with Leonard before the congregation that day, and Leonard has stood with me like a rock in the ministry I am leading at this writing (Peace on Earth Ministries). I had broken the bread of life that day in preaching. And like bread cast upon the waters, it has come back to me many times through the faithful support of Leonard and Patty Harris. I would be invited back to Des Moines to preach two more times later in the same month.

Then I received an invitation from A. K. Miller to come and preach in Indianola. This was also in November. Brother Miller was the one who had told me back in 1960 that he hoped that some day I would know the Scriptures as well as I knew the baseball statistics in the *Des Moines Register.* I preached at both the morning and evening services and enjoyed the day with A. K. and Annabelle. Their home absolutely radiated with love and happiness. I don't know of any two people who

★   ★   ★   ★   ★   ★   ★

ever demonstrated the fruit of the Spirit more than did the Millers. I wanted our home to be the same. They were just filled to overflowing with love, joy, peace, longsuffering, kindness, goodness, faithfulness, gentleness, and self-control. Brother Miller was never a "headliner" at any of the big preaching rallies or Bible conferences, but he was at the top of my list in the men I most admired.

Another invitation to preach came from Don Spencer, a student at Midwestern, who was conducting a student ministry at Promise City. This was indeed fortuitous because I would succeed him at Promise City when he graduated in the spring of 1967. Even though I preached an "old" sermon, "Faith, Like the Devil," I must have left a lasting impression on at least one listener, Mrs. Franklin Matsler. Years later she told Evelyn, "The first time I heard Victor preach, I knew he was going somewhere." That, too, was in November.

The final issue of the 1966 *Evangelism from the Heart of America* carried a news item titled **GREAT DAY AT HAMBURG**. "Sunday, December 11 proved to be one of the most edifying days that the church at Hamburg, Iowa, has had for a long time . . . when some of the Hamburg young people who are in training here took charge of the services . . . In the morning, Victor Knowles led the singing, and Kyle Koch preached. In the afternoon, Keevin Koch and Victor led a rousing Singspiration . . . In the evening, messages were brought by Earl Koch and Victor Knowles. The congregation is already looking forward to another such day in the Spring." It was special for me to stand in the same pulpit that my father had occupied during his happy ministry in Hamburg. I preached "Just One Glimpse" with everything I had within me. At the invitation a young girl came forward to reconsecrate her life to Christ, Deanna Cradic, Gary's sister.

★ ★ ★ ★ ★ ★ ★

LOVE IS IN THE AIR

My parents celebrated their 25th wedding anniversary on December 14. I couldn't go to California for the occasion but I sent them a card and called them on their special day. Then, the day before Christmas, I received the most wonderful Christmas present a young preacher could want: a letter of encouragement. It came from a lady in the church in San Luis Obispo where my father preached. Her name was Esther Phillips, a saint of God if there ever was one. A few years later when we met her in person, Evelyn said, "It was just like she had stepped out of the book of Acts because she was so godly; her whole demeanor, spirit, and words reflected the life of Christ." Sister Phillips had heard about my progress in Bible College and sent a little gift to help with my tuition. "May our Heavenly Father bless you in this ministry as you study and prepare for full-time work in His Kingdom." Her letter was filled with Scripture and words of encouragement. It was a "keeper" for sure.

By this time I wanted to give Evelyn a diamond engagement ring. She told me she didn't want a ring; she just wanted me. Well, she had me all right, wrapped around her finger like the ring I wanted to place there. No worries ever again there. She was just not into diamonds and pearls. Even when we were married eight months later, she desired only a simple matching wedding band. No wonder my mother said of her: "Evelyn is a lovely girl – far superior to most girls this day and age, Christian or not."

On Christmas day I preached at the church in Knoxville where Evelyn was now going with some of the students to assist Ted Stolz (no relation to Bonnie Stoltz), who was conducting a student ministry

*   *   *   *   *   *   *

there. It was a great way to end the year – preaching the Word and being with Evelyn. But the year was not over yet. On December 30 Evelyn and I attended the wedding of Terry Crist and Karen Runner in Spring Valley, Minnesota. I served as Terry's best man. In eight more months Terry would return the favor when Evelyn and I would become husband and wife.

I CONTINUE TO PREACH

Things were changing in America in 1967. Ronald Reagan, a former movie actor, was now the governor of California, the largest state in the union. In Massachusetts, Edward W. Brooke made history when he became the first Negro elected to the U. S. Senate. And on January 15, 1967, the first Super Bowl football game was played. The Green Bay Packers defeated the Kansas City Chiefs 35-10. The "Boston Strangler" was sentenced to life in prison on January 18. Three astronauts, Virgil Grissom, Edward White, and Roger Chaffee, perished in a flash fire that engulfed their Apollo I spacecraft during a simulated launching on January 27. I am sure that I used some of these news stories in my preaching as illustrations of one sort or another, for I was now beginning to clip items from newspapers and news magazines for future use. I had enough sermon outlines of my own now to warrant a black three-ring notebook that I probably purchased at Woolworth's. On the inside front cover I took a blue felt tip marker and wrote the following on the gray background.

- "Preach the Word" (II Tim. 4:2)
- "For we preach not ourselves, but Christ Jesus the Lord" (II Cor. 4:5)
- ". . . by the love of truth and the power of God . . ."

★   ★   ★   ★   ★   ★   ★

- ". . . I preached as never sure to preach again, And as a dying man to dying men . . ."
- "It pleased God by the foolishness of preaching to save them that believe" (I Cor. 1:21).

Preaching the word is what I had promised God I would do in the fall of 1964 and preaching was now a part of my monthly regimen. I began the year of 1967 by preaching at Ridgeway, filling in for Terry Crist who was on his honeymoon. On the 22nd of January the mercury plummeted to 20 degrees below zero. Evelyn and I drove to Sigourney in my "poor man's Porsche." The heater in the Corvair was not working that night and we were kept busy trying to remove the frost from the *inside* of the windshield. Evelyn had a scarf on but I had nothing to cover my ice-cold ears. She took pity on me and gave me her pink cardigan sweater, tying it around my head to keep my ears warm. I must have looked like Marley's ghost whose head and chin was bound with a kerchief. Our noses were so cold that I put to use the cigarette lighter in my car for the first time. We took turns warming our noses with the glowing cigarette lighter, being careful not to get too close! When we got to the church we hoped to warm up – but the furnace had quit working. I am sure that my teeth chattered all through my message. I am also sure it was the shortest sermon I had preached up to this time. I could actually see my breath as I spoke. This was the night for more than a perfunctory handshake. I am sure we all practiced a "holy hug" just to keep warm. I am also sure I may have broken all land speed records for a 1962 Corvair on the return trip to Ottumwa. Evelyn later made me a little red velvet "hat" to slip over the steel ball that was atop the stickshift.

One thing that warmed our hearts for sure was whenever we

★   ★   ★   ★   ★   ★   ★

talked about our future lives together. We started talking seriously about a wedding date and decided that spring would be a nice time in which to be married. After I asked my father to perform the ceremony, he mentioned that the whole family planned to come back in August for my sister Becky's graduation from Jennie Edmundson School of Nursing in Council Bluffs. Since it was fairly obvious that Evelyn's home church would not sanction our marriage in their building, we talked about where we would be married. We finally settled on the church in Hamburg, Iowa. I wrote to Brother DeVries asking for their permission and received the welcome word, as I knew we would, that we could be married there. The date was set: August 7, 1967, which happened to fall on my father's birthday. Stuart and Bonnie Fitzgerald gave us first chance at taking their apartment once Stuart graduated in May. After seeing the apartment we agreed that it would indeed be our new home once we were married.

The annual January Gathering featured a choir in which Evelyn sang. She had a beautiful soprano voice and I loved watching her sing. She looked like an angel. The conference that year also featured a preacher from the West Coast, Murrial Walker of Hayward, California. I not only listened intently to his preaching but also took note of his pulpit mannerisms. I did not copy them, but it was always interesting to observe a preacher's pulpit demeanor. Walker lived up to his name and walked around the stage quite a bit. I have never done much of that, preferring to "stand and deliver." The conference theme that year was "The Priesthood," and I took careful notes of one of Walker's messages on the priesthood of Christ.

In February I returned to Indianola to preach both morning and evening for Brother A. K. Miller. In the morning service I preached

★　　★　　★　　★　　★　　★　　★

Walker's "tweaked" tome that I titled "Jesus, Our Sinless, Spotless Savior." I have since thought that there could not be a greater contrast than Murrial Walker, the dynamic evangelist from California, and A. K. Miller, the quiet servant of the Lord in Iowa. Yet both men loved the Lord and served their Savior in the way that God had gifted them. It is not wise to compare one preacher to another because God has assigned to each a field in which to work and has equipped them especially for that field. I learned much from each minister in my formative years at Midwestern and could never understand why some people felt it necessary to exalt one and abase another when God had accepted them both. The ground is level when we stand behind the sacred desk and preach the message of the cross.

For some time I had been experiencing severe nosebleeds. One day in February I developed a terrible nosebleed during one of my classes on the second floor. After soaking up two large terrycloth towels I became faint. Nathalie Smith took one look at me and said, "Get that boy to the hospital as fast as you can!" Several of my classmates jumped up, picked me up, and carried me downstairs and out to a waiting car. I felt like the paralyzed man who was "bourne of four" in the Gospels. At the hospital I had my nose packed to stop the bleeding. I continued to have severe nosebleeds once or twice a year until 1970 when a doctor cauterized my nose with several sticks of silver nitrate.

THE DAY SAM BROWN WENT DOWN IN FLAMES

During the second semester of my junior year I added several courses to my already full class schedule: Song Leading under Lafe Culver and Advanced Life of Christ under Donald G. Hunt. I received A's in both classes as well as in my yearlong classes of Restoration

★   ★   ★   ★   ★   ★   ★

History and Christian Evidences. I was disappointed with myself when I slipped to a B in Church History. Rats! I wanted to get straight A's for the first time in my life. I had seen so many C's in my life that I was C-sick. I never wanted to see another C in my collegiate career.

One day in chapel Brother Hunt called on six young men to give a spontaneous, on-the-spot five minute sermon. One of those chosen was my good friend Sam Brown. The topic he was assigned was "Why a Christian Should Call." Striding to the front of the chapel I remember Sam quipping, "Now all you 'Dicksonites' are about to see the value of having a Thompson Chain-Reference Bible." We had this friendly rivalry at Midwestern between those of us who had a Dickson Analytical Bible and those who had a Thompson Chain-Reference Bible. I was a Dickson man and Sam was a Thompson man. In fact, Sam was a Thompson zealot, trying to convert anyone he could to use a Thompson. But poor Sam could not find anything in the back of his Bible on that particular topic. He spent the entire five minutes fumbling around, seeking in vain for an elusive text from which to pontificate, much to the delight of the Dickson devotees and greatly to the chagrin of the Thompson theologians. Finally he had to descend from the pulpit, crimson with shame, no homily delivered, to the good-natured hoots and hollers of the Dickson crowd. I have never enjoyed a "sermon" so much. Verily, I do believe that even the faculty had to smile the day Sam Brown, the Thompson Man, went down in flames.

KEEPING BUSY

I can't remember if I was even paid for my preaching that year. It wasn't even on my mind. Gas was only 31 cents a gallon in 1967 anyway. One day I filled up my Corvair for just a few dollars because a

★   ★   ★   ★   ★   ★   ★

"gas war" had brought the price per gallon down to 18.9. The March 8 *Evangelism from the Heart of America* carried a news item that read: "Student Victor Knowles keeps busy these days. On Feb. 19 and Feb. 26, he preached at Sigourney, Iowa. On Mar. 1, he preached at the Promise City, Iowa, midweek service. On March 5, he preached both times at Creston, Iowa. On Mar. 11, he is to preach on the youth rally at Brazil, Ind., and on the 12th he is to bring a message to the Brazil congregation." As the old song says, "I am happy in the service of the King." I certainly was all of that. I was also keeping busy working at a new grocery store, Giant Foods. I worked my way up to "third man" just behind the manager and assistant manager. One of the checkers there was a woman named Marie Box. In time she became a member of the River Road church in Ottumwa and told me that I played a part in her decision for Christ. I kept busy those days going to college in the morning, working in the afternoons and some nights, and always studying for class and preparing sermons in my Elisha Room. One night some of the fellows thought I was studying too hard, so they crept up to the third floor with shaving cream cans in hand and really let me have it. I showed them I still had some of the old spunk in me when I grabbed a couple of cans of Colgate shaving cream and went after them like Wyatt Earp with both "guns" blazing. It felt good to get "back in the saddle" again. For one thing, the old dorm never smelled so good.

On March 9 Josef Stalin's daughter Svetlana walked into the U. S. Embassy in New Delhi, India, and defected. Her defection was greeted with delight by all freedom loving people. The next day was Evelyn's 21st birthday. She joined me and two carloads of students from Midwestern to travel to Brazil, Indiana. My good friend Ken

*   *   *   *   *   *   *

Mickey was preaching at the Rio Grande church in Brazil and had planned a big area youth rally for the next day. Larry Mickey, Ken's younger brother, and I were to be the speakers. My assigned text was Romans 12:1, 2. I had worked for weeks preparing this message because it would be my first time to preach at a youth rally. I urged the assembled young people to present their bodies to God as "living sacrifices," to reject "conformity" to the ways of the world, and to experience transformation by the "renewing" of their minds. On Sunday morning I preached to the whole church on "The Children of Light." It was a great experience for me and I hope for everyone else as well. Two carloads of young people that were coming to the youth rally were involved in a 4-car accident, but no one was seriously injured.

The first Sunday in April I got to preach at my "home church" during my years at Midwestern, the Pennsylvania Avenue congregation. Brother Ellis was gone to Brazil to conduct a revival meeting and asked me to fill in for him while he was gone that Sunday. You don't know how that builds a young man's confidence until someone you really respect asks a favor like that. I worked extra hard on a new sermon, "The Imperative Need of the Church." I had picked up the word "imperative" from Marion McKee. It suggested *urgency* and urgency is what I was feeling those days. I wanted everyone to sense the imperative need of the church to be all that God wanted all of us to be and to do in His vineyard. I was young, just 21, but I took seriously Paul's admonition to Timothy: "Let no man despise thy youth." I was trying to be an example to the believers in word, in conduct, in love, in spirit, in faith, and in purity (1 Timothy 4:12). I was young but my grandparents were growing old. Sometime that same month my Grandma Brown, who had never recovered from the stroke, was moved into a

★　　★　　★　　★　　★　　★　　★

nursing home in Richmond. I felt so sorry for her and for my Grandpa who would be so lonely without her at home.

The next weekend I was back in my real "home church" in Hamburg, Iowa, along with Evelyn, the Koch brothers, and some other students from Hamburg for a return Singspiration. **ROUSING RALLY AT HAMBURG, IOWA** read the headlines in the April 26 *Evangelism from the Heart of America*. The Sunday service was planned and led by the three Koch brothers and myself. Brother DeVries wrote, "We highly recommend these brothers to all the churches. They employ local talent and fill in with their own male quartet and pianist . . . high quality music that is spiritually edifying." This would be the first of several male quartets that I would be a part of in the next year or so. Leland Vandeveer from Ashland, Kansas, was our highly talented pianist. Fellow students I would sing with in our traveling male gospel quartet in the next year or so, besides the Koch brothers, included Terry Crist, Sam Brown, Larry Mickey, Mark McDowell, Dave McSpadden, Don Hunt II, and Ron Hunt. The latter two were the sons of Donald and Margaret Hunt and were still in high school at the time.

The week following our "rousing rally" in Hamburg there were huge demonstrations in San Francisco and New York City against the war in Vietnam. I felt sorry for President Johnson and for our troops who were in harm's way, some of them my old high school buddies. But Vietnam seemed so far away from our little corner of the world in Iowa. The only war we were fighting at that time was against "spiritual wickedness in high places" – a never-ending war against the devil and his angels. We were young and unafraid and we knew that we had the "right stuff" to win that war – the sword of the Spirit, which is the word of God (Ephesians 6:17).

★   ★   ★   ★   ★   ★   ★

MINISTERING IN "THE PROMISED LAND"

Sometimes on Saturday mornings I would help senior Don Spencer deliver his orders for Watkins Products ("First in Home Service"). For two years running Don was one of the top Watkins student salesmen in the U. S. and Canada. Don would be graduating in a month and asked if I was interested in the student ministry he had conducted at Promise City for about a year. I certainly was. On May 3 I preached my "tryout" sermon. Several weeks later I received a call from the Promise City Church of Christ inviting me to come and be their preacher. I was to begin my student ministry with them on May 21. For me, this was a dream come true that had been conceived in 1958 at Camp Diagonal, developed in the fall of 1964 when I made my decision to preach, and now was about to be birthed in 1967 in what Evelyn and I came to call "The Promised Land."

To chronicle my first ministry, even though it was "only" a student ministry, I purchased a *Day-by-Day Ready Record: A Daily Record of Service for Christ*. It was published by 20th Century Christian in Nashville, Tennessee, and cost me all of $1.95. A whole page, naturally, was devoted to Sunday where entries could be made for sermons preached, responses, special announcements and attendance records for Bible school, Sunday morning and evening, and Midweek services. I used that red book with yellow spiral binding until the 1980s when I switched to a shirt pocket size *Planning Calendar for Growing Churches* provided free of charge by Standard Publishing in Cincinnati, Ohio.

Promise City was a little town of about 150 people. The little congregation met in a large church building that was located right on Highway 2, 63 miles from Ottumwa. The only other "competition" in

★   ★   ★   ★   ★   ★   ★

town was the Methodist Church. Three of the church ladies had first names I had not heard of before or since: Icle, Vesta, and Zula. The first two-and-a-half months of my ministry I traveled back and forth on Sundays and Wednesdays by myself. Evelyn was team-teaching small children at the church in Knoxville, so we didn't see each other on Sundays until I would drop by her house on my return trip Sunday night. I preached at both morning and evening services on Sunday and conducted the Midweek Bible study. I was paid the handsome sum of $20 a week for my ministerial duties.

I worked hard on my sermon preparation during the week and always had my Sunday morning sermon finished by Saturday night, but usually had my Sunday evening message only partially finished. After taking Sunday dinner with a different family each Sunday, I would finish my evening sermon preparation in the afternoon and sometimes make a few calls. My first sermon was titled "The Challenges We Face." The title was inspired by the book written by Richard M. Nixon, but of course I made spiritual, not political, applications to my audience of 11. The next Sunday we had 18 in attendance, including four visitors. We had "grown" to 22 by September 10.

"BUILDING OUR NEST"

Graduation Day came May 23, and I bade farewell to several seniors who had played an important role in my life at Midwestern including Terry Paul, Don Spencer and Stuart Fitzgerald (all three were from the Union Park church in Orlando, Florida). The June 14 *Evangelism from the Heart of America* read: "Don Spencer and his wife [Miriam] have been serving the church at Promise City. He has turned over the leadership of that work to student Victor Knowles that he

★   ★   ★   ★   ★   ★   ★

might seek labor elsewhere." Stuart and Bonnie had not left town yet, so I stayed in the boys' dorm until July 4th when I was able to take over their apartment where Evelyn and I would live after we were married.

Several married students before had lived in the apartment at 315 N. Marion Street in Ottumwa, just a few blocks from the boys' dorm. The one-bedroom apartment was on the second floor. Mrs. Baker, the landlady, lived in the front part of the house on the ground floor. She rented another apartment in the back part of the house to other married students. A flight of stairs on the side of the house led up to our apartment. When you entered the apartment, a storage room was immediately to your right and the bathroom to your left. Continuing down the hall you came to the bedroom on the right and the kitchen on the left. I set up my study in a little alcove where the hallway ended and the living room, the largest in the apartment, began. To the right of the living room was a door leading to a little balcony where one could sit on a summer night and catch a nice breeze. The apartment was completely furnished, and the rent was $50 a month, including utilities, although Mrs. Baker told me that if the electric meter went over a certain number by the end of the month, I would have to pay the difference.

Evelyn enjoyed stopping by our future home on her way home from work and quickly began her interior decorating magic. At one time she had wanted to enroll in the LaSalle School of Interior Decorating. She really didn't need to because she has always worked her magic in any home we have had since 315 N. Marion. She painted the walls, hung pictures, made a tablecloth for the kitchen table and curtains for all the windows, and painted the outside of the old-fashioned claw foot bathtub. As for me, I moved the library table to my

★   ★   ★   ★   ★   ★   ★

"anointed alcove" where I could study, write, and prepare sermons. I got a nice gooseneck fluorescent desk lamp with Gooches' Circles (like Green Stamps) from purchases made at Giant Foods where I also worked. I also got a green metal file box that I used for filing my sermons, clippings, and other data. Long hours into the night I sat at that oak library table working on my studies or sermon preparation.

"HOTTER THAN A PEPPER SPROUT"

On May 27 I preached at my second youth rally, this one sponsored by the Pennsylvania Avenue church in Ottumwa. All three speakers were the sons of preachers. Phillip Lyon, son of Raymond Lyon, brought the first message. Don Hunt II, son of Donald G. Hunt, preached the second sermon. Then I, son of Dale V. Knowles, and quite proud of it, closed the rally by delivering a new message titled "Why I Decided to Preach" from 1 Corinthians 9:16. I said that the two motivating factors in my decision were my father's earnest example and a vision of perishing people.

Evelyn had never met my beloved Grandma Knowles, so we took care of that on Memorial Day, May 30, when I drove her to Hubbard to meet her. They instantly formed a "mutual admiration society." Grandma gave Evelyn an old-fashioned picture of a young girl standing at a garden gate. We drove out to the cemetery to place fresh-cut peonies on Grandpa's grave.

On Monday morning, June 5, the day after I had preached "The Four Greatest Losses in the World," heavy fighting broke out between Israeli and Egyptian forces. The legendary "Six-Day War" was on. Led by Israeli Defense Minister Moshe Dayan, wearing a black eye patch, Israel smashed the Arab coalition of Egypt, Jordan, and Syria in no

★　★　★　★　★　★　★

time flat. By the end of the week Jerusalem was back under Israeli control. Soldiers prayed and wept openly at the Wailing Wall. Israel now occupied territories four times the size of their own nation. I thought to myself, "Now *that's* the way to fight a war!"

But during the Six-Day War, on June 8, I received a phone call from my father in California. He broke the sad news to me that my beloved Grandma Brown had passed away. I remember leaning up against the wall and being overcome with a huge feeling of loss and sadness that swept over me. I wept for her and for my Grandpa who now would be all alone in that empty house on Carol Drive.

Two days later I ordered the suit for my wedding. I had lost a lot of weight that summer, dropping from 125 pounds to 119, so the suit salesman at J. C. Penney had to take me downstairs to the boys' department and fit me with the largest suit in that department. I told him to remove the label on the inside of the suit so that Evelyn would not see it and think she had married a wimp. A few days later I was delighted to see my old pal from my freshman year, Mike "Hoot" Gibson, back in town. Mike was now married and I was about to be, so we managed not to get in any kind of trouble!

To celebrate the "Glorious 4th" and my moving into our apartment on Marion Street, we went with some of our friends to hear the famous Stamps Quartet. Gary Bryant and his fiancée Pat Britton went with us. I wanted Gary to be one of my groomsmen, and he wanted me to return the favor. The problem was, we were getting married on August 7 and they were getting married on August 14. Evelyn and I would be on our honeymoon when they got married, and he was busy helping Pat prepare for their own wedding, so it was not to be.

Our wedding was now only a month or so away. Everyone in

★   ★   ★   ★   ★   ★   ★

my family was looking forward to our marriage. Dad wrote that my 13-year-old brother David was "looking forward to kissing the bride." Dad himself wrote, "May your [wedding] day be the happiest, sweetest, and holiest wedding in all the world and history of time." But not everyone in the Saylor household was happy about our marriage. Evelyn's mother truly felt that if Evelyn married me and left "the one, true church" that she would be eternally lost. She pleaded with Evelyn over and over not to marry me. One day she collapsed on the floor with grief and this nearly broke poor Evelyn's heart. She loved her mother, of course, and she did not want to disobey her or hurt her, but she also loved me and wanted to spend the rest of her life with me. This went on almost up to the day that we were married. Evelyn's father, however, did not feel the way Ethel did at all. Bob approved of me as a future son-in-law and so did most of his family. Some days I knew that Evelyn was smiling at me through her tears. It made me love her all the more.

In 1967 Johnny Cash and June Carter came out with their hit duet, "Jackson." "We got married in a fever, hotter than a pepper sprout." The month of July was certainly "hotter than a pepper sprout" in America. Anti-war protesters were burning their draft cards. Race riots left 38 people dead in Detroit. "Black power" advocates Stokely Carmichael and Adam Clayton Powell, Jr. called for "armed aggressive violence" throughout the United States. During all this time Evelyn continued cleaning houses for three clients, while I worked at Giant Foods and drove to Promise City twice a week to preach. We were pinching our pennies, saving for the big day. At the end of July I checked the electric meter to see if I had gone over the limit and would have to study by flashlight. I had not. Whew!

★   ★   ★   ★   ★   ★   ★

"WHITHER THOU GOEST"

In the 1960s you had to get a blood test in order to get married, so we had that taken care of a week or so before the wedding. (With the AIDS epidemic and all the STDs today, I am amazed a blood test is not required now.) On July 12 we picked out a pair of matching 14K white gold wedding bands at the Bookin Jewelry Co. at 113 East Main Street in downtown Ottumwa. Evelyn's cost more than mine even though mine was larger. Maybe that was so the bride would feel special. Together they came to $40. I picked up my black wedding suit at J. C. Penney's, and then we drove to Roxy's Dress Shop ("Always the Newest in Fashions") and picked up Evelyn's white satin wedding gown. We packed our bags and headed to Hamburg in my Corvair. We had a grand total of $90 between the two of us. A month or so before the wedding a lady had backed into the passenger side of my car. The body shop had smoothed out the door but had not yet spray painted it. That explains the gray primer on the door in the wedding pictures.

The whole Knowles family was coming from different directions to Hamburg. Muriel flew into Omaha from San Juan, Puerto Rico. My parents and Bonnie and David drove all the way from California. Becky came from nearby Council Bluffs. Eddie DeVries had asked dad to preach on Friday and Saturday night and on Sunday morning. I preached on Sunday night. All the while Evelyn, my mother and sisters, and some of the ladies from the church in Hamburg and the church in Rock Port were busy setting things up for the wedding on Monday night, August 7. On Sunday afternoon the whole family went to Council Bluffs to see Becky receive her diploma from Jennie Edmundson School of Nursing. Talk about a wild weekend!

★ ★ ★ ★ ★ ★ ★

The day of our wedding finally arrived. I was staying with the Koch brothers and was nervous as a cat on a hot tin roof. Since it was "bad luck" so see the bride on her wedding day, I spent much of the day pacing the floor. Evelyn went to the countryside and cut armloads of a beautiful white and green flower called "Snow on the Mountain." She also cut some large ferns and arranged them along with the flowers in several tall wicker baskets on the platform where the ceremony would take place. The bridal bouquet (yellow daisies), candles, and other accessories came to a grand total of $17.91. Upstairs, the ladies were busy preparing for the reception that would follow the wedding.

Evelyn was pleasantly surprised when her mother, grandmother, and several family members that she did not think would come to the wedding did so. Her father did not come because he felt self-conscious about his size and his new dentures had not yet arrived. Her brother, Kevin, walked her down the aisle to give her away with the words, "Her mother and I." Two of Evelyn's sisters, Gloria and Lauraly, served as bridesmaids. She also selected Rowena Johnson, a good friend, and my sister Muriel, the first member of my family that she had met. My four groomsmen were some of my best friends on earth: Terry Crist, Gary Cradic, Eddie DeVries, and Sam Brown. I was only sorry that Gary Bryant and Mike Gibson could not be there. My sister Becky accompanied Kyle and Earl Koch as they sang two numbers: "Abide with Us" and "Whither Thou Goest."

My father performed the candlelight double ring ceremony. If he had not typed out the entire ceremony and given it to me with the certificate of marriage, I could not tell you one word of what he said that night! But when he said, "You may now kiss the bride," I was all ears. I took Evelyn in my arms and tenderly kissed her. Then I heard

★   ★   ★   ★   ★   ★   ★

my father say, "I present to you Mr. and Mrs. Victor Knowles." The photographer snapped a great picture of us as we came down the steps. We both gave my mother, who was just beaming, a pair of happy smiles.

My kid brother got what he had been dreaming of for months – a chance to "kiss the bride," and then we all went upstairs for a lovely reception. Marcia Emberton had made a beautiful three-tiered wedding cake and many of the ladies of the church served as hostesses. Outside my buddies were busy decorating my car with shaving cream. We were greeted with the traditional throwing of rice as we came down the front steps of the church, got into the car, and sped away into the night.

After a brief honeymoon in Des Moines, we drove to Hubbard to see my Grandma Knowles, who had not been able to attend the wedding. My family was there, and we spent a day or two visiting with them. One afternoon we went to the City Park where I made notes from some of dad's sermon outlines. I was back in the pulpit at Promise City on August 13 preaching one of them, "Four Words that Ought to Be Branded into Every Human Conscience." In case you are wondering – "Thou God Seest Me" (Genesis 16:13).

I carried Evelyn over the threshold of our little apartment on 315 N. Marion Street upon our return to Ottumwa. We now had our very own place to live and Evelyn quickly set about turning it into a home as only a woman can do. While I studied at my desk in the alcove, she would write letters at an old-fashioned drop-leaf desk in the living room. Stamps were only five cents then. We had lots of wedding presents to unpack and thank- you cards to send. My parents gave us a set of china and silverware and Evelyn's parents gave us a nice

★　★　★　★　★　★　★

area rug. Most of the presents were at Evelyn's parent's home. For our first meal Evelyn peeled some potatoes, put them on the stove to boil, and then we drove across town to pick up the presents. We stayed too long, however, and when we arrived back at the apartment with our wedding loot we were greeted with the smell of scorched potatoes! Evelyn said, "Oh, no! I burned the first meal I cooked for you!"

From the outset of our marriage we set Matthew 6:33 as our lodestar. "But seek ye first the kingdom of God, and his righteousness; and all these things shall be added unto you." Through forty-plus years of marriage God has kept His promise. We have always tried to put God's kingdom and his righteousness first in our lives. As a result, He has always provided everything we needed (but not everything we wanted).

MY SENIOR YEAR

We now settled into a fairly regular routine. Evelyn cleaned houses for three well-to-do ladies: Mrs. Erland, Mrs. Seabrooke, and Mrs. Evans. I would take her to work in the mornings and they would bring her home at the end of the day. I continued my work at Giant Food and my ministry at Promise City. Now I would not have to make the bi-weekly 125-mile round trip by myself. All of the folks at Promise City fell in love with Evelyn. Each Sunday we would have dinner with a different family, although the lion's share fell to Franklin and Icle Matsler. They were so good to us. Sometimes on Sunday nights when we got back to Ottumwa we would discover a grocery sack in the back seat that they had placed there. Sometimes it was potatoes or vegetables and once in awhile it was steak!

As always, the school year kicked off with the Centerville Rally.

★   ★   ★   ★   ★   ★   ★

My parents got to attend this event just before they returned to California. It was the first time they had heard me sing in the quartet that I had been a part of for most of the year. The quartet was composed of Terry Crist, Henry Neff, Chester Mullins, and myself. Leland Vandeveer accompanied us on the piano. We had sung in churches and even a county fair. We had done well enough to buy matching outfits – blue sports coats, black slacks, white shirts, and matching ties. I really enjoyed singing bass with the men's quartet, but it took a lot of practice to be prepared. Throughout my senior year I traveled with other quartets composed of different men from Midwestern.

Before my folks returned to California, they stopped by to tell us good-by at our apartment. As Evelyn and I stood at the curb to wish them a safe journey, I felt a wave of emotion sweep over me. My mother saw tears in my eyes, got out of the car and "rocked her baby" one last time. I remember her saying, "Oh Victor, now we know that you love us." As they pulled away, I realized that the apron strings had just been cut forever.

In September I enrolled at Midwestern for the first time as a married student. Had I really turned into one of "those" kinds of "old" upperclassmen? I carried a heavy schedule that year: 1 and 2 Corinthians (Weller), Advanced Preaching (Culver), Personal Evangelism (Hunt), Greek (Hunt), and Prophets (Hunt). The latter was my favorite, hands down. In addition I took an elective: Art Layout taught by Nathalie Smith, graphic designer for the *Voice of Evangelism*. I was also singing in the traveling male quartet from time to time. I was so busy I couldn't even keep up with baseball like I used to. If you would have asked, "Who's on first?" I would have had to say, "I don't know." On September 11 I also began working part-time at the school to help pay

*   *   *   *   *   *   *

my tuition. The work I enjoyed most was proofreading the weekly *Evangelism from the Heart of America* and the monthly *Voice of Evangelism*. Soon I was putting into practice my Art Layout class by doing some of the art design and graphics for the *Voice of Evangelism*. Other than preparing sermons and papers for classes, I had not yet written anything for publication, but I was quickly learning the publication business.

I was busy, far too busy, and it began to show in our home life. Sometimes I would not get home until early in the morning if we had to unload a truck at Giant Food. I would fall asleep, get up early to study, and be off to school. Evelyn was only taking one class, Mrs. Hunt's "Art of Home Management." Perhaps I should have sat in on a few classes. Several times I heard Evelyn crying in the night, and I just didn't know what to do. I had not learned how to balance marriage with ministry or schedule with a spouse. I was a louse for a spouse but I didn't mean to be. My super schedule caused my grades to slip from nearly all A's the year before to B's, only one A, and a C that I despised with all my heart.

BAPTISTS AND PRESBYTERIANS

The Promise City congregation was made up mainly of older people. I think we had three teen-agers who usually sat in on Franklin Matsler's adult class. Brother Matsler used *Clarke's Commentary* and would have a different person read each verse we were covering that day. Sometimes he would say, "I believe that verse means just about what it says" and then go on to the next verse. One day a family with Baptist roots started attending the church. They had three little boys and Evelyn was delighted to at last use one of the Sunday School

★   ★   ★   ★   ★   ★   ★

rooms and have a class for the little lads. All went well until one Sunday when I happened to mention the doctrine of "once saved, always saved" in my message. We were all sad when the parents, who really were nice people, stopped coming to church. Brother Matsler and I called on them a number of times but it was to no avail. John Calvin's terrible TULIP theology had done its work.

Dale A. Williamson invited our quartet to come to Lexington, Nebraska, for a weekend of special services October 27-29. We sang 30 songs over the weekend! Sam Brown, Terry Crist and I preached. My Sunday morning message was on Barabbas, "The Man for Whom Christ Died." A young girl, Lanay Strever, became the first person to respond to my preaching for Christian baptism. Brother Williamson sent a report to *Evangelism from the Heart of America* which stated that the weekend of special services was "a full and wonderful one here in Lexington." He wrote, "Good attendance marked all the services with people present from Tilden, Neligh, Holdredge, Hastings, Edgar, Lincoln, Overton, North Platte, and Cozad . . . Our appreciation for these young people deepened as we saw them depart after the Sunday night service, driving all night to return to their responsibilities in Iowa."

In November my first published article appeared in the *Voice of Evangelism*, "Journey into Hell," a fictional account of a lost sinner's descent into the lake of fire. It wasn't exactly Jonathan Edwards ("Sinners in the Hands of an Angry God") but it was mine, and I was excited to see my byline in print for the first time in a national publication along with those of Donald G. Hunt, J. Charles Dailey, and H. N. Solliday.

My sisters Becky and Muriel were among our first house guests on Thanksgiving Day, which happened to fall on my 22nd birthday

★   ★   ★   ★   ★   ★   ★

that year. We were glad to see them come and sad to see them go. We were even sadder around midnight on November 24 when I rushed Evelyn to the Ottumwa Hospital where she suffered a miscarriage. She fainted in the parking lot. Evelyn was in the hospital November 25-28. I went out to see her each day and had to go to Promise City alone on Sunday morning. The good people there told me not to stay for the Sunday evening service so that I could spend the rest of the day with Evelyn in the hospital. No doubt I continued my work on my Senior Chapel sermon that I was scheduled to preach on Tuesday morning. I don't remember much about it because I was still in a fog of concern about Evelyn. We wrote to my parents telling them about Evelyn's ordeal. Dad perceived that I was now showing "more lavish love and care" for Evelyn. And he was right.

One afternoon in December a man walked into the vestibule of the school where I was working and asked if anyone there would be willing to preach on December 31 for the Presbyterian Church in Hedrick, a small town a few miles from Ottumwa. I told him that I would be glad to do that for them. It was 15 degrees below zero the morning we drove to Hedrick in my car that barely produced any heat. The church parking lot was empty when I arrived, but the same gentleman who had invited me to come was there. He told us that the services had been cancelled because the furnace had broken down. He gave me a nice check for my troubles and said that they would still like to have me come and preach. I had never been paid before for *not* preaching. That check got us through the holidays and then some.

On February 11, 1968, I returned to the Hedrick Presbyterian Church. I preached from 2 Kings 22 and 23, relating the story of what happened in the nation of Judah when Hilkiah the priest discovered

*   *   *   *   *   *   *   *

the book of the law in the house of the Lord. I told them how the young king Josiah launched a successful movement to restore the ordinances of God. The people just loved that sermon, "Back to the Book!" and wanted me to come and preach for them on a regular basis. They were disappointed, and so was I, when word came down from the district superintendent that since I was not ordained and licensed with the Presbyterian Church, I could not preach for this group of people who were hungry for the Word of God. To this day I believe that the principles of restoration could have worked among those good Presbyterian people.

FINAL DAYS AT MIDWESTERN

The year 1968 was once compared to "a knife blade that severed past from future." Janis Joplin sang "Me and Bobby McGee" which contained a line that seemed to say what the year was all about: "Freedom's just another word for nothing left to lose." While we were snug and secure in our little apartment, "America shuddered. History cracked open: bats came flapping out, dark surprises" (*Time*, Jan. 11, 1988). The New Year, which began my final semester at Midwestern, began with the Viet Cong launching the Tet offensive and ended with astronaut James Lovell reading the Christmas story from outer space as Apollo 8 circled the moon.

When my second and final semester at Midwestern began, I added to my already busy schedule a 6:30 A.M. Journalism class under Hunt and a 9:00 P.M. Prison Epistles class, also under Hunt. The addition of these two classes made me come to a decision about my job at Giant Foods. Even though we needed the extra money, I knew I could no longer continue my work there and keep my grades up. They hated

★ ★ ★ ★ ★ ★ ★

to see me leave, and I hated to give up the job. Now my only salary came from preaching at Promise City. My afternoon job at the school continued to help pay down my tuition. Evelyn pretty well put me through school that final semester with her three house-cleaning jobs. One week we lived on nothing but potatoes and eggs – given to us by the Matslers. That was all we had, but we were grateful for what we had. I was amazed how many different and delicious ways Evelyn prepared our meals with just those two ingredients.

The first Sunday in January the church in Promise City hosted a Singspiration. Because of sub-zero temperatures only 45 people came, but we were encouraged because it was the largest crowd yet we had seen in the church. The blind poetess, Fanny J. Crosby, had written every song I selected. The next Sunday I preached my 100th sermon since making my decision to preach: "O Lord, How Long?" from Habakkuk 1:2. I am sure that this message was inspired by my class on Old Testament Prophets, but it was certainly relevant to the times in which we lived.

Evelyn and I were happy to open our little apartment to two couples during the January Gathering: Gary and Marilyn (Daly) Brennfoerder, and Eddie and Betty DeVries. We slept on the couch and floor so one couple could have our bed and the other couple could sleep on the now-famous "runaway rollaway." The featured speakers were Burton W. Barber and Carol J. Lankford. During the Bible conference I received an invitation to speak at a rally with Brother Barber later in the year. I also was approached by Russell Crum to see if I was interested in taking the church in Roberts Cove, Louisiana, when I graduated in May. This was pretty heady stuff, but it did not increase my hat size too much.

★   ★   ★   ★   ★   ★   ★

One day Evelyn was walking by the Singer Sewing Machine store in downtown Ottumwa when she saw a sewing machine on sale in the display window. She thought that this would be a great buy because she could save money by making clothing and household items like curtains, bedspreads, quilts, towels, washcloths, etc. She had been saving money from her jobs and had enough to purchase the machine and the nice wooden cabinet that came with it. This was the biggest purchase "we" had made – around $125.00. I say "we" because I was somewhat surprised when I came home that night and saw this "extravagant" purchase in our home. In time I did have to admit that Evelyn was a discretionary buyer because it is still being used by one of our daughters at this writing!

My "purchase," if you can call it that, was a portable Magnavox record player that my sister Becky had sold (or maybe given) to me. It had a great sound, and I loved nothing more than putting on a Blackwood Brothers' LP record while I was preparing for my Sunday sermons. Dr. Christiaan Barnard had recently made history when he conducted the world's first heart transplant in Capetown, South Africa. I used this current illustration as a springboard into my February 4 message at Promise City, "The Great Heart Transplant." This was another sermon inspired by my Prophets class for my text was taken from Jeremiah 31:31-33. I was quick to make use of what I was learning for the betterment of others. I have always tried to make my preaching relevant with the use of current happenings in the news.

PREACHING WHILE AMERICA BURNED

The same Sunday I preached "The Great Heart Transplant," we went to Albia for the monthly Singspiration. The weather was much

★   ★   ★   ★   ★   ★   ★

better and there was a full house with people standing in the back of the auditorium. Evelyn and I sang a duet, "Neither Do I Condemn Thee." This was not the first time we had sung together. The previous semester we had sung Myron LeFevre's "Without Him." We had also sung for Jerry and Vivian Harris's wedding in December. That was an adventure. We were singing "Each for the Other" to the accompaniment of the organ when the power went out. The organ wheezed and came to a stop but we kept going because Evelyn had been raised a cappella and this was no challenge to her. I followed suit and we finished the song while the organist was down on her hand and knees trying to find out what was wrong with the organ. My trusty logbook also says that we sang "Life like a River" at the March Singspiration in Centerville. Through the years we have sung duets, and I believe we do our best on Bob Ponchot's "God Still Cares."

I enjoyed singing but had no intentions of doing anything other than preaching when I graduated. Still, it was a blast to go on trips with various male gospel quartets from time to time. One of my favorite songs to sing in those years was "The Jericho Road." In March I was part of a quartet that appeared in West Concord, Minnesota. Kyle Koch and the Hunt brothers and I sang 15 songs, accompanied by Leland Vandeveer. I preached on Saturday night and Kyle preached on Sunday morning. Kyle had a sermon on the topic of courage that he would often ask me to give a new title to in order to "dress it up." On this occasion I gave it the title "The Bold and the Brave." I got a kick out of seeing his same sermon under different titles I had concocted for him that were published in the school paper. During the same month I preached at a weekend rally in Council Bluffs, where I had preached my first sermon back in November of 1964.

★   ★   ★   ★   ★   ★   ★

On March 31 President Johnson went before the American people and said, "I shall not seek and I will not accept the nomination of my party as your president." I felt sorry for LBJ. Nearly every time he appeared in public he was confronted by college students and anti-war activists yelling, "Hey, hey, LBJ! How many kids did you kill today?" Anti-war candidates Robert F. Kennedy and Eugene McCarthy were quick to throw their political hats in the ring.

Then, on April 4, at 6:01 P.M., Martin Luther King, Jr. was assassinated while he was standing on the second-floor balcony of the Lorraine Motel in Memphis, Tennessee. I could not understand how the death of a man who preached and practiced nonviolence could set off the incendiary and seemingly insane reaction that it did. Forty-six citizens died in terrible riots that spread to 125 cities including Chicago, Baltimore, Cincinnati, Kansas City and Washington, D. C. A few weeks later James Earl Ray was named as the suspect, setting off an international manhunt that ended, ironically, the day RFK was assassinated in Los Angeles.

My final year at Midwestern was coming to an end faster than a speeding bullet. During the month of April I was kept busy in the evenings practicing for a play that Donald G. Hunt had written, "Alive Forevermore!" Just as in high school, I was chosen to play two parts: Annas the High Priest and Philip, one of the twelve apostles. The play would be presented the week of graduation.

What would it be like to appear at a preaching rally with someone like the legendary Burton W. Barber? Sam Brown and I were about to find out. In mid-April we traveled to Rittman, Ohio, where Brother Barber was conducting a revival for Ed McSpadden. Dave McSpadden, Ed's son, and Don Hunt II made up the rest of our quartet. Brother

★   ★   ★   ★   ★   ★   ★

Barber opened and closed the rally while Sam and I brought one message each. Barber probably quoted more Scripture in just one sermon than we read in both of our messages! I had heard that the great man had committed most of the New Testament to memory. Appearing on the program with him was a special treat for us since we did not get to "sit at the feet of Gamaliel" our freshman year. On the way home we had a car wreck in Chicago. No one was seriously injured. And, no, I was not driving the car! In fact, I was sleeping in the back seat and have no memory of the collision. Let the record show that Sam was behind the wheel, and he was playing Rook while trying to traverse the freeways of Chicago!

Two days later I was part of a quartet in yet another great Sunday of singing and preaching in Hamburg, Iowa. Sam preached in the morning, Keevin Koch led another "rousing" Singspiration in the afternoon, and I preached the Sunday night sermon, "The Great Heart Transplant." The quartet, that also included Kyle Koch and Don Hunt II, sang at each service. We made it back to Ottumwa in the wee hours of the morning without incident or accident. Other than singing in the Graduation Quartet in May, this would be my last time to sing in a male gospel quartet at Midwestern. I enjoyed every minute of the ride. In another year or so Don Hunt II, Dave McSpadden, Mark McDowell and Leland Vandeveer formed The Sing-for-Christ quartet (later renamed The Gateway Singers). Orginally the group consisted of Dave McSpadden, Don Hunt II, Mark McDowell, and Leland Vandeveer. I had sung with every one of them at one time or another. Forty years later Dave and Don (and their wives) are still singing with that group!

On Saturday, April 27, it was my turn to plan a preaching rally. I invited Harold Buckles (who was conducting the revival in

★　★　★　★　★　★　★

Ottumwa) and Donald G. Hunt to speak at the area youth rally which was sponsored that month by the Promise City church. We had 150 people in attendance, more people in our church building than at any another other time during my student ministry there.

Harold Buckles, an evangelist who was full of interesting ideas and intrigue, conducted a two-week revival the last week of April and the first week of May. This cut into my final studies, but Evelyn and I managed to attend as many of the services as we could. One night he preached his famous sermon, "Christ in the Passover." In this presentation he set up a table with all the trappings of the Jewish Passover feast. He announced in advance the night that he would preach this particular sermon. There was a Jewish synagogue on the East Side of Ottumwa where Mr. and Mrs. Bookin attended each Sabbath. Mr. Bookin owned the Bookin Jewelry Co., where many of the students from Midwestern, including Evelyn and I, had purchased their wedding rings. The Bookins were sitting on the front row the night Brother Buckles preached "Christ in the Passover." Two things that happened that night impressed me. First, how interested Mr. Bookin was in the presentation. He leaned forward so as not to miss a single word. The second thing that impressed me was when Mr. Bookin raised his hand and asked permission to speak. Brother Buckles granted him permission. We all held our breath. What would he say? Mr. Bookin pointed out a mistake, a minor one, which the visiting evangelist had made in talking about one of the items on the Passover Table. We held our breath again. How would the preacher respond? Brother Buckles was most gracious, admitting his mistake, and complimenting Mr. Bookin on his perception. "Now this," I thought to myself, "is the way to 'win friends and influence people.'" The events of that night taught me that

★　　★　　★　　★　　★　　★　　★

no preacher is above being "entreated" and when he is corrected he should be as gracious in receiving correction as Brother Buckles was that night long ago.

QUO VADIS?

As graduation drew near I was still undecided as to what I would do. Entries in my *Ready Record* indicate I had 10 "possible places" to go: two on the West Coast, one in the South, and seven in the Midwest. Representatives of a new church in Spokane, Washington had spoken to my father to see if I might be interested, but I knew that I was not ready at all for a new church or even an established church for that matter. I was not yet Victor Mature.

Kyle Koch, who planned to marry Juli Winder in July, and I drove to Hamburg on May 11 to visit with Eddie DeVries about our future. We had heard that he was contemplating a move to Portland, Oregon. Would there be a place for us at Hamburg should he decide to remain? There would. We talked at length about what all that might involve but were sworn to secrecy and for good reason, as you will see shortly, about the specifics. Our friend and fellow graduate-to-be Terry Crist was ordained to the ministry in the afternoon, and I preached that night. Kyle and I returned to Ottumwa pondering the possibility of a move to Hamburg. What did the future hold for us? We committed ourselves to prayer about the matter.

On Sunday, May 19, almost a year to the day since I began preaching at Promise City, my student ministry came to close. I would be the last student preacher in the history of that church. Merle Dean Prater, the preaching brother of Malburt Prater, would move to Promise City once I left. At this writing he and his wife Mattie Faye are still min-

★   ★   ★   ★   ★   ★   ★

istering to that congregation! (I once got her name mixed up and called her "Fattie Maye," much to my embarrassment!) For my last sermon I repeated the first sermon I had preached there a year ago, "The Challenges We Face." There were lots of hugs and handshakes after the final amen. Brother Matsler said, "The church is in the best shape it has been in for many years" as he slipped a personal check for $50 into my hand. We pulled away from the church that night with a heart full of memories. I couldn't see the road very well, and it sure wasn't because it was raining. All the rain was in my heart and I used my index finger as a "windshield wiper" as we drove back to Ottumwa.

"FREELY YE HAVE RECEIVED, FREELY GIVE"

The motto of Midwestern School of Evangelism was a biblical one: "Freely ye have received, freely give." (When I began lecturing at the Pepperdine University Bible Lectures in 1998 I was thrilled to see that the motto of that great Christian university was the same as our small school in Iowa.) I was determined that I would always represent my school well, and that I would, on their behalf, be an "ambassador of good will" for Midwestern everywhere I went. To this day I believe that I have kept that self-imposed promise.

As Graduation Week approached, May 20-23, 1968, my mind couldn't help but go back to the day I had enrolled at Midwestern. Missing Registration Day to pay a traffic fine for careless driving. The "whirlwind year" that started with my decision to preach ended with a broken engagement. The terrible accident that took two innocent lives and turned my own life around. Meeting Evelyn – marrying Evelyn! All those classes, tests, papers, sermons and songs. How could all that happen in just four short years?

★   ★   ★   ★   ★   ★   ★

Thirty-nine of us had started out with high hopes and daring dreams in the fall of 1964. Two of our classmates, Peggy Wyatt and Susan Wood McGlumphry, were already in heaven. Only six of the original 39 would graduate. In alphabetical order: Sharon Agenter (by this time married to Darrell Bridgewater), Roger Deys (by this time married to another 1964 enrollee, Lois Williamson), Sam Brown (by this time married to Madaline Cross), Richard Geringswald (by this time married to Sandy Howard), and myself. But eight others graduated with us, making 14 in all, the largest graduating class in the history of Midwestern. They included, in alphabetical order: Lloyd Bradley (a transfer student from Central Christian College of the Bible), Madaline Brown, Mike Clement, Terry Crist, Gary Cradic, Sandy Geringswald, Kyle Koch, and Karen Koopman.

My father flew from Los Angeles to Omaha and took the train from Council Bluffs to Ottumwa. I met him at the train depot, and he stayed with us during Graduation Week. The three days of festivities began Monday afternoon with a prayer meeting for the graduates at the Administration Building, a softball game and picnic at Wildwood Park, and the evening service at the Pennsylvania Avenue Church of Christ. I was chosen to bring the first of nine sermons delivered by the male graduates in the next two days. All of the messages were taken from the book of Proverbs. I took my text from Proverbs 21:22, "A wise man scaleth the city of the mighty and casteth down the strength of the confidence thereof." I titled my sermon "Scaling the Walls of the High and the Mighty." Evelyn was sitting with my father and one of the ladies she cleaned houses for, Mrs. Seabrooke. Also present that day was Mrs. Marie Box, a checker at Giant Foods whom I had been witnessing to. When my sermon was done, Mrs. Seabrooke leaned over to

*   *   *   *   *   *   *

Evelyn and said, "I can see he's going to be a great preacher." (Evelyn chose not to tell me this for years lest I get the "big head.") I did not know it at the time, but a "scout" was also in the audience that night. Tom Sutherland, an elder in the Locust Grove Church of Christ in Galax, Virginia, had been "commissioned" by the minister, James E. Gibbons, to recommend one of the graduates to hold a revival at Galax in the future. When he got back to Galax, Tom told James, "The man you want is Victor Knowles." I knew nothing of this either until much later.

Tuesday night, after four more graduate sermons in the morning and afternoon, the play "Alive Forevermore!" was presented to about 750 people in the auditorium of Evans Junior High School. Terry Crist played the part of Christ, Kyle Koch was Caiphas the High Priest, and I played the role of Annas the High Priest and the apostle Philip. At one point in the play Marcia Williamson was to fall down at the feet of Christ and exclaim, "Blessed Jesus!" Somehow that struck me funny. From that day to this I have called her Marcia "Blessed Jesus" Koch (she later married Keevin Koch).

THE FINAL FAREWELL

Graduation Day, May 23, finally arrived. Evelyn bought me a yellow rose and pinned it on the lapel of my new suit. The graduation sermons were becoming a blur, but I never forgot something that Gary Cradic said during the ninth and final of the graduates' messages. "Some day we will not be defined by what 'camp' we are in regarding this issue or that issue. It will be those who believe in God and His Word against the whole world." I thought that was a pretty dramatic "prophecy" but today as I look at how believers are "surrounded on

★　★　★　★　★　★　★

every side" by the enemy I would have to say that Cradic was way ahead of his time in "prophetic perception."

I have two photographs before me as I write these words. The first is a black and white snapshot of our Freshman Quartet singing on stage at Midwestern. Jenifer Bradley is at the piano and there stand the "Four Freshmen" – Raymond Johnson, Roger Deys, Sam Brown, and myself. Now I am looking at a color snapshot of our Graduation Quartet singing on stage at the Pennsylvania Avenue church – Terry Crist, Roger Deys, Sam Brown, and myself. The accompanist is off camera but I believe she was Margaret Hunt. Three of us (Roger, Sam, and I) made it all the way. I am the only one living today as both Roger and Sam died in their 50s. You will excuse me for a moment, won't you? Thank you.

At 7:30 in the evening Jerry Weller brought the faculty message and Lafe Culver made the presentation of degrees. I have another photograph before me of my father, Evelyn and me standing together and holding my framed Bachelor of Sacred Literature degree. I could not possibly have made it to that moment without their love, prayers and support (both emotional and financial).

The June 22 issue of *Evangelism from the Heart of America* carried the graduates' pictures and future plans. Mine read, "Victor Knowles will be assisting Edwin DeVries with the work at Hamburg, Iowa." Dale A. Williamson, father of graduate Lois Williamson Deys, wrote the following eloquent words: "We were impressed with the fine caliber of young people graduating this year, and we were thrilled as we listened to the young men preach. Their messages showed good preparation and were clearly and powerfully presented. It is encouraging to know that such young people will be launching out for the Lord in var-

★   ★   ★   ★   ★   ★   ★

ious fields of labor . . . . Following the [final] message, degrees and certificates were presented to the graduates . . . and then as the young people stood with heads bowed, the faculty members offered prayers for them individually. We shall never forget the stirring scenes as loved ones and friends gathered around the young people to bid them Godspeed. And our hearts were also touched as students with tears streaming down their cheeks bade one another farewell after several years of wonderful fellowship and close association, realizing that for some it would be the final farewell on earth."

LEAVING OUR FIRST HOME

The day after my graduation from college we packed what few belongings we had and prepared to move to Hamburg. There I would become Assistant Minister with Eddie DeVries and my beloved Church of Christ at 1305 Main Street in Hamburg, Iowa. We took one final look around our first home, the little upstairs apartment at 315 N. Marion Street in Ottumwa. We handed over the keys to the apartment to Leland and Merna (Petersen) Vandeveer. We told Mrs. Baker good-by. There was nothing left to do but leave. But how do you leave a city where your wife has spent her entire life and I had just invested four years of my own life? Not easily, that is for sure. We got into my old 1962 Corvair, filled to the roof with our belongings. I remembered when the old gospel chariot wouldn't start and I had to coast down the hill and "pop the clutch" to start the engine. This time it was easy. I turned the key in the ignition and "Vair-Vair" (the nickname we had given it) purred like a kitten. We eased away from the curb and drove across the Highway 63 bridge that spanned the Des Moines River. I remembered the bitterly cold night I ran out of gas on that bridge and had to run to

★   ★   ★   ★   ★   ★   ★

get a canister of gas so that I could get back to the dorm. At the junction of Highway 63 and Highway 34 we stopped at the traffic light. I remembered the first time I saw the skyline of Ottumwa. Church steeples high on the hills gave "The City of Bridges" an almost European skyline look. The light turned green, and we turned west on Highway 34 and headed towards Hamburg.

Neither of us had any idea where the road ahead in our marriage and ministry would take us. We never dreamed as we drove into the west, that our setting forth together would eventually result in taking us from coast to coast and border to border of the United States. Or that some day we would stand in Communist strongholds and proclaim the gospel. Or that God would use us – two 23-year-old kids from Iowa – to help heal some of the wounds of a century-old division between two groups of people numbering in the millions.

But all that, and much more, was about to happen.

★   ★   ★   ★   ★   ★   ★

CHAPTER EIGHT
TRAINING FOR SERVICE

Being raised a preacher's kid and now a preacher myself, though not yet ordained as such, I considered Hamburg the closest thing I had for a home town. This would be my third, but not final, stint in the town bordered by the beautiful Loess Hills. We moved into a large room in the back of the church that would become our humble home for the next 13 months. The front half of the room we set up as our living room, and the back half became our bedroom. Helen Koch, the mother of the Koch brothers, gave us a full-size bed, chest of drawers, and a dresser. Off the bedroom was a full bathroom. I had taken many a bath in the old claw foot tub as a child. Well, maybe not as many as my mother would have desired! Evelyn used the fully equipped kitchen in the upstairs fellowship hall to prepare our meals. The refrigerator was used primarily to refrigerate the communion juice, so she had plenty of room to put our milk, butter and eggs. We lived as frugally as we could, trying not to spend more than $5 a week on groceries. Food prices were pretty low in 1968. Bread was 20 cents a loaf, 10 pounds of potatoes cost 49 cents, and oleo was two pounds for just 29 cents. I was not paid a salary by the church but neither were we charged any rent or utilities. When I was not holding revival meetings, I worked for some of the farmers in the church or did some odd jobs in the community.

Since our first home had been fully furnished, it was exciting to gradually make our first furniture purchases. One Saturday I went to

★   ★   ★   ★   ★   ★   ★

an auction and paid just $6 for a matching Mastercraft sofa and over-stuffed chair. No matter to me that they were a dreadful burgundy color. I brought them home with great pride like a hunter coming in from the field with his first kill. Evelyn thought the color was hideous, but she said, "Well, you did get a good bargain!" They were so well built that we had the set for years, somewhat to Evelyn's dismay. We started going to Bill Gold's auction house one night a week to scout out other bargains. Evelyn raised her hand one night, and I said, "Evelyn! They will think you are bidding!" She smiled and said, "I am!" That night she snagged a Scrabble set for only 50 cents and only one of the "E's" was missing. Our most "extravagant" purchase was $10 for a beautiful antique cherry wood table with a glass top. In the summer time a huge old window fan helped circulate the air in the room.

Evelyn told me she loved having her "old Victor" back. I had been so busy my senior year in college that she had wondered if it would always be that way. Now it seemed that we had some spare time to do things together as we had done in our courting days.

I BECOME AN "ASSISTANT MINISTER"

I set up my study stage left. My father's study had been stage right. That was now Eddie DeVries' domain. My office had a long black walnut church pew against one wall and an old black walnut table covered with a lace tablecloth where the ladies prepared communion on Sunday mornings. I took one corner of the room to set up my study, using a nice oak library table for my desk. I lined my books up on the back of the table against the wall, hung my diploma from Midwestern on the wall, plugged in my trusty desk lamp, placed my green file box under the table and declared my office "open for

★   ★   ★   ★   ★   ★   ★

business." In time I added a used Royal typewriter to my ministerial arsenal.

Terry Paul was Brother DeVries' Associate Minister so Eddie came up with a title of "Assistant Minister" for me. Eddie was an easy man to work with and work under. So were the elders of the church, Ronald Emberton and Marvin Sheldon. Brother Sheldon taught the large auditorium class on Sunday mornings while Brother Emberton taught Sunday morning high school class. One of my new duties was to teach the young people's class on Sunday evenings, before the main service. I used some workbooks on the New Testament church that had been developed by J. Charles Dailey. It was gratifying to see how hard the young people worked on those lessons. Evelyn was asked to teach the preschool class on Sunday mornings. The children loved her and she loved them right back. One Sunday she was telling them the story of how wicked men crucified Jesus on the cross. She noticed that one little boy, Kevin Paul, was becoming very upset. He finally scooted his chair back, stood straight up, and said, "Do you know what I would have done if I was Jesus?"

Evelyn smiled sweetly and said, "No, Kevin, what would you have done if you had been Jesus?"

"I'd of got a gun and shot them all!" declared Kevin. Evelyn had to hide a smile as she explained to Kevin how Jesus loved them in spite of what they had done and even asked God to forgive them.

I prepared a new church bulletin, which I dubbed *The Christian Persuader*, on Saturday nights, cranking them out on an A. B. Dick mimeograph machine, folding them, and having them ready to hand out on Sunday morning. I typed and printed a new church directory. I also typed some class notes for Wednesday and Sunday evenings. Evelyn

★   ★   ★   ★   ★   ★   ★

and I created posters for special occasions and maintained the bulletin board, the first thing visitors saw when they entered the auditorium. We made sure that it was neat, attractive, colorful, and that all announcements and church handbills were up to date. People notice little things like that and can make quick judgments about a church.

VISITATION OPPORTUNITIES

One of my first duties was to "visit the widows in their affliction" (James 1:27). I always took Evelyn with me on these visits. I believe we called on every widow in the church at least once if not more. They were so appreciative of a visit from a minister and his wife. If we were doing hospital visitation, we would limit our stay to just a few minutes, but we allowed ourselves much more time with them when we were calling on them in their homes. Ever since Hamburg I have always had a special place in my heart for elderly Christian women who have lost their husbands. Many times they will sit together in church, sometimes taking up an entire row. I called this the "Sweetheart Row" and always tried to make my way down that row shaking one hand after another. It is wonderful to see their faces light up when they see you paying them some special attention.

One evening we were spending some time with Inez Coffey in her home. We were playing Scrabble, and at the end of the game I confessed to her and Evelyn that I had cheated by turning over a tile and using it as a blank to help create a word that I had scored big on. They never let me forget that, but it sure made a good memory. I wonder tonight how many lonely church widows there are who would just love it if someone from the church stopped in to play Scrabble, even if they cheated! One of the greatest sins of the modern church is focusing

★   ★   ★   ★   ★   ★   ★

so much attention on the needs of young people while the elderly and their needs are neglected.

We also enjoyed calling on elderly couples, and we learned so much from them. One of the couples we liked to visit was Chris ("Bunjie") and Nannie Lloyd. I learned that he had been a part of the U.S. forces under General John "Black Jack" Pershing that had been sent to New Mexico to track down the notorious Mexican revolutionary Pancho Villa. Poor "Bunjie" had fought the tobacco habit all his life. He wanted to quit but just couldn't seem to shake the habit. He would go forward at revival meetings and tearfully ask for prayers. I grew to appreciate how some people have to fight battles that others never have. Sometimes he would sing a solo at church, and it seemed like it was always "I Come to the Garden Alone." I can never hear that song without thinking of him. One of my greatest regrets is that I never went fishing with him. He asked me many times to do so, but I was not much on fishing so I always found some reason not to go with him. If I had known then what I know now, I would have dropped everything and gone fishing with "Bunjie."

One Sunday afternoon Ronald Emberton took me with him to call on Nettie Dankof, a member of the church who was a widow and a shut-in. After serving her the Lord's Supper from the little black kit the church provided, Brother Emberton asked her if there was anything we could do for her.

"Oh, Brother Ronald," she said, "my toenails are just killing me. I can't bend over anymore to trim them. Could you do that for me?"

Secretly, I was glad she had not asked me. But I received a lesson in humility that day that was almost as good as the one Jesus taught His disciples when He knelt down in the Upper Room and

★   ★   ★   ★   ★   ★   ★

washed their feet. Brother Emberton reached into his coat pocket, pulled out a pair of nail clippers, knelt down on one knee and very carefully began trimming Mrs. Dankof's toenails. All the time he was talking to her gently about the Lord and His goodness to us. I saw her reach for a handkerchief and dab her eyes. These are the things they don't teach you in Bible College and that you will never learn unless you go calling with a godly elder who is not too proud to kneel down and minister to a fellow disciple, even if it means trimming toenails.

EDDIE AND EVANGELISM

Eddie DeVries had the gift of evangelism. He loved people and loved to lead them to a saving knowledge of the Lord. Sometimes he would take me on calls with him, cautioning me to be his "silent partner." I was to smile, be friendly, affirm what Eddie was saying with my body language but otherwise keep quiet. This was a good experience for me because I learned lots just by listening to his conversation with the unchurched. Had he sent me out "cold turkey," I would have failed miserably. He normally called by appointment, something I would learn to do in later years. Eddie was strong on building relationships with people, becoming their friend and confidant, before addressing their spiritual need to accept Christ. It was always a joy to see people make a decision for Christ when Eddie finally "called the question."

One Sunday afternoon I helped Eddie clear the stage in the sanctuary and set up a mock living room. We were going to put on a demonstration of how to call on prospects for the entire congregation during the evening service. I took my desk lamp and placed it inside a small wood cabinet with louvered doors to create the effect of a glowing TV. On a small end table next to my overstuffed chair I had placed

★   ★   ★   ★   ★   ★   ★

several pieces of white chalk, which would serve as my "cigarettes." We went through our script and were ready for the evening performance. Eddie was the Christian visitor and I was the town "heathen" who was supposed to become converted by the end of the night. Of course, I got carried away with the moment and started ad-libbing just like I had done in my high school play. Eddie did not know that I had been voted "First to Receive an Oscar." I could barely contain myself and the roar of the audience sitting in the darkness of the sanctuary was like music to my ears. Poor Eddie stammered and stuttered and the whole skit almost became a disaster until I finally realized I was undoing the whole effect Eddie had hoped to achieve. I put down my "cigarette," turned down the "TV," and started listening to Eddie and delivering the right answers. Somehow the heathen got converted that night, but it was touch and go for awhile.

IN THE PULPIT AND ON THE CHURCH ROOF

During my 13 months of ministry/internship with the Hamburg Church of Christ I was in the pulpit about a dozen times. That was very generous for a Senior Minister (although that term was not in vogue then) to do with a young Assistant Minister. I do believe that my best effort was the Sunday night I preached "Without a Prayer," a brand new sermon that I had developed. It was based on King Hezekiah's two effective prayers in 2 Kings 19 and 20. "But," I asked, "would all this have happened without a prayer?" I then showed how that "without a prayer" there can be no answer from above, burdens become heavier, sins remain unforgiven, and heaven cannot be attained. A dozen people from the Rock Port congregation came to be with us that night which was a great encouragement to me. Nearly

★   ★   ★   ★   ★   ★   ★

every Monday morning after I had preached on Sunday, Carl McSpadden came shuffling down the hall and knocked on our door. When I would open the door, he would say, "Good sermon, Vic," and tuck a $5 dollar bill in my shirt pocket. Sometimes that is what bought our groceries that week. At other times Ronald Emberton would show up with a box full of groceries.

Sitting under Eddie's preaching was quite an experience. One Sunday morning Eddie was preaching on the woman who for 18 years had been afflicted with a "spirit of infirmity" that caused her to be bent over. "She could in no wise lift up herself" (Luke 13:11). Eddie, a tall and lanky fellow, was in rare form that day. He did an amazing depiction of that poor bent woman, pacing back and forth across the stage, bent over and for all the world looking like a walking willow or a moving mini-version of the St. Louis Arch. His long black hair fell down around his face, ballpoint pens and combs fell from his shirt pocket, and his necktie nearly touched the floor. All the while he was saying, "Oh, this poor woman! Bent over and could not straighten up! And for 18 long years! Can you imagine how miserable was her life?" We had no trouble imagining it; we were seeing it played out firsthand. Then, still bent over, hair hanging and necktie dragging, he spoke words of Jesus: "Woman, thou art loosed from thine infirmity!" Immediately, like the woman of old, Eddie instantly shot up to his full height. I thought the place was going to go nuts! He deserved an Oscar for that performance!

On another occasion, a warm summer evening, when the congregants were drifting off and others were in full slumber, Eddie somehow managed to use his arms like one on the parallel bars and vault himself upwards until he was standing on *top* of the pulpit.

★   ★   ★   ★   ★   ★   ★

"Christians, awake!" he roared from his lofty position with arms outstretched. Everyone came out of their slumber; indeed, some came out of their very theater seats, as his voice echoed throughout the auditorium like the voice of the archangel.

Sometimes I would do a little song leading, and that was fairly easy to do because the Hamburg congregation was a great singing church. When we sang "In My Heart There Rings a Melody," the ladies chimed like bells during the refrain and it was really something to hear. The church was loaded with musical talent, and we had all kinds of solos, duets, trios, quartets, mixed quartets, and so on. I don't know that we ever ministered with a church that had as much musical talent or used as much talent as at Hamburg.

But all our work was not done inside that grand old auditorium at 1305 Main Street. One day found me on top of the church roof with Raymond Wise, repairing one of the brick chimneys. I still cannot believe I got up on that steep roof since I suffer from acrophobia (fear of heights). I couldn't stand on top of a pulpit, a la Eddie. But Brother Wise was much older than I was, so I guess I figured if he could do it, I could do it. Evelyn and I also helped Terry Paul and others mix cement and put in a new wide sidewalk leading up to the church steps. That was really backbreaking work. Evelyn and I also painted the church sign on the front lawn of the church. Sometimes I would take my turn at mowing the church lawn to keep everything looking nice and trim. I have always been a stickler for keeping my own lawn that way and do not understand churches that do not maintain their building and grounds.

★ ★ ★ ★ ★ ★ ★

EARNING A LIVING

So how did a nonsalaried Assistant Minister make a living and provide for his new bride? My 1968 *Ready Record* reveals that Evelyn and I earned a grand total of $1,716.00 for the year – and that includes the five months we were working in Ottumwa before we moved to Hamburg. Simple math says that we managed to live on an average of $33.00 a week for the year. I did some farm work for Ronald Emberton and his son-in-law Rex Bryant. One frosty winter day Rex rolled a big hay truck. We were taking hay to a bunch of cattle in a field when the tires slipped on the frost and over we went on Rex's side. I about broke my arm just trying to hang on to the door handle lest I land on top of Rex. I don't even remember how we managed to get out of the truck that lay on its side like a wounded animal. The Koch brothers and I also dug a well for their grandmother's country home. One night a heavy rainstorm did in all our hard work and we had to start over again a few days later. Then there were always the endless bean fields to walk, chopping down unwanted corn with a machete. One day I came home at noon for lunch and said to Evelyn as I came up the stairs to our upstairs kitchen, "Ev, guess what? I cut off my hand today!" Evelyn nearly had a heart attack and almost cut off my eating privileges that day. But mainly I put bread, burgers, and beans on the table by accepting preaching invitations from local churches, speaking at youth rallies, and conducting revival meetings. Of the $1,716.00 we made that year, $1,237.00 of it came from preaching.

THE SUMMER THAT SIZZLED

The summer of 1968 was a hot one in Hamburg and even hotter, politically and socially, in the nation. On a beautiful Wednesday

★   ★   ★   ★   ★   ★   ★

morning, June 5, I drove Brother DeVries to Shenandoah where he was to catch the noon bus for a meeting in Missouri. An old man in the bus depot spoke to Eddie.

"Do you think he'll make it?"

"Who?" replied Eddie.

"Kennedy," the old man said.

"What do you mean?" Eddie asked.

"Why, haven't you heard? Bobby Kennedy was shot this morning!"

I was to lead the Midweek service that night, but it was hard to concentrate on my lesson as I listened to the reports coming over the radio that afternoon. Just minutes after claiming victory in the California primary, the 42-year-old senator from New York was gunned down in the kitchen corridor of the Ambassador Hotel in Los Angeles. A bystander screamed, "Oh, God, it can't happen again!" But it did. A 24-year old Jordanian named Sirhan Sirhan shot Kennedy at point-blank range with a .22-caliber pistol. Five others were wounded in the shooting rampage. After the Midweek service was over, Evelyn and I stayed up late listening to the radio. Despite our prayers at church that night, and the prayers of a stunned nation, Kennedy was pronounced dead on June 6 at 1:44 a.m. In 1969 Sirhan Sirhan was sentenced to die in the gas chamber but the sentence was commuted to life in prison in 1972. At this writing Sirhan Sirhan, who is one year younger than myself, is serving that sentence in the California State Prison in Corcoran.

I wrote a guest editorial on the Kennedy assassination that was published in the June 1968 issue of the *Voice of Evangelism*. Among other things I pointed out that it often takes a tragedy to drive a nation to its knees in prayer, that death is no respecter of persons, and that,

★   ★   ★   ★   ★   ★   ★

unless America repented of her sins, outrages like this would continue to happen. I added that things we never dreamed could happen in our country would become a stark reality. I was certainly outraged by the brazen assassination. Even though I was a rock-ribbed Republican, I bought a painting of John and Bobby Kennedy in profile, which the artist titled "Brothers Slain," and hung it on my office wall. Somewhere in one of our moves the portrait was lost.

It was about this time that I discovered the brilliant conservative novelist Allen Drury. I went to the library next door to the church, where I had often read *Boy's Life* as a lad, and checked out Drury's first blockbuster political novel, *Advise and Consent*, which won the Pulitzer Prize for fiction in 1960. I was hooked for life and have since read every book written by Drury, including *A Shade of Difference, Capable of Honor,* and *Preserve and Protect.* A former writer for the *New York Times* and a staunch anti-Communist, Drury's knowledge of inside Washington and the Cold War fascinated me. He died on his 80th birthday, September 2, 1988.

It was also a hot year in the brotherhood. "Restructure" was in full swing and Hamburg was one of the churches that the Christian Church (Disciples of Christ) still listed in their annual Yearbook even though Hamburg had become an "Independent" congregation in the 40s. The Disciples had voted to become a full-fledged denomination in 1967 during their convention held in Kansas City. Many saw this as a betrayal of the nondenominational plea of the Restoration Movement. The hue and cry raised by conservatives, or "Independents," was to "Get Out of the Yearbook." So Hamburg, along with 3,500 other "Independent" churches wrote to the Disciples' headquarters in Indianapolis, requesting that our church be removed from their rolls. The

★　　★　　★　　★　　★　　★　　★

Disciples lost 750,000 "members" that year but continued in their set course of liberal theology and broad ecumenicity.

MY FIRST REVIVAL

A preaching scout at my graduation from college was directly responsible for my first revival meeting. And so it came to pass that on July 27 it was Eddie DeVries' turn to drive me to Shenandoah where I caught a bus for Cincinnati, Ohio. James E. Gibbons, preaching minister of the Locust Grove Church of Christ in Galax, Virginia, met me in Cincinnati. It was Brother Gibbons who had sent the "scout" to Ottumwa in search of someone to conduct a revival for the Virginia congregation. I believe he was in Cincinnati to pick up some printing supplies for the national paper that he edited, *The Sword & Staff*. I was one weary person when we finally arrived at his home, the parsonage next to the church building. Frieda, James' wife, called out a greeting from the kitchen as we took my luggage down the hall to the bedroom where I would stay. I said to James, "I didn't know your wife was a foreigner." She was not a "foreigner," of course, but I really thought she was. I couldn't make out one word of her Virginia drawl!

The meeting ran from Friday, July 19 to Sunday, July 28. The headline of the nicely printed handbill read:

HEAR GOD'S MESSAGE FOR TODAY
By One of Today's Generation

The handbills had been posted in nearly every store window in Galax. The picture that Brother Gibbons used on the handbill was my high school graduation picture! I'm sure all who received one thought, "What can I learn from this fresh-faced kid!" I preached 13 sermons in

★   ★   ★   ★   ★   ★   ★

10 days, including my first radio message on local radio station WBOB on Sunday afternoon, July 28.

While I was in Virginia, Evelyn went to Ottumwa to spend some time with her parents and family. I wrote to her nearly every day. From those yellowed letters I am reminded that it cost only $1.10 to get my suit cleaned at the dry cleaners. And that the crowd really "ate up" my sermon on "The Arks of Refuge." And that "Just One Glimpse" "came through again" with a 16-year-old girl, Terri Frazier, giving her life to Christ and being baptized. There were three decisions for Christ in all for the meeting. One of them was Debbie Sutherland, the daughter of Tom Sutherland, the elder who had scouted me out in Iowa. Brother Gibbons told me that it was their best-attended meeting the church had experienced. Lots of young people attended, and folks came from area Virginia churches and North Carolina as well, including a cappella and Independent churches. The New Home Church of Christ in Dobson, North Carolina, invited me to hold a revival for them sometime in the future. In the years to come I would return to Galax three more times for revival meetings.

I received $100.00 for my 10 nights of preaching. Brother Sutherland drove me to Wytheville where I boarded a bus at 10:30 P.M. the Sunday night that the meeting closed. The bus took me through Memphis and St. Louis before letting me off at the bus depot in Shenandoah at 4:40 A.M. on Tuesday, July 30. I waited until a decent hour to call Eddie to come and take me home. The endorsed $100.00 check went under the iron-grilled teller's window at Iowa State Bank and was deposited into our little account there. Now maybe we could have a chuck roast some Sunday instead of wienies or ground round. Or go to the White Spot and have two root beer floats instead of just sharing one!

★   ★   ★   ★   ★   ★   ★

I believe it was while I was in Virginia that a man named Victor Knowles was killed near Shenandoah, Iowa. The news was carried over KMA radio. When Evelyn walked into church that night, smiling as always, Stan Aistrope did a double take. He had heard the radio report and had assumed that I was the deceased. Evelyn assured him that I was safe and sound in Virginia. When I got back to town, I may have quipped, like Mark Twain did when he heard that his obituary had been published in the *New York Journal*, "The reports of my death were greatly exaggerated!"

ONE YEAR AS ONE

For our first wedding anniversary, August 7, we drove to Nebraska City and bought each other a few small gifts. I bought Evelyn two area rugs and she got me a new belt and some socks. That was about all we could afford. We did "splurge" by buying a nice two-drawer end table (which we still have) and going to dinner at a restaurant near John Brown's Cave. The cave was beneath the Mahew Cabin, believed to be the oldest cabin in Nebraska, and was used by abolitionists to hide and move slaves in the famous Underground Railroad.

I continued with my duties at the church. I wrote a number of articles, which were published in the *Voice of Evangelism*. One that I was particularly gratified with was "A Christian Review of *The Passover Plot*." The book, written by Hugh J. Schonfield, a Jewish British Bible scholar, posited "a new interpretation of the life and death of Jesus." I answered 10 claims made by Schonfield, including charges that Jesus was not born of a virgin, plotted his own crucifixion, and faked the resurrection, and answered them point-by-point from various scriptures in the four Gospels. Another one I was proud of was "Supporting Pillars of

★   ★   ★   ★   ★   ★   ★

the New Testament," a diagramed study of existing Greek copies, famous catalogues, ancient versions, early quotations, and internal evidences that proved the veracity of the New Testament Scriptures. I also had an article, "Profiting from the Prophets," published on the front page of James Gibbon's *Sword and Staff* in August 1968. I described the prophets as being "urgent in their appeal, powerful in their delivery, and honest in their truthful evaluation of a sinner." I also went into great detail about their sacrifice, humiliations, and loneliness. It was in Hamburg (or possibly while I was still at Midwestern) that I started contributing articles for an evangelical magazine, *Youth's Living Ideals*, that was published in Elon College, North Carolina. I cannot remember how I got in touch with them, but editor G. Berry published a good number of my articles for most of the years they were in existence (1967-1973). I have kept every article I have ever had published, numbering in the hundreds, but for some strange reason I do not have a single copy of that slick glossy magazine today. They must have come up missing in one of our moves; because all other published articles of mine are encased in clear plastic sheets and kept in five large three-ring notebooks today.

Our old college quartet (Terry Crist, Henry Neff, Chester Mullins, and myself, with Leland Vandeveer at the piano) got together to sing once more at the Centerville Rally in August. At the rally I was approached by Dale A. Williamson to come to Lexington, Nebraska, and conduct a revival meeting in the fall. During the rally the Soviets and four Warsaw Pact nations invaded Czechoslovakia. The free world was outraged by this brazen act. My old pal and fellow graduate Sam Brown came to Hamburg on August 25 and fainted during his ordination service. A combination of fasting all day, a really humid night, and

★　★　★　★　★　★　★

a long "charge" by Eddie DeVries combined to send poor Sam into a swoon. Over he went like a tree felled in the forest. We jumped up and crowded around him but Mary Margaret Solliday, a RN, came charging down the aisle crying, "Give the man some air!" She cleared us out of there in no time flat. Soon Sam came to and we propped him back up while Eddie continued the charge to "Preach the word; be instant in season, out of season; reprove, rebuke . . ." By this time all poor Sam wanted was a reprieve!

THE HAMBURG COLLEGE OF CHRIST

One of the reasons Eddie DeVries had wanted me to come to Hamburg was by this time out in the open. Kyle Koch and I had kept this secret for some time before we moved to Hamburg. The Hamburg College of Christ opened its doors in August 1968. The Hamburg congregation had been one of the biggest and best "feeders" of Midwestern School of Evangelism. Brother DeVries and the church elders believed the time was right to train their own young people, and anyone else desiring a good Bible college education, right in Hamburg. There were plenty of job opportunities in Hamburg including Vogel's Popcorn, the world's largest popcorn manufacturer; Interstate Nurseries, the world's largest flower nursery; Grape Community Hospital, and many other employers in nearby Nebraska City and Shenandoah, home of the Earl May Seed Company.

The original plans called for daytime classes, but the schedule was soon shifted to evening classes. The faculty included DeVries, Terry Paul, H. N. and Margaret Solliday, Kyle Koch, and myself. I was assigned to teach Homiletics, but I would not teach until the second semester. I did teach a few classes during the first semester, however,

★   ★   ★   ★   ★   ★   ★

when I filled in several nights for H. N. Solliday who taught Christian Evidences. No doubt I used my new chart for this class. (While we were starting a new college in Iowa, however, demonstrators at the Democratic National Convention in Chicago were starting a ruckus, engaging Mayor Daley's riot police with bottles, bloody noses, and blasphemies. The police responded with tear gas and nightsticks. Tears streamed down cheeks and blood flowed down faces. Television cameras caught it all as bystanders yelled, "The whole world is watching!" Vice President Hubert H. Humphrey won the nomination over Eugene McCarthy and would face Richard M. Nixon in the November election.)

We had 22 students enroll for the first semester. I believe I had seven or nine students in my Homiletics class. No doubt I used *How to Prepare a Sermon* by Harold E. Knott (Standard Publishing) as the main text. Had it really been five years since I had taken Homiletics at Midwestern and now I was teaching the same subject at the fledgling Hamburg College of Christ? I underlined in red the following words from Brother Knott. *"Preachers need to preach on positive, helpful, uplifting and inspiring themes, rising above their own sorrows and misfortunes, just as Jesus, almost under the shadow of the cross, staggering under the burden of His own grief, said to His disciples: 'Let not your hearts be troubled: believe in God, believe also in me.'"* I am sure that I gave my students the same advice an old preacher once gave to a young preacher. "When you preach, remember that in every church pew sits at least one broken heart."

I really came to appreciate fellow faculty member Horace Nichols Solliday and his good wife Margaret. We were in their home many times during our stay in Hamburg. Brother Solliday was a grad-

*   *   *   *   *   *   *

uate of Phillips University and a retired minister. He was also the great-grandson of J. Harrison Jones, a pioneer Restoration preacher and chaplain to General James A. Garfield. One of my treasured possessions today is a photocopy of a letter written to J. Harrison Jones by James A. Garfield when he was serving as a general during the Civil War. Brother Solliday, before graduating from Phillips University, had also studied under Ashley Johnson at Johnson Bible College. I learned so much just from listening to this fine man of God. His wife Margaret was one of the most hospitable and charitable Christian women I have ever known.

PREACHING IN CALIFORNIA

On October 3, one day after the St. Louis Cardinals' Bob Gibson set a World Series record by fanning 17 batters in the opening game against the Detroit Tigers, Evelyn and I took our first airplane ride – a nonstop flight from Omaha to Los Angeles aboard Continental Airlines. I remember two things about the flight. First, how scared we were when the big jet roared down the runway and lifted off. Evelyn wanted to kneel down on the floor, but I told her she had to stay belted up. Second, how scandalous the stewardesses' skirts were when they leaned over to serve someone. Evelyn put her hands over my eyes so I wouldn't see their garter belts! Remember: this was the era of the mini-skirt.

The Broad Street church in San Luis Obispo, California, had invited me to conduct a revival meeting for them. Dad had also arranged for me to speak in several other churches. I couldn't believe how living in California had changed my father's normally passive driving habits. Once we were on the freeway, he was honking his horn

*   *   *   *   *   *   *

and rapidly changing lanes like everyone else. Evelyn and I looked at each other in wide-eyed wonder. We weren't in Kansas anymore, that was for sure. When we pulled up to my parent's home, I saw this long-haired kid shooting baskets in the driveway.

"Who's that geek?" I asked.

My father grinned and said, "Why, son. That's your brother!"

My mother short-sheeted us the first night. The next night we found hangers in our bed. I thought, "Boy, California has really changed my parents! California is something else!" But by the time we left, some three weeks later, I had fallen in love with California, Californians, and especially the Christians and churches of the Golden State. Even though students at Berkeley seized campus office buildings during our meeting!

After one week of revival preaching, the church unanimously voted to extend the meeting another week. This was my first experience at what was then called a "protracted meeting." One Sunday night, as an added feature, the Moody film "Signposts Aloft" was shown. Up in the balcony, however, my brother David was shooting rubber bands at Evelyn and me. But his aim was off. When the film ended and the house lights were turned back on, we saw dozens of rubber bands resting on the beehive hairdo of a lady who was seated in the pew in front of us. I have often wondered what she thought when she got home that night and took down her hair! By the end of the second week, 10 decisions for Christ had been made. The third week was spent preaching at churches in Morro Bay and Bakersfield, and a Youth Retreat at Park Creek Camp near Sacramento. At Park Creek we counseled with a young man who one day would become a missionary to Africa, Paul Reyman. One day we went to see the

★   ★   ★   ★   ★   ★   ★

famous Hearst Castle in San Simeon. By the time we returned to the Midwest, I had preached 23 times and received a total of $420.00 for our labors. All the gold in California was *not* in the middle of a bank in Beverly Hills in somebody else's name! Kyle and Juli Koch met us at the airport in Omaha upon our return. As the passengers' luggage started coming down the conveyor belt, I saw a suitcase that had fallen open. Kyle and I started laughing until Evelyn gasped and said, "Victor, that one is ours!" I grabbed it, stuffed our dirty clothes back into it, and got out of there.

A CALL FROM NEBRASKA

On the first Tuesday in November Evelyn and I walked down to City Hall and voted for the first time in our young lives. We cast our votes for the winner and next president of the United States, Richard M. Nixon, who defeated Hubert H. Humphrey by a half-million votes.

On November 10 I received a phone call from Ken Mickey in Brazil, Indiana. He was going to be moving to Roberts Cove, Louisiana. Would I be interested in taking the church in Brazil? Six days later I received a phone call from Dale Williamson in Lexington, Nebraska. He was not feeling well. Could I come to Lexington and preach for him November 17? Our Corvair was about to give up the ghost, so Terry Paul loaned us his car to drive to Nebraska. I preached three times, and at the end of the day Dale told me he wanted me to come to Lexington and work with him for six months before turning the work over to me. No sooner had we returned to Lexington than Ken Mickey called again. We were faced with a decision. What would we do? We prayed about it, for what else could we do? Then the Lexington church called and asked us to return for a revival meeting November 26–December 1. This time a

★　★　★　★　★　★　★

friend in Council Bluffs, Bill Edwards, loaned us his brand new gold Corvette for the trip west. Each night the offering was taken up for me Brother Williamson would remind the people, "Now that fancy car that Victor is driving is a loaner. His is in need of repair!" I preached seven times, and we had three responses to the invitation. The following Sunday Brother Williamson announced his plans to step down in June 1969, after 17 years of faithful and fruitful ministry. The elders of the church, Ernest Hosea and Clyde White, called me to tell me that the church wanted me to be their next minister. We accepted their gracious call. In hindsight, I wish that we had followed Dale's advice for me to work with him for six months. He could have "shown me the ropes" in Lexington and thus prepared me better for ministry there. But the die was now cast. We would move to Nebraska in the summer of 1969.

Astronaut James Lovell, high above the earth in Apollo 8, read from the Bible on Christmas Eve. We brought 1968 to a close by trading in our 1962 Corvair for a 1964 Rambler Classic. The asking price was $1,050.00. The dealer allowed us $250.00 for a trade-in and we paid down $150.00, meaning that we got our "new" car for $650.00. So long "Vair-Vair" and hello "Lam-Ram." We felt blessed and celebrated Christmas and our new ride by having Christmas dinner with Inez Coffey and her daughter Helen Koch. But I still have a recurring dream about that first car, our little Corvair Sports Coupe. The dream is always the same. I step out into the backyard and there sits my old Corvair. The tires are flat and it needs a good car wash. I think to myself, "Hey, with a little work I can get this car fixed up and running again!" About the time I do, I wake up. No Corvair! Rats! Drat that Ralph Nader anyway!

★   ★   ★   ★   ★   ★   ★

"MRS. KNOWLES, YOU'RE GOING TO HAVE A BABY!"

On January 2, 1969, I took Evelyn to see Dr. Tom Largen at his office in Hamburg. Following the examination he smiled at her and said, "Mrs. Knowles, you're going to have a baby!" Evelyn's heart skipped a beat, and so did mine when she told me the good news. Dr. Largen calculated a July 5 delivery date. Patriot that I was, I hoped the baby would be born on the 4th of July. Two days later we drove to Deweese, Nebraska, in our Rambler Classic to begin a 15-night revival meeting with Ed Werner Sr., the minister of a small rural congregation. We stayed with our good friends Gary and Marilyn Brennfoerder. Three nights into the meeting Evelyn's little nephew Anthony Brown died of "SIDS." I drove her back to Iowa to attend the funeral, and Gary Werner filled in for me two nights. We finished up the meeting on January 19 and drove directly to Ottumwa for the annual January Gathering, very thankful for the $300.00 the church gave to us. The Brennfoerders left the next day to also attend the Gathering, but while they were gone, their home burned to the ground. We gave $50.00 to the Brennfoerders to help them in their loss.

GOOD-BYE TO MICKEY AND "IKE"

I taught my first Homiletics class at the Hamburg College of Christ on January 29. Gary Cradic, another hometown boy, was ordained on March 2. I preached the ordination sermon Sunday morning, "Bible Preachers God Has Blessed." Eddie DeVries delivered the charge and all of us were relieved when Gary got through the service without keeling over as Sam Brown had done! I was looking forward to my own ordination, which would take place in July. The day before

★   ★   ★   ★   ★   ★   ★

Gary's ordination one of my childhood heroes, Mickey Mantle, announced his retirement from baseball. He was only 37. The switch-hitting slugger played his entire career for the New York Yankees and finished with 536 home runs (at that time third on the all-time list). The Yankees retired his No. 7 and sent his uniform to the baseball Hall of Fame in Cooperstown. There was hardly a dry eye in Yankee Stadium when Mantle spoke, with a catch in his voice, and said, "I always wondered how a man who knew he was going to die [Lou Gehrig in 1939] could have stood here and said he was the luckiest man in the world. Now I know how Lou Gehrig felt." The newspaper clipping went into my Mickey Mantle scrapbook. Another of my childhood heroes, Dwight D. Eisenhower, died March 28 at Walter Reed Hospital in Washington, D. C. He had been the president of the United States for one-third of my life!

After giving a six-week exam to my Homiletics students, I headed for Lexington where I spoke at the annual Lexington Youth Rally April 3-5. My message, "Guard Your Hearts," resulted in six young people making a decision for Christ. Sometimes I would write down the names of those who responded. In this case I did: Debbie Conz, Vicki Williamson, Debbie Henry, Beverly Hesse, Jerry Guise, and Debbie Kursten. By now I was commuting to Lexington to preach on some weekends.

"TRANS"

I conducted my fourth revival meeting with the Church of Christ in Dayton, Ohio, April 27-May 4. Malburt Prater had preached for this congregation, located at the corner of Porterfield and Townfield Streets, before he formed the Prater-Mickey Evangelistic

★   ★   ★   ★   ★   ★   ★

Team. A young man from the congregation who was also a student at Midwestern, Herman Clark, was serving as the minister. I drove to Richmond before the meeting began to spend a few days with my Grandpa Brown. He had remarried by this time, but the new wife was a "gold digger." I felt so sorry for my dear grandfather. It was the last time I would see him alive. Only two things remain in my mind about the Dayton meeting. One night two black ladies attended the services. Afterwards they told me that they had enjoyed the sermon and that their brother, Hal, would have too had he been able to attend. Then they told me who their brother was – Hal Greer, 10-time all-star guard for the NBA team, the Philadelphia 76'ers. It would have been cool to meet him had he been in town for a visit. On a Saturday afternoon Herman and I took in a Reds-Padres game at the new Riverfront Stadium in Cincinnati, but I sure missed the aura of good old Crosley Field.

During the Dayton meeting Evelyn would write me nearly every day. By this time we were convinced we were going to have a boy because the baby was so active. Somehow we got to calling him "Trans." Why? One day I was carrying a stack of Bible translations from one part of the church to another. I was holding them in front of me and Evelyn said I looked like her with her protruding stomach. So we dubbed our little unborn one "Translation" – "Trans" for short. I called Evelyn my beautiful "beach ball" because of her size. In her letters Evelyn described how little "Trans" was moving all over the place. The third week in May I went with Ronald and Lorine Emberton to Ottumwa to attend the graduation of my pal Gary Bryant from Midwestern. Lorine and Margaret Solliday gave Evelyn a beautiful baby shower attended by many ladies from the Hamburg and Rock

★   ★   ★   ★   ★   ★   ★

Port churches. Letha Lu Solliday wrote down what every woman gave and even what Evelyn exclaimed when she opened each package.

OUR FIRST BABY!

The summer that sizzled moved on. My brother David, now a freshman in high school, flew from Los Angeles to Omaha to spend a little time with us. I picked him up at Eppley Airfield and drove him back to Hamburg. We fixed him up a bedroom in one of the back rooms of the church. By this time David was a big baseball fan, and I spent a lot of time with him playing wiffle ball in a natural "stadium" in the big back yard behind the library or playing home run derby at Clayton Field. I also introduced him to "All-Star Baseball," a popular board game designed by former baseball player Ethan Allen. The game was produced by Cadaco and was based on actual statistics of major league players. David still plays the game to this day!

As a child I had fallen in love with Judy Garland, star of "The Wizard of Oz." Her up-and-down life came to a tragic end on June 22 when the 47-year-old actor and singer took her own life in London. The day she died I had preached in Hamburg in the morning and at Rock Port that night. No Christmas is complete for me if I do not listen to her rendition of "The Birthday of a King." Sixteen days after Judy Garland's death we experienced the birthday of a princess!

July 4 came but the baby did not. July 5, the projected day of birth, also came and went with no projectile! On July 6, a Sunday, my beautiful "beach ball" was, amazingly, still able to reach down and touch her hands flat on the ground. Then came Monday morning, July 7. At 5:00 A.M. Evelyn jostled me and said, "I think the baby is ready to be born." I was so sleepy that I did not fully comprehend what she

★   ★   ★   ★   ★   ★   ★

said. I mumbled, "Um-hmm" and went back to sleep. Evelyn got up and did some ironing. About 6:30 she shook me and repeated the message. This time I aroused with a start. "What? It's time to go? Why didn't you tell me? Let's go!" After telling David the news, we headed for Grape Community Hospital, arriving at about 7:30. Then the long wait began.

I had told my Homiletics students that the delivery of a sermon could sometimes be a painful process. I had "delivered" 241 sermons up to this time. Now it was time for Evelyn to deliver our first child. I stood by her side, held her hand, wiped her brow, and agonized with her when the birth pangs came. I was beginning to appreciate what Paul wrote in Galatians 4:19, "My little children, of whom I travail in birth again until Christ be formed in you" as I watched the hands of the clock on the wall slowly move from one hour to the next.

Late in the afternoon a nurse came in to check on Evelyn's progress. "Oh," she said, "you're finally starting to do something." She patted her on the shoulder and said, "It'll be a long time yet." She was not out of earshot when Evelyn hit the buzzer and said, "The baby is coming!" The nurse came back in and checked Evelyn. Her eyes nearly popped out of her head. "Call the doctor!" she yelled over her shoulder. I was whisked away to the waiting room. Evelyn remembers a blur of white coats as everyone sprang into action. Dr. Largen was in nearby Sidney when he received the call and raced back to Hamburg just in time to deliver the baby.

Mindy Annette Knowles was born at 4:49 P.M. "Mr. Knowles, you have a baby girl. Mother and daughter are doing just fine." To this day I cannot recall who made that announcement to me. I thought, "Hmmm, it wasn't a boy after all." A few hours later I was able to hold

★　★　★　★　★　★　★

our little 7-pound, 12-ounce bundle of joy in my own arms. She had black hair and blue eyes. Her little mouth was shaped in a perfect "O." Evelyn thought it looked like a Cheerio.

In those days they kept new mothers in the hospital much longer than they do today. Evelyn was not released until Friday, July 11, five days after Mindy was born. In one of the strangest twists of fate possible, Susan Hand, my former fiancée, was one of Evelyn's attending nurses! She was now engaged to Chester Mullins, a member of my old quartet, who had transferred from Midwestern to the new college in Hamburg. (The college moved "lock, stock, and barrel" to Denver, Colorado when Eddie and Terry moved there in 1970, becoming Rocky Mountain College of Christ.) That night I made several rare long distance phone calls to tell the good news to my parents and Evelyn's parents. Bob and Ethel arrived the day Evelyn and Mindy came home from the hospital and my folks arrived a week later.

MY ORDINATION

The summer was really sizzling by now. It got so hot that Inez Coffey insisted that we move in with her because her house was air-conditioned. We had been busy packing for our move to Lexington and we gladly accepted her offer. At least we could rest at night in cool comfort. On Wednesday, July 16, I preached my farewell sermon at Hamburg, "A Church to Be Built," from Matthew 16:18.

Then came the night of my long-awaited ordination, Friday, July 18. I had seen some of my best friends ordained – Terry Crist, Sam Brown, and Gary Cradic. Now it was my turn. I fasted and prayed most of the day. My father preached the ordination message, "The Price of Telling the Truth." The prophets were stoned, John the Baptist

★   ★   ★   ★   ★   ★   ★

was beheaded, Jesus was crucified, and nearly all of the apostles, including Peter and Paul, were executed or assassinated. In years to come I would preach in places where other preachers had literally paid the price for telling the truth: Poland, Russia, Cuba, India, Africa, etc. Eddie DeVries issued the charge from 2 Timothy 4:1,2 to "Preach the word . . ." I took each charge seriously and answered them "I do" or "I will, so help me God." I didn't even come close to fainting. (Maybe that was because I had allowed myself a peanut butter sandwich late in the afternoon!)

I had carefully selected the men whom I wanted to participate in the laying on of hands, prayers, and signing my certificate of ordination. Some of them were a given. Because I was being ordained by the Hamburg Church of Christ, every officer of the congregation took part: Ministers Eddie DeVries and Terry Paul; Elders Ronald Emberton and Marvin Sheldon; Deacons Rex Bryant and Rex Dooley. In addition to these men there were: my father, Dale V. Knowles; fellow-faculty member H. N. Solliday; Don Jessup, preacher at Council Bluffs; and George Carmen, my youth leader at Mulberry Grove who was now preaching at Rock Port. I knelt before the Lord as these godly men laid their hands upon my head and shoulders and prayed for me to be "a good minister of Jesus Christ, nourished up in the words of faith and of good doctrine" (1 Timothy 4:6). I arose with tears in my eyes and thanked each man for their part in the service. Members of my family and church family surrounded me in love and gave me hearty handshakes, holy hugs, and best wishes for our new ministry in Nebraska.

The next day, Saturday, July 19, Clifford Strever came from the church in Lexington to help us pack our few belongings in a small U-Haul trailer and move to our new place of ministry. Evelyn held little

★   ★   ★   ★   ★   ★   ★

Mindy on her lap as I slowly drove out of my hometown and followed Cliff and the U-Haul trailer west to Nebraska. It was kind of like being in a small wagon train. Now we were a family of three. What adventures, dangers, joys, and heartaches awaited us in that little town on the prairie?

★   ★   ★   ★   ★   ★   ★

CHAPTER NINE

LITTLE CHURCH
ON THE PRAIRIE

The same day we were driving to Nebraska, July 19, 1969, Senator Ted Kennedy was driving off the Chappaquiddick Bridge in Massachusetts, leaving Mary Jo Kopechne to drown. He later pled guilty to leaving the scene of an accident and was given a suspended two-month sentence and placed on parole for a year. Late in the afternoon we pulled into the driveway of our new home, a three-bedroom, two-bathroom ranch style parsonage located at 1209 N. Pierce Street, within a few blocks walking distance of the church building. While we were unloading our belongings Evelyn took our first phone call. It turned out to be an obscene phone call. That "welcome" did not sit well with me and soured me on the town from day one. I must admit that it took awhile for me to warm up to Lexington.

The town of about 7,000 people was the county seat of Dawson County, located on U. S. Highway 30 (dubbed "Dirty Thirty"), which ran parallel to the Union Pacific Railroad. Originally the town was called Plum Creek and began as a trading post in 1860. Plum Creek was a wayside station on the Oregon Trail and Mormon Trail, and was also served by the Pony Express. The "Plum Creek Massacre" took place on August 7, 1864, when Chief Turkey Leg and a band of marauding Indians murdered several citizens. Fifteen years later Plum Creek was renamed Lexington, in honor of the Battle of Lexington during the Revolutionary War. Hence the nickname "Minutemen" for the sports

★   ★   ★   ★   ★   ★   ★

teams of Lexington. The main product was alfalfa, and the alfalfa mills along U. S. 30 were kept fired day and night during the alfalfa season, creating a foul-smelling aroma that wafted over the town.

Our new home seemed almost too good for us. Compared to our little upstairs apartment in Ottumwa and our humble one-room dwelling in Hamburg, the modern ranch house parsonage seemed like a large castle. It even had an attached garage where I could park the car. One of our first purchases was a used washer and dryer ($50) so Evelyn could keep up with the laundry, including Mindy's diapers. (Would you believe she raised all six of our children on cloth diapers?) "No child of mine will wear Pampers!" or something like that was her motto. We thought we had died and gone to heaven when we were paid the handsome sum of $70.00 a week. That was more than twice what we had averaged in 1968 ($33.00 a week). We stocked up on groceries at the local Safeway store and felt like robber barons.

Our first week in Lexington was as busy as it could be. My first sermon was the same one I had preached as my last sermon in Hamburg, "A Church to Be Built." I wanted my first fulltime church to be built upon the foundation of the apostles and prophets, Jesus Christ being the chief cornerstone, and for all of us to grow as a holy temple unto the Lord (Ephesians 2:21, 22). As soon as church was over, we headed to Camp-O-Cedar, a Christian service camp just a few miles from Lexington. And so it was that on Sunday, July 20, at 3:17 P.M. (CST), while we were setting up for camp, three U. S. astronauts set down the Apollo lunar module on the moon, right in the middle of the Sea of Tranquility. Houston, and at least one-fifth of the world, heard the first words spoken from the moon, "The Eagle has landed." Six hours later astronaut Neil Armstrong set foot on the moon and said,

★　　★　　★　　★　　★　　★　　★

"That's one small step for a man, one giant leap for mankind." I took my first step into the world of summer Bible camp by teaching two classes each day for five days and preaching two sermons. I also enjoyed directing a team and playing softball, especially the student-faculty game. Now, for the first time, I was on the faculty team!

LIFE IN LEXINGTON

Life in Lexington swiftly settled into its daily routine. I set up my study in the basement of the Church of Christ at 13th and Tyler Streets. The church in Hamburg had given me the nice oak library table as a parting gift, and I used it for my desk. The brick church building was well maintained and so were the grounds. The pulpit was made in the shape of the cross, and I liked that. I wanted to "hide behind the cross" when I preached anyway. Mary Strever, a talented artist, had painted a beautiful baptism scene on the back wall of the baptistery. Lucille Conz played the piano and Bertha Allen played the organ. Sometimes I led the music. We used a hymnal, *Church Service Hymns*, on Sunday mornings and Wednesday nights. But in one invitation song, "O, Why Not Tonight?" there was an error. It read, "O, do not let the *world* depart" instead of, "O, do not let the *Word* depart." So I jokingly referred to it as the "worldly" hymnal. Sometimes on Sunday nights we used a nifty book of youth choruses that Dale had compiled. I preached twice on Sunday and also taught the midweek class. In November the elders asked me to teach the Sunday morning high school class. I'm glad they did because the young people were the brightest part of my three-year ministry in Lexington.

Working with the elders as "the" minister at Lexington was a little different than working under the elders as an "assistant" minister

★   ★   ★   ★   ★   ★   ★

at Hamburg. One of my first mistakes was to call a meeting of the Bible School department without seeking the permission of the elders, Ernest Hosea and Clyde White. I meant no harm and had only good intentions of seeking ideas on how we could improve the department, and I was mildly taken to task by Brother Hosea the next day. But Ernie took a liking to me because we had a mutual interest in baseball. One Saturday we spent the entire day watching an American Legion baseball tournament. I forgot to wear my baseball hat and got quite sunburned. Sometimes I helped him on the farm, moving irrigation pipe in the summer and harvesting corn in the fall. I also helped a farmer from the Christian Church, Ben Rhodearmer, bring in the golden grain. Ben was always saying "By grannies" this and "By grannies" that. I got a kick out of working with the old gentleman who could, amazingly, blow a stream of snot out of one nostril by pressing his index finger against the other. I never tried it.

Clyde White, the older of the two elders, was still hoping to mend fences between the Tyler Street congregation and the local Christian Church from whom they had separated some years prior to my coming. Nearly every time I was in his home, he would quote Proverbs 18:19 to me: "A brother offended is harder to be won than a strong city: and their contentions are like the bars of a castle." But I was not yet inclined to be a peacemaker then and made little if any efforts to reach out to the offended party. Clyde kept us well supplied with sweet corn and Big Boy tomatoes in the summer time. Both men had us in their homes for meals, as did many of the people of the church. Not long after we were there, the church surprised us with a shower, the church in nearby Cozad joining in. We received many nice items that we needed to set up our new home.

★　★　★　★　★　★　★

For the first time in my life I was able to listen to a Christian radio station, KJLT in North Platte. The call letters stood for King Jesus Lives Today. I got most of my hard news over local radio station KRVN or in the *Omaha World-Herald*. August was one wild month. Sharon Tate and four other people were murdered in cold blood in Beverly Hills on August 9. Charles Manson was arrested and charged with master-minding the Tate-LaBianca murders. A sensational trial followed, and eventually Manson and three other members of his cult were sentenced to death (commuted to life when California ended the death penalty in 1972.) The weekend of August 15-17 saw 400,000 young people congregate on a farm in upstate New York for "Woodstock," a rock festival laced with LSD, anti-war rants, nudity, and sex. Five days after Woodstock, my parents and brother arrived in Lexington to pay us a visit. We were so glad to see them, but I think they were more interested in seeing little Mindy! She was a "show stealer" for sure.

MINISTERING IN MINUTEMAN CITY

Preparing two new sermons every week, plus a Midweek class, was a new challenge, but I rose to the occasion. Most of the time I got my sermons directly from my personal reading of Scripture, but sometimes I found good sermon starters in a book. One of those books was *Sidetracked Saints* by Douglas Dickey (Standard Publishing). Another book that proved helpful was *The Answers of Jesus to Job* by G. Campbell Morgan, the great British preacher who died the year I was born (1945). I have several of Morgan's books in my library today.

I also took my turn with other ministers in the city as "Chaplain of the Week" at Lexington Community Hospital. For some reason I did not feel as comfortable doing hospital visitation in Lexington as I had

★   ★   ★   ★   ★   ★   ★

in Hamburg. Perhaps it was because Evelyn was not with me (babies and small children were not permitted to visit in those days). But I did excel at recording the daily "Dial-a-Devotion" that patients could listen to by merely picking up their bedside phone and dialing a number. "Do with zest what you do best" was my motto. We were able to take Mindy with us, however, on visits to the homes of church members, former members, or prospective members.

My first baptism at Lexington was Ron Parks. I nearly capsized the both of us when I forgot to take that all-important step to the right when I lowered him into the water! Most of the baptisms I performed were young people who gave their lives to Christ at camp or as a result of my visiting with them about their spiritual condition. The most I ever baptized at one time was six. On another occasion I immersed four "the same hour of the night."

I made lifelong friends in area preachers Bill Paul (North Platte), Ira Cochran and Ed McSpadden (Cozad). Our churches enjoyed Fifth Sunday rallies. Not long after we arrived in Lexington, I developed a choking condition and could not preach for several Sundays. Ira filled in for me and did a great job. I will always remember his sermon "The World's Greatest Airlift," as he compared the Berlin Airlift with the Second Coming of Christ. All three of us worked together in revivals, rallies and youth camps. Bill Paul told us a great story one night when we were visiting their home. He and Bethel, like most preachers in those days, didn't have much money. One day they told their young son Tim that they were going to go to a restaurant that night. Tim was so excited that he ran to the window of their upstairs apartment, threw up the window, and yelled down to a neighbor boy below: "Hey, Johnny! Guess what? We're going to eat in *a restroom*

★   ★   ★   ★   ★   ★   ★

tonight!" Ed McSpadden, a Timothy of the Hamburg church, was a ham radio operator. His "handle" was GCKOGK, which stood for the Great Chicken Killer of Gobbler's Knob. He would often say to me, "Let's go wassail," so off we would go to "guzzle" some Root Beer.

In October we were delighted to have my Grandma Knowles stay with us one night on her annual trip to Denver for the winter. I got out my reel-to-reel tape recorder and "secretly" taped her as I plied her with questions about her youth. During a terrible blizzard she once carried her little sister Annie through the driving snow to safety. Annie, sadly, caught pneumonia and never recovered. I knew Grandma would not tell these stories with a microphone stuck in her face, so I hid it in a plant near her chair.

I was still a big baseball fan and listened in wonder to the Fall Classic as the "Amazing Mets," once the worst team in the National League, shocked the baseball world when they swept the powerful and heavily favored Baltimore Orioles in four games. During the winter months I would listen to Jack Buck on KMOX as he kept the "Hot Stove League" going. One night I called in and talked on the air with Mr. Buck. I tape recorded Harry Caray's last broadcast with the Cardinals. August Busch had not renewed his contract and by the 7th inning Harry was pretty ticked off. Buck, perhaps knowing he would replace Caray as the regular play-by-play man, wisely kept his mouth shut. I would be 25 in November, and I felt I was in my prime as a hitter. I was now batting left-handed most of the time, using a 35-ounce Carl Yastremski model. One afternoon I hit a shot that cleared the right field fence and two tennis courts. Old dreams die hard. I wrote to the San Diego Padres and they invited me to a tryout camp, but I never followed up on the opportunity.

★　★　★　★　★　★　★

The Vietnam Moratorium, the largest anti-war protest yet, took place October 15 with organized protests all over America, in cities both large and small. Presidents of 79 universities urged President Nixon to withdraw American troops from Vietnam. I felt sorry for Nixon. He had inherited this war from Kennedy and Johnson and nothing he did seemed to please his constant critics, especially Walter Cronkite, who acted like he knew more about running the country than did the President and his cabinet.

The decade of the 60s, "a decade of dissent," was coming to an end. We were delighted to have H. N. and Margaret Solliday in our home for Thanksgiving. I had Brother Solliday speak on our Thanksgiving Rally and the old gentleman did one great job of preaching. On Christmas Day we attended the wedding of Keevin Koch and Marcia Williamson at the Lexington church. Her father, Dale A. Williamson, performed the wedding ceremony. It was a nice way to say good-bye to 1969, and to our first half-year of ministry in Lexington.

COUNTERING THE CULTURE IN THE SICK SEVENTIES

America almost seemed like a different country to me in the 1970s. I was a World War II baby, a proud product of "The Greatest Generation," and had been raised in the fabulous 50s. Though we didn't have much of the world's goods in those days, the world in which I lived seemed good. I believe that the hinge point of history in my times was the assassination of JFK on November 22, 1963. The shocking deed cast a dark shadow over the land. For me life has never been quite the same. In my judgment that was the day the good life came to an end in America. Exit innocence and idealism. Enter the era of cyni-

★   ★   ★   ★   ★   ★   ★

cism, distrust and dissent. The 70s ratcheted up all that to dizzying new levels. Everything from music to fashion seemed discordant, decadent, and distasteful. I wasn't the only one who felt that way. One day I wrote an article (never published) in which I quoted May Craig who wrote a column "Inside Washington" for 50 years and was a regular commentator on "Meet the Press." "Unless there is a change, deepdown in the American people, a genuine crusade against self indulgence and immorality, public and private, then we are witnesses to the decline and fall of the American Republic." I agreed with her and was more than willing to lead that crusade in Lexington.

Since 1958 the Lexington church, under Dale Williamson, had published a weekly paper that was mailed to many churches and individuals beyond Lexington. I expanded the mailing list and gave the paper a new name, *The Lexington Lamplighter*. Doris Parks typed the stencils on Friday and Bob Conz printed them on the mimeograph machine on Saturday night. The paper became my bully pulpit to do my part in leading the crusade against "self indulgence and immorality" in America. I published a number of short but timely articles from Morality in Media, Inc. a pro-morality interfaith organization based in New York City. Founded in 1962, the nonprofit organization was in the vanguard of combating obscenity and upholding standards of decency in the media. I gave no heed to the argument "You can't legislate morality." I took on "Oh! Calcutta!" a musical that included nudity and obscenity. I also upbraided the Youth Department of the World Council of Churches for producing a hymn that included the lines: *"To hell with Jehovah, to the Carpenter I said; / I wish that a carpenter had made this world instead."* Some of my writings were picked up and reprinted in other

*   *   *   *   *   *   *

papers like the *Voice of Evangelism* and *Youth's Living Ideals*. I also brought some powerful speakers to the Lexington church to lead this crusade, my "four horsemen of the Apocalypse" as it were: Archie Word, Billy James Hargis, John Noble and Kenneth Goff.

THE WORD REVIVAL

Charles Foster, a veteran *Los Angeles Times* reporter who had covered the revivals of D. L. Moody and Gipsy Smith, among others, had at one time billed Archie Word as "America's Foremost Evangelist." In a 643-page biography I wrote about him 22 years after his revival in Lexington, *Archie Word: Voice of Thunder, Heart of Tears* (College Press, 1992), I called him "the Billy Sunday of the Restoration Movement." Word had run away from home at 16 to enlist in the Navy during World War I. He did most of his fighting in the ring, becoming his company's undefeated light-heavyweight boxer. When the war was over, he became a notorious bootlegger in California's San Joaquin Valley. Through a providential set of circumstances he wound up at Eugene Bible University (today Northwest Christian University) and was brought to the Lord by a band of brothers who prayed for him every night in their dorm rooms. In 1930 he and his good wife Florence entered the field of full-time evangelism – right in the middle of the Great Depression – and won 3,000 people to Christ in five years of conducting revival meetings on the West Coast. He then preached for the same church in Portland, Oregon, for 33 years, became editor of *The Church Speaks*, started nine new churches, and sent more men and women off to Bible College than any other preacher in the fellowship of Christian Churches and Churches of Christ. In the summer of 1968 he bought a 24-foot Silver Streak trailer and hit the revival road once

★   ★   ★   ★   ★   ★   ★

again. I was audacious enough to write him and invite him to come to Lexington and could hardly believe it when he called and booked a three-week revival meeting for February 1-22. It was an experience of a lifetime for me, a young untested minister of 24, only 7 months into my first full-time ministry. This would be my first – and most unforgettable – time to serve as host minister for a revival meeting.

I preached four sermons on "revival" before the meeting began. Each week in *The Lexington Lamplighter* I wrote or published articles on the theme of "revival." I designed, posted, and mailed out revival handbills and wrote news releases for the two papers in Lexington: *The Clipper* and *The Herald* (which later merged to form the *Clipper-Herald*). We had special prayer meetings at the Midweek services for the coming revival. I called on "prospects" and designed a list of people to visit with Brother Word. The Words rolled into town, literally, in their Silver Streak, which they promptly set up on a vacant lot near U. S. Highway 30. They had all the comforts of home inside their trailer, including their French poodle, Louis the XIV.

Each night Brother Word would teach for about 20 minutes from his large teaching chart, "The Church Revealed in the Scriptures," a large bed sheet which was artistically lettered and was strung on a wire in the front of the auditorium. He used a telescoping radio antenna for his pointer. "Whap!" That was the sound it made when he whacked the sheet to illustrate a point. No one went to sleep during an Archie Word revival! His sermons usually lasted about an hour and were punctuated with plenty of illustrations from real life that would touch the heart and cause tears to flow. Often his voice would break when he would tell about people whose lives had been ruined by sin or redeemed by Christ.

★   ★   ★   ★   ★   ★   ★

"I'D TAKE A GUN AND BLOW THEIR BRAINS OUT!"

Brother Word was an anomaly. That is seen in the subtitle of my book about him, *"Voice of Thunder, Heart of Tears."* It was also seen during a visitation episode during the meeting. The trial of Abbie Hoffman, Jerry Rubin and other members of the notorious "Chicago Seven" was in the news each day of the meeting. Judge Julius Hoffman (no relation to the defendant Abbie Hoffman) had endured all kinds of verbal abuse during the trial. William Kunstler, the lawyer for the Chicago Seven, was reprimanded for calling the judge "a racist, fascist pig." Defendants Hoffman and Rubin constantly used obscenities in the courtroom. It was a travesty of justice. One afternoon Brother Word and I were visiting in the living room of an extremely cultured woman who had shown an interest in spiritual matters. I considered her a good prospect. Somehow the discussion turned to the trial of the Chicago Seven.

"Reverend Word," the lady of the house said in her finest cultured voice, "What do you think of what is going on in the trial in Chicago?"

"Oh, no," I thought to myself.

Brother Word bristled. "Lady, do you know what I would do if I were Judge Hoffman?"

I nearly choked on my afternoon tea.

"Why, no, Reverend Word." She smiled sweetly, "What would you do if you were the good judge?"

My teacup started rattling in the saucer. I braced myself for what was to come.

"I'd take a gun and blow their brains out!" Archie thundered.

★   ★   ★   ★   ★   ★   ★

My smile was as weak as my tea.

"Oh! Reverend Word! You wouldn't!" Mrs. Culture was absolutely aghast.

But Archie was absolutely adamant. "I would! I'd take a gun and blow their brains out!" he said again.

Mrs. Culture, sculptured hand to lovely throat, nearly fainted.

I slowly took out my pocket notebook and carefully scratched Mrs. Culture off my prospect list.

That being said, Archie Word had a heart of tears to match his voice of thunder. During his last sermon of the revival, "The Peril of Resisting God," he broke down in tears when he recounted the wasted years of his own sinful life. Several responded to the invitation that night. We had a total of 439 visitors attend the three-week meeting.

It was wonderful to work with such veteran gospel workers as the Words. One night Evelyn and I sang with them in a mixed quartet. We took them to Pioneer Village in nearby Minden, a place they had always wanted to visit. On February 16, a "rest night" of the revival, the old boxer and I sat in his Silver Streak and listened to a radio broadcast from Madison Square Garden of a heavyweight championship fight. Joe Frazier knocked out Jimmy Ellis with a left hook in the fourth round. The Words adored our little Mindy; Brother Word called her "Pinky Tinky." During the meeting I fell ill with the flu. Evelyn wasn't feeling well either. The next morning the Words were on our doorstep with orange juice, groceries, and a steak. Brother Word believed a good steak was a tonic for all ills! He played with Mindy while Florence got down on her knees and scrubbed the kitchen floor. We were sad to see them pull out of town on the 23rd of February. I followed up that revival with my own 4-week "Crusade for Souls" to keep the revival

★ ★ ★ ★ ★ ★ ★

fires burning. We used a religious survey that my friend Gary Cradic had designed. In December we had an 8-night "Bible Crusade" with a different area preacher speaking each night with Brother Word returning to bring the final three sermons.

THREE "HEAVYWEIGHTS" COME TO TOWN

Like a good boxing promoter, I brought three nationally known "heavyweight" speakers to Lexington in 1970. I created publicity for all of them with articles in the local newspapers, radio announcements, handbills, and promotion in our church paper. The first to come to town was Billy James Hargis, founder and president of Christian Crusade, then located in Tulsa, Oklahoma. A former student at Ozark Bible College, Hargis had soared to national and international fame with his fiery preaching against the threat of communism. At his peak he was on 500 radio stations and 250 TV stations in America. Only Carl McIntire, a fellow conservative speaker, had a wider following. He brought his "For Christ and Against Communism" crusade to our church on February 27. The church building was filled to overflowing with 250 people that night. They heard Hargis speak on two hot topics of the day: the liberal National Council of Churches and the "sex revolution" in America. Several weeks later I accepted an invitation from Hargis to speak at a future Christian Crusade Convention. I don't recall any follow-up to the invitation, and so that's all it turned out to be – an invitation. In 1972 we hosted another Christian Crusade rally featuring Dr. Charles Secrest and Tom Hollingsworth, the latter being a former member of the Green Berets.

Kenneth Goff, a one-time member of the U. S. Communist Party and author of *Confessions of Stalin's Agent*, came to Lexington on

★   ★   ★   ★   ★   ★   ★

June 1 and spoke on the subject of "Campus Revolt." No doubt he must have addressed Kent State University, where on May 4, about a month or so before his appearance in Lexington, National Guardsmen had opened fire on rock-throwing anti-war protestors, killing four people and wounding eight more. Later that month thousands of homosexuals and those demanding liberal abortion laws marched in New York City in separate parades. Less than two years later Mr. Goff died of a heart attack while on a speaking tour in Chicago. The local newspaper fouled up my news release, and we did not have near as many come to hear Goff speak.

In November, just a few days after Janis Joplin died of a drug overdose, I brought a third nationally known speaker to Lexington, John H. Noble, founder and director of Faith and Freedom Forum. Evelyn and I liked him the best of the three. I had read his books, *I Found God in Soviet Russia* and *I Was a Slave in Russia*, when I was in college. In 1945, at the beginning of the Cold War, Noble, 23, and his father, who had a camera business in Germany at the time, were arrested by the Soviets on a trumped-up charge of espionage. Noble spent 10 years in the Soviet gulag system, working at hard labor. He managed to smuggle out a message for help that reached America. None less than President Eisenhower himself negotiated Noble's release in 1955. Noble gave a stirring account of surviving as Slave No. 1-E-241. He said that in the gulag Christians risked their lives to worship while in America we look for excuses not to go to church. We had a nice turnout, and it was an inspiring evening. Noble impressed us as a deeply spiritual man, something I did not discern as much from the other two guest speakers. Noble died in 2007 at the age of 84.

★   ★   ★   ★   ★   ★   ★

THE SPRING YOUTH RALLY

In addition to our Wednesday night midweek service, which started at 8 P.M. because of the farm families in the church, I tried something new at the time: Family Discussion Groups. Yes, we were doing "small groups" back in 1970! And it was inter-congregational (Lexington and Cozad) at that. A good number of folks from both congregations met in each other's homes for fellowship and study on Tuesday evenings, and it proved to be a successful innovation. Amazingly, there was no one our age in the Lexington church so we struck up a special friendship with Ron and Jeanie German of Cozad. Their little girl, Julie, was Mindy's age. We enjoyed being in each other's homes, especially on cold winter nights when the wind was fiercely howling on the prairie.

I directed the first of three Spring Youth Rallies at Lexington March 26-28, 1970. We had more than 250 young people from eight states come for the annual event. I chose as the theme "Fools for Christ's Sake" from 1 Corinthians 4:10. Among the speakers I invited to develop the theme were Lafe Culver, one of my instructors at Midwestern, and three former college classmates: Sam Brown, Terry Crist, and Mark McDowell. We received many glowing testimonies from young and old alike, which I published for several weeks in *The Lexington Lamplighter*. I chose the theme "We Shall Overcome!" as the theme of the 1971 Spring Youth Rally. A student at a Bible College in Gering didn't like the theme because civil rights protesters sang "We Shall Overcome." He took it upon himself to tear down handbills from church bulletin boards. I told him that God had used the theme of "overcoming" in the book of Revelation long before the Civil Rights

★   ★   ★   ★   ★   ★   ★

movement adopted it as their national anthem. This did not faze him in the least. In time Pete Peters left Gering and gained a following from those who shared his Aryan Supremacy or "Christian Identity" views. Among my speakers that year were retired Lt. Col. L. H. Tyree, my father, and my brother David. The rally came off without a hitch and was hailed by all as a success. In 1972 my keynote speakers were Eddie DeVries, Bill Paul, and Sam Brown. Several converted "hippies" came to this rally from Denver and caused "no small stir" with some of the older preachers because of their headbands, long hair, and hippie clothing. But there was no doubting their conversion to Christ or their love for the Lord. All three rallies were well attended and made a great impact on the lives of hundreds of young people who came to get their spiritual batteries charged up.

Out in California a man named Ralph Carmichael (a PK like me) was producing a new kind of music that young people really took to. I am still amazed that his songs like "He's Everything to Me" did not cause a rift in the church like some new music seems to do today. I liked Carmichael's songs, and we added them to our youth group songs. I believe his music drew young people closer to the Lord.

A young man lived right across the street from our parsonage, Dan Cunningham. His mother Betty became fast friends with Evelyn and proved to be the best neighbor one could ever want. One day Evelyn crossed the street to visit her. Betty's teen-age daughter Michelle seemed rather cool and told her that her mother was too busy to visit. Evelyn was a little hurt but didn't think too much of it. The next day Betty came to the house bearing with her a nice wicker rocker chair that she had picked up at a garage sale and had fixed up. She knew that we did not have a rocking chair and said, "How can you

★   ★   ★   ★   ★   ★   ★

rock your baby if you don't have a rocking chair!" Mindy liked playing with their beagle puppy, Heidi. I put up a basketball goal on our garage and Dan and I played many a game of "Twenty-one" and "Horse." My brother David came back from California each summer and he and Dan struck up a great friendship. The three of us would play catch in the front yard or play "Home Run Derby" at the one of the ball parks in town. One night I took Dan with me to hear the Blackwood Brothers sing at a nearby church, and Dan was hooked for life on Southern Gospel quartet singing, forming his own group in years to come. I volunteered to serve as a baseball coach one summer. I drafted Dan, and he became the star pitcher for our team, the Astros. David was my first base coach. We won the league championship that summer.

My dear Grandpa Brown died in Richmond on May 26, 1970. I wrote in our church paper, "He was the kindest and biggest-hearted man I have ever known." His second wife took everything he had, including what should have been rightfully my mother's home and inheritance. I felt my parents should have taken her to court, but they chose not to do so. Judgment Day will sort all that out. Still, I was incensed that mom had been robbed of a nice place to live if and when dad ever retired.

TRUMPET BLASTS AND WILD PANTOMIMES

During our three years in Lexington I taught and preached in several youth camps: Camp-O-Cedar, near Lexington; Camp Gering, in Western Nebraska; Camp Sharon Bluff, near Centerville, Iowa; and Boiling Springs Camp, near Mooreland, Oklahoma. I took my brother David, along with other young people from Lexington, to most of these camps. Because I was a wordsmith, I was chosen to edit the daily camp newspaper. It was a big hit with the young people. The campers

★   ★   ★   ★   ★   ★   ★

were my "cub reporters" and gladly supplied me with plenty of ammunition. My "shocking exposés" and other "breaking stories" spared no one. Sometimes I was merely "Ye Olde Editor" and other times I wrote under the name "E. Pluribus Unum."

One night at Camp-O-Cedar I preached on the Second Coming of Christ. I hid one of the senior campers, Ben Christianson, an accomplished trumpet player, backstage. I told Ben that when I reached a certain point in my sermon, I wanted him to cut loose with a blast on his trumpet that would make the campers think that Gabriel himself had sounded the Final Trumpet. Ben was right on cue. He hit a note that nearly caused old people in the audience to have heart attacks. At least one kid on the front row lost control of his bladder. Or was it the other way around? Whatever. When I extended the invitation, 15 young people gave their lives to Christ. I still have kids, now adults, who come up to me and say, "Man, that night you preached on the Second Coming of Christ and Ben blew that trumpet, I thought, 'This is really it!'" By the end of the week, Ben was actually signing autographs. (Later in the summer I preached the same sermon at Sharon Bluff Camp in Iowa and had 10 responses including five that were baptized.) That same week I taught a class, "Far Out!" The first day I wore a string mop head, round sunglasses, and had a fake cigar between my fingers. With the other hand I gave the class the "peace sign." The kids who were growing up in the "Age of Aquarius" were now ready to listen as I talked to them about "Mary Jane" (marijuana) and LSD and what it cost people like Jimi Hendrix and Janis Joplin to mess around with drugs.

We had some great Bible pantomimes in those camps. At Boiling Springs Camp my team did Jehu and Jezebel. My brother David was Jehu, and he nearly wrecked the dining hall with his mad

★　★　★　★　★　★　★

driving (his chariot being a serving cart pulled by several red-blooded boys). On another occasion David played Haman and nearly hanged himself choking on a little bag of ketchup that he was supposed to bite down on, thus producing "blood." I about died laughing when Bob Runner, a fellow faculty member, played Eglon, a fat king who was killed by a knife thrust from Ehud. The King James Version of Judges 3:22 says, "and the dirt came out." The New King James Version, which wasn't out then, says, "his entrails came out." We didn't have any entrails at camp that week, but we had plenty of dirt. Bob had a big Folger's coffee can full of Oklahoma dirt hidden under his robe and threw great handfuls of dirt into the air as he died a magnificent death. The greatest show on earth, however, was reserved for the evening presentation of Elijah (my brother) calling down fire to consume the altar of Baal. When the gas-soaked rag, representing the fire that fell from heaven, was sent down a wire from a kid up in a tree to the gas-soaked altar at the bottom of the hill, we nearly blew the place up.

GREAT ADVENTURE IN THE SAND HILLS AND ON THE STAR ROUTE

Each summer Ronnie German and I would take David with us to the famous "Sand Hills" of Nebraska for a "night under the stars." We packed our gear and set out across the prairie in Ronnie's Jeep until we found a good place to camp. There is nothing like a good steak sizzling over a campfire when you are out in the middle of nowhere. Our only "neighbors" were cattle that roamed the unfenced sand hills. One night heaven treated us to a real show – dozens, scores, it seemed like hundreds of "falling stars" streaking across the sky. We went on wild midnight rides in the Sand Hills, the lights from the headlamps of the bouncing jeep flashing all over the place, sometimes nearly straight up.

★　★　★　★　★　★　★

One morning we saw a nest of rattlesnakes sunning themselves on a pile of rocks. We left them pretty much alone. But I couldn't resist taking aim at a harmless can of beans bubbling on the makeshift grill. Dave and Ronnie nearly jumped out of their skin when the bullet I fired from the .22 rifle disintegrated the can of beans, spraying them (the beans, not the boys!) all over the place.

Phil Olson, the preacher at the local Christian Church, had a "Star Route" and asked me to be his substitute driver. A "Star Route," going back to the 1800s was different from a "Rural Route" in that it went to the lowest bidder. Federal employees were not allowed to bid. I hired David to work for me on days I had the mail route, which took us clear to the Custer County line. One old farmer expected his mail to be delivered at the exact same time every day. If we were even a minute late, he would curse a blue streak as we pulled up to his mailbox. But everyone else on the Star Route was very nice. Some even placed glasses of iced tea in the mail box for us. We got to know the reading habits of all the people on our route. You'd be surprised what people on the prairie read. Or maybe you wouldn't!

Sometimes Evelyn went with me on the Star Route. In August Dr. Elfeldt had informed us that we were about to become parents again! Evelyn's due date was February 27, 1971. Evelyn was experiencing "morning sickness" as we sped along the dusty Star Route. She was taking letters out of the mailboxes if the red flag was up and placing letters and packages in the mailboxes in return. A couple of times I had to throw the car in reverse lest she throw up right where the people had to pick up their mail!

In September I was scheduled to speak on a Labor Day Rally at Colorado Springs. While we were in Colorado, we took our first trip to Cripple Creek, a famous mining town which was now a "ghost town."

★   ★   ★   ★   ★   ★   ★

We also took time to see the Garden of the Gods, Pike's Peak, the Air Force Academy, and Evelyn's favorite place of all on the trip, Helen Hunt Falls. She told me later that she wished we could have been married at that place because it was so quiet and beautiful.

PACKING IN 1970

One fine day I spotted a sporty little 1968 cream-colored, two-door Chevy Camaro with bucket seats and a three-speed on the floor that was for sale for only $1,850.00. I quickly traded in my '64 Rambler Classic for it, now that I had a little extra cash. It was one sweet ride. Our first trip in it was in October 1970, back to Ottumwa for a 10-night revival meeting with the new Ransom Street Church of Christ where Bill Payne was preaching. We stayed with Evelyn's folks. I also spoke at my *alma mater* and on radio station KLEE. In November we made our first trip to Louisiana where I preached three nights for our friends Keevin and Marcia Koch at Ferriday (childhood home of Jerry Lee Lewis and Jimmy Swaggart) before opening an eight-night revival with Ken Mickey and the Roberts Cove Church of Christ. We had four rededications and two baptisms the first night of the revival in response to my message "Judgment Day Wishes!" I remember Ken striding to the platform and saying, "And now you know why I invited Vic Knowles to hold this revival!" The meeting ended with three more baptisms and another rededication. While in the Bayou country I went duck hunting for the first time in my life. I also got my fill of gumbo this and gumbo that. I had never before or since eaten so much rice in my life! The day we left Roberts Cove, one of the men of the church came running with a big 25-pound bag of rice under his arm. "Wait! Wait! Brother Vic, you must have some rice to take home!" I think

★   ★   ★   ★   ★   ★   ★

we used most of it that winter to spread on our driveway when we had ice and snow. If we needed some to toss at a wedding we had plenty!

One cold night in November I drove to Beaver City to hear Charles Selby speak. Brother Selby, a native of Nebraska, had gone to Cincinnati Bible Seminary with my father and was a veteran missionary to the Philippines. He and his wife Roberta had been in our home several times when I was growing up, as had Norval and Dondena Campbell, fellow missionaries in the Philippines. It bothered me that good men like Brother Selby and Brother Campbell were not given the "right hand of fellowship" by everyone in the network of churches that I was a part of in Nebraska. Some of them did not like the term "Christian Church" or anything that smacked of "Christian Churchy" (as they put it) ways of doing church. Just my going to Beaver City would probably cause some to raise their eyebrows and lower their estimation of me. But it also bothered me that I had sometimes "cast stones" too and was not man enough to stand up and say, "This man is a brother for whom Christ died, and he is my brother in Christ." It would be several years before I would do anything significant about *rapprochement* with the separated heirs of the Restoration Movement, including the a cappella Churches of Christ. But in my heart I always knew that the kingdom of God was far larger than our limited circle of fellowship.

ON THE AIR!

Ed McSpadden and I, on behalf of our respective churches in Lexington and Cozad, negotiated a contract with radio station KAMI in Cozad for a Monday through Friday 15-minute broadcast as well as a 30-minute broadcast on Sunday morning. We went on the air January 3, 1971. Once a week I would drive to Cozad to pre-record the broad-

★　★　★　★　★　★　★

casts with Ed. Our weekday broadcast featured Ed and me bantering back and forth about current news items and what the Bible might have to say about such things. For example:

Vic: "Ed, I see where a federal survey of marijuana use on college campuses has revealed that 31% of students have tried the drug and 14% are regular smokers. Are you surprised at these figures and does the Word of God say anything about drug use?"

Ed: "Well, Vic, those findings should be disturbing to every parent in America. I had no idea that one-third of college students had tried pot. Now let's turn to the Bible to see if we can find some help for these parents and these kids."

We discussed everything from "hot pants" to Ho Chi Minh to China being admitted to the U. N. One day we were talking about "women's lib."

Ed: "Vic, what do you think of this women's liberation movement?"

What a setup for an ad-lib! Ed should have known better.

Vic: "Well, Ed, I think we need to keep all the women barefoot and pregnant!"

Ed cracked up big time, and we had to rewind the tape and start over. We had a great time of fellowship during these broadcast recording sessions.

Immediately after our program "Encounter" aired, the local disc jockey cued up "The Assembled Multitude" (a Philadelphia instrumental group that had nothing in common with a church assembly!) before spinning Three Dog Night's "Joy to the World," which was a huge hit that year. The Sunday broadcast featured "tag team" preaching: Ed preaching one week and I the next. I normally preached from a prepared transcript but Ed would sometimes "wing it."

★   ★   ★   ★   ★   ★   ★

At the invitation of Donald G. Hunt, I also wrote a year-long column for the *Voice of Evangelism* that Hunt dubbed "From Knowles' Knoll." Like the radio broadcast "Encounter," it usually centered on current issues and news items with a biblical response.

COMMUTING TO TEACH

From January 26 to March 4 I commuted every week to Gering, a city in western Nebraska, to teach in the Church of Christ Bible Training School. The Bible institute was operated under the auspices of the Church of Christ at 7th and Q and was overseen by the local minister, Don Pinon. I was asked to teach Church History, which had been one of my favorite courses when I was at Midwestern. I had a great bunch of young men and women in my class, and I thoroughly enjoyed this assignment. I used two textbooks: *Christianity through the Centuries* by Charles E. Cairns and *The Church in History* by B. K. Kuiper.

Each Monday afternoon I would hop in my Camaro and drive the 215 miles from Lexington to Gering where I stayed with Herschel and Sue Stoner. On Tuesday and Wednesday mornings I would teach Church History. I would also preach in Chapel on Wednesday. Before heading back to Lexington I would have a steak dinner at Archie and Florence Word's home. He was still conducting revival meetings but had agreed to teach in the school as well. I had lined up several men in the church at Lexington to teach the Wednesday night class because I was usually worn out by the time I got home.

Everything about that weekly western trip enthralled me. I loved Ash Hollow, Windlass Hill, Chimney Rock, and of course, Scott's Bluff. Such places fired my imagination of what it must have been like to live in Nebraska a hundred years before. I took Evelyn, Mindy, and David

★   ★   ★   ★   ★   ★   ★

to climb Windlass Hill and see the other historical sites. I had always liked to read books about the Old West, but now I became an avid reader of western authors like Zane Grey, Will Henry, Allan Vaughan Elston, Luke Short, Max Brand, William McLeod Raine, and of course Louis L'Amour. Sometimes I would sit up and read tales of the West until long after midnight.

One snowy winter night I was late arriving home from Gering. About dusk someone knocked on the parsonage door. Evelyn answered the door and saw a patrolman standing in the doorway, hat in hand.

"Mrs. Knowles?"

"Yes," answered Evelyn.

"I have the sad duty to inform you . . ." the patrolman began.

Instantly Evelyn's heart sank. She knew right then that she had just become a widow. She thought I must have been killed in a car wreck.

But the patrolman continued. ". . . that your sidewalks need to be cleared of snow within the next few hours." Then, message delivered, he put his hat back on, got into his patrol car, and left.

Evelyn, who was "great with child" by this time, was relieved that nothing had happened to me but could not believe that the patrolman had not even offered to help by shoveling the walk. When I got home later that night, I am sure that I worked off my "steam" by clearing the walk in record time!

BRIDGET OLIVIA IS BORN!

Because our unborn child was so lively, we were convinced that this time we were indeed going to have a boy! But "he" was not to be. "She," rather, was to be. February 27, the due date, came and went. So did February 28, the last day of the month. Then came Monday, March 1, 1971. I spent the day at the office, going over my Church History

★   ★   ★   ★   ★   ★   ★

class I was scheduled to teach in Gering the next morning. Soon it became apparent I would not teach that class! I phoned some assignments to Gering, took Evelyn to the Lexington Community Hospital in the afternoon, leaving Mindy with Lillian Cochran, and spent the rest of the day in the waiting room. I was reading an article in *Guideposts* about the faith of the Dodgers' Gil Hodges when a nurse walked into the room and informed me that Evelyn had given birth to a girl at 9:30 P.M. As always, at least with us, "Mother and daughter are doing fine!"

We named our beautiful little 7-pound 6-ounce girl "Bridget Olivia." Bridget is an Irish name meaning "lively." At our meeting in November in Louisiana we had met a woman in the Roberts Cove church named "Olivia," and Evelyn had become quite fond of that name. So, in case you are wondering, no, she was not named after Hollywood actresses Brigette Bardot nor Olivia de Haviland! I left the next afternoon for Gering so I could teach my class and preach in Chapel on Wednesday. Evelyn was kept in the hospital only three days this time, so I arrived home in time to bring her and Bridget home on Thursday. Mindy, of course, was delighted to have a baby sister and "helped" Evelyn care for the wee little one with blond hair and blue eyes. Our neighbor Betty Cunningham and a lady from our church, Jessie White, were a tremendous help to Evelyn. Sometimes when I got home late at night after a trip or a call, I would thoughtlessly sneak into the baby's room and wake up Bridget so I could play with her. "Victor!" Evelyn would exclaim with some exasperation. "It took me two hours to get her to sleep!" I knew I should have let her sleep, but she was just so irresistibly cute that I could not restrain myself. Then, of course, Evelyn would have to nurse her and rock her to sleep all over again while I buried myself in a western. I was one "Bad Dad."

★　★　★　★　★　★　★

ON THE REVIVAL TRAIL AT YALE

During our ministry in Lexington I conducted 13 revival meetings. I have never considered myself a "revivalist" like Archie Word or Marion McKee, but for whatever reason I was in some demand in those days and in days yet to come. In college I had told the Lord that I would go wherever and whenever asked, so I did my best to keep that promise (with the blessing of the church elders, of course!).

One of the most interesting revivals I held in 1971 was in April in a small Iowa town called Yale. After finishing a week's revival with the church in Guthrie Center, I visited Yale. Eugene Lockling, the man who sold me my Dickson Bible, was the minister of both churches. (An aside: Lockling, at this writing, is still carrying on this dual ministry with these two churches and has since 1957!) By the time the Yale revival was finished, we had baptized six people including the wife of the local saloon operator, her daughter, and three of her daughter's children. It was a veritable "household conversion." In time the saloon even went out of business.

I had the privilege of working with the great Don Jessup in a three-week revival meeting in Council Bluffs, scene of my first sermon back in 1964. By now I had preached 500-some sermons. I held back-to-back meetings in New Home, North Carolina, in 1971 and 1972. This large church was built right in the middle of a big tobacco field and right next to a cemetery. I thought the juxtaposition was significant! The night I preached on smoking I didn't get too many "Amens!" John and Zella Dillon ministered with this church, and they were a delight to work with. John and I went calling in the afternoons. At the first home, which was a very nice home, I noticed a number of coffee cans

*   *   *   *   *   *   *

sitting on the floor. I thought that was rather odd until . . . WHANG! The lady of the house shot a stream of tobacco juice that hit the open coffee can dead center. She was a quid pro but alas, I had nothing to give in exchange! One night I was preaching away, and a well-fed Carolina horsefly started "buzzing" me in the pulpit. It bit me right on the seat of my pants! Brother Dillon rolled up a copy of a newspaper and came to my rescue. Thus began an epic battle between the preacher and a horsefly. The place just about went nuts as Big John vigorously fanned the air this way and that and finally . . . WHAP! He brought the winged beast down and brought down the house with the felling of the fly. The New Home church had not one but two pianos, and the two female pianists played in tandem. It was like hearing Jerry Lee Lewis and Mickey Gilley playing at the same time. I had never heard such singing and playing. The last night of the meeting I said those pianos had been worked so hard that they would probably have to be jacked up and given an oil change!

AMONG THE PAPAGO INDIANS

Not long after our arrival in Lexington, I read an article in the *Reader's Digest* on the plight of the Navajo Indians in Arizona. Somehow God put a burden on my heart for the Navajos and all Native American tribes in that part of the United States. Later I wrote to Gary Cradic asking him if he would be interested in going with me to Arizona to explore the possibility of doing some mission work with one of the Indian tribes. Both of us were more than a little disillusioned with the apathy of American churches in general at that time. He wrote back and encouraged me to make an exploratory trip, which I finally managed to do in late August and early September of 1971.

★ ★ ★ ★ ★ ★ ★

I wrote to Henry and Beulah Shaw, whom I had lived with for a short time when I was a child in Nebraska, about the possibilities of working with an Indian tribe. Henry, who lived in Maricopa County, told me about the Papago Indian tribe (at that time, the more usual name for the Tohono O'odham) that lived on the main reservation between Tucson in the U. S. and Ajo on the Mexican border. He knew a Papago Indian there who wanted to have a church started for his "Desert People" (the literal meaning of Tohono O'odham). That was all I needed to know. On August 1 I impulsively resigned at Lexington and informed the church of our intentions to pursue this possibility of working among the Papagos.

My folks had come back from California to see the new baby, and after their visit was over, we all set forth for Arizona. We stopped in Colorado Springs where dad and I preached on Wednesday night at the church where L. H. Tyree ministered. Once we hit Arizona, my folks headed West to go back to California while we continued on into New Mexico. When we approached Truth or Consequences, we encountered a first – a "motel war." It was just like a "gas war" with each owner dropping his prices to get your business. By the time we finally settled on a Best Western hotel we wound up paying only $4 – and we could have had one for as low as $2. It was unbelievable. On Sunday morning I preached in Tucson where our friends Don and Eileen Henry were ministering at the time. On Monday morning we headed to Sells, the administrative center of the Papago reservation, with a member of the Tucson church, Kent Kirkman. Right away we encountered difficulty with the Bureau of Indian Affairs. They informed us that no housing was available for non-Indians on the reservation for at least another year. Still, we spent several days on the reservation with Henry Shaw, who had driven down

★   ★   ★   ★   ★   ★   ★

from Phoenix. We met Floyd Harris, the Christian man who wanted a church started among his people. We drove clear to the Mexican border, visiting in the hogans and huts of the Papagos. They were made of cactus and had large gaps in places. Lizards and snakes came and went as they pleased. At one home a lady was making a raisin pie, or so I thought! She was actually making a large corn tortilla and it was covered with flies. The "raisins" lifted and flew away when she waved her apron at them! In another home a little baby that was drinking milk from a bottle was also covered with flies.

To make a long story short, Brother Shaw wisely suggested that we remain in Nebraska, and he would try to help Brother Harris get something started. The "old horse trader," as he referred to himself, was as good as his word. A large community center in Choulic was secured for a meeting place. It had benches, classroom space, even a pulpit and a piano – all rent-free! The church in Phoenix supplied them with a Communion set and hymnals, and I pledged a case of Bibles from the church in Lexington. Henry, or his son Paul, drove down every other week, and soon there were about 15 Papagos meeting for worship. Eventually Brother Harris became the minister and led many Papagos to the Lord. A few years ago I learned that he had been thrown from a horse and died of a broken neck. But the "little church on the reservation" continues because of that article in the *Reader's Digest*, the wisdom of an "old horse trader," and an Indian who wanted a church built for his "Desert People."

Looking at Evelyn, Mindy, and Bridget on our return trip to Nebraska, I wondered how they would have liked (or not) living in such a desolate place. Evelyn told me that her biggest concern was the health of Mindy or Bridget, should they become sick. But she also said

★   ★   ★   ★   ★   ★   ★

she was eager to serve. I wondered, too, how I would have done working as a missionary among Native Americans. Brother Shaw was a wise and patient man while I was still pretty impulsive and impatient. Maybe it was all just a foolish dream of mine, but if you never have a dream, how can dreams come true? And something good did come out of that dream inspired by a simple magazine article.

A GENTLE SOUL

Evelyn was always supportive of my dreams and was my number one encourager when my dreams died or were dashed into a thousand pieces. She was the best "helpmeet" a young minister could want. To this day I do not remember her complaining about anything. Like her mother, she was totally unselfish, industrious, and "the law of kindness" was always on her lips. She had never been to Virginia but had always wanted to see the beautiful Blue Ridge Mountains. So when David Kirk and the church in Galax invited me to conduct another revival meeting there in October, I took Evelyn and the girls with me. Evelyn instantly fell in love with those magnificent mountains and the people from the church. As to the latter, I will tell you why.

When we had been in Colorado in August, Evelyn was not feeling well. We went to a doctor and he told her there was nothing to worry about. But three nights into the meeting in Galax, Evelyn suffered a miscarriage. It was really bad. I rushed her to the hospital, and the next day the doctors told me that Evelyn had lost so much blood that she was going to need a blood transfusion. Members of the Galax congregation who shared her blood type came to the hospital to give blood. When someone gives his or her blood for you, hardly knowing you, that makes a lasting impression!

★ ★ ★ ★ ★ ★ ★

Meanwhile, David and Demoi Kirk, and their 12-year-old daughter Bonnie were caring for Mindy and Bridget. When Evelyn was brought home from the hospital, Demoi became her home "nurse," Bonnie played with Mindy, but only David could soothe little Bridget, who seemed the most upset by the whole episode. David would rock Bridget in his rocking chair, singing to her, and bottle-feeding her. From that day on Evelyn, with great affection, called David "Poppa Kirk." I kept on preaching each night and even went an extra three nights following the Sunday the meeting was supposed to end. In the years to come David and I would exchange sermon outlines and maintained a strong friendship. He was one gentle soul who loved the Lord and endeared himself to our family for life.

Leaving the Blue Ridge Mountains we traveled back to Iowa where we spent a few days with Evelyn's folks. I preached at the Ransom Street church, and Sam Sweeden talked to me about the possibility of moving there, but I was not interested at the time. I had once given some thought to trying to start a church in Hubbard, where my Grandma lived. Shenandoah had no New Testament church at that time, and I did make a trip there and talked to the manager of KMA about a position in radio broadcasting. Nothing came of these plans, so I continued on in the work in Lexington. However, something happened in November that made me determined that I would eventually move elsewhere. I surrendered the pulpit one Sunday morning to a visiting preacher who showed his gratitude by publicly "blasting" me for my miserable efforts (in his mind) at personal evangelism. That may have been the last straw for me. In December we took our first bona fide vacation and flew to California where we spent the Christmas holidays with my loving and supportive family in San Luis Obispo. We

★　★　★　★　★　★　★

saw in the New Year with my Aunt Lois and three sisters, and wondered what 1972 held in store for us.

MY FIRST FUNERAL

On Saturday, March 4, I received a frantic phone call from Jessie Hosea. Ernie was not moving. Could I come out right away? I hopped in my Camaro and was out to their farmhouse even before the doctor arrived. Brother Ernie had been diagnosed with phlebitis (the same condition President Nixon had) and was following doctor's orders, remaining quietly in bed with his foot propped up on several pillows. But the blood clot had broken loose and had hit his heart. My experience of going on death calls at Johnson's Funeral Chapel when I was at Midwestern told me that Ernie was dead. I hugged Jessie and gently told her that her husband was gone. The doctor confirmed that to her when he arrived at the house a few minutes later. It all seemed surreal. We had just gone to a "Travelogue" on Alaska with them two nights before.

Although I had been to scores of funerals, I had never conducted one. Brother Hosea was not only well known in the community, he was also a respected member of the Farm Bureau. People came from far and near for the funeral service on March 8. It was probably the largest crowd to fill the building (and basement) during my ministry in Lexington. I was not offended – in fact I was rather relieved – when Sister Hosea asked the former minister, Dale A. Williamson, to assist me in the service. I selected a passage of Scripture that I have since used in nearly every funeral I have conducted: 1 Thessalonians 4:13-18. That passage assures us of three things: the return of Christ, the resurrection of the dead, and the reunion with our loved ones that we will experience when we rise to meet them in the air.

★   ★   ★   ★   ★   ★   ★

LIFE GOES ON

I've always been amazed how quickly life goes on for everyone else after someone, even an important person, dies. Man is like grass which flourishes in the morning and withers in the evening (Psalm 90:6). He is cut down but life goes on. Two days after Ernie's death we celebrated Evelyn's 26th birthday. I took her to Elwood to hear one of our favorite gospel quartets, The Plainsmen. At five minutes to noon every weekday we would hear them sing "The Song of Inspiration" on an AM radio station in WaKeeney, Kansas, "The Christmas City of the High Plains." One day the radio announcer was giving a pitch for ladies nylons. He said that a certain store in WaKeeney had them on sale for 25 cents. Evelyn and I had a big laugh when the pitchman said; "Now, ladies, you know that's only twelve-and-a-half cents a leg!" The next Sunday the men of the congregation graciously asked me to stay on another six months, and I gratefully agreed to do so.

We often took Mindy and Bridget with us when we went to the Westside Care Home to visit the people there. It was sweet to see feeble hands reaching out to pat them on the head or touch their little fingers. One day when I was preaching at Westside, a lady on the front row kept saying, "Shut up!" throughout my entire sermon. I didn't take it personally! We had two ladies in the church, Mrs. Lake and Mrs. Herrmann, who were shut-ins. We often took the girls with us to see them before the Sunday evening service. One Sunday afternoon Mindy piped up, "Well, let's go see Lake and Herrman!" And so we did. Mrs. Herrmann lived in an upstairs apartment. Each time we would visit with her, she would end the visit with the same words: "I want to see Jesus as He is. Not as the artists have painted Him, but as He actually is." You could tell that 1 John 3:2 was dear to her because each time we visited her she

*   *   *   *   *   *   *

would quote it to us: "Beloved, now are we the sons of God, and it doth not yet appear what we shall be: but we know that, when he shall appear, we shall be like him, for we shall see him as he is."

One night in April the Lowell Lundstrom team from Sisseston, South Dakota, came to Lexington for a crusade that was held in the Church of God campgrounds on the edge of town. We went one night to hear them sing. But then Lowell launched into a full-blown sermon, ending the message by asking everyone who wanted to be saved to raise his or her hand. Mindy, avid listener that she was, and not yet three, shot her little hand high into the air! "I see that hand!" shouted Lowell. No doubt he meant someone else's hand. "Now all you people who have just raised your hand, come down to the altar." We decided it would be a good time to leave lest Mindy get more ideas!

Lexington had only one "fast food" place in those years: an A & W drive-in restaurant. The girls loved the foamy root beer that was served to them in baby-size mugs. I loved it too because the "Baby Root Beers" were free! We didn't eat out often, so it was always a treat when we went to the A & W.

I drove out to the Lexington airport to see a celebrity of sorts on April 25. Nebraska-born Sam Yorty, the fiery three-term mayor of Los Angeles (1961-1973), had thrown his hat into the ring to become president of the United States. Yorty, "the last of the big city conservative Democrats," gave a rousing speech at the airport. But his campaign never really took off, and he withdrew from the race just before the California primary in June. He then switched parties and became a Republican saying that he had not left the Democratic Party, the party had left him. The maverick mayor died June 5, 1998, on the 30th anniversary of RFK's assassination.

★   ★   ★   ★   ★   ★   ★

On May 15 we had just pulled up to the curb in front of our house after doing some grocery shopping when we heard on the car radio that Alabama Governor George Wallace had been shot during a campaign rally in Laurel, Maryland. Wallace was running for president as a Democrat. The would-be assassin, Arthur Bremer, was arrested and eventually sentenced to 63 years in prison. (He was released in 2007 after serving 35 years.) Wallace, however, was left paralyzed for life. Evelyn was so disgusted with all the assassination attempts in America that she said, "Let's move to Australia!"

THREE CALLS FROM OREGON

I received three phone calls from the Norvale Park Church of Christ in Eugene, Oregon, during April. Would I come to Eugene and consider becoming their minister? We would pray about it. On May 25 our family flew to Portland where James and Neola Willey, members of the Norvale Park congregation, met us at the airport. Both of them had been students at Boise Bible College when my father taught there; in fact, Neola had been one of my Sunday School teachers in Boise! We spent 10 days in Eugene, home of the University of Oregon. It was a beautiful city and we took to it right away. We ate in the homes of about eight families. I preached a total of seven times from May 28 to June 4. We were very impressed with the "faith, hope and love" of the Norvale Park church and returned to Nebraska feeling quite good about the possibilities of ministering there.

June 10-25 I was back in Virginia and North Carolina, conducting still more revival meetings at Galax and New Home. I think they must have liked me! The call to come to Eugene came the night I preached "16 Questions about Mark 16:16" at New Home. Norvale Park had voted

*   *   *   *   *   *   *

100% in favor of us to move to Oregon. Who was I to argue with a "fleece" like that? I told them we would make the move as soon as my obligations for the summer were completed: VBS in Lexington, a revival in Oakdale, Nebraska, and two youth camps (Camp-O-Cedar in Nebraska and Boiling Springs Camp in Oklahoma). In July Jane Fonda made a move of her own, traveling to Hanoi where she criticized the U.S. State Department on Vietnamese radio and posed for a picture on an enemy tank with North Vietnamese soldiers. If this was not treason, what was? For her despicable behavior she earned the title "Hanoi Jane."

We really enjoyed our time with the Oakdale church. Alvie Schwarting, the minister, was a good baseball player. He lived in near-by Tilden and had played high school baseball with Richie Asburn who played 13 years for the Philadelphia Phillies! I was really impressed. No wonder Alvie could slug that ball out of the park at our student-faculty games at Camp-O-Cedar! He had rubbed shoulders with a genuine Hall of Famer! This is what my father called "greatness by connection." We didn't have any difficulty finding babysitters for Mindy and Bridget at Oakdale: the Schwartings had eight children and the Petersen family had nine more! I had baptized some of them at Camp-O-Cedar. Both families overflowed with Christian joy and happiness.

ON TO OREGON!

On August 1 two *Washington Post* reporters broke the story on Watergate. When it was all said and done, they sold their research papers to the University of Texas for $5 million dollars. Our time in Lexington could now be measured by the days. My parents had moved from California back to Iowa, so we went to be with them on August 7, dad's 57th birthday and our 5th wedding anniversary. I drove my brother

★   ★   ★   ★   ★   ★   ★

David and Ron Parks to Ottumwa where they enrolled at Midwestern as I had done back in 1964. After spending a day or so with Evelyn's folks, we returned to Nebraska to begin preparing for the big move.

Our final Sunday with the church in Lexington was August 20. My Sunday morning message was "Why People Reject Christ." Two young men, Lloyd Sisneros and Paul White, responded to the invitation and I baptized them that afternoon at the church in Cozad since the two churches had gone together to have a farewell dinner for us at the City Park in Cozad. (Within a year or so young Paul would be dead, killed in an automobile accident.) My final message was "Worthy Is the Lamb!" from Revelation 5:12. I knew full well that Christ was worthy to receive power, riches, wisdom, strength, honor, glory, and blessing. I also knew full well the truth of Luke 17:10, "We are unworthy servants; we have only done our duty."

Our best and most lasting work with the church in Lexington was the many hours I invested in the young people. I had really loved teaching them each Sunday morning. We had some great discussions. They began a small paper with my help, *Our Testimony*. Nearly every one of them gave their lives to Christ at church, at church camp, or at the Spring Youth Rally. Several of them went on to Bible College. As far as I know nearly all of them are faithful to Christ today wherever they are living.

On Monday, August 21, Cliff Strever and Alan White helped me load the U-Haul truck I had rented. I had traded our 1968 Camaro for a larger car, a 1970 Ford Torino that I hitched to the truck, hoping I would be able to pull the load over the mountain grades in Idaho and Oregon. Saying good-by to our neighbors, the Cunninghams, especially young Dan, was hard. Soon the parsonage was empty, but it would be occu-

★　★　★　★　★　★　★

pied in a few days. Richard and Thelma Snell were moving from Cincinnati, Ohio, to minister in Lexington.

I had arranged for Evelyn (five months pregnant) and the girls to fly to Oregon, but they would not leave until the next day. So about three in the afternoon I kissed them all good-by and pulled out of Lexington and made it as far as Cheyenne, Wyoming, by nightfall. Evelyn and the girls stayed overnight with Earl and Jessie White and the next morning Jessie put them on a plane in North Platte. The airline had upped the tickets by $50 and Evelyn did not have that much money with her. Jessie loaned her the additional airfare. They flew to Denver where they boarded another plane for Portland. Little Bridget cried because of the air pressure on her ears. When they arrived in Portland, the family that was to drive them to Eugene was not there, but they had purchased tickets for Evelyn and the girls to fly to Eugene, so they boarded their third plane of the day that finally brought them to Eugene. Ralph and Ouida Gillette met them at the airport and took them to their home.

Meanwhile I was thoroughly enjoying my "Westward Ho!" trek in the truck. I did a lot of singing and praying and thinking and planning as I drove 14 hours to Heyburn, Idaho, the first full day. I hadn't felt this close to God in a long time. Spiritually energized, I got up early the next morning and drove 16 hours to Eugene. I loved every minute of that trip, especially crossing over the Blue Mountains and following the Columbia River into Portland. I was greatly struck by the majesty of Mount Hood and the glory of Multnomah Falls. By the time I left Portland and drove into the beautiful Willamette Valley, I was hooked for life on the state of Oregon! To this day it is my favorite place on God's good earth.

★   ★   ★   ★   ★   ★   ★

CHAPTER TEN

THE EMERALD CITY

One fine day in 1846 a fur trapper named Eugene Franklin Skinner built a cabin at the south end of the beautiful Willamette valley in central Oregon. The humble edifice was situated near the confluence of two rivers, the McKenzie and the Willamette. In a few more years Skinner turned the cabin into a trading post. In 1862 the enterprising trapper founded the city of Eugene. By the time we moved to Eugene in 1972, it had grown to become the second largest city in Oregon with a population of over 100,000. It was the largest city we had lived in up to that time, but it did not overwhelm us. We found the people in Eugene just as friendly as those in the Midwest, perhaps even more so. "Travel," said Mark Twain, "is fatal to prejudice."

Eugene was called the "Emerald City," I suppose because the abundant rainfall made everything so lush and green. It seemed like each tree was a different shade of green: evergreen, pine, blue spruce, etc. Timber and wood products were the main business in the Willamette Valley. Weyerhauser was a huge employer and there were all kinds of smaller logging outfits harvesting timber in the valley. This was before the tree-sitters and advocates for the spotted owl took over. Eugene was also called "Tracktown, USA" and "The Track Capital of the World." The University of Oregon track team, coached by legendary Bill Bowerman, was the perennial champion in the Pac-10. (Bowerman and Eugene native Phil Knight co-founded the Nike shoe company.) Steve Prefontaine was their big star. Mary Decker also ran in

★　★　★　★　★　★　★

Eugene. Both were world champion distance runners. I got to see "Pre" run several times at Hayward Field before he was killed in a car wreck in 1975. The 1972 U. S. Olympic Trials were held in Eugene. We were amazed at the number of walkers, runners and bicyclists we saw in Eugene. In Nebraska people walked only if their car was out of gas and ran only if there was some kind of emergency. Only kids rode bikes. But in Eugene it seemed like half the population was out walking, jogging or biking for their health.

In addition to the University of Oregon, Eugene was home to Northwest Christian University, originally Eugene Bible University, *alma mater* of Archie Word, Bill Jessup, Don Earl Boatman, and many other great preachers in the Restoration Movement. Today it is known as Northwest Christian University. They had a great library, and I made good use of it during my ministry in Eugene. The hippie movement was still big in Eugene in the 70s. Nearly every VW van in Eugene belonged to a hippie and was adorned with colorful flowers and the obligatory peace sign. Larry Jonas, a preacher with the West Broadway church, had led a good number of them to the Lord. Eugene was also home to Ken Kesey, author of *One Flew over the Cuckoo's Nest*. It was one wild and crazy town. And politically liberal. I wrote a number of letters to the editor of the left-leaning *Eugene Register-Guard*. Nearly all of my conservative missives were published.

MAKING A HOME

We stayed with Ralph and Ouida Gillette, a retired couple, for about 10 days before we found a nice place to live. The Gillettes were one of two couples who became our surrogate parents and our children's surrogate grandparents while we were living in Eugene. The

★   ★   ★   ★   ★   ★   ★

other couple, of whom I will have more to write about later, was Ken and Evelyn Sayles.

Our first home in Eugene was located in the southernmost part of Eugene, a nice two-story bungalow located at 4886 West Amazon Drive. Our landlord, Mr. Watson (whom we affectionately called "Dr. Watson" after the amicable character who was Sherlock Holmes' trusty companion), rented the house to us at a very reasonable rate. A carport was attached to the west side of the house with a storage shed stacked with wood that we occasionally burned in the living room fireplace. My second-story study had a magnificent view of Spencer Butte. (Skinner Butte was at the opposite end of the valley). The headwaters of Amazon Creek, which flowed right past our house, were located at the base of Spencer Butte. Ralph helped me build bookshelves for my growing library out of cinder blocks and planks of chipboard.

The girls had a nice yard in which to play and a paved drive-way on which to ride their tricycles. Not far from our home was Franklin Park (also named for Eugene Franklin Skinner) where we often took the girls to play. Evelyn quickly set about doing her magic of interior decorating, and before long we all felt at home in our new surroundings. We would have been content to stay there for the dura-tion of our ministry, but in 1974 we were given an offer we could hard-ly refuse by Blair and Ruth Howell, also members at Norvale Park, to live in one of their homes at a ridiculously low rate of rent. I will tell you more about that house later. God took care of us in both places by providing us with wonderful landlords.

THE NORVALE PARK CHURCH

I began my ministry with the Norvale Park Church of Christ as

★   ★   ★   ★   ★   ★   ★

soon as I rolled into town in the big U-Haul truck. Norm Fox, who was about my age and would become one of my best friends in Eugene, had set up a Jule Miller filmstrip showing at the home of a prospective couple, so Norm and I went to their home and conducted a Bible study our first night in town. On Saturday, August 26, while I was working on what would be my first "official" sermon at Norvale Park, the opening exercises of the 20th Olympiad were taking place in Munich, Germany.

The Norvale Park church, located at the corner of Rustic and Vernal Streets, was in the middle of a building program when we arrived. The congregation had pretty well run out of money to finish the new auditorium and classrooms. There were no elders when we were there, although a leadership team had been put together that served fairly well. One of the first crises we faced was a young married wife who had been unfaithful to her husband. She had left him but continued to come to church as though nothing was wrong. The leadership team and I tried to convince her of the error of her way with no results. Trusting God to lead us, we followed the procedure given to the church by Jesus in Matthew 18:15-17. It finally came to the point that we drew up a letter stating our intention to practice church discipline (withdrawal of fellowship). A few days before the letter was to be read to the congregation, the woman repented of her sin and was happily reconciled to her forgiving husband.

Evelyn and I got acquainted with the 75-member congregation by visiting in every home by the end of December. One of the families lived high in the hills overlooking Eugene. They had goats grazing in the flower-filled meadows, and one day we took a beautiful picture of our little Mindy in that meadow. She was offering a handful of flowers to a kid. It was like a scene out of *Heidi*.

★　　★　　★　　★　　★　　★　　★

THE CHRISTIAN LEADERSHIP TRAINING PROGRAM

The apostle Paul taught for three years in the school of Tyrannus (Acts 19:9). I taught for about the same amount of time in a school of Christian leadership cosponsored by the Norvale Park and West Broadway congregations. The school consisted of three instructors: Norm Fox and myself from Norvale Park, and Steve Holsinger, minister at West Broadway. From time to time we brought in special instructors like author Bruce Oberst. The school was really the brainchild of Norm, and I was happy to participate in the proposed 5-year program. Although most of the 40-some students were from West Broadway, classes were held at the Norvale Park building on Monday and Tuesday evenings. We launched on September 4, 1972, about a week after our arrival in Eugene. The very next day, September 5, Arab terrorists broke into Israel's dormitory at the Olympic Village in Munich and callously murdered 11 Israeli athletes.

I spent many long hours in my upstairs study preparing for my two Sunday sermons, a Sunday night class and a Wednesday night class (and in February of 1974 I added a Sunday night radio sermon as well). This was in addition to my Monday and Tuesday night classes in the leadership school. I was a regular preaching and teaching fool for Christ, but I enjoyed every minute of it. Many of the students were university-trained and their questions and comments kept me on my toes. The three-hour classes ran until 10 P.M., so Evelyn and the children were often asleep by the time I arrived home. Preparing tests and grading papers took additional time.

I taught Church History (Norm dubbed it "History of Religious Apostasy") to 25 students using the same texts I had used at Gering:

* * * * * * *

Cairns and Kuiper. I taught directly from the biblical text in the Epistles of James, Peter and Jude and also Paul's Epistle to the Galatians and Thessalonians, creating my own verse-by-verse commentaries in notebook form. For Intertestament History, I used Charles F. Pfeiffer's excellent *Between the Testaments*. (I think I learned as much in this class about the 400 years of silence between the Old Testament and the New Testament as the students did.) As I had done in Hamburg, I taught Homiletics by Harold Knott, author of *How to Prepare a Sermon*. Knott had taught the same course in the same city, at old Eugene Bible University! One night, to illustrate what an Introduction should be, I brought a record player and played for the class the opening bars of the William Tell Overture. I also assigned my Homiletics students to read *Elmer Gantry* by Sinclair Lewis so they would know how people often perceive preachers. For United Kingdom History (and later Divided Kingdom History) class I used a fine little book *The Birth of a Kingdom* by John J. Davis. For Restoration History I taught from James DeForest Murch's classic *Christians Only*. In all, I taught eight courses in my three years of teaching in the Christian Leadership Training Program. The school continued for a few years after I left Eugene and produced several qualified Bible teachers, elders, and preachers.

LINCOLN VAIL IS BORN!

On November 8 President Richard M. Nixon buried Senator George McGovern in a landslide. The victor pledged to secure "peace with honor" in Vietnam and to develop "a new era of peace" in the world. As 1972 came to an end (with seven inches of snow) we were wondering if our third child would be born on Christmas Day. We got

★   ★   ★   ★   ★   ★   ★

an early "Christmas present" when Lincoln Vail, our first and (as it would turn out to be) only son was born on Friday, December 22, at Sacred Heart Hospital in downtown Eugene. I had taken Evelyn to the hospital at 6 A.M., once the Gillettes arrived at the house to watch over Mindy and Bridget. After only two hours of labor, Lincoln was born at 8:36 A.M. He weighed in at seven pounds and four ounces. Evelyn was delighted with the quick delivery; I was delighted because she had delivered us a son! We were both admirers of Abraham Lincoln, so we named our son after the Great Emancipator. (Evelyn's paternal grandfather was also named Abraham Lincoln Stutzman.) Vail came, not from the city in Colorado, but from a combination of four letters from my first and middle name (The "v" and "i" from Victor and the "a" and "l" from Dale.)

The hospital in Oregon had a different philosophy from those in the Midwest. They believed in getting the mother up on her feet right away and out the door headed for home the next day! Evelyn was all for that. So we bundled up our little boy and brought him home for the girls to see on December 23. On Christmas Eve Sunday I preached "No Room for Jesus" from Luke 2:7, "And she brought forth her firstborn son, and wrapped him in swaddling clothes, and laid him in a manger; because there was no room for them in the inn." Christmas Day saw three families from the church – the Bradleys, Dicksons, and Willeys – bring us a full Christmas dinner with all the trimmings. We were one happy family all snug in our cheery home that day! The next day Harry Truman, the 33rd president of the U. S. – and the man who was president when I was born – died in Kansas City.

The Gillettes paid for a year of "Dainty Diaper Service" for Lincoln. Every other day the unique company would bring Evelyn a

*   *   *   *   *   *   *

stack of fresh cloth diapers and take with them the soiled ones. Evelyn thought it was one of the most wonderful and practical gifts she had ever received! I, who gagged at the thought of changing a dirty diaper, was equally grateful! Bridget was still sleeping in the crib so Evelyn made up a bed for Lincoln, whom we called "Wudlet," in the middle drawer of our larger dresser. No, we didn't close the drawer when he cried at night!

PREACHING ON KBMC-FM

Some members of the Norvale Park church owned and operated a Christian radio station, KBMC-FM. The call letters stood for "Keep By My Christ Forever More." Norm Fox handled a live call-in show. You had to be quick on your feet to handle callers with their amazing variety of questions and opinions, so I was glad that Norm had that assignment. On February 4, 1973, I preached "Newness of Life," launching "The Sunday Night Sermon," a half-hour broadcast beginning at 9:30 P.M. I recorded these sermons during the week, and they were put on the air at the station by the Sunday evening disc jockey. I prerecorded "The Sunday Night Sermon" for the duration of my ministry in Eugene. My "radio voice" was being put to good use. One year I narrated Donald G. Hunt's 52-chapter book *The Unfolded Plan of God*.

Ben Alexander, a delightful Englishman and a former spiritualist medium, who had been converted to Christ, had a Saturday night show, also prerecorded. Bernice Poling, a fine Christian lady in the church at Norvale Park, was the station manager. KBMC-FM had contracts with a number of "pay for play" ministries, but sometimes Bernice just couldn't take it when it came to airing the unscriptural "sinner's prayer." More than once I was driving down the road listen-

★   ★   ★   ★   ★   ★   ★

ing to a broadcast when suddenly music would replace the speaker's voice. I knew just what had happened: Bernice had had enough!

For some reason in April 1973, I stopped keeping a logbook of my sermons preached in April. My records show that Sermon #718 was "The Self-Discipline of Jesus" preached on KBMC-FM. I had preached 700-some sermons since May 1967 (when I started preaching at Promise City), an average of about 117 sermons a year for that 6-year stretch.

PUBLISHING *VANGUARD*

I had been called to Norvale Park, in part, because of my articles that had been appearing in the monthly national publication, *The Voice of Evangelism*. It was not long until we began our own monthly publication, *Vanguard*. While the paper was designed for making contacts in the Eugene-Springfield area, it was also sent to hundreds of people across the nation as well. Norm Fox and I served as co-editors. We met one night a month at his house to lay out the paper. Norm did the typing in a back bedroom while I did the paste-up on the kitchen table. All the while puns and insults would fly back and forth from one room to the other. We launched in February 1973. I had the front page article, "When the Master Marveled." Norm wrote the page 3 article, "Christ's 5-Point Peace Plan." The back page was everyone's favorite: The Vantage Point. It was a column filled with religious news (some quite offbeat) with witty commentary (usually penned by Norm). West Broadway and Norvale Park listed their times of services. In time, the 12th and C Church of Christ in Springfield, where Galen Farnsworth preached, ran their ad as well. By 1974 the national publication *Restoration Herald* was picking up some of our articles and reprinting them in their paper. Don DeWelt, publisher at College Press in Joplin,

★   ★   ★   ★   ★   ★   ★

Missouri, first became acquainted with me by receiving *Vanguard*. The paper grew in popularity and increased in circulation until it was going to several thousand readers in Eugene and across the nation.

Members at Norvale, including the youth group, met one night a month to fold, address, and bundle *Vanguard* after we picked it up at our printers, Postal Instant Press. These were great times of fellowship and bonding. To this day I call Paula Weitzel "George M. Poole" because that was one of the names she was addressing one night while we were making wisecracks about his name (sorry Mr. Poole, if you are still alive and reading this). Each month we had all kinds of free offers in *Vanguard*: a cassette tape-of-the month, gospel tracts, a 5-lesson Bible correspondence course, the Jule Miller filmstrips, etc. Occasionally we conducted reader opinion surveys. Norm excelled at writing on Christian evidences and Christian education while I took on everything from "streaking" to the SALT accords (strategic arms limitation talks). The articles that stirred up the most controversy were "Is Billy Graham Going to Heaven?" "Abortion Is Murder," and "Expelling 'The Exorcist.'" We lost a few readers (including West Broadway's ad over the unsparing exposé of "The Exorcist") but gained many more readers by our bold approach to writing. We didn't name it *Vanguard* for just any reason at all. We felt that we were at the forefront in the spiritual struggle to pull down strongholds and demolish arguments (2 Corinthians 10:4, 5).

GONE PREACHING

I conducted four revival meetings, taught Bible classes in three youth camps and preached on seven rallies during our three years in Eugene. Once I was gone almost three weeks preaching in Iowa. This was just not wise on my part. Evelyn and the children needed me at

★   ★   ★   ★   ★   ★   ★

home, but I thought the churches that called me to preach for them needed me more. During my third week of preaching in Iowa, the Norvale Park Church was short on funds and had no weekly check to give to Evelyn. One evening she was standing at the stove fixing the last of the food that was in the house. As she stirred the meal on the stove, she was thinking, "Well, this is it. This is our 'Last Supper.' There is nothing left in the cupboards or the refrigerator." Then she looked up on a shelf and spotted a glass jar full of layered dry beans, peas and lentils that were there only for decoration. She thought: "We can eat those!" The jar of decorative beans tided them over until some money finally came (either from the church or me). I was having some stomach "pangs" myself. It was during that three weeks of preaching (at my home church in Hamburg) in 1973 that I had my first experience with heartburn. It was so painful that I honestly thought I was having a heart attack. For 37 years I took a variety of stomach medicines until 2010 when I was forced to have surgery for a monster hiatal hernia. At last: no more antacids!

One of my meetings didn't take me too far from home. It was right across town with Galen Farnsworth and the Springfield congregation. Galen had been one of my dad's students at Boise Bible College. The first time I met him was in his garage where I found him making one of his famous grandfather's clocks. He had a great sense of humor and we got along great together. We had a full house every night for the preaching.

Once I took along my entire family for a meeting in Project City, California. The church had fixed up a small trailer next to the church building, but the first night the heating unit put off such noxious fumes that we had to move into the preacher's house. But John and Hazel Bell, the occupants, gladly made room for us and we enjoyed "close company" the rest of the week.

★ ★ ★ ★ ★ ★ ★

I also held a return revival with the Broad Street Church of Christ in San Luis Obispo, California. Bob Bowers was the preacher at that time. Bob had a fruitful prison ministry going on at the California Men's Penal Colony just outside San Luis Obispo. One day he took me with him to conduct a Bible study. I was hoping to meet Charles "Tex" Watson, one of the high profile prisoners incarcerated at CMPC. Watson, part of the infamous Manson family, had been sentenced to life in prison for his part in the murders of Sharon Tate and others. He had since turned his life over to Christ and had been baptized. But he was not in our study group that day. Bob gave me an opportunity to share in the Bible study. This was my first opportunity to preach Christ behind prison bars. I was impressed with how much the prisoners respected Bob. Watson, though still serving a life sentence, is now an ordained minister and maintains a Website at www.aboundinglove.org. We had five decisions for Christ in the meeting at San Luis Obispo.

It was my privilege to appear on several preaching rally programs in the Pacific Northwest with a number of excellent speakers including Tom Burgess, Bob Ballard, Harold Buckles, and Earl W. Chambers. Brother Chambers was a pioneer in preaching on television and had a weekly TV program "Eternal Good Tidings" which aired on KEZI-TV in Eugene. I preached for Tom Burgess at the Montavilla church in Portland on two occasions, and both times we had several responses to the gospel. I also baptized several young people at the three summer youth camps in which I participated.

WATERGATE AND WATER BAPTISMS

The year 1973 was one wild year. All year long Congress and the media were embroiled in Watergate. LBJ died in Texas on January

★   ★   ★   ★   ★   ★   ★

22, the same day that Roe v. Wade opened the floodgates to abortion on demand in the U. S. On January 27 the Paris Peace Accord was signed, "ending" the war in Vietnam, at least on paper. My high school classmate, Jimmy Scroggins, was one of the last men killed in Vietnam. In February militant Indians occupied the Pine Ridge Sioux Reservation at Wounded Knee, South Dakota. I did a take on that in the April *Vanguard* with "Bend the Knee at Wounded Heart." In the May *Vanguard* I wrote a piece on "The Energy Crisis," quoting a source who said that gasoline would soon be selling for 50 cents a gallon! In Eugene we were limited to five gallons of gas per trip to the gas station. Sometimes I got up early in the morning to get gas, but by the time I got to the Union 76 station I would have to sit in a line that was sometimes a mile long. In May a Senate panel began hearings on Watergate.

I baptized a fair number of people during our ministry in Eugene. Most of them were young people or young adults. One of the oldest people I ever immersed was May Nichols, a dear woman in her 90s, on the last day of a meeting my father had been conducting at Norvale Park that ended July 1. The largest attendance we had at Norvale Park was 140 the night Dale A. Williamson preached for us during a preaching rally. I learned that it was much harder to get people to come to church in the Northwest than it had been in the Midwest. Native Oregonians were rugged individualists who felt that they had pulled themselves up by their own bootstraps and didn't have much use for God. Indeed, Oregon is still one of the most "unchurched" states in the union.

MY FIRST WEDDING

I had never performed a wedding until August 11, 1973. It was my happy duty to unite in holy matrimony a young couple whom I had

★   ★   ★   ★   ★   ★   ★

taught and baptized earlier in the year, Fred Dickson and Debbie Bissell. The wedding was an outdoor affair, and the bride looked lovely in her white dress and floppy white hat. A farmer on a tractor in a nearby field was driving back and forth, but I managed to make my voice heard over the "put-put" of the tractor. I pretty much followed the order of service suggested by James DeForest Murch in his handy little *Ministers' Manual*, published by Standard Publishing. I have performed many weddings since that day, but I will always look back with fondness on that special outdoor ceremony. I do believe that marriage is a sacred institution that should be taken very seriously. The vows that Evelyn and I pledged to each other in 1967 mean just as much to us today as they did back then. I am always pleased with a marriage that "takes," and I am always saddened with a union that is dissolved. "What God hath joined together let not man put asunder" will always be the will of God.

THE SPORTING LIFE

Eugene was a sports lover's paradise. In the spring I enjoyed going to Hayward Field to watch collegiate track meets. In the summer I often went to Civic Stadium to see the Eugene Emeralds play baseball. At that time they were in the Pacific Coast League, Triple A, as high as you could go before entering the Major Leagues. The Emeralds were a franchise of the Philadelphia Phillies, so I saw some players going up and others on their way down. Jim Bunning, a former Phillies pitcher (and now a congressman in Kentucky) was the manager. After six innings had been played, you could get in for free. Our home was just a few blocks from the stadium. While I was reading or studying, I would have the game on the radio. After the top of the sixth I would drive to the stadium, arriving just in time to get in and see the final three innings. One night Norm Fox was driving by the stadium, listening to the game

★   ★   ★   ★   ★   ★   ★

on his car radio. He heard the announcer say, "There's a long drive to left field!" Norm looked up and saw the ball sail over the fence. He reached out his car window and fielded it cleanly as it bounced right into his hands! My brother David still spent the summers with us. One evening, right after picking him up at the airport, we stopped by Civic Stadium. We had not even taken our seats when a batter fouled one back and it ricocheted right into David's hands! I took Lincoln to his first game when he was about two, but all he cared about was ice cream and a hot dog. He was covered with mustard and chocolate by the time we got home. The first game I took Evelyn to featured a great "rhubarb" between the home plate umpire and the visiting manager. Even Evelyn, my mild-mannered wife, cheered lustily when the ump gave the argumentative manager the old "heave-ho"! But the best thing she liked about baseball games was listening to the stadium organist. "That's the way the organ should be played at church!" she exclaimed.

When fall rolled around, sometimes I would go to Autzen Stadium, home of the University of Oregon Fighting Ducks. All-American Dan Fouts was the quarterback then, who later wound up playing in the NFL. After the first half they opened the gates and you got in for free. So I would listen to the game at home on Saturdays and at half time head for Autzen. I witnessed some exciting finishes in the second half, including a big upset of Stanford. I never got to go to "The Pit" to see the Ducks play basketball, however. The place was packed every time UCLA or USC came to town. I contented myself by just listening to the play-by-play on the radio. Sometimes on Monday nights I would visit with Ken Sayles to watch Monday Night Football. Many people despised Howard Cosell, but I, for one, took special delight in listening to his amazing vocabulary. I think I learned a new word each Monday night!

★   ★   ★   ★   ★   ★   ★

412   V I C T O R :   S I N C E   1 9 4 5

TURMOIL AND TROUBLE AT HOME AND ABROAD

As summer turned to fall in 1973, "turmoil and trouble" seemed to be the operative words for much of what was happening in the U. S. and the Middle East. Egypt and Syria launched a surprise attack on Israel on Yom Kippur (October 6), the holiest day on Israel's calendar. Iraq and Jordan were only too happy to leap into the fray to assist their Arab allies. Israel was on the brink of annihilation. Although he was an Austrian Jew, Secretary of State Henry Kissinger coldly advised President Nixon, "Let the Jews bleed a little." Nixon received a frantic phone call from Israeli Prime Minister Golda Meir at 3 A.M., begging him to intervene. Nixon said Meir's voice became his mother's voice. When Nixon was a little boy his Quaker mother read him Bible stories about the Jews. One day she told him, "Richard, some day you are going to be in a position to save the Jews." Remembering his mother's "prophecy," Nixon promised Meir immediate support, and as a result, Israel's beefed-up armed forces quickly defeated the Arab coalition. Before long they were knocking on the door of Damascus. To punish the United States for their support of Israel, oil-producing Arab nations placed an embargo on oil shipments to the U. S. Nixon asked gas stations to close on Sunday, and 99% of them agreed to do so. The national speed limit was lowered to 55 mph to cut gas consumption. On December 9, I preached "The Worst Oil Shortage of All Time!" – from 1 Kings 17:8-16.

Spiro Agnew resigned as Vice President October 12 and was soon replaced by Gerald R. Ford. Agnew pleaded *nolo contendre* to charges of income tax evasion. (As I write these words, Congress has just approved a man who failed to pay his taxes to become Secretary of the

★   ★   ★   ★   ★   ★   ★

Treasury.) Later in the month Nixon, facing possible impeachment, agreed to turn over some White House tapes that had been subpoenaed. It seemed like Watergate was on the front page of each day's *Eugene Register-Guard*. It was relentless. I wrote several letters to the editor during this time frame. Here is an excerpt from but one that was published. "I find it extremely difficult to believe that I'm the only one writing, or who has written, to the *Register-Guard* in pro-Nixon language. Does the overwhelming majority of anti-Nixon letters reflect the actual ration of such mail received? Is it possible that all writers are immersed in this maelstrom of impeachment?" To this day I believe that the liberal media never gave Nixon the credit due him for opening up dialogue between the U. S. and China and Russia. In my opinion Nixon was the best foreign policy president we have ever had, but was tarnished for life by Watergate. The drumbeat for Nixon's impeachment continued nonstop until he finally resigned as President in August 1974. That was one sad day for me, a Nixon loyalist to the bitter end.

But Christmas was still a season of "peace on earth, good will to men." We celebrated Lincoln's first birthday on December 22 with my sister Bonnie who had flown to Eugene to help us celebrate the holidays. The Sunday before Christmas I preached "Christ and the Common People" from Mark 12:37: "And the common people heard him gladly." We had our first Christmas tree that year. Mindy, now four, had saved her nickels and dimes to buy a Christmas tree for $2 that looked almost like Charlie Brown's famous Christmas tree. She was so proud of it. We set up the little tree on a table in front of the picture window and let the girls decorate it with shiny green and red glass balls. It was a bright and happy moment and was a nice way to bring the year of "turmoil and trouble" to an end.

★ ★ ★ ★ ★ ★ ★

ALL IN THE FAMILY

"Children are a heritage of the LORD . . . Happy is the man that hath his quiver full of them" (Psalm 127:3,5). Our quiver was half full by this time – three children. Evelyn was studying one day and discovered that a Hebrew archer's quiver held six arrows, so we still had three to go! She was expecting our fourth child in late May 1974. We decided to keep it a secret from our parents back in the Midwest so we could surprise them with the news. But it was no secret that our three children, Mindy, Bridget and Lincoln, were a constant source of joy and happiness to us. Whenever they said something cute or witty Evelyn would stop whatever she was doing and write it down. She has two or three boxes full of their wit and wisdom. Perhaps some day she will put them into a best-selling book so we can retire in comfort!

A MAN ON A MISSION

I'm still not sure how I got on the mailing list for W. Carl Ketcherside's provocative paper *Mission Messenger* when we lived in Eugene. Maybe someone sent my name to the unity-minded word-smith in St. Louis, or perhaps we just exchanged our papers as editors are wont to do. Of all the papers and journals I received, *Mission Messenger* challenged my thinking the most. Here was a man who had been raised in the ultra-right wing of the Churches of Christ, had been a combative and effective debater, and then had his whole way of thinking and living dramatically changed by a visit to Belfast, Northern Ireland in 1957. Of course, I had no way of knowing then that some day I would preach in that same church – from that same elevated pulpit – where he had been so wonderfully transformed.

★   ★   ★   ★   ★   ★   ★

Brother Ketcherside planted the seeds of peace and peacemaking in my heart as I read his paper from cover to cover each month. Evelyn knew who he was; indeed, he had once visited her church in Ottumwa. I had heard people talk about him – sometimes in uncomplimentary terms. He was a lightning rod for many and a whipping boy for others. But as I read what he was writing, I found that what his critics were saying were often mischaracterizations or outright distortions. I sent for some back issues of *Mission Messenger* so I could get the whole picture. In time I started collecting bound volumes of the paper, never dreaming that some day the ministry I would direct would publish a handsome 12-volume set, *The Complete Works of W. Carl Ketcherside*. His book *The Twisted Scriptures* was perhaps his best work, in my young judgment at that time (I was not yet 30).

Still, I was only reading and assimilating what the great man was thinking and writing. It would be a few more years before I would actually put into practice, in word and deed, the pertinent peace principles of W. Carl Ketcherside. Someone had to plant those latent seeds in the furrow of my mind, and for me that man was the sanguine scribe of St. Louis. "The fruit of righteousness is sown in peace of them that make peace" (James 3:18). What he wrote took root in my heart until I could almost quote from memory gems like the following.

- "Make nothing a test of fellowship that God has not made a condition to salvation."

- "Wherever God has a son or a daughter there I have a brother or sister."

- "If a man is good enough for God to accept, he is not too bad for me to receive."

★   ★   ★   ★   ★   ★   ★

Sometimes, when people tell me that my writings remind them of W. Carl Ketcherside, I feel good all over.

Starting in Eugene I also exchanged papers for several years with Lindy McDaniel and his *Pitching for the Master*. Lindy was a member of the Church of Christ and was a fine relief pitcher with the St. Louis Cardinals and New York Yankees. McDaniel's paper was also sent to many major league players and coaches. He also sent me an autographed picture. McDaniel pitched for 21 years in the big leagues and wound up with a very respectable 141-119 record. He now blogs for Pitching for the Master.

DARKNESS AND LIGHT

Watergate continued to dominate the headlines in 1974. How much more of this could America take? Eugene was a bastion of liberalism, and every day President Nixon took hits in the *Register-Guard*. On January 11 I sat down and wrote a letter to the beleaguered leader of the country. I don't remember what I wrote, but I did receive a nice note from President Nixon in return, thanking me for my words of support. On February 4 members of the radical Symbionese Liberation Army kidnapped Patty Hearst, daughter of millionaire publisher Randolph Hearst. This led to a string of bank robberies, with Patty evidently joining her captors in the capers, perhaps a victim of the "Stockholm syndrome." Even a church was not a safe place in America in the 70s. On June 30 Alberta King, the mother of Martin Luther King, Jr., was murdered while attending services of the Ebeneezer Baptist Church in Atlanta!

The Norvale Park church in Eugene, however, was a "haven of rest" in contrast with all that was going on in the mid-70s in America.

★   ★   ★   ★   ★   ★   ★

Week after week we enjoyed the fellowship of the saints. One of those saints was Evelyn Libby whom I visited every week in a nursing home in Springfield. Evelyn was a beautiful woman who had a beautiful spirit. As her physical suffering increased, her Christian attitude toward suffering increased even more. Every time I called on her, it seemed that she was able to cheer me up more than I could her. One day she was in such agony, she asked me to rub her back. I was hesitant to do so, but her plea touched my heart and so I did as she had asked. When I conducted her funeral on March 22, I quoted from Isaiah 9:2, "The people who walked in darkness have seen a great light." I know this passage is referring to Messiah, but I felt that Evelyn had lived such a Christlike life that she deserved this recognition. Never once did I ever hear her complain about her suffering. Never once did I hear her blame God. Her daughter, "Frankie" Weitzel, who was also a member at Norvale Park, was so grateful for the attention I had given her mother that she did something very special for me. I had always admired the painting of Christ that was on the dust jacket of Fulton Sheen's *Life of Christ* – actually a painting done by the great Salvador Dali. Frankie painted the scene of Christ on the cross on a large oil canvas, had it professionally mounted and framed, and presented it to me before we left Eugene in 1975. It has hung on my study wall wherever I have lived since, and I would not trade it for anything. To this day it reminds me that the sufferings of Christ are to be ours too. The great apostle Paul even desired to know the sufferings of Christ. Evelyn Libby shared in those sufferings, and if I am ever called upon to do so, I hope I can remember her shining example of Christian faith and hope.

Another "Evelyn" who manifested the spirit of Christ was Evelyn Sayles. Ken and Evelyn were our other "surrogate" parents

★   ★   ★   ★   ★   ★   ★

while we were in Eugene. Many times they had us in their home for waffles with fresh Oregon strawberries covered with whipped cream. Ken always asked me to pray before the meal, as he was not able to. He had been shot down over Germany during World War II and received terrible treatment from the Germans in a prisoner of war camp. In later years he wrote the account of his imprisonment and the effects that it had on him, and I printed it in *One Body* ("Special Delivery at Stalag-17"). Ken ran a barbershop next to their home on River Road and gave our little Lincoln his first professional haircut. He always called him "shortstop" and said he would have to stretch out his legs if he were ever going to play for the New York Yankees. Evelyn possessed one of the sweetest spirits I have ever seen in a Christian woman. She would always see the best in others and would never utter a word against anyone. To this day no one has given as large a gift to Peace on Earth Ministries as did Ken and Evelyn Sayles – and they did it while they were still living! I often think of them when I hear the old adage: "Do your giving while you're living; then you're knowing where it's going!"

James and Neola Willey had been students at Boise Bible College when my father taught there in the mid-50s. In fact, Neola had been one of my Sunday School teachers at the church at 18th and Eastman where my father was also an associate minister. I called Neola "Mouse" because she was quiet as a church mouse – such an example of "the incorruptible beauty of a gentle and quiet spirit" as Scripture commends for all women (1 Peter 3:4). Betty Wickwire was another of my father's students at BBC who was a member at Norvale Park. One day Mindy accidentally called Harold and Betty the "Wickedwires."

Two days after the funeral for Mrs. Libby I flew back to my

★   ★   ★   ★   ★   ★   ★

hometown of Hamburg, Iowa, to conduct a revival that stretched out for three weeks. Beforehand I had helped organize a men's retreat that Norvale Park was to host. One or two of the men thought I should be present to host the event, but I felt that they could do just fine in my absence. I do believe that this decision would eventually lead to my untimely departure from Eugene in 1975. While I was preaching in Iowa, Hank Aaron hit his 715th career home run, breaking the record of 714 long held by Babe Ruth. I never thought that record would be eclipsed, and I kind of felt sorry for the old Bambino.

AMANDA JANE IS BORN!

We had always let our parents know when we were expecting a child, but we decided to surprise them when we knew that our fourth child was coming. The folks at Norvale Park knew, of course, but we asked them to keep "mum" about our little secret. At a most respectable hour of 9:15 A.M. on May 28, 1974, our Amanda Jane was born at Sacred Heart Hospital in Eugene. For the first (and last!) time I accompanied Evelyn into the delivery room for the birth. I do believe the nurses had more concern for me than they did Evelyn, for I was quite queasy during the whole process. I am sure they wondered if I would throw up or faint first!

Later that day I got on the phone and called my parents back in Iowa. The conversation went something like this.

Me: "Hi, mom and dad. How would you like to have another grandchild?"

Them: "Oh, wonderful! That would be just fine with us. When do you think it will happen?"

Me: "How about right now?"

★   ★   ★   ★   ★   ★   ★

Them: "What? What do you mean?"

Me: "Well, Evelyn just delivered a little girl a few hours ago. Her name is Amanda Jane and she is beautiful!"

Them: "What? What? You have a baby girl? Oh, that is wonderful! Say, why didn't you tell us this was going to happen!"

Me: "Oh, we wanted to surprise you this time."

Them: "Well, you surprised us all right!"

The next day, in true Sacred Heart fashion, Evelyn was released, and we brought our new baby home. Mindy, Bridget and Lincoln were fascinated, delighted, and eager to help take care of the baby in any way they could.

We took Amanda to church with us on Sunday, June 2. Everyone "oohed" and "ahhed" over her as we knew they would. My *Ready Record* says that I preached "What Kind of Person Ought You to Be?" from 2 Peter 3:11. Baby Amanda's first Sunday at church was almost her last, for on the way home we were broadsided in an intersection, and all six of us were sent to the hospital for observation. Oregon law did not require seat belts in 1974. A young man from Cottage Grove ran a red light and smashed into us on the driver's side at a high rate of speed. Evelyn was holding the new baby on her lap and the three other children were in the back seat of our four-door sedan. Evelyn, with a mother's instinct, leaned over Amanda, protecting her with her arms, but was thrown into the windshield, breaking her nose. I suffered tension in my arms for several weeks after the crash from gripping the steering wheel so hard. The children were tossed around in the back seat, but miraculously suffered no injuries. Our 1970 Ford Torino was a total loss. A few days later Evelyn spotted

★   ★   ★   ★   ★   ★   ★

a 1969 Oldsmobile Delta 88. Because of the national oil crisis, big cars were selling cheap. We were able to buy this beautiful car for only $970.00! It was the nicest car we had ever owned and rode whisper-soft on the highway as we motored back to Iowa later in the month for our annual vacation to see our folks and show off our new baby. Another mouth to feed, of course, put a crimp in our finances. Even though we loved our home on Amazon Drive, we were grateful when a couple from the church, Blair and Ruth Howell, invited us to move into one of their rental homes at 2885 Ava. The rent was much cheaper, and we could hardly say no to such a generous offer (they could have received much more from more affluent renters). The new home was much roomier and more modern. The big back yard had lots of fruit trees loaded with apples, nuts and cherries, and there were also plenty of blackberries and raspberries to pick and enjoy. Amanda was born with hip dysplasia and had to wear a special brace for the first year of her life. Even with it strapped on she could still crawl around the house and even turn over, cartwheel style. Eventually she learned how to get the contraption off. Then she would crawl off on all fours with a squeal of delight as Evelyn would chase her down.

A REUNION AND A RESIGNATION

In July I flew back to St. Louis. My high school buddy Larry Dothager was there to greet me at Lambert Field. I had not seen "Doe" for 10 years. The occasion was the 10th anniversary reunion of the Class of 1964. While there I was asked to preach at the church in Mulberry Grove where my father had once preached. I took as my text Ephesians 3:21; "Unto Him be Glory." Later that month Evelyn and I took our children to the Holgate Rally in Portland and enjoyed staying in a

★   ★   ★   ★   ★   ★   ★

rustic cabin on the campgrounds. Even though it was in the heart of Portland, the campgrounds were nestled in the middle of a forest with tall Douglas Fir trees and evergreen trees everywhere. It was a delightful week, and we were refreshed both physically and spiritually. Each summer we were in Eugene, we also attended the Lane County Fair. Evelyn was in "seventh heaven" the year she got to hear her favorite country singer, Marty Robbins. In other years we heard The Statler Brothers and Loretta Lynn sing at the fair.

In August the church launched the Willamette Valley Christian School, and our little Mindy, now five years old, was one of its first preschool students. From here on there was no going back. Just as I had gone to school in Whiting, Iowa, in 1950, so now all our children would follow the same routine. "And with all thy getting, get wisdom." We celebrated our seventh wedding anniversary on August 7, and on the next day President Nixon announced that he was resigning as President of the United States. Nixon said, "I have never been a quitter. To leave office before my term is completed is opposed to every instinct in my body." He stated that he had decided to put "the interests of America first." I, a Nixon loyalist, was not a happy man. I continued my summer duties: teaching at youth camps, teaching night classes at our Vacation Bible School, preaching, recording, writing, and editing. In fact, in September I started a new paper, *Venture*, a bimonthly that was designed for church leaders. This was in addition to our monthly paper *Vanguard*. I managed to produce seven issues of *Venture* before I put it to bed when we moved away from Eugene in 1975. In retrospect I probably could have used my "extra" time better than by starting a second journal.

And just about the time I thought things could not get much

★   ★   ★   ★   ★   ★   ★

worse in America in 1974, my favorite singer, Connie Francis, was brutally raped by a stranger who broke into her motel room while she was performing in Long Island, New York. Like many boys growing up in America in the 60s, Connie had been my poster girl, and the thought of her being savagely violated like that just made me sick. The rape led to her having a mental breakdown and a long road to recovery for the little Italian girl who sang such pretty songs in my adolescent growing-up years.

A SAD DEPARTURE

Twenty-nine days into the New Year (1975) the Weather Underground Organization, a radical leftwing group that declared war on the United States in 1970, bombed the U. S. State Department in Washington. Earlier they had bombed the U. S. Capitol (1971) and the Pentagon (1972). Bill Ayers was a member of the WUO and is unrepentant to this day of his actions against the United States. It staggers the mind that this man is a friend of our president and that Mr. Obama has not renounced his ties to the unrepentant bomber.

Try as I might, however, I could not seem to set a fire and help get the Norvale Park church up and going. James Willey and a few others donated time in the evenings to work on the new auditorium, but the finances were just not there. As the minister of the congregation, I felt that I was letting them down by not producing new members who would, if properly taught about finances, produce the necessary capital to finish the building.

The first issue of *Vanguard* in 1975 was a special one. My father, my brother David (a third-year student at Midwestern), and I combined to write on that great Corinthian trilogy of faith, hope and love.

★ ★ ★ ★ ★ ★ ★

I wrote, "Hope is the vital need of the hour. It will make life bearable and death beautiful. It will steady us when tempted, sustain us when grieved, spur us on when weary, and at last save us." But my hopes for getting things going at Norvale Park seemed to be going nowhere. When I told one of the men that I planned to go back to Iowa in May to hear my father preach his 5,000th sermon, he responded, "Maybe you should look around for another church while you are back there." He told me that another man agreed with his assessment. I knew and loved both these men and so, acting on their suggestion, I announced to the church on April 13 that I was resigning as their minister. Everyone seemed sad. Sometime later I took my car to Cecil Bradley, a godly man if I ever knew one, and as he was working on my engine he asked, "Why are you resigning?" When I told him what had been suggested to me, Cecil replied, very seriously, "One or two men do not speak for the entire church." After conducting a second revival meeting at San Luis Obispo, we left for Iowa. But Brother Bradley's words troubled me all the way back to Iowa. No sooner had I arrived at my parent's home than I received a phone call from Eugene. It was Steve Holsinger from the West Broadway church, asking for my "blessing" to merge West Broadway and Norvale Park into one congregation. Somewhat stunned, I rather curtly gave him my "blessing" and hung up the phone. Now what was I to do? The fall of Saigon was nothing compared to the fall of my spirits. We returned to Oregon with nothing in hand. I loved Oregon and I loved the people in the Norvale Park church. In hindsight (which is usually 20-20), I should have called for a congregational meeting to see if they really wanted us to leave because deep down I really wanted to stay.

The summer wore on. In July I flew to Denver and met with

* * * * * * *

Don Heese and William E. Paul. They wanted me to join them in kingdom endeavors, but I would have to raise my own support. Don suggested that I interview with the *Denver Post* for a sports writing position, but my heart wasn't in it. Also, at that time, the relationship between the two brethren and Eddie DeVries was somewhat strained. I could not see myself getting into a situation where I could not work with all three, so I declined. I taught for a week at Tremont Bible Camp, a young people's camp in Colorado, and then moved on to another camp in Minnesota, where I taught for another week. While I was teaching in Minnesota, I met with some men from the Church of Christ in West Concord, a small town near Rochester. I don't remember whether I was invited to move to Minnesota before I returned to Oregon or after, but the result was the same. They were good enough to ask a man who was out of a job to come and preach for them, and I, grateful for their kindness, accepted.

One of the last things we did in Oregon was to take the children to the see the Pacific Ocean. We had been to other magnificent sites like snow-capped Mt. Hood, the plunging Multnomah Falls, and the beautiful Columbia Gorge, but we wanted one last trip to the ocean. It was a windy day, but how the kids enjoyed building sandcastles and playing on the shore. However, I was rather sad because I was seeing my own sandcastle disintegrating and blowing away in the wind.

Ed Weitzel generously put four new tires on our Oldsmobile and then it was Departure Day. Not until I looked over at Evelyn the first day out of Eugene and saw her crying did I realize what I had done. She did not want to leave these loving people. Why hadn't I asked her how she felt about moving? But I never asked and she never questioned. She just felt like I must have considered it to be the will of God.

★   ★   ★   ★   ★   ★   ★

I do not blame her for her silence; rather, I blame myself for failing to seek her advice and ask her how she felt about things. Each day that we drove back to the Midwest, my heart sank lower than the sinking sun. By the time we pulled into the big farmhouse in Minnesota on August 25, I was lower than the lowest lake in "the land of 10,000 lakes." Had it not been for a providential visit from our old friends Ronald and Lorine Emberton from Hamburg, Iowa, on the very day we moved in, I honestly do not think I could have had the strength to go with them to the new church, and there preach my first sermon.

★   ★   ★   ★   ★   ★   ★

CHAPTER ELEVEN

THE COLD COUNTRY

Our new home was a nice old two-story farmhouse in the country, about seven miles from the town of West Concord. It belonged to Dana and LaVonne Campbell, members of the church who graciously allowed us to live there rent-free. The church paid the utilities, which was another blessing. The heating bill would often be more than $400 a month during the long, cold winter. There were three bedrooms and a bathroom upstairs. The downstairs consisted of a large kitchen, dining room, living room, and a room off the living room that I used for my study. We had a large yard where the children could play, an old garage where we parked the Oldsmobile and a big windmill covered with luscious grapes. The windmill was adorned with a star at the top and when lighted during the Christmas season it could be seen for miles around. The front yard sloped down into a deep ditch next to the highway. One day we heard Lincoln crying but could not find him. We followed his voice to the ditch and found him at the bottom, crying his eyes out. To him it must have seemed like he was lost at the bottom of the Grand Canyon. Dana had a dairy herd on the farm, and the children liked it when the cows came up to the fence and visited them.

The town was not much to look at, and for some reason I barely remember it. The congregation was not a large one, but they had an earnest zeal to spread the word of God. It was made up primarily of three families: the Averys (Tom and his brother Lloyd) and the Campbells. All of them had big families and some of the children were

★   ★   ★   ★   ★   ★   ★

now married and starting their own families. Eva Campbell, Dana's mother, was a quiet and godly woman who was very knowledgeable of the scriptures. The West Concord congregation was begun when these good people had left the Concord Church of Christ some years previous to start a new church. Concord, or "Old Concord," was just a spot in the road on the way to West Concord, a Norwegian community of about 800 people. My new duties included preaching on Sunday mornings and evenings, leading the midweek service, and doing something I had never done before – teaching a "Release Time" class one day a week at the small parsonage (which was being used for classrooms). In Minnesota the public schools would release junior high and senior high students one hour each week for religious instruction at their local church. I imagine that this was due to the influence of the Lutheran Church in Minnesota.

OVERCOMING MY NEGATIVISM

Tom Avery was a Christian businessman who believed in the power of positive thinking. He was a big encourager and influenced my life when I really needed some help. Tom supplied me with some good books and recordings by Earl Nightingale that helped me to be more optimistic in my thinking and approach to life. Nightingale, the "Dean of Personal Development," was a motivational speaker and radio broadcaster. Evelyn has always been by nature a positive person, but I have been the opposite. I have to constantly work at being positive. To paraphrase the apostle Paul: "The positive approach I want to take, I don't; and the negative approach I don't want to take, I do." I have fought this battle all my life, but it was positive-thinking Tom Avery who set me on the road to right thinking. Not long after arriving in

*   *   *   *   *   *   *

West Concord I received a negative letter from a church leader on the West Coast who took me to task for an article I had written for the final Oregon edition of *Vanguard.* He wrote something like, "Why don't you climb out from behind that typewriter of yours and join the real world?" Do you know how a negative letter or comment stays with you longer that a positive one? I let that letter bug me until one day when I burned it along with other trash. You can't let other people run your life or ruin your living.

The famous Dutch painter Vincent Van Gogh once said, "In spite of everything I shall rise again: I will take up my pencil, which I have forsaken in my great discouragement, and I will go on with my drawing." I soon discovered that even when you are discouraged – as I was when I began my work in West Concord – that the best thing you can do is to pray to God for strength and then plunge into your work. And then find even more work to do to keep busy. So, like Van Gogh, I took up my pencil and went back to my work. I introduced myself to the editor of the local newspaper and showed him my portfolio. He immediately invited me to cover the local high school football and basketball games. The *West Concord Enterprise* certainly wasn't the *Denver Post,* but I really enjoyed covering the Cardinals' games. I wore a red and white checked sport coat and walked the sidelines of the football games and was seated at the scorer's bench for the basketball games. Sometimes people in the community would stop me on the street and comment favorably on my weekly sports column. In this way I was able to quickly introduce myself to the community.

One night Dana Campbell, an avid Minnesota Vikings fan, took me to Minneapolis to see an exhibition game between the Vikings and the visiting Miami Dolphins. This was the first NFL game I had ever

★   ★   ★   ★   ★   ★   ★

been to, and I was somewhat taken aback by the nature of the crowd. I dis-covered that NFL fans are more like fanatics. At a baseball game you can sit back and relax, but at a professional football game the atmos-phere is quite raucous. Even mild-mannered Dana, wearing his trusty Australian cowboy hat, with one side pinned up, was up and roaring with the rest of the crowd while I watched in wide-eyed wonder.

I was very happy to be reunited with my old friend from Hamburg and college days, Gary Cradic, who was now leading in a new church plant at nearby Owatonna. We started team-teaching some night classes at West Concord for about 16 members from both congre-gations; a good mix of eager young couples and mature older mem-bers. Gary taught Genesis on Monday nights while I taught Thessalo-nians on Tuesday nights. We also started a "5th Sunday Rally" where the two churches came together as "one body" four times a year. As with the Lexington and Cozad congregations in Nebraska, we were manifesting an "interdependent" spirit, not an "independent" spirit that is the unfortunate practice of most churches.

A WALK IN THE WOODS AND A CLIMB UP A WINDMILL

Evelyn was due in October, so we wasted no time in finding a doctor in Owatonna. When our children were sick, which was often in the harsher climate of Minnesota, we often took them to a medical clin-ic in Wanamingo. Mindy rode the big yellow school bus into West Concord. She looked like Little Red Riding Hood dressed to the nines in her red coat and red fur cap. One day after school she and Evelyn went for a walk through the timber. Evelyn spotted a foxhole and cried to Mindy, "Look, a foxhole!" When there was no reply Evelyn turned and saw Mindy – a blur of red – running as fast as she could back to

★   ★   ★   ★   ★   ★   ★

the big farmhouse. Our entire family enjoyed listening to a profession-al narration of Kenneth Grahame's "The Wind in the Willows" over Minnesota National Public Radio. The children fell in love with Ratty, Mole, Badger, and of course, the vain, obsessive, and self-destructive Toad of Toad Hall. They would march around the house singing "When the Toad Came Home!" Maybe it was the atmospheric condi-tions in the cold Minnesota countryside, but at night I could pull in radio stations from Detroit and even Pittsburgh. I enjoyed listening to Ernie Harwell call the Tigers' games over WJR and Bob Prince doing the play-by-play of the Pirates' games over KDKA.

On September 5 I had the radio on and heard the shocking news that a woman had tried to assassinate President Ford. Lynette "Squeaky" Fromme, a member of the notorious Charles Manson fami-ly, had pulled out a .45-caliber handgun and aimed it at the president. An alert Secret Service agent grabbed the gun before she could pull the trigger. Fromme was sentenced to life in prison. (A bit of irony here: I am writing these lines on August 15, 2009, at my daughter's home in Texas. The front-page story in today's *Dallas Morning News* is: "Fromme freed, but not from past." The would-be assassin was released today from a Fort Worth federal prison after serving 34 years for her misdeed.) Seventeen days later, perhaps emboldened by Fromme's actions, Sara Jane Moore got off a shot at President Ford when he was in Sacramento, California, earning herself a life sentence. She was paroled in 2007. How unlikely is it that two women would try to assassinate a president – harmless Gerald Ford no less – within a two-and-a-half week span? What were women like these thinking, eat-ing, or taking in the 70s?

And what was my three-and-a-half year old son Lincoln think-

★ ★ ★ ★ ★ ★ ★ ★

ing when he attempted to climb our big windmill one crisp fall afternoon? Mindy and Bridget spotted him halfway up the windmill and raced to the house to get Evelyn. I was upstairs at the time, and by the time I made it outside, Evelyn, eight months pregnant, was climbing up the windmill to rescue Lincoln! Even though I have acrophobia (fear of heights), I went up after them both. The windmill was covered with a huge grapevine. Lincoln had started eating his way up the fruit-laden windmill, hanging on with one hand while stuffing his face full of grapes with the other hand. Far below at the base of the windmill was a concrete pad. One slip and he would have fallen to his death. Evelyn was talking to him as calmly as she could; though her heart was racing. "Lincoln, I'm coming up to be with you. Hang on tight until mommy gets there." Lincoln climbed a little higher, in search of bigger grapes. Guardian angels were working overtime that day as Evelyn finally reached Lincoln and I caught up with them both. We descended downward an inch at a time, somehow navigating in reverse as I guided Evelyn's feet down one rung at a time. By this time she had Lincoln on her hip but he was still stuffing grapes in his face all the way down. To this day I shudder when I see grape jelly. The whole family breathed a big sigh of relief when we were back on *terra firma*. Little wonder that our son would in time become a fearless rock climber!

EMILY MAE IS BORN!

After Lincoln was born, I guess it was only natural that I was hoping our next child would be a boy so that he could have a brother to play with. Evelyn's due date was late September. On October 1 Mohammad Ali defeated "Smokin'" Joe Frazier in the much ballyhooed "Thrilla' in Manila." Finally, on October 5, Evelyn gave birth to a baby

★   ★   ★   ★   ★   ★   ★

girl whom we named Emily Mae. The "Mae" was for my mother, Ethel Mae. Evelyn's parents had come up for the birth, and Grandpa Saylor had the honors of carrying baby Emily to the car when we left the hospital. My parents came to see the new baby in mid-November. Dad and Gary Cradic teamed up to preach on a rally at West Concord, attended by some 125 people, our largest attendance up to that time. It was nice having our parents live within a day's driving distance. Now we did not have to make that long trip across the desert to see them each year.

My 30th birthday fell on a Sunday, November 23, 1975. Gary had secretly made an arrangement with both churches that we should switch the preaching hour to the Sunday School hour so that he could take me to Minneapolis to see the Minnesota Vikings play the San Diego Chargers. What a nice birthday present! We had front row seats on the 50-yard line, second deck. The gusty winds and arctic temperature were something else, but we were dressed for the occasion. We shared a thermos of hot chocolate and had warm fellowship as Fran Tarkenton scrambled on the gridiron far below. I noticed that the Vikings had big hot air blowers on their sidelines but the poor Chargers, from southern California, were not afforded any such amenities.

We now had five little mouths to feed. Dana allowed us to tap the big milk vats of his dairy farm anytime we needed milk. One day Mindy came down with strep throat and scarlet fever. Eventually everyone in the family (except Evelyn and Emily) was suffering from both illnesses, myself included. Evelyn was up day and night tending to the sick, caring for a newborn baby, doing her best to keep the house in order. It was a rare Sunday when all of us could go to church together. Most of the time Evelyn would have to stay home with one or more of the children who were sick. She was still pining for her friends in

★   ★   ★   ★   ★   ★   ★

Oregon and was having a difficult time adjusting to life in the cold country. Nordics are known for their independent spirit and think everyone can take care of himself or herself. No inquires were made or perhaps even thought of being made. Then Emily came down with colic and was a very sick baby for three months. One blessing was that Emily never cried. She just gave out sweet little "breathy" sounds. It was nearly a year before she ever said "Mommy." One night there was a terrific thunderstorm and a house-shaking crash of thunder brought her standing upright in her crib. "Mommy!" she cried. Evelyn sprang out of the bed and raced to her and shouting to me, "Mommy! She called me 'Mommy!'" (She had called me "Daddy" long before and I sometimes teased Evelyn about that.)

THE THREE-TREE CHRISTMAS!

Rochester was the nearest big city, and so I would drive there once a week to buy groceries. As Christmas approached, it became apparent that we would not be able to afford a tree. Doctor bills and pharmaceutical bills were eating us alive (we never had health insurance until 1987 when we moved to Carthage, Missouri). One day I simply stuffed all our bills in an envelope, wrote "God" on the envelope, and put it in a desk drawer because I knew there was no way I could possibly pay them. But we continued to give our tithe to God. We did not want to rob God of His tithe and our offering. Somehow we always managed to pay the bills. Many times it was because an unexpected check came in the mail from our parents or our friends back in Oregon.

While I was in Rochester getting groceries, Evelyn told the children, "Let's go outside and see what we can find." They all bundled up

★   ★   ★   ★   ★   ★   ★

and together managed to break off a large branch of an evergreen tree and had it all decorated by the time I returned home. But in the meantime I had found a rather pathetic looking Christmas tree at a Christmas tree lot for only $3. It resembled the sparse tree in "A Charlie Brown Christmas." So now we had two trees in the living room. Then, after Christmas, I found an artificial tree that was on sale. So we set that one up as well. The year 1975 became the year that we had *three* Christmas trees when we thought we would have none at all.

TROUBLESOME THOUGHTS AT THIRTY

Those who are familiar with the life of Christ and are concerned about their own life generally have some serious thoughts when they turn 30. I certainly did. Jesus began His public ministry at the age of 30. He had only about three-and-a-half years to fulfill His ministry. I had gone through four years of training for the ministry and was now entering my eighth year of ministry. Nearly 12 years and exactly what did I have to show for it? What had I accomplished for the glory of God? Not very much – not nearly enough! My self-analysis and ruthless introspection troubled me. Our little congregation was just that – little. A few people had joined our fellowship, but only a few. One family was from Church of Christ (a cappella) background.

In those days I exchanged my *Vanguard* paper with a number of journals edited by men from the Churches of Christ. Many of them were filled with bitter invective and projected nothing of the spirit of Christ (*Mission Messenger* was a happy exception). While the church at West Concord was at peace, there were others in our close-knit fellowship who were not "keeping the unity of the Spirit in the bond of

★   ★   ★   ★   ★   ★   ★

peace." All of this would lead me to make several big decisions in 1976. In many ways 1976 was a watershed year for me.

CELEBRATING INDEPENDENCE/PRACTICING INTERDEPENDENCE

America celebrated her 200th birthday in 1976. To do his part in the nationwide celebration my father produced his first book of poems: *76 Selections for '76 (The Bicentennial of My Country)*. It included a 10-stanza poem, "Hymn for America's Tribulation." The United States Supreme Court made two controversial rulings that year. On March 29 the court ruled that states may prosecute people for homosexual acts and on July 2, two days before Independence Day, they ruled that the death penalty was not "cruel and unusual punishment." Crime and punishment was very much a part of the bicentennial year. Sara Jane Moore was sentenced to life in prison for her attempted assassination of President Ford. Newspaper heiress Patty Hearst was sentenced to seven years in prison for her participation in the robbery of a bank in San Francisco, but was freed the same year on a $1.5 million dollar bond. Caril Ann Fugate, the teen-age accomplice of Charles Stark-weather during the 1958 killing rampage, was finally released from prison. In July the first victim of the "Son of Sam" killings was gunned down in New York.

But all of this was far away from our humble church in Minnesota. I started the new year by teaching three classes in our fledgling Bible institute: United Kingdom History, Galatians, and Church History. The spring semester found me teaching James, New Testament Translations, and Church History II. Gary Cradic started a 5th Sunday Rally that alternated between West Concord and Owatonna. Just like our experience in Nebraska with Lexington and

★   ★   ★   ★   ★   ★   ★

Cozad, the fellowship and interaction were wonderful. We were show-ing that we were "interdependent" rather than "independent" church-es. In addition to editing *Vanguard* (which was now printed nine times a year) I took on the task of writing a 30-year history of the *Voice of Evangelism* which was published in serial format in that publication. All the while I was finishing up writing my first full-length book, *The One Cup Faith*, which I had started when we were in Oregon. I asked Donald G. Hunt to review the manuscript, and he wrote the following in the March *Vanguard*.

> The author has spent three years and much research in compil-ing this material. The research is reflected not only in the con-tent and quality of the material, but also in the over 200 refer-ence footnotes in the book. His love for writing makes it a free-flowing, easy-to-read work. It was my privilege to have him in my classes, and the present work causes me to recall his special love for Church History.

I had hopes of seeing it published by College Press of Joplin, Missouri. I received a kind letter from Don DeWelt saying that while he person-ally liked the book, he was sorry that College Press could not print it at the time. Undaunted, I started raising the $4,000.00 it would take to see the book published. Many readers of *Vanguard* generously contributed to the cause.

A DEBATE, A DEATH, AND A WEDDING

On March 10 Evelyn celebrated her 30th birthday. Her parents drove up from Iowa, and we had a wonderful time with them. One night Bob and I played a terrific game of Scrabble. I don't remember

★　　★　　★　　★　　★　　★　　★

who won (probably him) but we loved the competition. Any time they would visit us, they would attend church with us on Wednesday night. And I would always forgo the use of instrumental music because of Ethel's conscience in the matter. The morning they were to return to Iowa, Bob came downstairs and found Evelyn sitting in the living room with baby Emily. No one else was up and the house was quiet. Evelyn felt an urge to say to her dad, "Daddy, I just want you to know how much I love you and Mommy." He was touched and replied, "Well, honey, we love you too." Evelyn had no idea that it would be the last time that she would ever see him alive.

I attended my first religious debate on March 16 at Mason City, Iowa. It was a lively but cordial five-night discussion between Dwaine Dunning of Dakota Bible College and Rubel Shelly of Freed-Hardeman College. The topic was the use (or non-use) of instrumental music in the worship services of the church. I was impressed how both men conducted themselves in a Christian manner and even embraced one another at the conclusion of the evening's activities. I never dreamed that some day I would publish both men in a national magazine that I would edit, nor that I would speak alongside both men in national unity meetings.

I invited Jerry Weller from my *alma mater* to come to Minnesota and address our students for three days, which he was glad to do on March 19-21. During those days Jerry also reviewed many of my class notes (from Eugene and West Concord), my published articles and my yet-to-be published book. He determined that the hundreds of hours of study I had put into preparing these lessons, class notes, and published articles were more than enough to allow Midwestern to bestow their new fifth-year degree upon me.

On March 31 we received a phone call from Evelyn's oldest

★   ★   ★   ★   ★   ★   ★

brother Paul. He told her that her father was sick and had been admitted to the Ottumwa Hospital. We had no idea how sick he really was. The next day, April 1, Bob Saylor died of Coomb's disease, a rare blood disorder. We were shocked that he had gone so quickly. The night before we left for Iowa, Evelyn put the children to bed and then went out on the big side porch. Outside the moon cast its ghostly light on the bare trees and snow-covered ground. She thought, "It's so much the same and yet it's so different now." Early the next morning we drove to Ottumwa to attend the funeral of Robert K. Saylor. He was only 61 years of age and was the first of our parents to leave us. I later wrote a tribute to him that I published in *Vanguard*, including these words, in part.

> Bob's sudden passing was a blow to all who knew and loved
> him. Like Barnabas, he was "a good man, full of the Holy Spirit
> and of faith." And, as with Stephen, "devout men carried him to
> his burial and made great lamentation over him." His life was
> rich and full; his experiences many and varied, his friends and
> acquaintances innumerable. We shall miss him greatly.

We stayed for a few days to comfort Ethel and help wherever we could. I was asked to speak at the Ransom Street Church of Christ and at the chapel services of Midwestern. We returned the next month for the graduation of my brother David from Midwestern. It was a unique night in that he received his four-year Bachelor of Sacred Literature degree, and I was the recipient of the five-year Bachelor of Theology degree. My graduation sermon was "I Believe" and David's was "I Appreciate." We both appreciated our parents who were there for the graduation on May 18 and had our picture taken with them: two proud parents and two grateful sons.

Ten days later, May 28, we found ourselves in Hamburg for the

★   ★   ★   ★   ★   ★   ★

wedding of my brother David to Pamela Henshaw, who was also a student at Midwestern. All my family was back for the wedding, and it was great to see everyone again. Had it really been nine years since we were gathered in the same church for our wedding? Dad performed the ceremony and I served as my brother's best man. One of David's groomsmen did not show up on time, and so once I walked the maid of honor down the aisle, I exited stage right, raced down the hall alongside the auditorium, then calmly walked another bridesmaid down the aisle, much to everyone's amusement. It was also our Amanda's second birthday, and we were so busy with the wedding that Evelyn didn't have time to bake her a cake. So we just stuck two candles in a piece of wedding cake and celebrated anyway!

LIFE IN THE PARSONAGE

One night Lincoln wanted me to sleep with him in the smallest of the upstairs bedrooms. I had just about drifted off when I heard him say, "Dad, it's stuck. I can't get it out."

"What do you mean?" I said. "What is stuck?"

"My finger," he replied. "It's stuck in my hair and I can't get it out."

I switched on the light and started to laugh for there was Lincoln with his right index finger so firmly wrapped in his hair he could not get it out. It was actually beginning to turn purple, because the blood supply had been restricted. He had been twirling his hair in the dark as we had chatted about this and that. It took both Evelyn and me several minutes to carefully cut the hair away from his finger with a pair of scissors. He grinned sheepishly and we all went back to sleep.

That summer we were informed that the Campbells had other

★   ★   ★   ★   ★   ★   ★

plans for the farmhouse, so we moved in town into the little parsonage next to the church building. And I do mean little. We had to store much of our belongings in the garage for the house had three small bedrooms, a small bathroom, and a small kitchen. The only redeeming factor was a large living area. We used one end for a dining area and the other end for a living room. The Mastercraft couch and easy chair separated the two areas. When my folks came to visit, Lincoln entertained them by running pell-mell from the end of the dining area, hitting the couch like a gymnast would the somersault, vaulting himself into the air and making a perfect landing on his feet in the living room. My mother would laugh, clap her hands, and call for a repeat performance.

At that time Gary Cradic was doing some remodeling in his home so we bought two of his glass wall bookcases for my books. I moved my study into a small office at the church, stage right. The parsonage had been used for Bible classrooms for some time, so we had to make sure the house was tidy for Sunday School after getting the children ready for church.

One of the young married men, Ross Clark, often stopped by to give the children a ride around the church grounds on his motorcycle. All of them except Amanda loved to make the circuit, crying, "Faster, faster!" Amanda would say, "Slower, slower! I'm fraidy scared!"

REVIVAL AND EVANGELISM

I was called back for return revival meetings at Galax, Virginia (June 13-20) and New Home, North Carolina (June 20-26). I closed the Virginia revival in the morning and the same night opened the North Carolina meeting: 14 straight nights of preaching it straight. I had left Evelyn and the children with her mother in Iowa. While I was gone,

★   ★   ★   ★   ★   ★   ★

Lincoln and Amanda found a box of Rolaids and, thinking they were candy, devoured several rolls of the antacid. Evelyn called the emergency room at Ottumwa Hospital, and the doctor on call recommended that the children's stomachs be pumped because there was just too much antacid in their system for their own good. En route to the hospital Evelyn tried to prepare Lincoln and Amanda for the painful procedure that was about to happen to them. Lincoln quickly responded, "Let's go see Daddy!"

The church in West Concord was trying to reach out to their community and beyond. July 14-18 the church had an exhibit at the Dodge County Fair. We offered Christian literature and Bible correspondence courses. I manned the exhibit for much of the week and had many interesting conversations with those who stopped by to ask questions about the Bible or religion. I had taught in young people's summer camps before, but I had never managed one until we moved to Minnesota. Dana Campbell asked me to manage Milliken Creek Camp July 26-30, and I was happy to do so. I asked my father to bring the evening messages and God blessed with nine decisions for Christ that week. Of course my mother came too so she could spend some time with her grandchildren! Sometime during the week of camp Lincoln became very ill and we had to rush him to the hospital. We thought it might be appendicitis. But it turned out to be just a giant tummy ache. Lincoln had eaten one too many green apples at camp! I also managed the family camp August 10-13. I remembered how impressed I had been with Gary Werner, a student at Midwestern when I was contemplating college, and so I asked him to speak at both the morning and evening services. In addition to all this, the church had a VBS and Joy Club where many children were introduced to

★   ★   ★   ★   ★   ★   ★

Christ, some for the first time.

When I was in Galax, I finished my work on a small booklet I had been writing: *The Christian and Divorce*. I asked my friend L. H. Tyree, a minister in Colorado Springs (and retired lieutenant colonel in the U.S. Army) to vet the booklet before it went to press. He wrote,

> I believe you have covered the subject very thoroughly. I cannot see at the present where one could take exception to the manner that you chose to present the material nor where you have been very emphatic in those scriptural verses covering the subject. I hope your material enjoys a wide degree of distribution among the brethren as I believe it is needful.

James E. Gibbons, editor of *The Sword & Staff*, published one of my articles in tract form in the summer of 1976: "The Last Broadcast." It was billed as a "fast-moving" and "exciting" account of the return of Christ as covered by anchorman Wilbur Thotrite (a guise for Walter Cronkite) and other thinly-veiled news correspondents. One day I got a phone call from Alvin Jennings, publisher of Star Publications in Ft. Worth, Texas. Star was an a cappella Church of Christ publishing house. Brother Jennings asked for my permission to print "The Last Broadcast" in their famous "flip-top" tract series. I gladly said yes but let him know that I was from the Churches of Christ fellowship that used instrumental music. "I know that," he replied. "But souls are at stake here. We want to print this because it is a great evangelistic tool." It was my good fortune to meet Alvin Jennings at a large gathering in Tulsa, Oklahoma, many years later. I was somewhat surprised to see that I was taller than he was. I guess I figured that being from Texas, he would be a "long, tall Texan."

★   ★   ★   ★   ★   ★   ★

MY FIRST BOOK

In August my first full-length book, *The One Cup Faith*, rolled off the presses in Iowa City. My brother-in-law Gary McGlumphry had done the typesetting and cover design. By this time I had formed my own book publishing company, Vanguard Books. The softbound book contained 200 pages, 13 chapters, and 209 footnotes. It sold for $5.95 and everyone who had contributed to help get it printed received a complimentary copy. I was pleased as punch when Edward Fudge, a highly respected scholar from the Churches of Christ (a cappella) wrote the Foreword. In part he wrote,

> Victor Knowles has done his homework in this book. It is no "mosquito" to be simply "shooed away" by those who insist on one container in the Lord's Supper. It deals with solid facts of history and with clear arguments from Scripture. It is the kind of careful study which can help break down the barriers among brethren on all subjects – when accompanied by an open mind to the Word of God and an open heart toward brethren with whom one has differences of understanding.

Many people who read the book would say that the chapter on "Inconsistencies" was worth the price of the book. The fact that Edward Fudge saw it as something that could "help break down barriers among brethren on all subjects" meant a lot to me. The divisions I had studied about in college and had seen firsthand in my relatively young life had discouraged and disheartened me. Today I believe that Fudge's Foreword did more for me than perhaps the book did for readers. It set me on a path that I would follow for the rest of my life – doing what I could to "break down barriers among brethren" and also "build bridges between brethren." Every time I see Edward Fudge

*   *   *   *   *   *   *

today, usually at the Pepperdine University Bible Lectures, I thank God that he put his own reputation on the line to write a Foreword for an untried and unknown young man like me.

TAKING ON DIVISION

In September I wrote a front-page article for *Vanguard* that made a few waves, at least as far and wide as my paper was being read in 1976. Don DeWelt, down in Joplin, Missouri, was one of my readers, and he certainly took note of it. I took the Restoration Movement to task for not only dividing, but being content to just live with division. The article was titled "DI-VI-SION: The 'Acceptable' Sin." I offered three remedies for division. (1) Declare a moratorium on division. (2) Avoid divisive people. (3) Make love supreme. I closed with these words: "Let's quit accepting division! God doesn't approve of it and neither should we. Jesus prayed, 'That they all may be one.' Let's make that our prayer, our project, and our priority." Most of the response to this article was positive, but I did receive a few negative letters too. One in particular cut me to the quick, but I remembered my father's ordination sermon, "The Price of Telling the Truth." If this is the price I would pay for taking a stand against division and for unity, so be it.

THE SERMON THAT CHANGED MY LIFE

On October 8 I received a phone call from Fred Miller, administrator of the Dorr Drive School of the Ministry in Rutland, Vermont.

"Where are you?" he asked, almost in a demanding tone.

"I'm right here in Minnesota."

"Well, you're supposed to be here in New Hampshire, preaching tonight!" Fred thundered.

★   ★   ★   ★   ★   ★   ★

"What?" I exclaimed. "What do you mean?"

About a year earlier Brother Miller had asked me to speak on a rally program, and I had told him I would be happy to. I had not heard from him since. I had no idea of the dates, place, or preaching assignment. So I told him these facts. I could tell he was frustrated but I felt that I had nothing to apologize for. The phone went dead and I figured that was that.

But an hour later the phone rang again. It was Fred.

"Do you still want to preach out here?"

I replied, "Of course. I always did. But I never heard back from you."

You've got to know Fred Miller to appreciate this story. "O.K., I've booked a flight for you from Minneapolis to Boston. Can you get there in time to make the flight?" I looked at the clock. Maybe if I really rushed I could. We lived about an hour from Minneapolis. So, just as rashly, I told him I would come.

Evelyn threw some clothes in a suitcase; I grabbed a handful of sermons, kissed Evelyn and the kids and was off to the airport within the hour. I couldn't believe I was making this crazy trip. But God knew what He was doing. He knew what was in store for me long before I arrived in Boston later than night. Fred met me at Logan Airport, looking rather sheepish I thought, but I said nothing to him that would make him feel bad. We drove about 115 miles through the night until we reached a retreat center in Groton, New Hampshire. I fell into bed in the wee hours of the morning, exhausted by the whirlwind trip.

Groton, New Hampshire, I was to discover much later (for I had no time to explore the premises) was incorporated in 1796. Henry David Thoreau once visited Groton, perhaps because of the good fish-

★   ★   ★   ★   ★   ★   ★

ing in Newfound Lake or the natural marvels of Sculptured Rock. It was also the home of Mary Baker Eddy, founder of the Christian Science Church. But I was not in Groton to explore or sightsee. I was there to preach. I reached into my briefcase and began to look over what I had quickly pulled from the files before I left for the airport. I settled on one that I would preach that night, October 9. I am looking at it even now as I write these words. On the back of the last page of the notes I notice that I had preached it in 1972 in Lexington, Nebraska, and again in 1974 in Eugene, Oregon. So it was not a new sermon by any stretch of the imagination. There were three pages of paper, written on front and back for a total of six pages of notes. The text was from Ecclesiastes 3:3, "A Time to Break Down, and a Time to Build Up."

I may have preached earlier in the day. I know I also preached on Sunday morning. But it was the Saturday night sermon, October 9, 1976 that I shall always remember. As I look at it now, I am struck that I actually quoted Henry David Thoreau! "You cannot kill time without injuring eternity." I had not the faintest clue that he had once visited Groton! I noted that "time" is mentioned 29 times in the full text of Ecclesiastes. Then I launched into my first point: A time to break down the walls of partition that separate brethren. It is true, I said, that Christ has already broken down the "middle wall of partition" that separated Jew and Gentile" (Ephesians 2:13, 14). No longer should there be divisions between anyone, for Christ has made us one (Galatians 3:26-28). If memory serves me correctly, it is then that I departed from my script. I became so convicted by the power of these passages that I said: "I here and now dedicate the rest of my life to breaking down these walls between brethren!"

In the back of the room Fred was sitting with his head down,

*   *   *   *   *   *   *

following along in his Bible. But when I said those words I remember how he lifted his head and lifted his voice as well: "God help him!" I doubt that anyone else in the congregation took note of what had just happened. But I did. Fred Miller did. Most important of all, God did. A young preacher had just "come down the aisle" while still standing in the pulpit. The Word of God had just mightily convicted the one who was preaching from it. The Bible is like a sword without a handle. It cuts both the hearer and the speaker. It was indeed an epiphany, a sacred moment, a special moment I'll always treasure.

I went back to my manuscript and mentioned four modern "walls of partition" that need to be broken down. One was the "race issue" partition, another the "strong brother vs. weak brother" partition, another the "clergy-laity" partition, and finally the "rich-poor" economic partition. I closed by citing three things that need to be built up. First, the broken altars of prayer and faithfulness; second, the body of Christ itself; third, the walls of reproach. Here again I touched on the sin of our divisions that ultimately stem from pride. I did not fully realize it then, October 9, 1976, but that night in Groton, New Hampshire, was the starting of a long road that I have traveled to this very day. Some day I hope to return to Groton, New Hampshire, where I can see the sights. Just give me a little more time to pack my suitcase, please!

OUR FAMILY IS PROVIDENTIALLY SAVED

One thing about living in the cold country – I had many days to write when we were all but snowbound. When we still lived in the country, I had a single bed in my study on the ground floor. That was so that when I wrote late into the night (or the early hours of the morning), I could just fall into bed and go to sleep without going upstairs and

★   ★   ★   ★   ★   ★   ★

waking anyone. One night it proved providential that I had a bed in my study. It was a literal "dark and stormy night" of which I speak. Lightning struck an electric pole outside the house and blew out the fuse box in the basement, starting a fire. I awoke at the crash of thunder and just happened to see through a small crack in the floor the flicker of light in the basement. I knew something was amiss because there were no lights or power in the house. I went down the steps to the basement and saw that water was already up to the first step. The fuse box and the wood trim around it were ablaze. Sparks were flying everywhere. Electrical wires were exposed and I knew that I should not step into the water lest I be electrocuted. You will never guess how I put that fire out. I prayed for strength and then, from the second step, I literally *blew* that fire out. God must have seen that sweet wife and those five babies slumbering peacefully above and given me the lungs of Samson to do what I did. The next morning Dana Campbell came to inspect the damage. He looked at the scorched wall and asked how I had put out the fire. When I told him, he just took off that crazy Aussie hat of his and shook his head in amazement. I had no rational answer either.

In December it was a joy to have Donald G. Hunt come to our church and bring several messages. I never had anything but respect for the life and ministry of the cofounder of my *alma mater*. We had a wonderful time of fellowship, and I believe it was also at this time that he examined my many writings and determined that I would now be given a sixth-year degree from Midwestern, the Master of Sacred Literature degree. The busy year came to an end with our family celebrating Christmas in the cold country with just one tree! That winter we had so much snow that the drifts went clear up to the roof of the parsonage. The children could actually walk up the huge drift right onto the roof.

★　★　★　★　★　★　★

A NEW YEAR AND A NEW LIFE

Jimmy Carter was sworn in as our nation's 39th president on January 20, 1977. The peanut farmer from Georgia had somehow managed to defeat the incumbent president, Gerald R. Ford. He was the first Democrat since LBJ to hold office. Since he was a Southern Baptist I expected good things from him, but I soon became disillusioned with his liberal agenda. It was not long into the new year before I received one or two phone calls from the Church of Christ in Oskaloosa, Iowa. They wanted to know if I was interested in moving there to lead the congregation. At the time I was not interested because things seemed like they were starting to gel for us in Minnesota. But a seed had been planted, and seeds eventually start to grow. Something had also started to grow in Evelyn. Back in October the doctor had informed Evelyn that we could expect a new addition to our family around Mother's Day. That certainly seemed like an appropriate day to have a baby!

MEETING W. CARL KETCHERSIDE

Minnesota Bible College was in nearby Rochester. My father had studied for nearly three years at MBC (when it was located in Minneapolis), and so I naturally wanted to visit the campus. Each year the college sponsored a Mid-Winter Conference so when I heard that W. Carl Ketcherside, editor of *Mission Messenger*, would be the keynote speaker February 2-4, there was no question in my mind but that I would go and hear the man speak. The conference opened on February 2, a Wednesday night, and I knew that I could not attend that evening because of my teaching duties at the church. But on either Thursday night or Friday night (February 3 or 4), probably Friday, we went to

★　★　★　★　★　★　★

hear Ketcherside speak. Evelyn wanted to go with me because she had heard so much about Brother Ketcherside from people in the church in which she had grown up. (To the best of our knowledge this was the only time we had a night out together in the two years we were in Minnesota.) We arrived at the place of meeting, the Zumbro Lutheran Church rented by the college for their conference, on the corner of 3rd Avenue and 6th Street S. W. The theme of the conference was "Fellowship and Unity in Christ." I remember nothing at all about his sermon, but I thought his voice was similar to that of Norman Vincent Peale, whom I had heard speak on the radio.

When Brother Ketcherside had finished his sermon and the closing song and benediction were over, we respectfully waited for some time to shake his hand. After everyone had opportunity to visit with him, I introduced ourselves as Victor and Evelyn Knowles. He immediately connected the dots because by this time I was exchanging my *Vanguard* for his *Mission Messenger* as fellow editors were wont to do in those days. He first turned his attention to Evelyn, for indeed he had once visited her congregation, the Finley and Adella Church of Christ in Ottumwa when Evelyn was about a 7th grader. He had come unannounced and had proved by his cordial visit that he was not the "troublemaker" that some thought him to be. Evelyn's father had told her after the services that morning that their visitor was none other than the much discussed W. Carl Ketcherside. He asked Evelyn about her family and about our own family. I thought that was very gentle-manly of him to do so.

Then Brother Ketcherside turned to me and began to commend me for my work that he had been following. Here I had come to thank him for the great influence he had on my life, and all he wanted to do

★　★　★　★　★　★　★

was talk about me. His interest was genuine and his commendation was sincere. I had all kinds of things I wanted to say to him, but that night all he wanted to talk about was us – not himself. I have thought about that meeting so many times since. A great man doesn't want to talk about himself; indeed, he does not need to talk about himself. He wants to help others, to encourage others, and to build other people's esteem. "Let nothing be done through strife or vainglory; but in lowliness of mind let each esteem other better than themselves" (Philippians 2:3, KJV). He made us feel like the King and Queen of Minnesota, even if we were not Norwegian! That was the one and only time I ever had a personal conversation with the great W. Carl Ketcherside, but it left a lasting impression on me. Yes, even tonight as I write these words on this cold February night, February 2, 2010, exactly 33 years to the night that the Mid-Winter Conference at Minnesota Bible College began!

OUR BIBLE INSTITUTE

Later that month, February 27 – March 6, I invited Fred Miller, *quid pro quo*, to come to Minnesota from Vermont and conduct a series of lectures on the Book of Revelation. (Yes, we took care of his travel arrangements far in advance!) Brother Miller was fluent in both Hebrew and Greek and presented his Revelation lectures in a most positive and exciting manner. Some years later he produced a 404-page commentary, *Revelation: A Panorama of the Gospel Age*.

I continued preparing and delivering my own lessons on Hermeneutics and the Epistles of John in our nightly Bible institute. Art Deys, the friendly minister of the Fridley church in Minneapolis, asked me to come and teach Church History on Sunday nights in the months of March and April. So we had a "pulpit exchange" as it were. He preached

★　★　★　★　★　★　★

in West Concord on Sunday nights while I was teaching an extension course, using B. K. Kuiper's *The Church in History* in Minneapolis. It was a unique, profitable and edifying experience for all. I have always enjoyed the robust repartee between students and teacher. If I didn't have the answer to a question, I would try to have it for them in the next session. Speaking of questions and answers, I ran a year-long question and answer series in *Vanguard* called "Vanguard Bible Study." Each month I asked "Twenty Questions" on key topics like: "The Word of God," "Sin and Salvation," "The Grace of God," "Faith and Works," "Turning from Sin," "Buried in Baptism," and "The New Testament Church."

THE "BROTHERHOOD" ARTICLES

The months of March and April are also important to this story because I followed up on my previous and provocative "Division" article in *Vanguard* with a two-part article on *Brotherhood*. As I review them today I can imagine that I was inspired by Carl Ketcherside's sermon in Minneapolis (I must have taken notes), but I did not quote him *per se* in the article. Rather, I quoted Donald G. Hunt. In Part I, I wrote,

> True brotherhood is neither trying to see how large the boundaries of brotherhood can be expanded or how small the lines of fellowship can be drawn. Brotherhood is receiving each other in spite of our differences of opinion. Brotherhood is not a sectarian exercise of tabulating the totals of the "faithful." Since we are only a *part* of God's massive adoption agency, let us not be so presumptuous as to become a god knowing exactly who is and who isn't our brother. How could any mortal, belonging to such a huge adopted family that "no man can number," know exactly who all the faithful brethren are?

★ ★ ★ ★ ★ ★ ★

Part II closed with these words.

I must love *the* brotherhood, not "our" brotherhood. The term
"brotherhood" is just as singular as the term "church" in Matthew 16:18. The brotherhood is not ours – it is God's! Brotherhood could not exist without Fatherhood. God is the Father of
His immense adoption agency and spiritual birth clinic. He
keeps the books. The brotherhood is His baby, so to speak . . .
Isn't it about time we started treating those in the brotherhood
as *brothers* instead of *hoods*?

The article received a wider circulation when Eddie DeVries published
my "Brotherhood" series in his Nationwide Youth Roundup newspaper.

PORTIA BABETTE IS BORN!

In May I was invited by Eddie DeVries to come to Colorado to
conduct a revival meeting for The Church at 59th and Vance, something I was most willing to do. It was so good to once again work with
this veteran evangelist and successful soul winner. Seven people made
decisions for Christ during the week of preaching. Later that month I was
awarded the Master of Sacred Literature degree by Midwestern School
of Evangelism, although this time I did not attend the actual ceremony, probably because Evelyn's due date was drawing nigh. Mother's
Day came and went. No baby and not even a sign that the baby was
close to coming. The days stretched on. Finally, on June 7, four full
weeks *after* her due date, Evelyn gave birth to little Portia Babette
Knowles in the Owatonna Hospital. You know that Lincoln and I were
rooting for a baby boy. This would be our last chance to get Lincoln a
little brother. I think that both of us shed a tear – not that we weren't
glad to welcome Portia into the family – we just wanted a little guy.

★   ★   ★   ★   ★   ★   ★

Evelyn's mother had produced five daughters and my mother had given birth to three daughters, so I guess the "girl gene" ruled in both our families and that's the way it would be. On the way home from the hospital I stopped and bought Lincoln a new football. We played a game of tackle football on the front lawn and the tussle was good for both of us. Then, a day or so later, we all welcomed Portia into the family as we brought her and Evelyn home from the hospital in our 1972 Oldsmobile Custom Cruiser station wagon that we were now driving.

GOOD TIMES IN MINNEAPOLIS

Living close to Minneapolis provided me with the opportunity to attend a variety of events. One was a 32-hour Basic Youth Conflicts seminar conducted by Bill Gothard, founder of the Institute in Basic Life Principles. Gothard taught seven biblical, non-optional principles of life. The event was held in the Met Center where the Minnesota North Stars played in the National Hockey League. Of course I still loved baseball, so I made several trips to Metropolitan Stadium to see the Minnesota Twins play. On one occasion Gary Cradic and I had box seats down the first base line for a game between the Twins and the Yankees. Reggie Jackson, normally a right fielder, was playing first base for the Yanks that night. All night long Gary surreptitiously flipped chocolate malt balls Jackson's way at first. Jackson kept looking over into the box seats to spot the culprit, but Gary could keep a straight face no matter what. I kept whispering, "Cradic, you're going to get us tossed out of the game!" By the end of the game the ground around first base was littered with dozens of malt balls, courtesy of my good friend. I'm sure Bill Gothard would not have approved.

★   ★   ★   ★   ★   ★   ★

CALLED TO IOWA

The church in Iowa would not take "no" for an answer. And so, just when Evelyn felt that she was getting to know the Norwegians in Minnesota a little better, I said "yes" to the plucky and persistent congregation in Iowa. About two months after Portia was born, we left "the land of 10,000 lakes" for the fertile farmland "where the tall corn grows." What had started out as a very difficult ministry for me personally had turned into something beneficial. I had learned to work through my times of discouragement. I had used the time of solitude in "the long winter" to think, ponder, study and write. I had experienced some watershed moments: my own convicting sermon in New Hampshire, meeting Carl Ketcherside in Minneapolis, and dealing with some vital issues through *Vanguard*. Lincoln and Evelyn (and yet-to-be born Emily) were spared death high atop the windmill. Our whole family had been providentially saved the night I slept downstairs when the lightning struck. Now we would be returning to Iowa where we would have our most fruitful located ministry. The cold country had prepared us for a season of planting and bountiful harvest.

★   ★   ★   ★   ★   ★   ★

EPILOGUE

"The unexamined life is not worth living." — Socrates

Evelyn tells me that the sign of a good book is when the reader gets to the end and says, "Oh, I wish it would continue!" I don't know how good this book has been to the reader, but at least I can tell you that this story is going to continue!

When I set out to write my life story, I had no idea of how long the book would be. Then, when the actual writing began, I could see that it was going to have to be told in two takes. As it turned out, this first volume covers the first 33 years of my life (1945-1977). If all goes well – and I pray that it will – the second volume will span the next 33 years of my life (1978-2011). God willing, I will be 66 when the autobiography is finally finished.

As I stated in my Preface, I have chosen to write about my life just as I remember it happening. I could have left a lot out; indeed, much was left out. But I also wanted to tell it like it actually happened. I have tried to write with the feelings and emotions that I was experiencing at the time I lived those events. I believe that those who revise or deconstruct history are doing a terrible thing. I have tried to tell my story as honestly and accurately as I possibly could.

When I was a boy, I can remember reading stories in *The Saturday Evening Post* that would end, "To Be Continued." I was disappoint-

★   ★   ★   ★   ★   ★   ★

ed that I would have to wait another week before picking up the story again. But at the same time it heightened my anticipation for the arrival of the next week's *Post*. Here follows a "preview of coming attractions" (to borrow from another media term).

This book ends with our leaving Minnesota in the fall of 1977. Our family was complete by this time: six wonderful children. From there we migrated south to Oskaloosa, Iowa, where we started a ministry with the Osklaloosa Church of Christ that would last almost seven years. It was our longest and finest ministry. The congregation grew from an attendance of only 35 on our first Sunday to an attendance of 233 when we finished a building program and moved into a brand new auditorium. The Lord blessed us with 140 additions and giving increased by 53 percent. It was in Oskaloosa that I would begin to apply the unity principles that I had been learning. I started writing for *Christian Standard* in 1980, *The Lookout* in 1982, and was named president of the Iowa Christian Convention in 1983. Don DeWelt asked me to become the editor of a new paper he was starting, *One Body*, in 1984.

That same year would see us move to Portland, Oregon, at the invitation of Northwest College of the Bible. There I would work as the Director of Development for NCB. In reality I functioned as a fund-raising president, academic dean, recruiter, and part-time faculty member. It was one busy year. While we were in Oregon, I was invited by Don DeWelt to attend the first Restoration Forum in Joplin, Missouri. Little did I know that we would move to the Joplin area in 1987.

When my mother died on Good Friday of 1985, I felt a need to move back to Iowa to be closer to my father. As a matter of fact, dad became my "Assistant Minister" with the Hamburg Church of Christ, just as I had been Eddie DeVries' assistant in my first ministry there.

★   ★   ★   ★   ★   ★   ★

I worked very hard to build the church back up to where it had been in former years, continued my work with *One Body* and the Restoration Forum, and wrote three books for College Press.

I hated to leave my hometown, but when Don DeWelt urged me to move closer to Joplin, we accepted a call from the Fairview Christian Church in Carthage and served there from 1987-1992. This would be my last located ministry. We would triple our midweek attendance when we went to small groups, saw a high attendance of 447, and remodeled the auditorium. All six of our children would graduate from Carthage High School. I began my overseas travels in 1988 and my kingdom heart would no longer be content serving in just the local church. I would resign in 1992 and start One Body Ministries (now Peace on Earth Ministries).

The remainder of Volume 2 of *Victor: Since 1945* will cover my work with POEM from 1992 to the present time, my increasing involvement in unity efforts (the Restoration Forum being one example), my writing and editing ministry, teaching and preaching trips abroad, preaching in hundreds of churches, appearing at national and international conventions and conferences, serving on a number of parachurch boards, my association with many interesting leaders, and my father's passing in 2009. The final chapter will be "If I Had Life to Live Over Again."

I hope you will "stay tuned" for Volume 2.

★   ★   ★   ★   ★   ★   ★

TIMELINE

1945 — Born 11/23, Seymour, Indiana
1946 — Family moves to Polo, Illinois
1947 — Family moves to Clay Center, Nebraska
1949 — Family moves to Whiting, Iowa
1950 — First day of school
1951 — Family moves to Hamburg, Iowa
Hears Archie Word preach in Inglewood, California
1952 — Big flood hits Hamburg
1954 — Family moves to Boise, Idaho
Meets Donald G. Hunt
1955 — Plays first baseball game for United Airlines
1956 — First call of God, Cottage Grove, Oregon
Family moves to Rock Port, Missouri
Sees Budapest Uprising on TV
1957 — Family moves to Goldfield, Iowa
Second call of God, Diagonal, Iowa
1958 — Third call of God, Eldora, Iowa
Converted at Pine Lake Bible Camp, Eldora, Iowa
Has Russell Boatman as camp teacher
Sees first major league game, Cincinnati, Ohio
1961 — Hits first home run for Goldfield Indians
1962 — Family moves to Mulberry Grove, Illinois
Plays for Mulberry Grove Aces
1963 — Church divides in Mulberry Grove
JFK assassinated
1964 — Graduates from MGHS
Spends summer with Grandparents, Richmond, Indiana
Plays last baseball game for Richmond Lions Club
Desires to attend Cincinnati Bible Seminary
Enrolls at Midwestern School of Evangelism,
    Ottumwa, Iowa
Preaches first sermon, Council Bluffs, Iowa

★   ★   ★   ★   ★   ★   ★

1965 — ├─ Makes decision to preach
               Becomes engaged to Susan Hand; later breaks
                 engagement
               Meets Marion McKee
1966 — ├─ Turning Point: Fatal crash takes two students' lives
1967 — ├─ Begins student ministry at Promise City, Iowa
               Marries Evelyn Saylor 8/7, at Hamburg, Iowa
               First article published in *Voice of Evangelism*
1968 — ├─ Graduates from Midwestern with BSL
               Ordained at Hamburg, Iowa
               Becomes Assistant Minister, Hamburg, Iowa
               Conducts first revival, Galax, Virginia
1969 — ├─ Mindy Annette born 7/7
               Begins first full-time ministry, Lexington, Nebraska
1971 — ├─ Bridget Olivia born 3/1
1972 — ├─ Begins ministry with Norvale Park Church,
                 Eugene, Oregon
               Lincoln Vail born 12/22
1973 — ├─ Begins editing *Vanguard*
1974 — ├─ Amanda Jane born 5/28
               Published in *Restoration Herald*
1975 — ├─ Begins ministry at West Concord, Minnesota
               Emily Mae born 10/5, in Owatonna
               Begins correspondence with Don DeWelt
1976 — ├─ Publishes first full-length book
               Portia Babette born 6/7, in Owatonna
               Receives BTH from Midwestern
               Preaches watershed sermon in Groton, New Hampshire
               Meets W. Carl Ketcherside in Minneapolis
1977 — ├─ Denounces division, promotes unity in *Vanguard*
               Receives MSL from Midwestern
               Begins ministry at Oskaloosa, Iowa

★   ★   ★   ★   ★   ★   ★

The art of biography

Is different from geography.

Geography is about maps,

But biography is about chaps.

— Edmund Bentley

★ ★ ★ ★ ★ ★ ★

★   ★   ★   ★   ★   ★   ★